Paint in America

Paint in America

THE COLORS OF HISTORIC BUILDINGS

ROGER W. MOSS, EDITOR

THE PRESERVATION PRESS

NATIONAL TRUST FOR HISTORIC PRESERVATION, WASHINGTON, D.C.

WILEY

Preservation Press

JOHN WILEY & SONS, INC.
NEW YORK • CHICHESTER • BRISBANE • TORONTO • SINGAPORE

Copyright © 1994 The Barra Foundation, Inc.
Published by John Wiley & Sons, Inc.

Reproduction or translation of any part of this work beyond that permitted by Section 107 or 108 of the 1976 United States Copyright Act without permission of the copyright owner is unlawful. Requests for permission or further information should be addressed to the Permissions Department, John Wiley & Sons, Inc., 605 Third Avenue, New York, NY, 10158-0012

Printed in Singapore
5   4   3   2

Library of Congress Cataloging-in-Publication Data
    Paint in America : the colors of historic buildings / edited by Roger W. Moss
        p.   cm.
    Papers from Paint in America — a Symposium on Architectural and Decorative Paints, held in Lexington, Mass., 1989
    Includes bibliographical references and index.
    1. Paint — Congresses. 2. Color — Conservation and restoration — United States — Congresses. I. Moss, Roger W., 1940– . II. Paint in America — a Symposium on Architectural and Decorative Paints (1989: Lexington, Mass.)
    TP934.P317 1994   94–7463
    698'.14'0973— dc20   CIP
    ISBN 0-471-14410-X (casebound)
    ISBN 0-471-14411-8 (paperbound)

Produced by Archetype Press, Inc., Washington, D.C.
Project Director: Diane Maddex
Editor: Gretchen Smith Mui
Art Director: Robert L. Wiser
Designers: Robert L. Wiser and Lisa Markowitz

Front cover and frontispiece: The variety of textures, irregularity of plan, exposed structural members, and small panes of glass in the upper sash—all characteristics of the Queen Anne style—call attention to the need for careful outlining and color changes, as clearly shown in this flank elevation from The Painter *(March 1885). (The Athenaeum of Philadelphia)*

Back cover: H. W. Johns's miniature color chart (New York, 1890) teaches primary, secondary, and tertiary colors. (The Athenaeum of Philadelphia)

CONTENTS

Preface

R O G E R   W .   M O S S

In the 1950s I often accompanied my father to the Campus Martius Museum in Marietta, Ohio. It wasn't much of a museum by modern standards: the usual American Indian potsherds arranged in dusty cases and the twisted metal remains of a crashed dirigible stacked in the corner like so many excavated mastodon bones—in short, little to stimulate a child's imagination. But the largest artifact in the collection was another matter. The principal reason for the museum and its greatest treasure was the two-story, clapboarded Rufus Putnam House (1789), around which the museum building had been erected in the 1930s. By permanently enclosing the house, the museum's designers eliminated several chronic problems faced by anyone who owns or cares for wooden buildings exposed to the weather, especially the necessity of maintaining protective paint finishes on trim and siding.

However much we might wish to protect our buildings from the elements, the Campus Martius solution to historic preservation is one that few owners would—or could—adopt today. Consequently, we protect our buildings from exposure to the elements by the periodic application of paint. But what do we mean by the term *paint* in a historical context? And since paint is more than protection, how do we determine appropriate colors, textures, and placement? This book, which has drawn on the expertise of many individuals and organizations interested in the history and replication of historical finishes, attempts to answer some of these questions.

Paint in America is a collection of essays that grew out of a public symposium presented in 1989 at the Museum of Our National Heritage in Lexington, Massachusetts, and sponsored by the Society for the Preservation of New England Antiquities in Boston. It was followed by a colloquium of specialists in the analysis of architectural finishes hosted by the Colonial Williamsburg Foundation, Williamsburg, Virginia. The final papers were reviewed by an editorial committee chaired by the executive director of the Athenaeum of Philadelphia, and the book was published by the Preservation Press, Washington, D.C. The symposium, colloquium, and publication were made possible by the financial support of The Barra Foundation, Inc., Wyndmoor, Pennsylvania.

Not all the symposium presentations are included here. Andrew L. Ladygo and John Canning delivered an important talk entitled "Preparation, Application, and Protection of Painted Surfaces" that has been subsumed by other papers, and two symposium presentations—

Joseph W. Prane's "The Nature of Modern Paints" and Richard Wolbers's "Issues of Paint Selection and Compatability"—have been omitted from the book because they related to the physical properties of modern architectural coatings. The editorial committee felt that these two papers contributed greatly to the understanding of the subject for those individuals able to attend the 1989 symposium but if published might date the book because of rapid changes now occurring in the field of modern architectural coatings.

In addition to the presenters and authors, many other individuals deserve thanks for their creativity, dedication, and generosity in the completion of this project. The editorial committee is pleased to acknowledge the central role of Nancy R. Coolidge, former director of the Society for the Preservation of New England Antiquities, in planning the symposium and this publication. Sara B. Chase, Nancy Hamilton, Leslie Fox, Richard Nylander, and Jocelyn Young—several of whom have left SPNEA for other positions—also helped plan and execute the symposium. Patricia L. Weslowski is due special thanks for coordinating the project from preliminary proposal to final editing; she is the thread that has held *Paint in America* together over several years. The encouragement of SPNEA president Jane C. Nylander is also appreciated.

Clement M. Silvestro, president of the Museum of Our National Heritage, permitted the use of that institution's excellent facilities, and June Coob, general services administrator, helped with logistical support. At the symposium, documents donated to SPNEA by the Edward K. Perry Company were displayed with guidance provided by Samuel and Elizabeth Perry. Patricia Lescalleet coordinated the exhibition. Following the symposium Minxie Fannin, Pamela Hawkes, Christy Cunningham-Adams, and Daniel Coolidge led tours of Boston landmarks illustrating decorative paint restoration and conservation.

The colloquium at Colonial Williamsburg was organized by Nicholas Pappas, FAIA, then-Foundation architect, and Thomas H. Taylor, Jr., Foundation architectural conservator. The following persons, in addition to the organizers, took three days from their busy schedules to share their professional expertise and exchange ideas on the future of research in historical architectural finishes: Penelope H. Batchelor, Ian C. Bristow, Douglas G. Bucher, Marijene H. Butler, Andrea M. Gilmore, Matthew J. Mosca, Roger W. Moss, Catherine S. Myers, Carole L. Perrault, Morgan W. Phillips, Judith E. Selwyn, Frank S. Welsh, and Patricia L. Weslowski. Marijene H. Butler, head of conservation, Philadelphia Museum of Art, assumed the additional burden of bringing order out of the colloquium discussions by drafting a summary narrative of great value to both the participants and the editorial committee.

The editorial committee consisted of Abbott L. Cummings, Jonathan Fairbanks, Andrea M. Gilmore, Roger W. Moss, and Patricia L. Weslowski. They are particularly grateful to Robert L. Feller and Regina Ryan for valuable assistance in reviewing papers at various stages during the editorial process. Thanks are also due Gail H. Fahrner, The Barra Foundation, who kept track of both participants and finances over the course of the project; Buckley Jeppson and the Preservation Press for publishing the book; and Diane Maddex and her associates at Archetype Press, Washington, D.C., who fashioned a complex manuscript into a book.

For all the creativity, dedication, and generosity of the individuals mentioned here, *Paint in America* ultimately reflects the vision of Robert L. McNeil, Jr., president, The Barra Foundation, Inc. Without his interest and encouragement this publication would not have been possible.

Authors

Ian C. Bristow, an architect living in London, has specialized in the use of paint color in eighteenth-century British interiors and has served as adviser for the redecoration of many noteworthy British interiors. He is a Fellow of the the Society of Antiquaries of London and serves on a number of statutory committees concerned with the care of historic buildings in England.

Richard M. Candee is professor of American and New England studies at Boston University, where he directs the preservation studies program. He is the author of *Housepaints in Colonial America* and has written extensively on the architecture of southern Maine and New Hampshire as well as New England's nineteenth-century textile industries.

Sara B. Chase, formerly director of the Conservation Center of the Society for the Preservation of New England Antiquities, is an independent preservation consultant. She helped plan and execute the syposium Paint in America.

Abbott Lowell Cummings, author of *The Framed Houses of Massachusetts Bay, 1625–1725* and many other works, was formerly executive director of the Society for the Preservation of New England Antiquities and recently retired as the Charles F. Montgomery Professor of American Decorative Arts at Yale University.

Christy Cunningham-Adams is a fine arts paintings conservator whose practice includes wall, easel, and panel paintings. Among other projects her firm has recently completed are wall paintings at the U.S. Capitol and the Library of Congress.

Eugene Farrell is the senior conservation scientist at the Center for Conservation and Technical Studies, Harvard University Art Museums, and a lecturer in fine arts.

Andrea M. Gilmore is director of architectural services at the Conservation Center, Society for the Preservation of New England Antiquities. Her paint research projects include Lindenwald,

Kinderhook, New York; Sagamore Hill, Oyster Bay, New York; the Old State House, Hartford, Connecticut; and the Old South Meetinghouse, Boston.

Matthew J. Mosca is a consultant and lecturer in the field of historic paint research and restoration. Several of his projects have received national awards for excellence in the field of historic preservation.

Roger W. Moss is executive director of The Athenaeum of Philadelphia and adjunct associate professor of architecture, historic preservation program, University of Pennsylvania. His several books include *Century of Color, Lighting for Historic Buildings, The American Country House,* and *Victorian Exterior Decoration.*

Richard Newman, formerly conservation scientist and assistant conservator of sculpture and objects at the Center for Conservation and Technical Studies, Harvard University Art Museums, is research scientist in the department of objects conservation and scientific research, Museum of Fine Arts, Boston.

Nicholas A. Pappas, FAIA, recently retired as foundation architect of the Colonial Williamsburg Foundation, where his primary charge was the preservation and enhancement of the physical authenticity of the Historic Area.

Morgan W. Phillips, a specialist in conserving and replicating historic architectural materials, is a consultant in architectural conservation in Canajoharie, New York.

Brian Powell is an architectural conservator at the Conservation Center, Society for the Preservation of New England Antiquities. In addition to dealing with materials problems, he conducts documentary and physical studies of historic buildings. His projects have included the U.S. Treasury Building, the New York State Capitol, and Boston's Old South Meetinghouse.

Myron O. Stachiw was trained and worked as a historical archeologist, social historian, and architectural historian throughout the northeastern United States. He is director of research, interpretation, and education at the Society for the Preservation of New England Antiquities, Boston.

Thomas H. Taylor, Jr., is architectural collections manager and chief architectural conservator, Colonial Williamsburg Foundation. He is responsible for overseeing the preservation, maintenance, and conservation of the foundation's architectural collection of six hundred structures, several thousand architectural fragments, and approximately fifty architectural models.

Frank S. Welsh is a professional microscopist specializing in scientific research and microscopical analysis and color analysis of historic architectural finishes. Since 1974 he has been in private practice in Bryn Mawr, Pennsylvania consulting to national foundations and private citizens.

Introduction

S A R A   B .   C H A S E

According to a Victorian writer no worker was more welcome than the painter. Indeed, since the time of the Lascaux caves (ca.10,000 B.C.), which harbor the first known examples of the use of animal hair brushes to apply coloring to walls, we have been painting our shelters. From the Parthenon to Pompeii to Portland and Pittsburgh, paint has enhanced and protected buildings.

That paint beautifies while it provides a protective film over the surfaces of buildings is doubly gratifying—no doubt the basis for the somewhat extravagant claim of the Victorian author. The craft of making and applying paint in the United States and the history of its evolution in terms of both chemistry and color has engaged writers for almost two hundred years. And for at least seventy years researchers and historians have been digging into the paint layers of the past to discover as much as possible about architectural paint in America.

In 1989 Paint in America: A Symposium on Architectural and Decorative Paints brought together sixteen experts on every aspect of historic paint from history to chemistry. They presented slide lectures to an audience of several hundred during two days and submitted their information as chapters for this book. In addition to the symposium lectures, this book includes a chapter on the English background of the early paints of British settlers, a recent survey of early American paint colors, and a glossary of historic pigments. The chapters reflect the varied points of view of those who approach paint and its use from different backgrounds. The authors are architectural historians, paint investigators, and painting conservators. Yet as various as their backgrounds and points of interest may be, taken together the authors provide a unified and virtually complete reference work on historic architectural paint in this country.

Publications about paint in the United States began, as far as we know, with Hezekiah Reynolds's *Directions for House and Ship Painting,* printed in New Haven, Connecticut, in 1812. Certainly, long before the nineteenth century, paint was in use—as colors mixed in a liquid form and applied to buildings, furniture, canvas (portraits), ships, and more. It was used by native Americans and Spanish settlers and by other early colonists. If any of them published information about their colors or their craft, however, their work has not yet been discovered.

In his introduction Reynolds suggested that "the fruits of his observation and experience" in the business and the "Art" of house painting, together with "correct and useful . . . information from other persons of long and extensive experience" would be of assistance to others.

Now, two centuries later, the need for accurate and precisely documented information about historic architectural painting is even greater. Not only painters but also historians, conservators, museum administrators, educators, and owners of old buildings wish to have an understanding of the old paints on their structures. Some may have an interest in colors only, but many, including craftsmen and conservators, must know the materials and practices of earlier painters to save or recreate the original appearance of rooms. This book, like Reynolds's book, does indeed represent information from "persons of long and extensive experience."

Paint in America has four parts. First are chapters on the history of paint in American buildings from the seventeenth century to the end of the nineteenth century. This historical perspective includes a brief survey of painting practices and materials in England. The second part of the book presents the current state of knowledge about historic paints and their uses based on case studies of actual paint investigations at Mount Vernon and other historic properties. The third part lays out the specifics of modern paint research and interpretation. Over the past twenty-five years the study of historic paints has become more sophisticated. As experience accumulates, interpreting the findings of paint investigators has become more complex and demanding. The chapters in this part discuss paint study in general, the technical identification of pigments and media, preparation of surfaces for paint, and paint application. The fourth part provides basic technical information on the nature of paint in general and the properties of oil and glue distemper paints in particular. At the end is a glossary of pigments commonly used in historic paints, arranged by color.

The beauty of paint may be only skin deep—as deep as the paint film thickness—but there is far more to paint and architectural painting than meets the eye. For more than three hundred fifty years paint in America has been protecting vulnerable wood, masonry, plaster, and metal surfaces while giving them a pleasant appearance. Much is asked of the thin paint film: hardness and flexibility, adhesion and removability, practicality and beauty. The relative simplicity of early paints has given way to the great complexity of modern coatings, for which there is an almost equal diversity of means of application.

Nevertheless, the paint on American buildings still enhances both the architecture itself and the context of our buildings. It is now time to bring to the study of historic paint the intensity and depth of the study of structural engineering or materials science. Hezekiah Reynolds concluded his introduction with this hope:

… to others whose Trades are connected with building, as well as to those whose taste and genius qualify for, and invite to the practice of this useful and ornamental Art … [may] these directions be important as a substitute for experience. Should this expectation be realized, [the author's] object in laying them before the public will be obtained.

It is the hope of those who have contributed so generously to this book—a compendium of the best and most current work on historic architectural paint in America—that the reader will indeed have the benefit of all this experience. Technically, historically, and practically may the reader see, understand, and appreciate in a fresh and informed manner both historic and modern paint.

Historical Perspectives

Colonial and Federal America

ACCOUNTS OF EARLY PAINTING PRACTICES

ABBOTT LOWELL CUMMINGS AND RICHARD M. CANDEE

Extensive accounts of the day-to-day work of colonial painters exist only for Boston, but similar if less abundant records in other major port towns begin about the time of the American Revolution and continue into the early years of the new republic. Craft practices of this period can be discerned from the work of several urban painters in New England, whose records also indicate patterns of color choice and usage and provide a documentary background that can be compared with practices in other regions of the country. Visual images of painters at work are virtually unknown until the early nineteenth century (**fig. 2**), although the products of their craftsmanship—from portraits to painted wall surfaces—abound to be studied and enjoyed.

COLONIAL AMERICA

Painters or "painter-stainers," as they were originally called, were at work in colonial America long before we begin to find the physical evidence of paint used on buildings. Augustine Clement of Dorchester and Boston, Massachusetts, trained as a painter-stainer in his native Reading, England, embarked from Southampton for New England in 1635 on the *James* of London, together with his servant, Thomas Wheeler.[1] They were preceded by one "Will. Johnes," who in 1634 was described as "late of Sandwich now of New England, painter."[2] We know as little of these men as other painters of record who arrived later in the century. Not until shortly before 1700 is there any reference in New England to such craftsmen painting houses with what were called colors "laid in oil" (oil paints), but documents are fairly clear that colored surfaces appeared first and fairly early on the interior of houses.

EARLY WHITEWASHES AND DISTEMPERS

Both written and physical evidence points to the widespread use of whitewash and other non-oil-based media. It may be said quite simply that few (if any) surviving colonial New England houses do not show some indication that whitewash was applied early and liberally on interior woodwork and plastered walls. Physical evidence confirms that whitewash often covered

Figure 1. *Portrait of Capt. Elijah Dewey by Ralph Earl, 1798, showing his house in Bennington, Vt. (The Bennington Museum, Bennington, Vt.)*

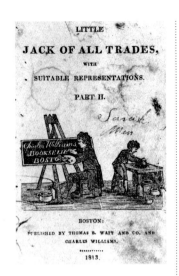

Figure 2. *"The Painter's Shop," an early nineteenth-century woodcut from the cover of* Little Jack of All Trades *(Boston: Thos. B. Wait and Charles Williams, 1813). The sign painter works next to an apprentice grinding pigment and mixing it with oil. (American Antiquarian Society)*

virtually every interior surface, as we also learn from such contemporary documents as the August 4, 1718, bill of Richard Richardson to one "mr. Stoder" in Boston for "Whitwashing" Stoddard's "Diningroome," "Best Chamber," "Stayer Case," "Littell Roome & ye shop sealing," "Parlor," and "Entereway."[3] Traditionally whitewashing, when performed professionally, was the work not of painters but of masons or plasterers after that craft was represented in the colonies, probably because of the use of lime and ancient divisions of labor between the crafts.

Even after oil paints came into general use in the eighteenth century many plaster ceilings, service rooms, and less formal apartments continued to receive whitewash as the only finish. The November 15, 1736, *Boston Gazette,* for example, advertised for sale a "well built brick House" with "four Rooms on a Floor," two chambers of which "in the first story [were] hung with Scotch Tapestry, the other Green Cheney," while the "upper Chambers [were] well Plaistered and white wash'd...."

Evidence for the pervasiveness of whitewash in even the most stylish eighteenth-century houses can be found in the accounts for the maintenance of Boston's Province House, the official residence of the colonial governors. Several long, itemized bills for periodic whitewashing exist for the 1730s and 1740s, of which the following is characteristic:

> To Saml. Heath of Boston Brick Layer ...
> To work Done at yᵉ. province House: in Boston ... May: 1738 ...
> To: whitewashing 3 upper Chambers ...
> To: Do. one Little Chamber aloft ...
> To: Do. 3: Cielings in yᵉ. second story ...
> To: Do. the Lanthorn [cupola] ...
> To: Do. the front stair Case and Entry way ...
> To: Do. the back stair Case and Entry way ...
> To: Do. 3: front Lower Room Cielings ...
> To: Do. 2 Small Lower Rooms ...
> To: Do. a Large Kitchen Chamber ...
> To: Do. yᵉ. Kitchen stair Case ...
> To: Do. 2. Large Clossets ...To: Do. yᵉ. house of office [privy]

In addition, Heath billed for outside work, which included "pointing and whitewashing yᵉ front wall under ye pale fence" and "pointing and whiteing ye stone work under ye front of yᵉ House...."[4]

In June 1785 Francis Hopkinson, signer of the Declaration of Independence, writing from Pennsylvania to a "friend in Europe," indicates that whitewashing was still very common: "the latter end of May is generally fixed upon for the purpose," he noted. "The walls are stripped of their furniture—paintings, prints, and looking-glasses lie in huddled heaps about the floors ... chairs and tables, beadsteads and cradles crowd the yard.... The next operation is to smear the [plaster] walls and ceilings with brushes, dipped in a solution of lime called WHITEWASH."[5] The continued widespread use of whitewash as a means of freshening the house interior has not been sufficiently appreciated. In rural New England the practice continued well past the middle of the nineteenth century. Lucretia Stow Cummings, born in 1851 in Southington, Connecticut, reported in the course of her reminiscences of childhood: "We always had all the

Figure 3. *Reconstruction of the original paint scheme (ca. 1665), second-floor chamber, Eleazer Gedney House (ca. 1664), Salem, Mass. (David Bohl, Society for the Preservation of New England Antiquities)*

Figure 4. *Reconstruction of the second paint scheme (ca. 1675–80), second-floor chamber, Eleazer Gedney House, Salem, Mass. (David Bohl, Society for the Preservation of New England Antiquities)*

Figure 5. *Reconstruction of the third paint scheme (ca. 1700), second-floor chamber, Eleazer Gedney House, Salem, Mass. (David Bohl, Society for the Preservation of New England Antiquities)*

walls white-washed every Fall, to have them nice and white for winter (as they were not in summer)." For this service they depended on one "Mr. Amon Ames, the village whitewasher."[6]

The earliest known appearance of paint pigments in seventeenth-century New England occurs in conjunction with distemper and related paints.[7] The upstairs hall chamber of the Eleazer Gedney House (ca.1664), 21 High Street, Salem, Massachusetts, reveals several successive color transformations, all designed to pick out or highlight certain exposed structural members of the interior frame. The earliest application of color, dating perhaps to the period of construction, consists of an optical green formed by mixing yellow ocher and charcoal black with calcite. Traces of copper suggest that some copper green was used to reinforce the optical green created by combining yellow and black. The pigments were applied in an animal glue binder, making this a distemper paint (although positive traces of oil may have come from a prepared layer next to the wood). This optical green color-wash covers the surface of posts, end- and chimney-ties, plates, and the summer beam. The green extends no higher on the sides of the summer beam than the lower edge of the joists. The green is found, too, on the bottom of the joists but not on the sides or on the underside of the attic floorboards that form the ceiling overhead (**fig. 3**).

In a subsequent color transformation of this room the entire frame was redone with the summer beam and its supporting posts overpainted for contrast with a thin application of soot black with gypsum (plaster) and a gum binder. Again, this black extends up the side of the summer beam only as far as the bottom of the joists framed into it (**fig. 4**).

Use of plaster instead of slaked lime (as in whitewash) to which a gum was added is difficult evidence to interpret. It has not been determined whether the gypsum was a filler or served as a binder with the gum. Moreover, this unusual type of distemper is found in two separate paint layers in this house. Before the final color transformation of the Gedney hall chamber occurred, a ceiling of lath and plaster was applied to the underside of the attic floorboards between the joists. The final finish was a thick layer of an animal glue distemper in which particles of fine-grained calcite with traces of yellow ocher are evenly distributed. This yellow-tinted wash covers almost the entire frame and also (where fragments remain) the surface of the added plaster ceiling. However, the summer beam and its supporting posts were again overpainted with a thin wash of another plaster and gum distemper, this time colored by natural red ocher with traces of carbon black. This red plaster and gum distemper extends over the entire surface of the summer beam up to the plaster ceiling (**fig. 5**). This final redecoration, whether before or just after 1700, and the color layers beneath it were all concealed and preserved when the interior frame was cased sometime during the eighteenth century and a new ceiling of lath and plaster was hung from the joists of this room with handwrought nails.

Because these colors were previously assumed to be some sort of whitewash, the absence of lime and the presence of plaster raise many questions. The optical (rather than chemical) green is not unknown, as Rembrandt is said to have used it. But the fine arts are no source for the plaster and gum. Was it an urban version of a long-lasting wash that used plaster rather than lime with gum to help hold the paint to the surface? The three redecorations of the Gedney chamber over a thirty- or forty-year period would suggest that its longevity matched that of oil-based paints and differed from colored lime-based washes, which were often renewed.

Similar evidence of pigmented washes and finish trim picked out in color has been uncovered in other seventeenth-century houses in New England.[8] Two pieces of seventeenth-century molded wall sheathing have been found in Ipswich, Massachusetts, with their original surface condition preserved (they had been reused in the buildings where they were discovered). For the first of these, from the Ross Tavern, the surface of the sheathing is perfectly clean without finish of any kind. For the second, found when a mid-eighteenth-century house at 28 East Street was demolished about 1960, the surface had early been covered with what is assumed to be whitewash. In both of these fragmentary pieces of finish, the molded edges are picked out in color, a condition one finds commonly in the identical creased moldings of seventeenth-century chests and cupboards. The color of the Ross Tavern example is light brick red and has the flaky character of whitewash (although it has not been tested). On the second sample, the presumed whitewash surface continued into the molding, which was picked out with an overlay of lampblack.

Soon after 1700 color also began to be used to create freehand patterns in either whitewash or distempers. In the lean-to of the White-Ellery House (ca. 1710), Gloucester, Massachusetts, for example, a simple decoration of semicircular slashes, alternating in direction in two vertically arranged bands, was found on the surface of the exposed ceiling joists. Here the decoration is again lampblack over whitewash. At the south end of the same lean-to is a spatter decoration in black on whitewash applied directly to the original plaster wall.

One ceiling of early floorboards, reused in the construction of a mid-eighteenth century house in Dartmouth, Massachusetts, shows an extraordinary combination of colors and materials. Both the boards and floor joists were exposed and painted with a high-quality natural red ocher. On this base a white paint creates commas and an occasional chevron pattern; moreover, there is a loose freehand use of a copper acetate or verdigris in bold splashes. The red and verdigris, at least, were both in a pine resin binder (fig. 6).

The most common early eighteenth-century freehand decoration is that often called "sponge-painting." A well-known example is preserved in the upper entry of the William Boardman House, 17 Howard Street, Saugus, Massachusetts. The house dates to about 1687, although the decoration was added probably in the early 1700s. The original sheathing of the upper entry was prepared with a ground of whitewash tinted yellow, over which a series of "dots" about one and a quarter inches in diameter were painted in lampblack about three or four inches apart. These dots have been dabbed on with a spongelike agent, hence the common name. In other examples, however, like the board that formed part of the lean-to ceiling at the Joseph Blaney House (ca. 1700; demolished 1914), 280 Humphrey Street, Swampscott, Massachusetts, the decoration of black spots on whitewash was made with a round brush (the typical colonial paint brush form) twirled in the painter's fingers.

Figure 6. *Red ceiling with green and white decoration, from a house formerly in Dartmouth, Mass. These eighteenth-century ceiling boards, removed from their original location, used pine resin and also perhaps glue as a paint binder. (Society for the Preservation of New England Antiquities)*

One of the most interesting examples of this type of spotted decoration survives on the ceiling frame (under a later plaster ceiling since removed) of the first-floor east room of the John Sherburne House (ca. 1695), located on the grounds of Strawbery Banke in Portsmouth, New Hampshire. This room was added to the original house sometime before 1703, and the spotted ceiling actually sits over an earlier layer of gray distemper paint.[9] The sheathed fireplace wall as well as the framing members of the ceiling in this addition were originally all painted the light gray distemper. Later, perhaps in the 1730s or 1740s, when a central chimney was removed (the first gray is preserved unaltered on reused sheathing from the first fireplace wall) and rear corner chimneys were installed, the ceiling was repainted red and spotted with darker gray dots from some 2½ to 3 inches in diameter. Again, the dots were created by twirling a round paint brush in the fingers. The Province House in Boston, although we know nothing of the colors used, was also repainted with spots; Samuel Heath charged the province of Massachusetts for "Collouring and spotting a Large Kitchen" there in May 1738.[10] Perhaps many more surviving spotted ceilings and walls in old houses should actually be dated to the 1730s or thereafter.

At the Sherburne House the underlying light gray paint, the iron oxide red base, and the darker gray spots are all water-soluble distemper paints. Like whitewashes, with which they are often confused, distemper paints were common in colonial America and had ample English precedent. One English guide, published in 1725, directed that wood first be "laid . . . over with [a] white" sealer; next ocher was to be ground "very fine with water . . . then put size [glue] to your color and having mixed it well upon a [painter's grinding] Marble, you shall therewith Paint your Wood."[11]

Probably predating the introduction of freehand painting was the practice of painting a "baseboard" in lampblack directly on the plaster wall, a decorative device that at times was used to outline the risers and treads of the staircase and extended inside the fireplace as well, where it could be terminated in a decorative flourish. One of the earliest examples known of the painted baseboard was discovered in the chamber of the Abraham Browne House (1694-1701), 562 Main Street, Watertown, Massachusetts, when the house was restored in 1919–20. The practice was by then well established in England, as we learn from Joseph Moxon in 1700: "The *Pencil* [brush], or *Drawing Tool*, is used in blacking the bottoms, or lower ports [sic] of Rooms, &c."[12] Examples of black banding that follow the outline of the treads and risers can be found along the main staircases of the Robert Peaslee House (ca. 1710), 790 East Broadway, Haverhill, Massachusetts, and the Parson Barnard House (ca. 1715), 179 Osgood Street, North Andover, Massachusetts. Nor is this technique limited to New England; a painted baseboard appears on the whitewashed vertical-sheathed wall along the attic staircase in the Ashton House (ca. 1704), St. Georges Hundred, New Castle County, Delaware.[13]

One of the handsomest examples of painted banding within the fireplace can be seen in the left-hand front room of the Moses Pierce-Hichborn House (ca. 1711), 29 North Square, Boston (fig. 7). The scrolled bands were restored in 1949–50 from fragmentary evidence. The perfectly plain banding found in the original fireplaces when the Peter Sargeant House (1679), later the Province House, in Boston was demolished in 1922, if contemporary with construction, represents the earliest example of any such decoration in New England.[14]

At a less formal level, examples of overall coloring have been found within eighteenth-century fireplaces. Both flanks of the fireplace in the Judson House (ca. 1750) in Stratford, Connecticut,

Figure 7. *Fireplace decorated with a black band and scroll, Moses Pierce-Hichborn House (ca. 1711), Boston. (George M. Cushing, Society for the Preservation of New England Antiquities)*

when it was restored as a house museum were found to have been painted red, perhaps in association with whitewash. In May 1741 John Kneeland, mason, billed for "Blacking Backs of Chimneys" in the course of whitewashing and other services at Boston's Province House.[15] Documentary corroboration for the decorative use of color in fireplaces is found in many accounts. In Salem, Massachusetts, mason Gibson Clough charged Mary Pickman in May 1779 for "Coloring the Chimeneys of the house of Mr Hiller"[16] and the Pennsylvania journal of Elizabeth Drinker notes, on August 25, 1794, "Sam Spriggs came up this morning with paint and brushes to black and redden our hearths."[17]

PAINTING IN OIL

When the appraisers of the estate of Boston merchant Robert Gibbs inventoried his possessions in February 1675, they were sufficiently impressed with one room to call it the "Painted Chambr."[18] In 1672 Lawrence Clenton of Ipswich, Massachusetts, about whom little is known, was credited with three and a half days' work in painting a room for a Mr. Baker.[19] While we cannot be certain that these were colors laid in oil, in 1681 a painter named Daniel George arrived in Boston, the 1684 inventory of whose estate includes entries for "Sixty gall. Linseed Oyle," "comon Varnish," six hundred pounds of white and red "Lead," and an array of other pigments.[20] These are of particular interest, for from this period we find the earliest surviving physical evidence in New England of decorative oil painting of architectural elements. The Paul Revere House in Boston's North End was newly built when the property was conveyed to merchant Robert Howard on November 2, 1681.[21] When the house was restored in 1907–8, an original or early single-board pine door with applied moldings was found in a reused position. The flat surface within the spaces defined by the applied moldings had been painted in simulation of two widely feathered panels of oak. The seventeenth-century English preference for the appearance if not the reality of oak as a building material was also found elsewhere in the house. Traces of oak graining were also found on the originally exposed interior house frame, beneath later eighteenth-century casings, as was decorative painting in imitation of hardwood panels on the plastered side walls. Precedent can easily be found for this elaborate painted decoration in seventeenth-century England.

From 1700 on, documents show that painting in oil was becoming increasingly popular among the urban elite. We also find a growing number of professional painters, at least two of whom, Thomas Child and John Gibbs, had served their apprenticeships with the London Painter-Stainers Guild. Child, who graduated into the ranks of that company in 1679, arrived in Boston by July 1685.[22] Gibbs, apprenticed in 1690 for seven years, arrived in Boston by March 1703.[23] Records of their activities are important for they include the earliest references to both decorative and common painting practices that would shortly become routine. Child, for example, billed Capt. John Miles in May 1706 for "Oyle Worck Don In your hous," including "Painting your c[h]amber stone [color]" and "To ye stares wenscot." Throughout the colonial period, graining and marbleizing were often described as colors or named by reference to the type of material they simulated. On February 25, 1707, following Child's premature death the previous year, his widow, Katherine, who carried on the business using the talents of her husband's "Servants," billed Captain Miles for additional painting of "26 yds green Marble color" and "24 yds Walnut colour." Together with Child's 1706 bill for "wenscot" they are the earliest unequivocal documentary references to these forms of decorative painting on woodwork in New England.[24]

Similarly Gibbs sent a statement to Thomas Banister for "Painting work done ... At the house you dwel in measured July yᵉ eighteenth 1714" that includes certain entries that rank as the earliest known references in their respective categories:

> To 116 yds of pearl colour at 2s/
> To painting & gilding the beaufait [cupboard]
> To gilding the Shelf in ye Library
> To gilding the frame & painting Landskip.... [25]

Particular interest centers on the last item, "To gilding the frame & painting Landskip," for this is the only known early eighteenth-century Boston reference to landscape painting in an architectural context. The 1714 date also suggests that Gibbs may have been the painter of the important painted landscape panels salvaged from the north parlor of the Clarke-Frankland House when the North End mansion was demolished in 1833 (fig. 8). William Clarke, merchant and member of the Governor's Council, purchased the site on December 10, 1711, and the house, one of the most opulent of its period, was built over the next two or three years.[26] Thus, Gibbs becomes an excellent candidate, with respect to training and background, for having painted the reported eleven landscape panels (of which two are known to survive) as the house neared completion. Nina Fletcher Little, whose pioneering investigations of American decorative wall painting form the foundation of all later research, concluded that these panels are the "earliest presently known examples of the English school of architectural landscape painting in the New England colonies."[27]

Figure 8. *Decorative landscapes on panels (ca. 1714), attributed to John Gibbs, Clarke-Frankland House, Boston. These two surviving panels were salvaged from the north parlor of this large estate when it was demolished in 1833. (Society for the Preservation of New England Antiquities)*

THE PAINTER'S SHOP

Craft practices of the common painter in colonial American society are still only partially understood because they evolved from English guild "mysteries" that were designed to protect their practitioners by excluding from others all knowledge of oil painting.[28] The English guild tradition in America is best illustrated by the 1697 coat of arms of the London Painter-Stainers Company used in Boston by Thomas Child. While the English guild system did not continue in this country, the ability to mix paint colors from imported dry pigments and oils still required training. Apprenticeship continued to provide the skills that made oil painting the nearly exclusive prerogative of this craft well into the nineteenth century. For this reason, at least among trained urban practitioners, the same painter who provided house owners with plain or decorative architectural painting also provided clients with landscapes and portraits, other crafts with protective finishes for their products, and tradesmen of all sorts with signs. Child, for example, practiced not only decorative painting of houses, as we have seen, but also painted signs, ships, and carriages, made picture frames, japanned (lacquered) metal objects, and painted coats of arms.[29] Records of four other early Boston painters suggest not only the diversity and status of their craft but also, from detailed lists of materials, tools, and craft products, help draw a composite picture of the colonial painter's workshop.

Edward Stanbridge, who arrived in Boston before 1714, was the nephew of Thomas Child's widow, Katherine. Sometime before 1725 she leased the house and painter's shop to Stanbridge, who continued the business until his death in 1734.[30] His estate inventory lists typical pigments such as red and white lead, whiting, Spanish brown, and lampblack, as well as "sundry small Collours in Drawers," seventy-five pounds of blue paint, and twenty-six pounds of India red. More than 120 brushes are listed (large, small, hair, and so forth) as well as the normal clutter of "Sundry Potts Bottles, Jugs, Jars, Measures, Brushes & remnants [of] Paint In Shop."[31]

Edward Pell, born in Boston on October 19, 1687,[32] became apprenticed to Child, whom Pell called "my mastor."[33] Pell was one of the servants who remained after Child's death in 1706 and, at age nineteen, was old enough to be entrusted with outside commissions under the management of Katherine Child. It was Pell, for example, who did the later painting at Captain Miles's house. In 1710 Pell married Sarah Clark in Boston and was launched on his own by March 23, 1714, when he was paid fifty-four pounds by the First Church of Boston "for painting yᵉ Brick meeting house," then newly built, and November 19, 1714, when he was paid fifteen pounds "for painting Outside & Inside" the "Ministeral house [of] yᵉ Revᵈ Mr Benja[min] Wadsworth."[34] Both these commissions were a recognition of his skill by Boston's most prestigious religious society.

Within a decade he petitioned the selectmen for permission "to Erect with Timber a smal Building in Gibbs's pasture near sheafe street . . . to be imployed for a Horse Mill for the making of Linseed Oyl, the building to be thirty two feet long twenty seven feet broad and about fourteen or fifteen feet studd."[35] His petition was granted on February 25, 1726,[36] and when his estate was inventoried in 1737 he had a "Mansion House and Land with Painters Brick Shop" worth 1,150 pounds plus an "Oyle Mill with it's appurtanences" valued at another 800 pounds, all located near Hull and Sheafe streets in Boston's North End; the whole estate totaled more than 3,567 pounds. The appraisal lists among the contents of his shop the provocative item of "8 Draughts of Landskips." It also indicates the presence in the household of "Negro Robbin" and three other blacks named Harry, Jenny, and Betty Mingo.[37] The two men may well have been involved in the painter's business—the training and employment of blacks for skilled labor are well documented in the South, particularly among Thomas Jefferson's slaves, but the subject has neither been investigated nor well understood in the colonial North.

If Pell operated on an extensive scale, he also associated with the leading public institutions of his day. In 1720, for example, he was a member of the committee appointed in December by a group that seceded from Boston's Second Church "to agree with workmen to erect, build, and finish a brick house, suitable for the public worship of God . . . according to a plan offered to the society by Edward Pell. . . . "[38] That Pell furnished the design of what became known as the New Brick Church (no longer standing), adding a new name to the short list of early eighteenth-century New England architectural designers, is not so surprising. In an era before the professional architect had appeared in America, the design of public buildings involved the services of "skillfull" persons of diverse backgrounds: for example, Peter Harrison, "gentleman-designer" of Kings Chapel in Boston; John Smibert, artist, who furnished the design of Boston's Faneuil Hall; and Thomas Dawes, mason, credited with the design of the Brattle Street Church.

In light of this record, one is not surprised to discover that Pell received forty shillings in March 1725 "for Drawing a fresh Draugh[t] of St. Georges River & of ye Fort there for his Honour the Lieut Gov.r"[39] His appointment on March 13, 1733, to a committee to review Boston waterfront fortifications may have been with an eye to his service as a draftsman (an unsigned plan of proposed changes to the existing fortifications was filed with their report) or related to his military counsel as he is listed as "Capt. Edward Pell."[40] Thus, his public services were related in one way or another to special skills. Pell pursued an active painting career until his death in 1737, when he was not quite fifty years old.

Thomas Johnston of Boston, who variously styled himself as "Painter-stainer," "Escutcheon maker," and "Japanner," is also remembered as an engraver and builder of the first American organ.[41] His 1767 estate inventory indicates that he kept tools and products of both his engraving and the painting of coats of arms in a bedchamber in his house. These included a dozen prints and a parcel of books including singing books, examples of his copperplate engraving, a diamond used to cut glass for windows or picture framing, and a book of heraldry as a guide for his coats of arms. Perhaps "a picture half length" valued at thirty-six shillings indicates his own or a son's artistic pursuits. His workshop, listed separately from the household contents, further contained "2 Burnishers 2/. 15 Copper plates 40/" as well as his own engravings: "12 plans of Kennebec, 8 of Canada, 6 of Louisburgh" valued at twelve shillings. The painter's craft is evidenced by "3 paint stones," "paint knives," an "Easel," a variety of jugs, jars, brushes, and iron kettles. Japanning or varnishing is seen in the gums amber, seed lac (a resin ground from twigs of the *Coccus lacca*), and "shellack" (derived from melting seed lac). A variety of furniture—"3 Clock Cases," "a Chest of Draws," "2 Spinett Desks"—located in the shop may have been awaiting finishing. Planes, "Moldings for 6 frames," three "Holdfasts," forty wooden screws, and thirty-seven iron screws testify to his framing business, while his musical interests are reflected in "5 Fiddles," "a Base Bow" in the workshop, and "An organ unfinished" described elsewhere in his inventory.[42]

When painter John Moffatt died in 1779, he owned, among other more common items, a "Parcell of Heads &ca in Plaister of Paris," surveying instruments, and an "Electrical Wheel wth Glass Globes." In his Queens Street shop were "Three casks of American Oacker"—an early indication of the mining of native earths—together with bottles, jars, ironware, a painted counter with "a number of draws," a stone roller, and "Mullett." The latter, usually called a muller, was a stone ground flat on one end that apprentices rotated on a marble or glass slab to mix the oil and pigment into paints just as paint shops continued to do for the next century.

That Moffatt, like Pell and others before and after him, was also called on for decorative painting is well documented. His household inventory included a substantial library, "Six Large Pictures," twenty-two pasteboard books "with various draughts," and pictures numbered "from No. 1 to 64" and thirty more of a "Smaller sort," all valued at more than 365 pounds. In addition to these print sources, his shop contained "2 Images over the Chimney in the painting room" and a "painted Chimney Board," which we may assume were products of his own hand.[43]

Colonial Boston painters such as these were multitalented and often successful. As all were fully proficient in the technical aspects of painting in its many forms, it is little wonder that John Singleton Copley lamented that the people of Boston regarded the fine artist "as no more than any other useful trade, as they sometimes term it, like that of a Carpenter or a shew maker."[44]

Some painters also took a step toward becoming merchants by specializing in the sale of imported pigments, oils, and related painting supplies. John Howard played the "colourman" role in Boston during the 1720s, and his widow continued his business into the next decade. In the 1730s John Merritt of Boston advertised more than thirty pigments for use in oil or water. By the 1760s John Gore seems to have taken the lead in this field, advertising four white pigments, nine reds, ten yellows, seven blues, four greens, and five blacks as well as gold and silver leaf, oils, varnishes, chalk, whitings, driers like copperas and litharge (in the eighteenth century a byproduct of red lead). Gore also advertised "colours ready prepared for House or Ship Painting" and "Watercolours ready prepared in shells."[45]

Throughout the eighteenth century the number of pigments remained nearly static. We count just over three dozen pigments imported from Europe and available to the American painter, of which only three were products of eighteenth-century invention. Their description and manufacture have been well detailed by Candee and Penn and need not be repeated here.[46] Only a few earth colors were locally mined in this country, and lampblack was manufactured from waste oils of New England fisheries as early as the 1760s.[47]

The painter bought or imported dry pigments or "colours" and mixed them with oil either by hand with a stone muller and slab or with the aid of a paint mill. Edward Pell's 1737 inventory listed "2 paint Mills out of Repair" and valued at only fifteen shillings. Such machines may have been used as later mills were—for grinding with oil the more dangerous pigments and thereby avoiding physical contact with poisons like common orpiment and verdigris, vermillion and cinnabar (red mercuric sulphides), as well as red and white leads, which caused lead diseases that disabled many painters. Just as the American Revolution began, John Gore ordered a paint mill from his suppliers in England. They wrote back: " ... we have omitted sending the Colour Mill as you have not described what sort of one you would chuse to have, whether a Wood one or an Iron one Single or double." Their cost estimate for a double iron mill was twenty-four pounds but ten pounds for a single wooden mill. Gore responded in January 1775 requesting "one [of] the best Double Iron paint Mills & one single wooden one.... "[48]

With this as background, we can better understand the estate of Edward Gyles, a Boston painter who died in 1785. When the inventory of his possessions was made, the first item listed in the shed that served as a shop was "A Painter's Mill" worth twelve pounds. It also contained "a Painters small mill," "3 painters Stones ... 6 Mullers," and a variety of iron utensils for boiling oil or mixing paints. Listed between these tools and casks of Spanish brown and spruce yellow were a feather bed and "Sacking bottom Bed Stead," perhaps an indication of where an apprentice slept. Gyles also had pigments and painter's supplies scattered throughout his Charter Street house. In the garret were a cask, twelve bottles, a box of tools, and "50 squares of glass," as glazing was a commonly allied trade. In the upper chamber, among his household furniture, were found "16 [one pound] Baggs of Vermillion" and a "lump of white Copperass or Litherage." In the paint shop Gyles had a cask of whiting, more than three casks of yellow ochers, a cask of "Yellow or spruce Oaker," a five-hundred-pound cask of red ocher, and another two hundred pounds of "damaged red oaker," red chalk, two kegs, and a pail of red lead, one keg of white lead, a box of smalt (grains of cobalt glass for decorating signs), a hundred-weight firkin of venetian red plus twenty-six gallons of oil and "On the Shelf sundry Paints in Oil &c mixed."[49]

Before we turn to the explicit use of these materials in house painting, it is useful to understand how painters charged for their services. Different methods of measurement provided the traditional basis for payment in architectural painting, as amply documented by London price guides as well as builder's dictionaries of the early eighteenth century:

For painters work in building, the taking of the Dimensions, is the same with that of Joiners, by girting over the Mouldings, &tc. in taking the Height, and it is but reasonable that they should be paid for what both their Time and Colour are expended in. The casting up after the Dimensions have been taken and reduc'd into Yards, is altogether the same with that of Joiners Work; but the Painter never reckons work and a Half; but reckons his work once, twice or thrice colour'd over.[50]

English painters measured by square yards and number of coats; window sash and frames were priced by the piece, while cornices were priced by the running foot. Although prices for different forms of work might vary according to local circumstance, these units of measurement continued in America throughout the century and beyond. Painter's bills and account books confirm this, as does George Fisher's *The Instructor, or American Young Man's Best Companion* (Worcester, Mass.: Isaiah Thomas, 1789), an almost verbatim copy of an English guide containing similar rules for figuring painting costs.

EXTERIOR PAINTING

It is clear from both physical and documentary evidence that a majority of rural houses remained unpainted on the outside for much of the eighteenth century. The earliest urban painters' accounts, on the other hand, reveal a different situation. Wealthier clients, at least, were concerned with the exterior finish of their houses. In May 1706, for example, Thomas Child billed Capt. John Miles for painting "30 Casments," "ye Cornich in ye front," and "ye [down] spouts" of his Boston home. A year later the Child firm charged Henry Gibbs for "39 yds flatworke in ye Outside at 6d p yd," together with "56 window lights at 4 d p Light."[51] A most explicit account is that of John Gibbs to Thomas Banister on July 18, 1714, for "Painting work done ... At the house you dwel in," with the "outside" work carefully differentiated:

> To 188 yds~ of plain work at 1: 6 p yd . . .
> To 35 large window frames at 45/ each . . .
> To 8 Carved Cantilevers . . .
> To 4 Window frames primed . . .
> To 209 yds of priming at 6d- . . .
> To 15 Modillions. . . . [52]

For rural buildings during this period we are confined almost entirely to physical evidence. In contrast to urban documents, which suggest that the walls of wooden houses were covered

Figure 9. *Fragments of the original molded girt and other exterior trim with red paint (late seventeenth century), Ross Tavern, Ipswich, Mass. Only the window trim and other exterior trim were painted. (David Bohl, Society for the Preservation of New England Antiquities)*

Figure 10. *Ross Tavern, Ipswich, Mass., with paint colors restored. (David Bohl, Society for the Preservation of New England Antiquities)*

with "flat work" or "plain work," traces of original paint when found on the earliest eighteenth-century houses in New England farms and villages are consistently confined to the trim.

For example, the late seventeenth-century Ross Tavern in Ipswich, Massachusetts, has surviving evidence of the girt, molded sheathing, and dentil course picked out in red **(figs. 9 and 10)**. This trim color was restored by Daniel Wendell when the house was moved and combined with another early frame in the 1940s. Unfortunately, it is not certain whether these exterior elements were originally painted in oils during the seventeenth century or whether the physical evidence dates from a slightly later period. In at least two well-authenticated Massachusetts cases—the French-Andrews House (ca.1718) in Topsfield and the Gen. Sylvanus Thayer House (ca.1720) in Braintree—the paint or stain was the familiar "Indian red" (an iron oxide) found protected by finish trim at the cornice level during twentieth-century restorations. In each case the paint had clearly been applied to the trim only and not to the clapboards.

Changing fashions in paint colors are perhaps nowhere as marked as on the exterior of eighteenth-century buildings. Before the Revolution strong hues in contrasting patterns of wall and trim colors dominated. This was particularly true of the New England meetinghouse. Few structures survive, but well-kept church records yield an abundance of documentary information, especially for the second half of the eighteenth century. In Pomfret, Connecticut, for example, the town voted in April 1762 that the newly erected meetinghouse "be colored on the outside of an orange color—the doors and bottom boards of a chocolate color—the windows, jets, cover boards and weather boards [i.e., the exterior trim], colored white."[53] Shortly thereafter, in 1769, the neighboring town of Killingly, Connecticut, voted "that the cullering of the body of our meeting house should be like that of Pomfret, and the Roff should be cullered Read."[54] That same year in the upper Connecticut River Valley the town of Deerfield, Massachusetts, directed that the exterior of its meetinghouse be painted a "Dark stone Colour," the window frames white, and the doors "a Chocolate."[55]

Evidence of color schemes at the domestic level before the Revolution is severely limited but reveals the same pattern of strong contrasting hues for the more stylish houses. A mid-eighteenth-century overmantel panel painting preserved in Fairfield, Connecticut, portrays a local gambrel-roofed house painted a stone gray color, with the door rendered in blue and the trim uniformly white; its barns are red **(fig. 11)**. Further pictorial evidence can be found in the portrait of Capt. Elijah Dewey of Bennington, Vermont, painted there by Ralph Earl in 1798. Earl has included a literal "portrait" (image) of Dewey's house, built probably in the 1780s, as a background detail **(fig. 1)**. The color scheme is a strong yellowish "stone" color with trim picked out in white and the roof painted red. Still another roof color appears when the South Church in Portsmouth, New Hampshire, voted in 1796 to "paint the out side of the [1731] Meeting House, the Walls of house of a light stone colour, & the Roof of a chocolate colour."[56] Pictorial evidence seldom fails to emphasize the practice of picking out the trim in white, and documentary corroboration of this can be found in a contract of 1758 in which Joseph McIntire of Salem, father of carver-architect Samuel, agreed "to Paint yᵉ Sides & Ends" of a house "once over & yᵉ Window Frames & other Parts *Usually Painted white* twice over" [emphasis added].[57]

Figure 11. *Detail, over-mantel painting (mid-eighteenth century), Elisha T. Mills House, Fairfield, Conn. (Fairfield Historical Society)*

A late eighteenth-century Boston fireboard depicting the grand Thomas Hancock House on Beacon Hill reveals a situation that, if correctly portrayed, may or may not have been common for masonry buildings in eighteenth-century New England. The house was erected in the 1730s using, as contracts reveal, local "Mistick or Medford Stone" for the walls and imported Connecticut brownstone for the trim.[58] However, the fireboard shows that by the late 1700s the darker brownstone trim had been painted white, perhaps to suggest a lighter stone color or attempt to control brownstone decay.

In 1796 George Washington recorded: "Some years ago, I had ... a quantity of fine white Sand for the purpose of Sanding my houses anew" and then asked whether sand or pounded stone "will look best and most resemble stone" when thrown against the freshly painted surface.[59] Evidence for a closely related treatment was discovered in 1988 during repairs to the Porter-Phelps-Huntington House in Hadley, Massachusetts. Built as the country seat of a prosperous local resident in 1752, both its raising and subsequent alteration in 1799 from a pitched- to a gambrel-roofed house are well documented in family diaries. In 1799 the original exterior walls were reclapboarded as well, and this covering has survived to the present. Beneath the clapboards three main walls of the house and an early added kitchen ell were originally covered with sheathing deeply scored to resemble masonry. Above the principal exterior door the scoring of the woodwork simulates a flat masonry arch with voussoirs and a keystone, and over the window the scoring traces the arc of a segmental pediment. This whole "rustication" of the exterior was covered with a dark red paint or stain and heavily impregnated with sand, the scoring picked out in white.[60]

Other evidence for contrasting color schemes exists in western New England. The original door surround of the mid-eighteenth-century Samuel Fowler House in Southwick, Massachusetts, found in a reused position and acquired by Historic Deerfield in 1984, reveals that the deeply scored rustication was early if not originally painted in an alternating pattern of a deep burgundy red color and deep purple. Again, the scored joints of this rustication were picked out in white. An even more delicate juxtaposition of colors was discovered in 1988 when the segmental door head of the Elisha Root House (ca.1765) in Southington, Connecticut, was stripped of its later paint layers. The surface of the door head was decorated with a pattern of rosettes and leafy stems, shallowly carved and incised in the woodwork. The paint decoration here, which is original or very early, consisted of picking out the rosettes in red and the leafy stems in green. The background color was found to be a very light white or off-white, and the house seems otherwise to have been uniformly painted red, including the rest of the trim.

Only rarely in the colonial period does one find reference to the use of white as an overall exterior paint color, as for example the 1737 Edward Pell estate bill to Daniel Henchman for "179 yds white out side" and "2 Luthorns [or dormer windows] painted white. . . . "[61] Accounts for painting the Ipswich, Massachusetts, meetinghouse in February 1765 suggest a similar treatment in that "White Lead and Oyl" constituted the major expense.[62] Given the predilection throughout the later colonial period for differing color schemes, the occasional use of white, if not related to progressive style trends, may perhaps be seen as just another "color" option. On the other hand, when the province of New Hampshire built a lighthouse at the mouth of the Piscataqua River, for which Joseph Simes billed "290 [pounds] White paint Ground in Oyl" and twenty days work in December 1771, the color may have had the functional purpose of helping make the landmark recognizable from the sea.[63]

INTERIOR PAINTING

Documents and physical evidence reveal an interior color distribution of oil paints ranging from houses in which each room was painted a different color to a restricted use of no more than one or two colors throughout. Both sources suggest that the wealthier urban population enjoyed the greatest diversity. The Edward Pell accounts of the 1730s tell much about color distribution and the equally important consideration of changing fashions in paint colors. Pell billed Boston housewright Thomas Foster for "Inside work" that included "painting a Boffat," "6 double prim'd Shutters," " 20 y^{ds} 8 Feet of Cedar [graining in] Chamber & Entry," "28 y^{ds} Marble in the Lower Room," and "20 y^{ds} Lead Colour in the Kitchen." Even more varied is Pell's 1737 account with Daniel Henchman of Boston, father-in-law of Thomas Hancock, which includes "141 y^{ds}: in Great Entry Wainscott" and "46 y^{ds}: Kitchen, Wallnutt" (the only lower story spaces mentioned), and a full range of colors in the upper stories: "75 y^{ds}: lead Collour, Garretts," "29 y^{ds}½ marble Chamber," "28 y^{ds}:½ Blue Chamber," "44 y^{ds}: Green Chamber," and "54 y^{ds}: 6 feet Ceder Chamber."[64]

A similar diversification of colors, with repetition of colors on upper and lower stories, is revealed in the statement of "Samuel Cutts & Com^p" for a partial redecoration of the Massachusetts Province House in Boston in October 1741:

> To painting front Lower room Light Blew 155 Yds 6 f . . .
> To D° Green Chamber 78 Y 2 f . . .
> To D° Vermillian 6 Yards & 7 feet . . . in ye Green Chamber
> To D° Front Chamber Light Blew 102 Y 2 [f] . . .
> To D° Back Chamber pearl Colour 55 Y . . .
> To D° Back Lower Room Winscot Colour 59 Yards 2 feet . . .
> To D° Counting Room pearl Colour 20 Yards. . . . [65]

It is clear from such accounts and from physical evidence that there typically was a correlation between color and the social distinctions they expressed in various public and household spaces. In larger houses, for example, lead color is apt to be associated with rooms of lesser rank, as in the Henchman and Foster accounts. The same was true of George Tilley's house on Pleasant Street, Boston, near the Hay Market, described in 1753 as having "eight Rooms in it, seven of which are fire rooms ... four of the said Rooms is cornish'd, and the House is handsomely painted throughout, one of the Rooms is painted Green, another Blue, one Cedar and one Marble; the other four a Lead colour...." [66] While the spaces painted lead color are not named, the hierarchical distinction is clear.

Earlier, when Katherine Child billed Henry Gibbs on July 8, 1707, for "Painting worke in y^r Houses," the account confirms a less formal and less costly role for lead-colored paint from the beginning of the century:

To 19 yds in ye Shop Lead colour at 18d p yd ...

To 15 yds Walnut colour at 2s p yd ...

To 9 yds 8 foot in ye Chamber Olivewood at 2s p yd ...

To 15 yds in Entry & Staircase Led colour at 18d p yd ...

To 25 yds in ye upper Chamber Led colour at 18d p yd.... [67]

While Henry Stanbridge, son of Edward, billed Thomas Hancock in 1754 an indiscriminate three shillings a yard for "Lead Colour" and "Seader" alike,[68] accounts more often reflect a price scale with lead color the lower-priced item.

Both typical and somewhat unusual conditions were found in the original paint colors discovered and restored in 1987–88 when the Elisha Root house (ca. 1765), in Southington, Connecticut, was dismantled and relocated to Redding, Connecticut. Measured against other buildings in the eighteenth-century farming community of Southington, Root's was clearly among the two or three best houses built in the town before the Revolution. The principal staircase was located, unconventionally, in an entry at the rear that was painted a lead color. For the balance of the ground story of this stylish rural house, color distribution was limited. A small rear bedroom was painted yellow ocher, as was the buttery, but the parlor, keeping room, and front entry between them were all rendered, unexpectedly, in the same strong shade of blue. Within this restricted range, the only other color was red, found in the original kitchen.

A thin red stain was found also as the only paint applied to the original parlor floor boards, long covered by a later floor (these parlor floor boards were narrower than the other original floor boards throughout the house). If contemporary with construction, this iron oxide red paint represents an exceptionally early example of floor coloring. References to painted floors generally do not appear until after the Revolution.

DARK RED PAINTS

While pigment analysis may distinguish between "red lead," "Spanish brown," and "vermillion"—terms that appear often in colonial records—we have become accustomed at a more popular level to describe all those darker shades of red paint that appear so commonly in eighteenth-century buildings as "Indian red" or "oxblood." Among the pigments inventoried following the 1684 death of Boston painter Daniel George, "red Lead" or pigments of "red colour," together with small amounts of "Vermillion," totaled more than 504 pounds, leading all other pigments in bulk and rivaled only by those described as "best Oaker," "Sprues Oaker," or "English Oaker" (400 pounds).[69] While flat painting of red does not appear in these

Figure 12. *Overmantel land-scape and chimney breast marbleized in red-and-white and black-and-white panels, Pitkin House (1740–60), East Hartford, Conn. (Wordsworth Athenaeum)*

Figure 13. *Marbleized pilasters, Rocky Hill Meeting-house (1785), Amesbury, Mass. (Arthur Haskell, Society for the Preservation of New England Antiquities)*

painters' accounts, it is the first color to have been discovered so far in New England as an over-all interior paint. The beaded frame of the William Clough house (1696–1700) on Vernon Place, Boston, had as its first coat of finish a thin red stain, applied perhaps when the house was built. Similarly the Moses Pierce-Hichborn house (ca.1711) on Boston's North Square and the nearby Ebenezer Clough house (ca.1715) at 21 Unity Street have only a thin red stain as the first finish coat of the wooden trim of their principal rooms, presumably contemporary with construction.

Throughout the eighteenth century red was customarily used in the service sectors of the house, but for simple rural houses red often played the dominant role in the whole interior color scheme. Its use also as an inexpensive priming coat is documented at the outset when on July 18, 1696, Thomas Child billed Capt. Isaac Jones for painting materials that included "20 pound of red primar ground"[70] and even later when Daniel Rea, a Boston painter, debited Edward Lyde, merchant, on November 17, 1772, for "9 yds of Priming Red @ /4" and "16 yds of Lead Col-lour Priming @/6."[71]

PAINTED GRAINING AND MARBLEIZING

The decorative effects of painted graining and marbleizing, together with the use of glazes, have been thoroughly explored by Nina Fletcher Little.[72] The descriptive terms that appear in the earliest documents are generally explicit, and the full range of recorded American ex-amples have ample precedent in English work of the period. The somewhat indeterminate designation "Wainscot Color" or simply "wenscot," as previously noted as occurring in many of the earliest documents, is the single exception. Architect and historian Thomas T. Water-man, from his experience with historic houses in Virginia, believed the term refers to "painted woodwork grained to imitate English oak,"[73] and this would clearly describe the condition found and recorded when the late seventeenth-century Paul Revere house in Boston was re-stored. The only other known example of oak or wainscot graining from this period in New England survives on the summer beam and chimney girt of the north parlor at the Kingsnorth-Starr House in Guilford, Connecticut, built probably just before 1700. This graining is very much worn as a result of continued exposure, but it is combined with early geometric painted decoration on the end girt suggestive of Mannerist patterns.

Both marbleizing and decorative grained effects were practiced extensively in the eighteenth century, and many examples, ranging from the naturalistic to the bizarre, survive **(fig. 12)**. Contemporary documents not infrequently imply that quite literal, even trompe l'oeil, representation was intended. The June 26, 1760, *Maryland Gazette*, for example, noted that a "convict servant man named John Winters" had run away from his employer. He was described as "a very compleat House Painter," who could "imitate marble or mahogany very exactly...." In this connection marbleizing was

Figure 14. *North parlor, Lady Pepperrell House (ca. 1765), Kittery Point, Maine. The room's restored paint and paper is based on surviving physical evidence. (David Bohl, Society for the Preservation of New England Antiquities)*

thought especially appropriate for columns and pilasters. John Gibbs billed Christ Church in Boston on April 9, 1737, for "painting ye pillar white marble and Stone Coulour of ye Pulpitt"[74] and a later rural example of marbleized pillars and pilasters survives in original condition at the Rocky Hill Meetinghouse (1785) in Amesbury, Massachusetts **(fig. 13)**.

One variety of graining that does not appear in the urban documents and seems on the basis of physical evidence to be confined to rural areas is that which simulates knotty pine. Such highly individualistic work seems to mark the progress of those decorative painters who abandoned a fixed urban clientele and took to the road.[75]

OTHER DECORATIVE INTERIOR PAINTING

The use of different colors within a single room provided unusually rich effects and is not uncommon in the more ambitious houses of the colonial elite. During the 1741 redecoration of the Province House in Boston, as noted earlier, the "Green Chamber" received 78 yards of paint (presumably green) together with "6 Yards & 7 feet" of "Vermillion." In the Lady Pepperrell house (ca. 1765) in Kittery Point, Maine, color analysis of the original paint color (now restored) in the north parlor revealed that the woodwork as a whole was a light green, the doors were painted a delicate salmon pink, and the baseboard was picked out in a dark mahogany color **(fig. 14)**. It can be matched with evidence of an English wallpaper installed at the same time. The wallpaper, of which only fragments remain, consisted of a series of pastoral vignettes framed with rococo borders set against a pink background.

Of critical importance in any study of the colonial house interior is the well-documented crossover relationship between the artist and the decorative painter seen earlier in the bills for decorative effects and painting landscapes of the Boston painter John Gibbs. Winthrop Chandler is perhaps the classic case of a rural artist-craftsman. Working before the Revolution in his native Windham County, Connecticut, he is known to have painted a number of overmantel compositions as well as portraits. At his death in 1790 the *Pennsylvania Packet* of September 1 reported: "By profession he was a housepainter; but many good likenesses on canvas shew he could guide the pencil of a limner."

Certainly work like this of a highly skilled painter is found less commonly than purely plain painted surfaces that have been grained or marbleized, but this may be a function of cost or demand. The work of more sophisticated painters often was little more than patterns based on stylized naturalistic forms inspired from textile designs or imported wallpapers, but such designs appear early in New England and continue with increasing popularity into the nineteenth century. Two examples of trailing vines painted on plaster walls in houses built about 1725 are known in Massachusetts Bay.

THE FEDERAL ERA

While colonial documents provide no more than a few tantalizing clues of the painter's actual daily employment, the evidence changes by the late eighteenth century. For this period detailed records of shop practices are found in painters' accounts, and unpublished "Painter's Prices" and "Rules of Measurement" describe the economics of craft practice after 1800. No American painter's guide is known until 1812, when Hezekiah Reynolds (1756–1833), a rural Connecticut painter, published *Directions for House and Ship Painting, Shewing ... The Best Method of Preparing, Mixing and Laying the Various Colours Now in Use* in New Haven. This rare pamphlet gives directions for paint preparation with a unique compendium of native Federal-era paint recipes. Account books of rural painters, such as that of Stephanus Knight (1772–1810), who practiced as a jack-of-all-trades in Enfield, Connecticut, are uncommon. That exteriors often remained unpainted and that rural account books are so scarce raise questions about how viable the trade really was in rural areas during this period. Shop records from seaport towns, however, provide a wealth of information about the work of common painters and the colorful urban world they made possible in colonial and Federal America.

THE REA AND JOHNSTON ACCOUNTS, 1767–1803

Daniel Rea, Jr., was apprenticed to Thomas Johnston, a Boston painter and father of a clan of portraitists. Johnston's accounts between 1726 and 1764 are lost, but we have manuscripts that cover the last two years of his life to 1767, when his wife, Bathsheba, inherited the business. She remarried the next year, and Daniel Rea, now her son-in-law, purchased all her property and took over the painting business. Rea ran it alone from 1769 to 1772, when he took John Johnston, one of Thomas and Bathsheba's sons, into partnership. (This arrangement lasted until 1789, when John Johnston left the business to work primarily as a portrait artist.) From 1789 to his death in 1803 Rea worked with his son, Daniel III.[76]

Computerizing nine volumes covering the work of all four periods (from the mid-1760s to just past 1800) allows us to categorize entries into six major types of painting as well as associated sale of art supplies and other materials.

Table 1 shows a shift in their business over the four decades, with house and ship painting generally increasing at the expense of carriage and other work. A solid majority (51 percent) of Johnston's last customers were other craftsmen for whom he painted their products, such as carriages, ships, furniture, funeral hardware, and other utilitarian objects. Merchants and urban gentry accounted for less than a quarter of the individual entries in the accounts.

Table 1. *Percentages for Types of Painting in the Rea and Johnston Accounts*

Type of Work	1765–67	1769–72	1773–76	1777–80	1781–85	1786–90	1791–95
House painting	9.1	20.0	18.6	17.5	15.3	23.2	33.2
Carriage painting	15.0	12.0	11.4	17.1	14.5	7.0	4.8
Ship painting	2.6	2.8	5.7	12.1	7.2	9.8	8.3
Sign painting	5.3	12.0	5.7	2.6	5.1	5.0	9.1
Small objects	39.8	31.7	32.8	33.2	25.3	24.7	33.2
Art work	1.1	0.8	1.0	0.9	0.6	0.4	0.3
Paint supplies	20.9	20.0	14.0	16.4	31.0	27.6	10.1

After Johnston's death the first three years of Rea's business involved less painting for other craftsmen (39 percent) and a rise of work (43 percent) done for the local merchant elite, in part because in 1770 Rea associated with such men as a militia member of the Ancient and Honorable Artillery Company. Between 1770 and 1795 more than seventy new customers from the ranks of this 260-man militia account for nearly a quarter of all the shop's customers. Like most painters in Boston, Rea never advertised in newspapers; merchants and professionals were attracted through association in volunteer organizations outside the craft.[77]

Rea's new patrons were customers for more house painting, carriage painting, and decoration of utilitarian consumer goods than were the craftsmen-producers who had been the mainstay of the Johnston shop. Even during the British occupation of Boston during the war, which forced Rea and his family to move temporarily to Weston, Massachusetts, Rea continued to find work with merchant-patriots. He also did military work by painting privateers, gun carriages, and in 1773 more than thirty drums for Samuel Ridgeway, a Boston drum maker. In the years after the Revolution painting the products of other craftsmen designed for resale became a smaller and smaller part of the business; in the final years of Rea and Son the only significant work for other craftsmen was decorating toleware for tinsmith Joseph Howe. Carriage painting, which in former years had as often been done for chaise makers as for the merchant gentry, dropped to its lowest point. Ship painting, on the other hand, increased hand in hand with the growth of merchant ship-owning customers and the revival of Boston Harbor as a major port.

The accounts provide a long list of architectural elements painted between 1765 and 1803, sometimes indicating the colors used. The earliest work was primarily exterior painting: walls, windows, doors, and gutters. By the end of the eighteenth century among the merchant elite, at least, there are also descriptions of painting outbuildings, garden architecture, and ornamental fences. Interior painting is seldom specified until after the Revolution; the only specific features mentioned in prewar accounts are the fireplace, chimney, and the kitchen. Nor does painting of floors, walls, or shutters typically appear in these or other painters' accounts until after the Revolution—for example, the Rea bill of September 24, 1791, to Thomas K. Jones for "paintᵍ Kitchen floor, yellow."[78] Not only floor colors but also decorative treatments are noted, such as painting for Samuel Parkman a "Kitchen Floor done 4 Times with a Border" or another account for painting a chamber floor with "a dog in the center."[79] Dog designs were apparently popular in Federal Boston, for in 1795 another painter, George Davidson, recorded: "John Hayward Dr

Table 2. *Floor Cloth Designs in the Rea and Johnston Accounts*

Design	Number	Known Location
Cubes	1	+ 1 in parlor
Black and yellow diamonds	1	
Turkey fashion	1	in entry
Plain	7	
Plain with borders	4	+ 2 in entry
Plain with borders and center	4	+ 1 in room and entry
Plain with borders, center, and corners	3	
Straw work	2	+ 1 in back parlor
Straw work with border and center	1	in entry
No design given	40	+38 in named rooms

to Painting a Carpet Plain with a Bourdur Round and a Dog in the Midle."[80] At the turn of the century, as floor carpeting became more common, Rea's 1799 account for Stephen Gorham makes reference to painting the "Floor round yᵉ Carpett, and some more Small Jobs."[81]

Painters also painted floor cloths. Edward Pell's 1737 inventory of his "Cellar and Painters Shop" listed a "Floor Cloth on yᵉ Fence," which shows how the canvas was prepared.[82] One of the most informative aspects of the Rea and Johnston accounts are 149 floor carpets painted and recorded between 1767 and 1803, of which there are nearly a dozen known designs **(table 2)**. While no pattern is usually cited, it may be significant that Hezekiah Reynolds's 1812 directions for making "Floor Carpets or Oil'd Cloth" recommended painting white and black "squares or diamonds" and notes the "margin may be ornamented ... by using paper patterns."[83] From extant building evidence, stencil borders began to replace the larger freehand designs found on walls and floors during the Federal period.

Just as important as the designs, the Rea and Johnston accounts show that Boston floor cloths were used in the same room setting as those found in rural household inventories.[84] Moreover, painted floor cloths were not merely a "poor man's carpet" but were commissioned by the merchant elite and more prosperous craftsmen. Rea charged at least twenty-seven to people of title (such as ministers and government officials), eleven were made for other professionals, fifty-seven for merchants, and fifty-four for a wide range of craftsmen and others.

These painted floor cloths were designed primarily for the front entry and, somewhat less commonly, an adjoining room or the kitchen, where wet and muddy feet could damage a real carpet **(table 3)**. Only after the war do individual floor cloths appear in other locations, and even then the entry was the preferred location. Nor was this unique to New England. A visitor to Thomas Jefferson's Monticello in 1823 noted that the entry hall was "covered with a glossy oil cloth," although the 1805 floor color was a grass green recommended to the president by the artist Gilbert Stuart.[85]

Rea's accounts also mention with some regularity the painting of "window shades," "Venetian" shades, or "blinds," terms that were interchangeable. These canvas and slatted-wood

Table 3. *Known Room Locations of Rea and Johnston Floor Cloths by Date*

Rooms	1768–76	1777–85	1786–95	1796–1803	Total
Kitchen	2				2
Stairs	1				1
Entry	6	1	9	4	20
Room and entry	1	2	6		9
Dining parlor and entry			1		1
Dining parlor			2		2
Room			4		4
Parlor			2		2
Back parlor			1		1
Middle room			1		1
Drawing room			1		1
Chamber			1		1
Church pew			1		1

shades were a luxury product throughout the period of the accounts, perhaps partly because of the difficulty of painting them. Where color is noted, the window shades or blinds are always green. Merchant and professional customers account for the great majority. Only in the economic recovery in the late 1780s and 1790s did the occasional housewright, tailor, silversmith, and painter-glazier also have "Canvas Window Shades" painted. These interior shades are clearly differentiated from "Outside Window Shades," which appear only in postwar accounts. Those were probably the louvered exterior window shutters known in the South since the mid-eighteenth century but not otherwise documented in New England until the beginning of the nineteenth century. By 1792 Jefferson apparently had louvered "blinds" or shutters on the exterior of Monticello as well as solid paneled shutters inside.[86]

While notation of colors used in specific architectural contexts is rare in the Rea accounts, patterns in the use of colors for specific features can be discerned by studying the accounts as a whole. Shop doors, signs, and shutters were generally painted black. Often this formed a background for gilding the name, trade, or street number of the shop. The other place Rea used black as a primary color was in the fireplace, at least toward the end of the century—for example, in 1799 he charged Stephen Gorham for "Black backs & Jambs of four Chimneys."[87]

Red, probably common Spanish brown, was used early and late for exterior details. Windows, doors, gutters, coving, and cornices, as well as a lean-to and one room, were specifically described as red. Blue and green, both more expensive colors, appear in the records as wall colors in the interior of a few homes. There are blue walls in the dining room, staircase, and parlor as well as in a privy. Green, besides being used for window shades and shutters of all sorts, inside and out, was used in the garden for "Boarder Boards, Hott Bed and Flower Boxes, done green." Green was also found on one Boston chimney breast and was the primary color for the "Walls of the Great Entry" of the Lincoln "Mansion house" of John Codman.[88] Specific pigmentation, if not color, is noted in the 1796 charge for painting the front of the William Woods house in Boston "the Colour mix'ᵈ with Verdisgreae."[89]

Yellow was used on a floor and for painting a nursery, "Straw Colour" used for a shop door, and white (rather than the earlier black) was used for mop boards and a cistern top. Mixed colors and those in imitation of fine woods appear in several Rea accounts. "Lead Colour" appears before the war as an interior color, while later it is mentioned for shop fronts. "Stone colour" is mentioned for "Priming [a] Room & Entry" for Dr. Lloyd. Chocolate was used once as an exterior house color and later on mop boards of an entry and two window seats inside one house and four chambers and entry of another. Mahogany was used for house or shop windows, as well as an insurance company office. In 1798 Samuel Barrett was charged for "Painting your Parlour, Clossetts &tc Complete—Vizᵗ ... Extra work of Mahoʸ & Marble" and the doors and shelves of two closets.[90]

THE ACCOUNTS OF GEORGE DAVIDSON, 1793–99

The career and accounts of George Davidson, another Boston painter, offer a stark contrast to the Reas' work. Apparently working in Charlestown before 1790, Davidson shipped out as a ship's painter on the second voyage of the 212-ton merchant ship *Columbia* under the command of Capt. Robert Gray. This eighty-three-foot, three-masted ship is famous as the first American ship to circumnavigate the globe and its discovery of the "great river of the West" to which the ship's name was given, thereby furnishing the new nation with Pacific northwest coast claims.[91]

The ship left Boston September 28, 1790, and arrived at the Northwest coast in June 1791. During this voyage in April 1792 Gray "discovered," charted, and named the Columbia River. The *Columbia* sailed for Hawaii that fall, reached China in December, and began its return in February, reaching Boston on July 29, 1793. During this voyage of exploration and trade, Davidson not only painted the decks, masts, and other ship's work but also acted as ship's artist, recording the events of the voyage in a series of wash drawings, for which he became known as one of "the most talented of the seaman-artist" in the early republic.[92]

While scholars have assumed that Davidson "made many copies of his drawings of the trip" for friends, one writer suggested that it was "likely that some were also made to sell."[93] Unrecognized until now, Davidson's daily accounts from 1793 to 1799 survive in the manuscript collection of the Old Sturbridge Village library.[94] These accounts show that the known Davidson paintings were, indeed, copied in sets, perhaps from originals or from those later owned by Captain Gray. In December 1793 for Samuel Yendell, *Columbia*'s ship carpenter, he records "Painting three Pictures at 36 /[shillings] Pʳ Each." In March 1794 for Benjamin Popkins, the ship's armorer, he painted five pictures at five dollars each.[95] The same week he painted a small set of three unidentified pictures at forty shillings each for a "Mr. Blake the Cabinetmaker," whose identity is not otherwise known.

In February 1795 he charged ship carver Simeon Skillin three dollars for "a Picture of the *Concord*," and there are several entries like the one in October 1796 for "Canvas & Painting a Masons Badge of Masonry," which suggests that he, like Daniel Rea, belonged to a lodge. On November 28, 1798, he records another aspect of his art, charging Daniel Bowen for

"Brightening up his Pictures in his Museum" as well as painting his sign. Over the next two months Bowen's museum account included finishing a picture for thirty dollars, a large gilt frame and strainer, a pint of copal varnish and "laying it on his picture" as well as "varnishing Mrs Pricherd Picture & frunt Peice Extraordnery."[96]

Davidson's accounts begin September 9, 1793, only six weeks after the *Columbia*'s return, when he "Agreed with Mr Bull the Baker for a small shop at Eight Dollars p^r Quarter of a year." In October he began to board "at M^r [Thomas] Trumans at 12/ p^r week," and in May he "Took half a Pew in the New North Meeting house." The 1797 Boston *Directory* lists him as George "Davison [sic] ... painter," with a shop located on Prince Street (which ran from North Square to the Charles River bridge), living in a nearby house on Salutation Alley off North Square. The accounts end in August 1799, the year he apparently shipped out as captain of the ship *Rover*, bound again for the Pacific but reported lost at sea in 1800. Davidson may have turned to sailing during absences of several weeks each year for which there are no painting charges. In any event, his portrait from sometime just before his final voyage survives.

Davidson's work was primarily carriage painting, but like other Boston painters he also engaged in ship, sign, and house painting as well as decorating furniture, fire buckets, and floor cloths. Like the better-known John Gore, he regularly painted coats of arms (compared to only three ever listed in nine volumes of Rea and Johnston accounts). One was for his former commander, Captain Gray, for whom he also painted fire buckets in August 1794 and July 1795.

He also did sign painting. In September 1793 Davidson charged Nathan Copeland, a shoemaker, for "painting 3 Window shutters Black" and painting them with "54 letter"—the same pattern of blacking shop shutters as a background for signs also seen in the Rea accounts. For a Cambridge tavern keeper Davidson painted a sign "with a flag &c" in May 1796, a few days after charging William Williams for "Painting his Sine hat Boxes and a Wooden Hatt Seventeen Dol[lars]."

For two Boston furniture firms—Alexander and Stone and Howard and Blake—he painted a number of bed cornices. These were usually plain like the 1795 "Sett of cornices Edged with Red" for Alexander and Stone, but for Howard and Blake in January 1794 he painted "a sett of Bed and Window Cornices Resembling the Cop[p]er Plate" curtains that would hang below them. A year later he did another set of bed cornices in "Emitation of Coper Plate," and in March 1795 he charged five dollars for "Painting a sett of Window Cornices in imitation of Calico." This is not the first known case of such a cornice. Daniel Rea charged a John Miller on July 15, 1793, for a bed cornice "in Imitation of the Copper plate" and in 1791 painted one for himself with double scalloped edges.

The new Federal-style architecture of postrevolutionary Boston is rarely recognizable in these accounts. In August 1795 Davidson was at architect Charles Bulfinch's "Tontine Building" "Painting Two Window Cornices" for Mr. Carnes in "No. 14," and later that year he charged John Coffin Jones for "Painting five Window Cornices and gilting the same." For pastor Thomas Badger in September 1794 Davidson painted the "Meeting house Windows and over the top [in] Imitation of glass," perhaps creating the illusion of an arched window. While there are accounts for painting "4 window Shutters stone Colour" and painting the front of a house "done Mahogany Colour," there is generally little mention of architectural colors.

Davidson supplemented his income by measuring the work of other painters, in cases of disagreement between a painter and his customer about the proper cost of the work, at a fee of a half cent per yard. While Boston's carpenters regularly published their own rules and prices, there was no similar printed source for painters. A handwritten source, however, does exist. Perez Loring, whose brothers helped write *The Rules of Work of the Carpenters, in the Town of Boston* (Boston, 1800) added in handwriting two sets of rules and prices for house painting in the end papers of his own copy of the book.[97] These prices were established by local painters in 1800 and 1815.

The painters' prices Loring recorded in 1800 are cited in dollars and cents, a departure from the traditional pounds, shillings, and pence in which Davidson, for example, still figured most accounts. Loring lists the cost for painting one coat (12½ cents per yard), two coats (20 cents), and three (25 cents); special charges for mahogany "color" or graining (50 cents a yard), marbleizing (41 cents), and green (two coats, 33 cents; three coats 50 cents); as well as piecework charges for priming and cutting sash, painting window frames of various sizes, mahogany doors ($1.00 per side), and plain and fret dentils. All other painting was to be measured and priced "by Judgement."

These prices and special charges seem to be reflected in the accounts of Boston contemporaries. The Reas' work on June 10, 1800, for Stephen Gorham included

Painting your House Inside & Out	
Outhouses, Barn Fences &c Intire	
Measuring 3400 square yards——	[$]680.—
as Agree'd for at 20 Cents Pr Yard	
To d° 56 Window frames at 75 Cts	42.—
To d° 624 Large Sash Squares at 6 Cts	37.44
To d° 144 Small Squares at 3 Cts	4.32

Such bills suggest that if Rea followed the local prices the house, window frames, and sash were painted twice over. Whatever colors were used did not include the more expensive green or mahogany that would have been separately listed.

The introduction of new Adamesque architectural joinery may have prompted a more detailed attempt to provide standards for measuring and pricing painters' work. But in a period of much new construction and harsh economic cycles, price guides were also designed to foster craft uniformity and sustain the trade by reducing competitive prices. This is evident in the 1815 prices and rules of measurement recorded by Loring, which had been "Unanimously Adopted by the Painters of Boston" that year. This action established separate prices for brick and wood; repainting old surfaces now cost less than new wood; blue as well as green cost more per yard, but Spanish brown was lower than the norm. Rules for pricing various sash, doors, signs, stairs, cornices, and other architectural features were carefully detailed for the first time.

One short painter's manuscript in the collection of the Essex Institute supplements the extensive run of Daniel Rea and George Davidson in Boston.[98] William Gray (1750–1819) was one of five men by that name in Salem, Massachusetts, including his father (1727–1806), also a painter.[99] A single ledger lists customers of his work spanning the years 1774 to 1811. The younger William practiced the whole range of painting—ships, houses, and other forms of utilitarian painting—as well as glazing and wallpapering. In 1774, for example, he painted, outside as well as in, the house of Capt. William Bartlett in nearby Beverly, Massachusetts. One room was painted blue, and a chamber was painted in imitation of "Seder" (cedar). In 1783 he also charged Jeremiah Sheppard of Salem for painting a "Seder Chamber."

While formal rooms were usually painted in oil, Bartlett's kitchen, chamber, and entry were all done in size (distemper). The use of glue (size) and pigment for utilitarian rooms is common throughout his accounts. Four years later he charged Samuel Ward of Salem for "Sizing Kitchen, painting front room & Entry 3 days @ 5/pr." In 1781 he painted Capt. Josiah Batchelder's chamber blue and charged him for two pounds of glue and an equal amount of Spanish brown "For sizing 2 rooms in the Tavern."

In May 1800 he moved to Portsmouth, New Hampshire, and in July advertised a partnership with John Gray, Jr. Probably a nephew, John may have apprenticed under William Gray in Salem, as William debited John for paints and oils as well as "Boarding you from May 1 '97 to Nov.ʳ 5, '98." By the end of November 1798, however, John Gray was in Portsmouth advertising painting and gilding at his shop on "Jeffrey" (Jaffrey) Street. By February 1799 he was living at a local inn; a year later he married the innkeeper's niece. John and William Gray's "copartnership" lasted less than a year; newspaper advertisements soon announced its dissolution. It appears that William then concentrated on ship and house painting while John specialized in sign, furniture, and coach and chaise decoration. Like painters elsewhere, they also sold paints and pigments "both dry and ground" (white lead in kegs and Prussian blue in bladders) as well as varnish, window glass, and wallpapers.[100]

At first glance it would appear from William Gray's Portsmouth accounts that he painted and papered two houses in Durham, New Hampshire, some twelve miles upriver from the port. Both Capt. John Bickford and Col. Ebenezer Thompson are listed as "of Durham," and it appears that in June 1800 he may have traveled to that town to paint Bickford's house. One room was "Seder Colour" and another "Stone Colour"; he also charged for "Papering the front room and Bordering 4 Rools" as well as papering both a chamber and the "Seder room with Bordering." On the other hand, when in October he painted and papered the house of Col. Ebenezer Thompson "of Durham," it is certainly the large, L-shaped three-story home on Haymarket Square in Portsmouth. Thompson had just purchased the land and constructed a new house while still residing in Durham, and Gray's accounts provide the first accurate date for its completion. He later returned in 1803 to paint one of its chambers.[101]

Together with Gray's earlier work around Salem and Beverly, we get a picture of a semi-itinerant urban craftsman who responded to work in surrounding towns that may have had no local painter of their own. If, indeed, Bickford's house was in Durham and not an unidentified building in the burgeoning port town, Gray's work may show that some settled Piscataqua communities relied on painters from Portsmouth. If so, it is understandable that the least affluent people in more distant rural communities all over New England might forego house painting almost entirely.

HEZEKIAH REYNOLDS'S 1812 PAINTING GUIDE

Not until the early nineteenth century do we have a firsthand account of an American house and ship painter that describes both the method of making paints and the proportion of specific pigments used to make the colors familiar from other documentary accounts. Hezekiah Reynolds (1756–1833) was born in Waterbury, Connecticut, married in North Branford, and later worked in Wallingford. His book *Directions for House and Ship Painting; Shewing in a plain and concise manner, the Best Method of Preparing, Mixing and Laying the Various Colours Now in Use, Designed for the Use of Learners* was published in New Haven in 1812. On the basis of thirty years' experience, he offered the secrets of his trade to other craftsmen—"the Cabinet and Chair Maker, the Wheelwright, the House and Ship Joiner; and to others whose Trades are connected with building."[102] Thus, although this country painter does not propose making Everyman his own painter, he does recognize the needs of other crafts for practical information about his trade.

Among the distinctions Reynolds makes, for the first time in print, was that exterior and interior paints were mixed differently. Rather than using an imported paint mill to pulverize the pigments, he used a "smooth iron kettle of middling size" with a twelve- to twenty-four-pound ball hung over the kettle to grind the pigments while still in their dry form. When enough was ground, six to eight pounds of the pigment was placed in the kettle and ground, using the iron ball, with oil that had been boiled with red lead to speed its drying. He provides directions for making ten exterior paints: white, cream, straw, orange, pea green, parrot green, grass green, red, slate, and black.

For interior painting, colors were individually ground in boiled oil, to which copal varnish or turpentine was added. The painter then ground white lead and oil using a muller on marble slab. Small quantities of other pigments were each ground in oil separately, unlike those for the exterior, before being mixed together. Reynolds provides directions for three whites (including "light stone color"), sea green, both Prussian blue and navy blue, dark stone, red, purple, claret, chocolate, mahogany, red cedar, cherry tree wood, and marble. These are not only the same fancy hues and "colors" for graining or marbleizing that we find in painter's account books but also those listed in the Boston prices for 1815.

CHANGING PATTERNS OF EXTERIOR TREATMENT

Reynolds's colors suggest that traditional red and orange exterior colors were then in competition with the new fashion for lighter hues. Strong paint colors like these, preferred throughout the colonial period, were used even later in conservative situations. Capt. Daniel Willard, born in 1784, writing of his native Newington, Connecticut, could "remember well when there was not a white house in the place, one was of a greenish color, a few were painted Spanish brown, all the others of the natural wood color."[103] Willard's recollections remind us that exterior paint still remained something of an exception in all but the finer houses throughout

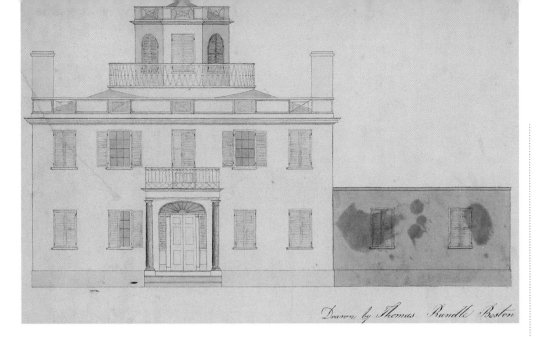

Drawn by Thomas Rundle Boston

much of the period. As late as 1833 one New England writer noted, "Most of the Dwelling Houses in the country are erected and suffered to continue years without painting; this they suppose a matter of economy to save expense." He went on to argue the benefits of periodic painting to keep "the exterior in a state of fine preservation."[104]

Willard's reminiscences of strong exterior paint colors can be matched in other rural documents, including the all-important meetinghouse (which in rural areas retained its traditional form until the beginning of the nineteenth century). The town of Gilsum, New Hampshire, for example, voted in 1791 to paint the clapboards of its meetinghouse "bright orring" [orange] and the doors stone gray.[105] This situation began to change in the years following the Revolution in keeping with neoclassical style trends in building and furniture. The Middleborough and Taunton (now Lakeville, Massachusetts) church voted on June 16, 1794, that "the outside walls" of its mid-eighteenth-century parsonage "be painted a stone colour." When, on the other hand, its 1759 meetinghouse was substantially repaired and modernized, the society voted in March 1799 to paint the body of the house white and the doors and trim they called "wast boards" a chocolate color.[106] In many documents of the Federal era when white is not specified, a lighter hue at least is indicated. The 1792 contract for a new meetinghouse in Durham, New Hampshire, specified that "the outside wholly to be painted, the roof with Spanish brown & linseed oil, and the remainder of a Straw or light couler."[107]

Architectural drawings for the period just after 1800 are often given a wash of color to represent exterior paint. While in general these washes are unreliable guides to actual colors, one pair of drawings in the Society for the Preservation of New England Antiquities collections is of particular interest. Drawn on paper watermarked 1801, they are designs for a house in Medford, Massachusetts. One for a brick dwelling is by the noted architect Asher Benjamin, and the other for a wooden version is signed by Thomas Rundle, a housewright of Cambridge and Boston, who may have been Benjamin's student.[108] The yellow wash on the Rundle facade elevation is confirmed as an actual yellow paint in a later set of watercolor landscape views of the house (fig. 15). This house was built between 1808 and 1816 on Forest Street in Medford for Thompson Kidder of Boston, "gentleman" and "Broker" and was demolished

Figure 16. *Watercolor (1808–10) by James Kidder of the house and gardens of Thompson Kidder, Medford, Mass. As first built, the ocher facade was apparently unrelieved by a different trim color. (David Bohl, Society for the Preservation of New England Antiquities)*

in 1925 after being photographed. The Kidder house was the center of an elaborately landscaped estate with adjoining stable, privy, and gardens. Two unusually complete sets of perspective watercolor views of the house and its grounds document the site at different dates **(figs. 16 and 17)**. These watercolors are here for the first time attributed to Kidder's brother, James Kidder (1793–1837), an artist whose earliest known landscape aquatint was published in 1813. The attribution is based on his 1818–19 pencil and watercolor painting of the Old Feather Store, in the Massachusetts Historical Society, which shares identical measurements within a drawn frame and much similarity in technique and handling.[109]

The clapboarded side and rear walls as well as the flush-board facade of the Kidder house are depicted as uniformly yellow with the only different color the green shutters (shown closed for the summer as was traditional). The fences and trellis work in the gardens are the only elements painted white. The absence of a distinct trim color on the window frames, door surround, or cornice of the house or its outbuildings is a change from the eighteenth-century practices previously described. Beginning about 1800 less and less mention is made of a contrasting color being used for any architectural trim except for doors and shutters. Henry Wansey, an English textile manufacturer, traveling from Boston to New York along the inland route in 1794, noted, "The houses which we passed in the woods are ... all sashed, and ... neatly painted; some of a free stone colour, others white with green doors and window shutters."[110] By 1796 Timothy Dwight, president of Yale University, observed while passing through Suffield, Connecticut, "The houses on both sides of the street are built in

a handsome style; and being painted white, (the common colour of the houses in New England,) … exhibit a scene uncommonly cheerful."[111] A foreign visitor to the Mid-Atlantic states in 1797 described the same conditions: "One sees a very large number of … country houses all around Philadelphia … for the most part of wood, built in a manner both light and elegant. All of them are painted white with green blinds."[112] And while many farmhouses may have remained unpainted well into the nineteenth century, change was at work here at the rural level too, as we know from the recollections of S. G. Goodrich (Peter Parley), who wrote of his boyhood in Ridgefield, Connecticut: "My memory goes distinctly back to the year 1797, when I was four years old. At that time … we removed from the Old House to the New House … painted red behind and white in front.…" Using less expensive red paint on the backside was a common New England "economy" which survived well into the twentieth century. He noted, for comparison, that "most of the dwellings thereabouts [were] of the dun complexion which pine-boards and chestnut-shingles assume, from exposure to the weather."[113]

This image of the Federal New England agricultural landscape—many small unpainted houses interspersed with those of strong colonial colors or the newer light facades on homes of the country elite—is hard to imagine. Landscape artists after 1800 painted a more prosperous countryside of farm, factory, and center village. A century more of inaccurate colonial images and revival restorations has colored New England a monochromatic white. In truth it was both far more vivid and more unpainted than we have generally recognized.

Figure 17. *Watercolor (1810–16) by James Kidder of the house and gardens of Thompson Kidder, Medford, Mass. A porch, balustrade, and shutters have been added to conform with Rundle's elevation. (David Bohl, Society for the Preservation of New England Antiquities)*

House Painting in Britain

SOURCES FOR AMERICAN PAINTS, 1615 TO 1830

IAN C. BRISTOW

lthough from the seventeenth century on there are many documentary references to the use of paint in American buildings, the earliest known American work dedicated to the subject of house painting from a technical viewpoint is the short book *Directions for Ship and House Painting,* published by Hezekiah Reynolds in New Haven in 1812. To provide a context for this book and for information on earlier practice it is necessary to turn to European sources. From these it is possible to assemble a good outline of house painting methods, which, as is clear from documentary sources, were used on both sides of the Atlantic (fig. 1).

From 1615 to 1830 three major categories of paint were used for house painting: water-based paints, oil paints, and varnishes based on natural resins dissolved in a variety of organic solvents. Water-based paints were generally applied to plaster, although during the seventeenth century they were also used on timber, a practice that seems to have persisted in France until at least the end of the eighteenth century. Oil paints were used with equal facility on both plaster and joinery but were much more expensive than water-based paints. Varnishes could be used to provide a more or less glossy transparent finish, as a medium for pigment, or as an additive to oil paints to provide an enhanced gloss or harder paint film.

WATER-BASED PAINTS

The simplest type of water-based paint was commonly known in the seventeenth and eighteenth centuries as "whiting" or "whitening." It consisted of a suspension of pigment in water and was applied by brushes of the type illustrated by Joseph Moxon in 1703 (fig. 2). It found widespread use on plaster ceilings, where the unbound friable finish it provided was not subject to abrasion. Its principal advantages were its complete porosity, which allowed application to newly completed work, and lack of yellowing that an oil binder would cause. The pigment commonly used was powdered natural chalk (calcium carbonate), easily recognizable under the microscope by the presence of small fossil coccoliths. This was prepared by crushing the chalk, separating coarse particles by settlement in water, and then drying. During the seventeenth century it was commonly known as "Spanish white" or simply "Spanish," but by

Figure 1. *Staircase, No. 1 Greek Street, Soho, London, reflecting fashionable coloring of mid-eighteenth-century England, when the house was built. The use of stone color on the walls and deep blue on the ironwork is typical of the period.*
(Ian C. Bristow)

the latter part of the eighteenth century it was also supplied as "Paris white," a term that may at first have been applied to finer grades. In addition, slaked lime (calcium hydroxide) was also used, but in such instances the finish was often referred to as "limewash" or "lime white."

References to "whiting" are commonly found in seventeenth- and eighteenth-century building accounts, a typical instance being the application of this finish to the ceiling of the King's Withdrawing Chamber at Greenwich Palace, Kent, in the fiscal year 1616–17.[1] A few decades later the gentleman-architect Sir Roger Pratt (1620–85) noted that new ceilings should be "whited with the best Spanish white.... "[2]

The friable nature of such finishes precluded their use at low levels, where clothing might come into contact with the surface. To overcome this, animal-glue size was used as a binder. During the first half of the seventeenth century this was often prepared on site by boiling off-cuts of leather in water, a practice illustrated by a reference to work at Newmarket, Cambridgeshire, one of the king's houses, where in the accounts for 1627–28 an item appears for "Leather shriddes to make Size" together with "wood to boile Size."[3] Outside London this practice persisted at least until the end of the eighteenth century,[4] but by the 1730s size could be purchased in the capital and probably in other towns and cities prepared in two strengths, known respectively as "single size" and "double size."[5]

Finishes bound with size were commonly known as "whitewash," and although similar to "whiting" or "whitening," there is some evidence that this term was often used to distinguish size-bound from unbound formulations. Size-bound types were also known as "distemper," the anglicized form of the French *détrempe*. A good description of their method of preparation was given by T. H. Vanherman, a London house painter, in the late 1820s. Twelve pounds of the best whiting, he directed, should be barely covered with cold water and soaked for five or six hours. The mixture was then stirred and two quarts of double size added, after which it was allowed to stand overnight to become a jelly, in which state it was applied.[6] Instances of the use of distemper on ceilings and plaster walls are ubiquitous, but examples of its use on timber paneling and other joinery elements in seventeenth-century England may also be encountered. Thus, in 1625–26 the wainscoting in one of the bedchambers at Dover Castle, Kent, was painted timber color in distemper,[7] and in 1674 items appear in accounts for Whitehall Palace, London, "ffor paynting white in distemper 3 times in a place the playne waynescott Cornish doores & windowes in yᵉ Duke of Yorks bedchamber withdrᵍ & presence."[8] Other references show that distemper on joinery was sometimes finished with a coat of varnish, as on the linenfold paneling in the Tiltyard gallery at Whitehall in 1627–28.[9]

No eighteenth-century British examples of joinery painted with distemper have yet been identified, however, and it seems likely that by then oil was commonly substituted, at least in high-class work. In the 1770s, however, when paneling had fallen out of fashion in England, the French author J. F. Watin advocated a complex multilayered system of varnished distemper for *boiserie,* which, he claimed, would offer to the ostentatious great richness and the most sumptuous embellishment while exhibiting the freshness of porcelain, a quality that, he stressed, the finish would keep.[10] In this and other instances he advocated the use of white lead in the upper layers of distemper in place of whiting, probably with the intention of producing a cleaner color. This substitution may also be found in later eighteenth-century English

Figure 2. *Early eighteenth-century brushes, illustrated in Joseph Moxon's* Mechanick Exercises, *3d ed. (1703), pl. 2.*

accounts for distemper work, notably in a bill of 1789 for painting sculptures at the Mansion House, London, which includes items such as "white lead done in distemper."[11] Although similar references to the use of white lead have been noted, this was clearly not everyday practice.

Another water-based system was true fresco, described notably by the Italian artist Cennino Cennini in the early fifteenth century,[12] in which pigment suspended in water is applied to the surface of wet lime plaster. It appears to have been reserved for the use of artists and was referred to by Roger Pratt in the mid-seventeenth century and by Roger Neve in the early eighteenth only in that context.[13] No references to its use for the common purposes of house painting have been encountered to date. In preparing pigment for use in fresco, however, Neve included milk or skimmed milk among alternative vehicles, his suggestion indicating that the properties of casein were current knowledge in early eighteenth-century Britain. Watin too described the use of colors *au lait* but remarked that the method had fallen into disuse because of the smell.[14] In Europe, as in America, not until after the French writer Cadet de Vaux attempted to revive the method at the end of the eighteenth century does it appear that its use was again considered,[15] but the absence of references to it in any early nineteenth-century British painting accounts examined to date suggests perhaps that the technique was more written about than practiced.

OIL PAINT

The chemical principle behind the drying mechanism of oil paints is described by Morgan Phillips in "The Composition and Nature of Paints" (in this volume). The first stage in their preparation was the thorough wetting of individual pigment particles with oil by grinding the two together until they were fully integrated in the form of a paste. The simplest method of grinding—by means of a slab and muller—was known from very early times. Cennini, for example, described the process,[16] and in the second half of the seventeenth century the method was related at length by John Smith, author of the *Art of Painting in Oyl*.[17] By the 1740s, however, at least one paint mill driven by horsepower was in use in London. Reference to it is found in a newspaper advertisement thought to date from 1741, in which claims for the superior nature of the product were made,[18] and it is illustrated at the head of the "Directions for Painting" issued by Joseph Emerton, the British Museum copy of which has a bill dating from 1744 made out on its reverse **(fig. 3)**.[19] Both this and a better illustration dating from the latter part of the eighteenth century, when the firm had become Emerton and Manby,[20] indicate that the mill was constructed on a rotary principle, probably similar to that used in the hand mill described by Andrew Ure in 1839, in which flat horizontal millstones similar to those used in corn grinding were used **(fig. 4)**.[21] This indicates that the conical elements seen in Emerton's illustration at the feet of the drive shafts are funnels used to feed the dry pigment into the space between the stones.

Although it seems possible that even in the early nineteenth century some painters preferred to purchase the more costly pigments, such as vermilion and verdigris, in dry form,[22] during the seventeenth century those of which larger quantities were regularly required were available from merchants ready-ground into oil. Their supply in this state is mentioned by Smith,[23] and an instance may be found earlier in the century in connection with work at Greenwich Palace, where "Englishe oker grounde" was supplied in 1619–20.[24] Small quantities of ground

Figure 3. *Opening illustration for* Directions for Painting *issued by Joseph Emerton in the 1740s, showing a horse mill for grinding pigment into oil. (British Museum, Print Room, Heal Collection, 89.55)*

pigment were preserved in bladders, which were pricked with a pin to release as much color as needed from time to time. Larger quantities were preserved in wooden casks, and any un-used color was covered with water to prevent it from hardening. Bladders and a color barrel may be seen in the view of Emerton's works **(see fig. 3)**.

Most oil paints were based on the use of white lead, which was ground with linseed oil and tinted with varying proportions of other pigments to produce the color required. Various qual-ities of white lead, made throughout the period by the stack process, were available under dif-ferent names—such as ceruse, flake white, or Nottingham white—at different periods, mak-ing concise discussion difficult. Of primary note, however, was its adulteration by cheaper pigments, generally a legitimate practice (rather than dishonest sophistication) designed to make the comparatively expensive pigment go further, especially in undercoats. Until the lat-ter part of the eighteenth century whiting was commonly used for this purpose, but by the early nineteenth century barytes (barium sulfate) was extensively used, and other whites may have been used from time to time.

To turn the ground white-lead paste into paint of a consistency suitable for application, it was necessary to dilute it with oil or a mixture of oil and oil of turpentine. (The latter was usually the distillate of pine resin, American species of which were quickly exploited during the seventeenth century.)[25] Evidence for the quantities used is sketchy but would in any case have varied from pigment to pigment and would also have depended on the stiffness of the paste at hand and the proportion of oil of turpentine included. General advice was given by Smith, who recommended the addition of oil until the colors "be so thin as not to let the ground on which they are laid be seen through them,"[26] but Watin and the early nineteenth-century Swiss author P. F. Tingry provided a different criterion. The latter advised that when diluted "the colour on being taken from the pot ought not to drop from the brush when turned round two or three times in the hand, raising it obliquely to check the thread which is formed."[27] A typical consistency was probably that advocated by Joseph Emerton's predecessor, his brother Alexander, who advised that six pounds of his paste should be diluted with a quart of oil, a figure approximately matched by a number of later suggestions.[28]

The proportion of oil of turpentine used depended on the function of the paint. For exterior purposes it was regarded by Smith as harming its weathering properties;[29] but for interiors it became widely used, and in the mid-eighteenth century Robert Dossie referred to the practice as if it was a matter of course.[30] The proportions usually recommended for ordinary finishes by later English authors are either one part oil of turpentine to two parts of oil, or their combination in equal quantities.[31] Of course, the greater the proportion of oil of turpentine, the lesser the sheen with which the paint will dry, and from about 1740 a taste arose in England for completely flat paint in fine interiors. This was achieved by diluting the paste for the final coat with pure oil of turpentine. The resulting finish was known as "dead white" or "flatting" and was often expressed as an additional item in accounts of the period in phrases such as "painted twice in oil and flatted." Oil of turpentine was, however, a comparatively expensive commodity, and the lesser rooms of even grand aristocratic houses did not receive this treatment.

Undoubtedly, one attraction of flatting was that it reduced the amount of oil in the finish and thus minimized any tendency to discoloration. This could also be achieved by substituting walnut oil for linseed oil, a practice not uncommon in the seventeenth and early eighteenth centuries before the fashion for flat paint. Sir Roger Pratt, for example, specifically mentioned the use of walnut oil in preventing the yellowing of paint;[32] and accounts of the 1690s and early 1700s for painting Kensington Palace and Montagu House in London include items for white paint in nut oil.[33]

During this period the use of glossy paint was often advocated. Smith, for example, stated that "all simple Colours used in House Painting, appear much more beautiful and lustrous, when they appear as if glazed over with a Varnish." One method of achieving this was, he noted, by the use of boiled oil for dilution of the paste.[34] This was prepared by heating linseed oil with one or more metallic compounds, the primary purpose of the operation being to increase the speed with which the oil would dry (that is, polymerize). A side effect of the process, however, was to increase the viscosity of the oil, and this led to the production of a higher sheen in the dried paint film. Furthermore, Smith noted, the addition of crude turpentine would "make those Colours shine when dry ... with an extream glasey surface," although it is unclear whether he had in mind the use of raw pine resin or one of the better varieties such as Venice turpentine, obtained from the larch.[35] Suggestions may also be found for the addition of varnish to the paint, a technique mentioned by the seventeenth-century French writer André Félibien, although probably in connection with fine art or decorative painting rather than house paint. Elizabeth Raper noted in her domestic receipt book of 1756–70 that white lead should be mixed with an equal part of turpentine varnish for a finishing coat, adding "and you my depend on't you'll have a clear gloss."[37] Another practice in interior work that should be noted is that of applying a coat of hot weak size between the undercoat and finish, a process advocated by Alexander Emerton, who observed, "The Use of Size is to make the Paint look Glossy."[38]

The addition of boiled oil to increase the speed at which paint would dry has already been mentioned. The substances with which it was heated were generally the lead oxides (commonly known as litharge and red lead), but formulas calling for lead acetate (sugar of lead),

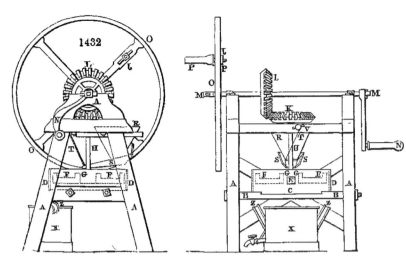

Figure 4. *Illustration of paint mill published in 1859 in Andrew Ure,* A Dictionary of Arts, Manufactures, and Mines *(London, 1859), 916, s.v. "Paints, grinding of."*

zinc sulfate (white coperas), and umber (a pigment containing manganese) may also be found.[39] Oil treated in this way is, however, darker in color than raw oil, and this precludes its use in white or fine pastel tints. Boiled oil is nevertheless a convenient additive in dark greens and browns and was extensively used for exterior paints where a little yellowing could be tolerated. Smith observed, probably for this reason, that when posts and rails were painted white the finish was called *stone color,* a term then implying a pale creamy off-white.[40]

To aid the drying of fine tints, common practice was to add to the paint small quantities of one of the substances mentioned earlier, ground in oil. Of these lead acetate was regarded as the best, but it was also the most expensive. Zinc sulfate, which was significantly cheaper, was probably the most commonly used, its use being mentioned by authors including Smith and Dossie.[41] Litharge and red lead would, of course, discolor the finer tints, but because they were much cheaper than zinc sulfate, they were often used in undercoats or primers.

Oil primers in the seventeenth century generally used red ocher as the base pigment and may often be seen under the microscope at the bottom of prepared cross sections. Smith, for example, recommended the use of Spanish brown (a cheap red ocher often, in fact, of British provenance) on its own;[41] and Dossie observed that this pigment was much used by house painters for grounds and primings in coarse work.[42] A more complex formula was given by William Leyburn in 1700, which combined Spanish brown and Spanish white with about a fifth part of red lead.[44] During the second half of the eighteenth century such primers were supplanted by those of a pale pink color, probably reflecting a response in technique to the change in taste that in the first half of the century had led to the almost universal use of white on joinery in British neoclassical interiors. Primers of this type were made by adding a proportion of red lead to white lead in oil and may commonly be observed on cross sections of paint from interiors of the period, although suggestions for their formulation do not appear in published literature until the nineteenth century. A typical reference is that by Peter Nicholson in 1825.[45]

On plaster it was not uncommon to apply a coat of hot linseed oil as a primer. Smith recommended this for plaster clock dials, and the French writers Félibien and Watin referred specifically to the practice in interior work.[46] On indoor joinery, however, it was also common to prime the work in size. Alexander Emerton, for example, observed, "Outside Work must be primed with Oyl Primer; but Inside Work may be primed with Size,"[47] and in 1662 payment was made for a quantity of work at the Queen's House, Greenwich, "Layed in Sise & couered over with oyle."[48] Although condemned by Dossie,[49] the practice persisted into the nineteenth century.

Another essential in preparing new joinery for painting was the local application of "knotting" to prevent the resin in knots from bleeding through the dried paint film and disfiguring its surface. Various types were used, the simplest consisting of red lead in size,[50] although oil-based formulations, often containing red lead, litharge, or white lead, were also advocated.[51] In work of the highest class Nicholson suggested the use of silver leaf on gold-size, a method used in the saloon at Uppark, Sussex, in about 1770.[52] References to the use of shellac in alcohol, the formula common today, have not been encountered.

The brushes used in applying paint were round. Smith noted that they were made from hogs' hair and varied in diameter from one-fourth inch to two inches.[53] The two on the right side of Moxon's illustration of plasterer's brushes (see fig. 2) appear similar to later depictions, which occur frequently on eighteenth-century trade cards, including that of Joseph Emerton (see fig. 3), and round brushes continued in use well into the present century. The minimum number of coats generally recommended for new work during this period was three, representing (in modern terms) priming, undercoat, and finish. When an oil primer was used the sequence was referred to as "three times in oil," but where the work was primed in size it was known as "twice in oil and primed in size." In high-class work, particularly in interiors, more coats might of course be used. A 1771 estimate for painting the principal rooms at the Shire Hall, Hertford, for instance, contains items for five coats in oil on plaster.[54]

In everyday repainting of old work, two coats appear to have been the norm. In good-quality work both would be in oil, often expressed in painting accounts as "second colour and finish." A cheaper method, often used in humbler interiors, was that known as "clearcole and finish." Its undercoat consisted of a layer of size-bound distemper, and it was thus unsuited to exterior work.

VARNISHES

The varnishes used in connection with house painting during this period can be divided into three main classes depending on the solvent used: ethyl alcohol, linseed oil, and oil of turpentine.

ALCOHOL, OR "SPIRIT," VARNISHES

The simplest spirit varnish, commonly known today as "French polish," was prepared by dissolving lac in alcohol (spirit of wine). Lac is the only varnish resin of animal origin and consists of the sticky exudation with which the lac insect *(Laccifer lacca,* formerly known as *Coccus lacca)* coats the twigs of certain trees indigenous to India and neighboring countries. It is refined by crushing and washing to remove the crimson-purple lac dye with which it is associated, in which form it was commonly imported into Britain in the seventeenth century and known as seed lac. A product further refined by heating and drawing out the lac into thin sheets, known as shellac, was also available in London in the seventeenth century. John Stalker and George Parker, whose *Treatise of Japanning and Varnishing* was published in 1688, gave a formula in which one and a half pounds of shellac were added to a gallon of spirit, allowed to stand for twenty-four hours, and then strained. To fit it for use on houses, two or more ounces of Venice turpentine were added.[55]

A second type of spirit varnish used sandarac, which is exuded from trees of the species *Tetraclinus articulata,* native to the mountains of North Africa. It was particularly advocated by Watin, who gave a series of sandarac-based formulas for different house-painting purposes, all of which also contained Venice turpentine and in some cases further resins, including shellac.[56]

A third type of spirit varnish contained alcohol-soluble copal resins. The term "copal," although originally of American origin,[57] has been used for a wide variety of material obtained both as fresh, soft products of living trees and as hard fossil resins from long-dead trees buried in the ground. The species yielding the resin belong to the genus *Hymenaea*, and historical sources of soft, spirit-soluble material include certain Caribbean islands, Central America, and northern countries of South America. Similar resins were also obtained from African species of the same genus, although the history of their exploitation before the nineteenth century is unclear. Modern material is obtained from various species of *Agathis* growing in the Far East. Although reserved by some modern authors for hard fossil resins, the term *animi* was also applied historically to spirit-soluble material, and such soft resins were clearly known and used in seventeenth-century London. Stalker and Parker, for instance, included "Gum-Capal" and "Gum Animae" in a spirit-based formula (in which, however, sandarac predominated);[58] and comparable early nineteenth-century formulas calling for the use of soft copals may also be encountered.[59]

OIL VARNISHES

The principal resins used in good-quality oil varnishes were the harder copals, although amber, a fossil resin obtained from the Baltic, is also often mentioned as providing a varnish of the highest quality. Historic sources of hard copal that were exploited by the eighteenth century are not easy to pinpoint, but the northern countries of South America and parts of East Africa are likely candidates, since such material was certainly being imported from these regions in the nineteenth century, when West African sources became increasingly important.

To dissolve them, even in hot linseed oil, hard resins had to be "run"—that is, melted—before being mixed with it. This process was described by William Salmon in 1672,[60] and a notable formula for copal varnish was given by Watin: four, six, or eight ounces of hot linseed oil were allowed for each pound of melted resin, and one pound of oil of turpentine was later added.[61]

TURPENTINE VARNISHES

The principal resin soluble in oil of turpentine is mastic, which was known to the ancients and used throughout the Middle Ages. It is obtained from the small Mediterranean tree *Pistacia lentiscus,* the principal source of supply being the island of Chios. Damar, from various species of the Dipterocarpaceae family, found over a wide area of the Far East, including the Seychelles, Philippines, New Guinea, Malaysia, and Indonesia, is also soluble in oil of turpentine, but no references to its use in connection with house painting have yet been encountered.

A formula using mastic was given by Watin. Intended as a vehicle for pigment, it called for four ounces of the resin to be dissolved in one pint of oil of turpentine, to which a half pound of crude turpentine of unspecified type was then added.[62]

USE OF VARNISHES

The most obvious use for varnish is as a transparent finish on timber or on painted imitations, including graining and marbleizing. For this purpose turpentine varnishes were unimportant, probably because, as Watin pointed out, they were lacking in luster.[63] Accordingly, their primary use was for pictures. Spirit varnishes, on the other hand, were capable of producing a fine polish but would not stand the weather and could not be used externally. For outside elements, therefore, oil varnishes were used. The balance between the use of oil and spirit varnishes in interiors in Britain is difficult to judge on the evidence at hand, but Watin clearly envisaged spirit varnishes as the type typically used indoors, although he suggested that in public buildings, such as the choir of a cathedral, oil varnishes were preferable.[64]

The typical method of applying varnishes was by brush. The brushes used differed from those used for oil paint and were flat. Watin described them as made from badger hair.[65] It is noteworthy that none of the authors studied to date mentions the application of spirit varnishes in the way currently practiced—by impregnating cotton wool with the material, wrapping it in a clean cloth, and rubbing it over the surface. Instead, much is made of the need to polish the varnish between coats, a procedure described by Stalker and Parker.[66] The abrasives commonly used were tripoli or rotten stone. Tripoli took its name from a variety of diatomaceous earth obtained from North Africa, but the term was later applied to a range of suitable earths including, no doubt, rotten stone, which is found in several parts of Britain. As usual, Watin provides the most detailed description of the process, indicating that it consisted of four stages: (1) rubbing the surface with powdered pumice in water; (2) rubbing with powdered tripoli and olive oil; (3) polishing with a soft linen cloth; and (4) finishing off with starch or French chalk and the palm of the hand.[67] That such an elaborate procedure was commonly practiced in Britain other than in connection with coach painting seems doubtful, since painting accounts generally refer only to applying a certain number of coats of varnish. Nevertheless, a model specification provided by Alfred Bartholomew in 1846 calls for each coat of copal varnish on marbled columns to be "polished thoroughly to a perfect gloss," suggesting that this may have been done on occasion, at least in the nineteenth century.[68]

In addition to being used as a transparent finish, varnishes could be pigmented to provide an opaque paint film. In the second half of the seventeenth century it was fashionable to decorate rooms in imitation of oriental lacquer or "japan," a taste enthusiastically advocated by Stalker and Parker, who used a lac-based spirit varnish for the purpose.[69] Watin too used spirit varnish as a medium for black or vermilion but also proposed a number of oil-based formulas, notably for preparing black and gray paint for ironwork.[70] However, both he and Tingry, who based many of his ideas on Watin's publication, appear to have regarded turpentine varnishes as the best choice for the purpose; and Tingry in particular provided comprehensive directions for their use with different colors.[71] Whether nineteenth-century British practice was influenced by their books is unclear, but from the lack of references to such formulations in painting accounts after the demise of the fashion for japanned rooms in the early eighteenth century, it seems unlikely that they were much used in fashionable house painting in the intervening decades. They were, however, probably used on furniture. A likely instance is a pair of chairs supplied by Thomas Chippendale to David Garrick in 1772 and described as "Japan'd Green & White"; examination of these suggests that the color was provided by means of a copper resinate.[72]

To date no evidence has been found for the use in Britain of green glazes above oil paint on joinery similar to those encountered in New England.[73] Colored transparent spirit varnishes, known as lacquers or "changing varnishes," were, however, used in the seventeenth century to make silver leaf look like gold; their reddish or orange-yellow tint was imparted by a range of spirit-soluble dyes or resins.

SPECIAL PAINTING TECHNIQUES

Among the special techniques used in painting were strewing of smalt, sanding, coloring Roman cement to imitate stone, and graining and marbleizing.

STREWING SMALT

Before the introduction of Prussian blue in the early eighteenth century, the number of blue pigments available for house painting was limited. Only natural ultramarine provided a really satisfactory blue, but it was far too expensive for application to large areas. By contrast, smalt, a crushed blue glass, while less costly, bright in color, and of similar hue, went dark when ground in oil on its own, was gritty in texture, and could not be mixed with white lead without losing its intensity. The solution was to strew the dry pigment on a ground of wet white lead in oil, a process described by Smith in connection with the painting of clock dials.[74] On occasion, however, the technique could be applied to architectural elements and has been found, for example, on the ceiling beams and entablature in a room at the Queen's House, Greenwich, designed by Inigo Jones for Henrietta Maria in the late 1630s.[75] It was also commonly used on both interior and exterior ironwork in royal and other grand buildings.

SANDING

An allied technique was that of sanding, in which dried colorless or "silver" sand was dusted onto the surface of wet white lead to imitate stone, generally in an exterior context. This was described in the 1730s by Alexander Emerton, who noted that after the first coat of sanding a second should be applied.[76] Sanding has been found on a number of eighteenth-century buildings in Britain, including the timber cornice on the north side of Ham House, Surrey, which dates probably from a mid-eighteenth-century alteration of the building.[77] Restoration of this finish has recently been completed, and the experience proved that two coats were necessary to achieve an even color.

COLORING ROMAN CEMENT RENDERING TO IMITATE STONE

Roman cement, obtained by roasting nodules of septaria found in Kent and Essex, was patented by James Parker in 1796 and quickly found a use for the exterior rendering of buildings. It was often lined out to look like ashlar masonry and could be treated by a technique misleadingly known as "fresco" to imitate the natural variations in color found in a wall constructed of stone. The method was used by the architect Henry Holland at the Royal Pavilion, Brighton, Sussex, in 1802 and 1803,[78] and other examples may also be found.[79] As described by Peter Nicholson in 1823–25, the technique consisted of the preliminary application of a wash made from Roman cement and fresh lime tinted by the addition of a solution of five ounces of ferrous sulfate per gallon of water. This was followed by the application of different concentrations of ferrous sulfate solution to vary the color of the individual blocks imitating ashlar, and the work was finished by marking the joints with umber to complete the illusion.[80]

GRAINING AND MARBLEIZING

The imitation of decorative timbers and marbles was a conceit practiced from early times and used extensively in seventeenth- and early eighteenth-century Britain. After a dip in popularity, graining and marbleizing regained favor about 1800, when new techniques based on the manipulation of glazes were introduced, probably from France.

The early techniques appear from surviving examples to have involved little use of glazes and to have been based on the building up of the figure in body color. This is the case, for example, with the 1694 marbleizing in the Balcony Room at Dyrham Park, Avon, cross sections from which illustrate well the opaque nature of the oil paint used.[81] Early descriptions of graining and marbleizing methods are slight. Smith, for example, simply mentioned that the imitation of "Walnut-Tree" was effected by means of a ground of "burnt Umber, and White vein'd over with the same Colour alone, and in the deepest places with Black," noting that the method for the imitation of timbers and marbles "must be attained by ocular inspection, it being impossible to deliver the manner of the operation by precept."[82] The American writer Hezekiah Reynolds appears to have given the best description of early methods, although by 1812 these had been superseded in fashionable work in England and France.[83]

The new and much finer technique introduced in the late eighteenth and early nineteenth centuries resembles that still practiced in the trade. In graining, a ground color matching the lightest tone in the timber to be imitated was applied first and overlaid by a glaze of darker tint. This was brushed out and manipulated with various tools, including brushes of various types, combs, sponges, and feathers, to thin or remove it locally, allowing the color of the ground to provide the highlights in the figuring. On joinery the ground was generally in oil, but for the imitation of marble on plaster walls it might be in distemper. On the latter the glaze might be applied in size or milk, but on an oil ground stale beer or an oil-based "megilp" was commonly used. The latter was often formulated from linseed oil and beeswax. Finally, darker veins could be added with a small brush or "pencil," and when dry the completed work was varnished. Good descriptions of the methods for imitating individual timbers and marbles were given in the late 1820s by Nathaniel Whittock and T. H. Vanherman.[84]

FRONT ELEVATION.

Nineteenth-Century Paints

A DOCUMENTARY APPROACH

ROGER W. MOSS

From the colonial period through the middle of the nineteenth century there was virtually no change in the working methods of the painter's craft. As for the colors used in the early decades of the nineteenth century, the literature suggests that the developing taste for architectural forms inspired by classical Greece and the wide availability of carpentry guides by authors such as Peter Nicholson (1765–1844), encouraged the use of colors in addition to common white—among them straw, gray, green, and fawn.[1]

READY-MIXED PAINTS

The major change in both the craft of painting and the colors used for American buildings occurred in the years immediately following the Civil War, when a successful ready-mixed paint industry was developed. Earlier efforts had been made to develop ready-mixed paints in both England and America, but as far as we know they had minimal impact on color use in this country. Paint is capital intensive when produced in commercial qualities; it is also bulky to package, ship, and store. Therefore, it should come as no surprise that the ready-mixed paint industry developed slowly in America. It is one thing to manufacture white lead and other pigments—as was being done in Philadelphia by the beginning of the nineteenth century— leaving it to the painter to purchase these in bulk for mixing to suit the tastes of clients. It is a different matter, indeed, to ship a product that has been blended to color at the factory, considering the attendant problems of container size, shelf life, and inventory variety. In addition, the limitations of the transportation system and the inability to create a market through advertising all retarded the development of a large ready-mixed paint industry. [2]

In the meantime, demand for such a product was growing. In 1800 the population of the United States stood at approximately 5.3 million. On the eve of the Civil War that number had grown to 31.5 million and by 1900 to 76 million. In the same century, even allowing for territorial growth, the population density increased from approximately six persons per square mile to twenty-five per square mile as the entire nation became more urbanized. These raw figures suggest a similar growth in residential and commercial construction along with a concomitant expansion in the market for architectural finishes, which American manufacturers rushed to supply **(fig. 3)**.[3]

Figure 1. *This "neat and convenient homestead" in the Italianate Revival style cost $5,150 to build on the eve of the Civil War. It illustrates several important painting details: green shutters, oak-grained front door, and striped porch roof. John Riddell,* Architectural Designs for Model Country Residences *(Philadelphia, 1861 and subsequent eds.), design 13. (The Athenaeum of Philadelphia)*

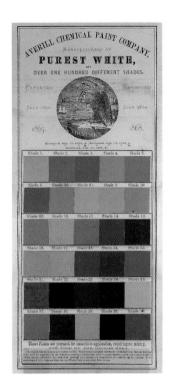

Figure 2. *Color sample card (above), Averill Chemical Paint Company, 1869. (The Athenaeum of Philadelphia)*

Figure 3. *Flyer detail (opposite, top), Averill Chemical Paint Company, ca. 1876. (The Athenaeum of Philadelphia)*

Figure 4. *Card (opposite, middle), F. W. Devoe & Company, ca. 1869. (The Athenaeum of Philadelphia)*

As nearly as can be determined, the earliest successful ready-mixed oil paint produced in America was green. John Lucas and Company of Philadelphia advertised "French Imperial Green for Blinds, &c." by 1866, and F. W. Devoe and Company of New York City touted its "Park Lawn Green For use on Window Blinds [shutters], Ornamental Iron Work, Machinery, etc." by 1869. Even the most cursory examination of the architectural literature of the mid-nineteenth century confirms the wisdom of this choice. A. J. Davis, Andrew Jackson Downing, William H. Ranlett, and other nineteenth-century American architects and critics specified green for the shutters and ornamental metal trim of both masonry and frame houses, regardless of the other colors that might be selected. In short, green, because of its universal application, was the most promising color for a manufacturer testing the market. Devoe wrote to its dealers in the spring of 1869: " ... we pack [Park Lawn Green] in 50 lb. cases, holding assorted cans of 1, 2, 3 and 4 lbs. weight ... and in kegs and casks of any desired quantity,— of Light, Medium, and Dark shades."[4]

The earliest ready-mixed paints suffered from the difficulties of inadequate grinding and mixing techniques, which caused pigment settlement and shortened shelf life. These problems had to be solved, as they were in the 1860s and 1870s, and resealable cans had to be invented if the manufacturers hoped to sell directly to the consumer rather than professional painters. In 1867 the Averill Chemical Paint Company issued a range of ready-mixed colors, and its sample card, one of the earliest dated American examples, is shown here in a reissue from two years later **(fig. 2)**. The card confirms the growing availability of ready-mixed paints in the years immediately following the end of the Civil War.[5]

Expanding modestly on the success of its green, Devoe introduced a line of earth and stone colors—three of which were illustrated with sanded finishes—such as those suggested by the celebrated author-architect Samuel Sloan, who argued in 1852 that "soft neutral tints are only proper to be used" for architectural painting. "For the exterior of a dwelling," he continued, "nothing is more beautiful than the soft delicate tint of the Connecticut brownstone. The depth of the shade must be varied to suit circumstances. In truth, it is a safe rule, to adopt, for artificial purposes, the colors of natural objects. These seldom fail to suggest the most beautiful tints." The Homestead Colors sample card **(fig. 4)** is undated but is located in an archive of Devoe publications at the Athenaeum of Philadelphia in materials from the late 1860s. Whether it predates the more extensive Averill card is uncertain.[6]

Sloan's views on proper exterior decoration echo the criticism of white trimmed with green that appeared first in England in the early decades of the nineteenth century with the growing movement toward picturesque design in landscape gardening and architecture. English authors such as Robert Lugar and John Papworth, who were influenced by Humphrey Repton and Uvedale Price, argued for "light-coloured sand-stone, or brick, tinted of stone-colour ... " or buildings "done in stucco with Stone-lime and sand ... " **(fig. 5)**. Downing picked up this appeal for "subdued tone" in color and particularly argued for colors that "copy those that [nature] offers chiefly to the eye—such as those of the soil, rocks, wood, and the bark of trees— the materials of which houses are built. These materials offer us the best and most natural study from which harmonious colours for the houses themselves should be taken."[7]

Of equal significance, if ready-mixed paints were to enjoy more than local availability, was the maturing of the American transportation system, which meant that virtually any American could obtain these new products. The Civil War encouraged the growth of the railroad network (at least in the North and West), and the war's ending released venture capital to expand the capacity of the paint industry. Also, once manufacturers moved from providing raw materials for painters to factory-mixed paints in an ever-growing array of colors, a demand developed for colorful advertising literature to reach the consumer—both painters and building owners themselves.[8]

A NEW COLOR PALETTE

In an article entitled "What the Art of House Painting Owes to the Manufacturers of Ready-Mixed Paints" in the magazine *House Painting and Decorating* (1885), an industry representative stated that " . . . as soon as ready-mixed paints, or paints ready for use, began to be introduced a field of new and rich design was opened to the painter and owners of property, which circumstances had previously barred. Shades and tints of color were prepared, which had hitherto been beyond the painter's reach." In addition, the publication of advertising literature had a major impact. These "enabled tints and shades of color to be seen and their effect in combination determined."[9]

As the color schemes became more complex in the post–Civil War years, architects and paint manufacturers began to specify rules based less on personal judgment and more on the growing body of color theory. Most writers relied on the work of David Ramsay Hay of Edinburgh, Scotland, a house painter and author of *The Laws of Harmonious Colouring*, published in 1828. Many articles on the subject of color during the 1850s and 1860s referred to Hay's work, including *Godey's Lady's Book*, the most popular magazine for women in America. Consequently, Hay's theories were well known to many American homeowners. John W. Masury, in his *House-Painting: Plain and Decorative* (1868), included Hay's theories and described two approaches to color harmony. The first was "harmony by analogy"—that is, using those next to one another on the color wheel. Masury's examples included crimson and purple, yellow and gold, crimson and rich brown. The second was "harmony by contrast"—that is, using complementary colors, those colors opposite one another on the color wheel, such as scarlet and green or orange and blue (see back cover).[10]

Sophisticated studies of the effects of adjacent colors on one another also influenced the palette used for exterior decoration. The most significant of these was the work of Michel Eugène

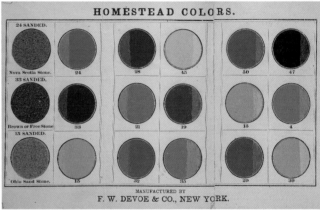

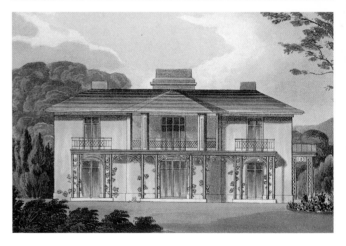

Figure 5. *Illustration (above) from John R. Papworth,* Rural Residences *(London, 1818), pl. 14. (The* Athenaeum of Philadelphia)

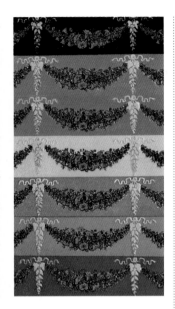

Chevreul (1786–1889), director of dyes for the Gobelins tapestry works in Paris. His text on colors was published originally in France in 1839 and followed by an English translation, *The Principles of Harmony and Contrast of Colors and Their Application to the Arts* (1854). Chevreul's principles appeared in America in *The Painter, Gilder, and Varnisher's Companion,* which ran to sixteen editions between 1869 and 1873. The magazine *House Painting and Decorating* considered Chevreul's work so important that it urged readers to consult the English translation because "it is an error . . . to suppose that the art of arranging colors so as to produce the best effects in painting is entirely dependent on the taste of the operator; for harmony of coloring is determined by fixed natural laws."[11]

From his work with tapestry dyes Chevreul observed that certain colors placed adjacent to some hues appear to shift in hue or value while the same colors adjacent to other hues might intensify **(fig. 6)**. Chevreul was not the first to witness these phenomena, but he was the first to record them systematically. He remarked, for instance, that complementary colors adjacent to one another in patterns appear more intense because the retina of the eye produces an after-image of the complement of each color—for example, the afterimage caused by looking at red is green and that of green is red. The human eye responds this way to all colors; thus, yellow will cause a purple afterimage, and orange will cause a blue one. Because of the afterimage, two colors adjacent to one another but not complements will appear altered in hue. Chevreul's studies showed that red next to orange appears as a purplish red next to a yellowish orange. Furthermore, he discovered that white, black, and gray also affect the hues adjacent to them, making them appear deeper, lighter, and richer respectively. Chevreul's findings regarding color relationships greatly influenced critics and through them the decoration of buildings in the 1870s and 1880s.[12]

This growing self-consciousness about the choice of color provides the later student of paint in America with a rich and useful documentary history. As a historian rather than a scientist I have leaned heavily on what is often called prescriptive literature, particularly the writings of certain architects and critics as well as the publications of the paint industry itself. These sources have certain inherent problems, discussed below.

HISTORICALLY AUTHENTIC COLORS

In 1976, in response to a growing interest in nineteenth-century architecture in America and an accompanying demand for historically authentic colors, the Athenaeum of Philadelphia republished the countertop display book of F. W. Devoe and Company originally entitled *Exterior Decoration: A treatise on the artistic use of colors in the ornamentation of buildings and a series of designs, illustrating the effects of different combinations of colors in connection with various styles of architecture* (New York, 1885). This

large-format book contained twenty color lithographs and fifty color samples that were reproduced as faithfully as possible **(fig. 7)**. A new introduction by Samuel J. Dornsife, a pioneering student of color use by the Victorians, was added to the reprint along with a brief bibliography prepared by the Athenaeum's staff. In my foreword I remarked, "Ideally a restoration should be based on a careful, detailed microanalysis of original painted surfaces, but such scientific archaeology is expensive, and there are few persons qualified to conduct the studies." Consequently, the Athenaeum believed that a straightforward reproduction of the color plates and the paint chips would provide guidance to the restoration community.[13]

Exterior Decoration succeeded beyond our wildest dreams. Although expensive for the time, the book sold out rapidly, and it is still coveted by those unable to acquire one of the five thousand copies. Two years later the California literary agents Elizabeth Pomada and Michael Larsen published *Painted Ladies,* a photo essay on the modern painting practices of San Francisco. Fantastically colorful and published in an inexpensive paperback, this often tongue-in-cheek record of a Bay Area phenomenon has subsequently been embraced by large numbers of well-meaning Americans thinking too often that they were following a historical precedent **(fig. 8)**. *Painted Ladies* and its sequels say more about the taste of the 1970s and 1980s than they do about the 1870s and 1880s.[14]

My response to the publication of *Painted Ladies* was an equally slim and inexpensive book of prescriptive literature entitled *Century of Color: Exterior Decoration for American Buildings, 1820–1920* (Watkins Glen, 1981). The intent of that book was to "encourage the owners of American houses built in the last century to select colors that are historically proper for the age of the structure and to place those colors to emphasize correctly the rich character and detailing intended by the original builders." The unspoken assumption was that *Century of Color* would provide a foil to *Painted Ladies.* To a degree it was; forty thousand copies were distributed before the book went out of print. The Sherwin-Williams Company also issued its "Heritage Colors" paint line keyed to the book and based on original color samples in the

Figure 8. *The handsome late Victorian houses of San Francisco's Steiner Street at Alamo Square, among the most publicized examples of the "painted lady" approach to Victorian exterior decoration. (Roger W. Moss)*

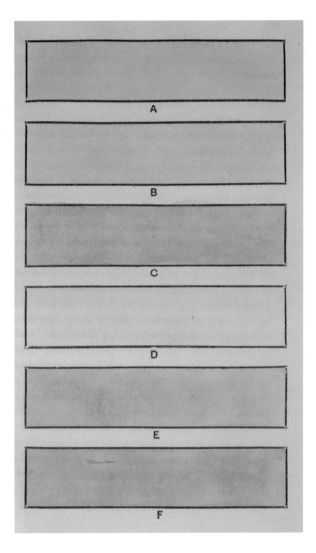

Figure 9. *Andrew Jackson Downing's hand-colored plate in* Cottage Residences *(New York, 1842 and subsequent editions), one of the first American books on architecture to provide actual colors. (The Athenaeum of Philadelphia)*

Athenaeum collection. Unfortunately, Sherwin-Williams did not continue the document line of colors, and the publisher decided not to reprint *Century of Color*.[15]

In an effort to improve the deficiencies of *Century of Color* and avoid the perception of association with a single manufacturer, Gail Caskey Winkler and I wrote *Victorian Exterior Decoration* (New York, 1987) as a companion to our *Victorian Interior Decoration*, which had been published the year before. Again we relied principally on the prescriptive literature supplemented by many photographs of actual buildings that had been painted following the plates published in *Century of Color*. In *Victorian Exterior Decoration*, however, we introduced through the text and extensive footnotes much of the technical literature by many of the authors in this book, and we attempted to match colors from the standard lines of four major paint manufacturers to thirty-five commonly used ready-mixed colors from the late nineteenth century.[16]

LIMITATIONS OF THE SOURCES

Books such as *Exterior Decoration*, *Century of Color*, and *Victorian Exterior Decoration*, based primarily on historic photographs, specifications, and prescriptive literature as well as physical documentation, have certain inherent problems. I am, in effect, taking this opportunity to critique my own work of the past decade—work that resulted in three publications to date that have, if the number of copies sold is any indication, influenced the repainting of thousands of American structures. Let us examine each source in turn.

The most obvious sources, common to all three books, are the color illustrations issued by architects, color theorists, and critics, as well as the publications of the paint companies themselves. Unlike my colleagues dealing with seventeenth- and eighteenth-century paints, who have few of these seductive documents to tempt them away from mixing formulas and scientific analyses of surviving surfaces, the student of nineteenth-century paints has first a trickle and then a flood of rich visual documents. The earliest of these are colored illustrations—that is, the plates actually have a wash of pigment dissolved in water applied by hand after the printing process. The first and most famous example of this process in America appearing in a book of architecture is A. J. Davis's *Rural Residences* (New York, 1837), which had plates colored by hand in the manner of many English books of the period, particularly those illustrating the cottage orné. These illustrations are of limited use except to suggest the adoption of such colors as buff with scoring for stucco, as recently uncovered at Montgomery Place in Annandale-on-Hudson, New York, or bronze green for ironwork.[17]

More didactically intended is Andrew Jackson Downing's hand-colored plate in *Cottage Residences* (New York, 1842) **(fig. 9)**. "As it is difficult to convey in words a proper ideal of delicate

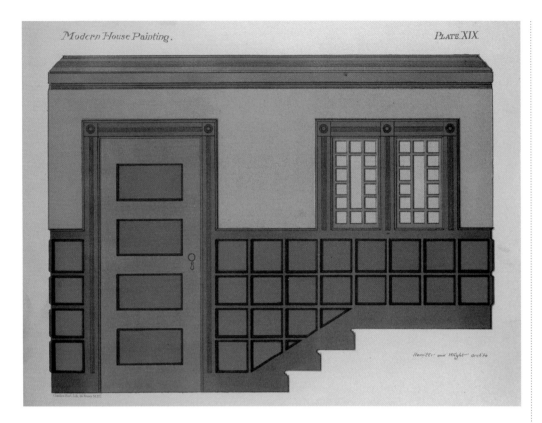

shades of colour," he wrote, "and as we think the subject one of very great importance in domestic architecture, we have given specimens … of six shades of colour highly suitable for the exterior of cottages and villas. A, B, and C, are shades of gray, and D, E, F, of drab or fawn colour; which will be found pleasing and harmonious in any situation in the country." Hand coloring cannot be precise, of course, and each copy of the book may differ slightly from the next depending on the skill and color sense of the watercolorist.[18] By the mid-nineteenth century printers were capable of producing color lithographs of high quality that involved several lithographic stones, one for each color. The color separations had to be performed by eye, of course, and as with the hand-colored prints of the early nineteenth century there was a fair degree of room for differences between copies or for variations between what the author had intended and what finally appeared. Regardless of these problems, the structures in the most handsome pattern book of the mid-nineteenth century, John Riddell's *Architectural Designs for Model Country Residences, Illustrated by Colored Drawings of Elevations and Ground Plans* (Philadelphia, 1861), were shown "in suitable tints, which add much to the appearance of a rural residence" **(fig. 1)**.[19]

A quarter of a century later, however, Ehrick Rossiter and Frank Wright complained about the limitations of color printing in the second edition of their *Modern House Painting,* first published in 1882. The colors of some plates in the first edition were so unlike what they had specified that they had the plates redone. Alas, the revisions were worse than before. With extraordinary candor they remarked that they could not commend their own plates to the reader **(fig. 10)**. Little wonder that there appears to have been no third edition.[20]

Other technological advances in color printing—the development of inexpensive wood-pulp paper in continuous rolls and high-speed, steam-driven presses—encouraged paint companies to print and distribute colorful advertising brochures and architectural pattern books that reached thousands of Americans building residential, commercial, and institutional structures (fig. 11). Taking into account the limitations of all nineteenth-century mass printing techniques, it is questionable how accurately the color in these documents is portrayed. In the foreword to the *Exterior Decoration* reprint I warned of this problem: "The nineteenth-century printer had less control over his inks than modern pressmen. Consequently, readers are cautioned to work from the paint chips rather than the plates when selecting colors. The plates serve best today as in 1885: 'as a means of illustrating the effects than can be produced by a judicious and artistic use of colors.... '"[21]

Figure 11. *A late-nineteenth-century example from the Sherwin-Williams Company of literature featuring color printing and actual samples of paint. In an effort to teach theories of "harmonious" combinations, paint companies produced a wide variety of such literature. (The Athenaeum of Philadelphia)*

Even if color rendition in the nineteenth-century documents had not already been flawed, the modern process of reproducing these plates carries inherent problems. In most cases the printer works from photographic transparencies rather than from the document. Consequently, another step is introduced before the press operator separates the image and inks the drum. It is little wonder that the color reproductions in *Century of Color* had drifted so far from the documents that the colors gave little more than general guidance. When we came to *Victorian Exterior Decoration* each image was rephotographed with a color scale for the separator, and a proof run was compared to the original before being approved for the book (fig. 12). As a result the fidelity to the original was retained, however limited that original might be.

Many of the paint company publications, such as Devoe's *Exterior Decoration* (1885) or the larger John Lucas and Company's *Portfolio of Modern House Painting Designs* (Philadelphia, 1887) contained actual color samples of ready-mixed paint to which consumers were directed so that they would not rely on the limited capabilities of nineteenth-century color printing. These one- or two-inch-square samples were not printed but consist of actual sheets of paint cut to size, often coated with varnish, and glued into the book. These samples, mounted on acid paper and shielded from the light for more than a century, have often suffered some of the same discoloration found in samples removed from historic structures. Consequently,

Figure 12. *A Second Empire–style mansard-roof house painted straw or fawn with dark brownstone and Indian red trim as published by the Seeley Brothers Paint Company (New York, 1886). Originally it was photographed with a color scale to assist the separator. (Collection of Mr. and Mrs. Lewis Seeley, The Athenaeum of Philadelphia)*

when Frank S. Welsh conducted microanalysis on the Devoe and Harrison Brothers' cards of 1869 and 1872 for inclusion in *Century of Color,* it was necessary to remove the coating of varnish before examining the sample.[22]

A systematic examination of ready-mixed paint cards, which survive by the hundreds in the collections of independent research libraries such as the Athenaeum of Philadelphia, the Eleutherian Mills-Hagley Foundation, and the library of the Society for the Preservation of New England Antiquities, would result in a far more accurate and representative palette for the second half of the nineteenth century than a similar sample of structural case studies where the surfaces have suffered far more severe environmental and mechanical stresses. Such an examination is also more likely to produce a viable result than modern efforts to recreate vague nineteenth-century mixing formulas with the many variables in the proportions and purity of pigments. Unfortunately, such a study remains for future researchers.[23]

Figure 13. *A frame house near Philadelphia, photographed in the late nineteenth century. Such photographs are helpful for color placement but not color value. (Collection of Robert Skaler, AIA)*

CONFIRMATION BY PHYSICAL EVIDENCE

Ultimately, of course, the inherent limitations of prescriptive literature demand that it be confirmed by actual case studies. Just because Downing said that buff should be used for stucco in the 1840s or because colorful brochures of the Sherwin-Williams Company touted its latest shade of olive green in the 1880s does not mean that the advice was followed in either instance. Written specifications, such as those by the mid-nineteenth-century architect John Notman, however, provide a rich source of nonvisual information on both color choice and finishing techniques. In 1849 Notman submitted specifications for Glencairn, an Italianate house to be erected of stone for Isaac Pearson in Trenton, New Jersey. Notman wrote:

The whole of the wood work as usually painted will have 3 coats of white lead and oil of best quality. The last coat on the shutters to be green [,] that on the doors of principal rooms to be of shades of colour as may be desired conditioned they are plain colours ... the sash and frames will be painted stone colour outside, the porch and bow window to be sanded, the roof of the balcony to be painted in stripes bronze and pale yellow, the iron work of bronze.

Here Notman is recommending the common technique of sanding paint—that is, blowing sand on the paint while it is still wet to simulate cut-stone trim. He also suggests painting striped veranda roofs in alternating bronze green and pale yellow, as suggested by a mid-nineteenth-century photolithograph from *Villas on the Hudson* and as restored at the National Historic Landmark Athenaeum building in Philadelphia.[24]

Prescriptive literature also does not allow for regional or ethnic variations in color choice and placement, even though the widespread distribution of late nineteenth-century tertiary colors strongly suggests the homogenization of American color use by the 1880s and 1890s, especially in more heavily populated areas. The careful historian will nonetheless always check for local variations from the norm. Unfortunately, the siren lure of such local variations—however improbable—is so compelling that it may overwhelm contradictory evidence. This once happened to me in a neighborhood of high-style Queen Anne houses in Alabama where regional conservatism was advanced as the reason why rich, tertiary colors had never caught on. Of course the buildings themselves were telling a different story as they exfoliated several layers of twentieth-century white paint to expose the expected deep olives and brownish reds of the 1880s. Nonetheless, some architects and building owners have taken the prescriptive literature from my books as gospel and forced it down the throat of communities that passed through the "high Victorian" colors of the 1880s as if the ready-mixed paint factories of Philadelphia, New York, Cleveland, and Chicago had never existed—communities where white and gray mixed by local painters had continued to dominate.[25]

The palette of the mid-nineteenth century—grays and other stone colors—doubtless continued to be used by most Americans throughout the century except for the more exotic styles of the 1880s, particularly Queen Anne, for which the rich, multicolored paint schemes seem so appropriate **(see front cover)**, and the more self-conscious Arts and Crafts styles, particularly the Shingle Style and its offshoot, the bungalow. Also keep in mind that late nineteenth-century critics continued to complain about Americans who had not adopted the new colors and that the paint industry continued to argue the merits of ready-mixed paints to the end of the century. This suggests that many older painters continued to mix their own colors from bulk materials and satisfy their customers with the more limited palette that had become popular earlier. Until this hypothesis is tested under a microscope it will remain only a hypothesis.

Finally, we come to photography. Photographs are a particularly popular document for understanding the use of nineteenth-century paints, and I have reproduced many of them drawn from collections throughout America. Fortunately, architecture has long been a favorite subject for photographers; lighting is rarely a problem, and the subject does not twitch or blink. Nineteenth-century photographs, of course, are color blind, and while we often use them for color placement, we may also unwittingly make certain assumptions about the relative value of the original colors **(fig. 13)**. We do this because we are used to modern panchromatic black and white film, which renders all colors in a fairly uniform range of grays.

Nineteenth-century film, however, was less sensitive to reds and yellows. A print made from one of these negatives renders yellow much darker than modern film would, and reds will appear even darker, virtually black. Conversely, blues become lighter to the point that light blue will appear to be white. This limitation of pre-1900 photographs must be kept in mind whenever such documents are interpreted.[26]

In discussing some of the limitations of the prescriptive literature and various documents used by historians seeking to understand the use of nineteenth-century color, I have suggested some of the rich variety of sources not generally available to the student of earlier color use. Ultimately, of course, these more literary sources should be tested against the physical evidence. Only through a combination of both techniques will we come to understand fully the history of paint in America.

Case Studies in Paint Research

The Early American Palette

COLONIAL PAINT COLORS REVEALED

FRANK S. WELSH

Americans in colonial times frequently used paints, whitewashes, and wallpapers not only to protect their houses from weather and wear but also to enhance their homes' appearance with color and design. Their choice and placement of colors can tell us a great deal about regionalism, geography, and history as well as provide interesting insights into style, social fashion, and personal taste. Even though some of these early footprints of our culture have been washed away or disguised by nearly two centuries of weather, repainting, stripping, restoring, yellowing and graying, fading, and in many cases neglect, a substantial amount of evidence does remain for us to excavate and to analyze using ever-improving scientific methods.

The paints, styles, finishes, and colors popular in the eighteenth and early nineteenth centuries have drawn considerable interest for many generations in this century. Beginning in the 1920s and into the 1940s, the Colonial Williamsburg Foundation took the lead in researching the colonial American palette of paint colors (figs. 2 and 3). Because of the foundation's efforts, Colonial Williamsburg is still in the minds of many the official source of "authentic" colonial colors.

The paint archaeology efforts begun at Colonial Williamsburg were continued by the National Park Service and others. In the 1950s Penelope Hartshorne Batcheler, restoration architect at Independence National Historical Park, initiated use of the stereomicroscope as an archaeological tool at Independence Hall, thus opening up a new route of discovery. Through the 1970s especially, in preparation for America's Bicentennial, the Park Service pursued the discovery of historic paint colors.

Today, hundreds of colonial sites have been investigated, and many have been restored. Yet after almost seventy-five years of our modern fascination with colonial American paints and colors, there still exists no resource that illustrates or documents authentic colonial colors as analyzed and evaluated microscopically. Further, there may be confusion surrounding what constitutes an "authentic" colonial color.

Some evidence at last is in hand. On the basis of twenty years of studying and microscopically analyzing paint from early American buildings, I have compiled a very large data base that now contains more than one hundred hues from more than 175 colonial structures from a broad cross section of buildings dating from 1715 to 1815.

Figure 1. *Charles Willson Peale,* Staircase Group, *1795. A typical colonial American interior is exemplified in this well-known late eighteenth-century painting. The baseboards are painted black, the walls are papered in blue with a pattern, and there is a border paper at the top of the baseboard. The stair treads and risers are unpainted and unfinished, a treatment typical of the colonial period. (Philadelphia Museum of Art, The George W. Elkins Collection)*

Figure 2. *Colonial Williamsburg paint color card, produced in 1957 by the John Masury Paint Company, the first licensee for reproducing Colonial Williamsburg paints. This is virtually identical to the first card, produced in 1936. The colors are marketed as either interior or exterior colors, but their original source use may not have been the same. Some of the blue, ocher, gray, and brown colors are representative of the eighteenth-century palette. (Colonial Williamsburg Foundation)*

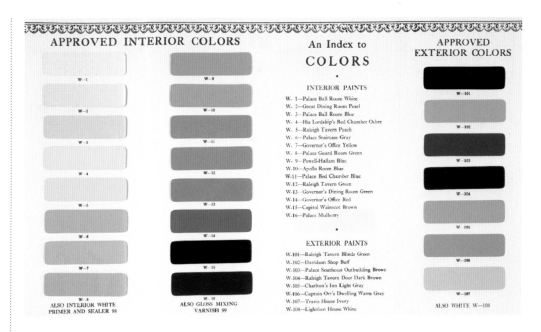

APPROVED INTERIOR COLORS

W—1
W—2
W—3
W—4
W—5
W—6
W—7
W—8
ALSO INTERIOR WHITE PRIMER AND SEALER 98

W—9
W—10
W—11
W—12
W—13
W—14
W—15
W—16
ALSO GLOSS MIXING VARNISH 99

An Index to
COLORS

INTERIOR PAINTS

W. 1—Palace Ball Room White
W. 2—Great Dining Room Pearl
W. 3—Palace Ball Room Blue
W. 4—His Lordship's Bed Chamber Ochre
W. 5—Raleigh Tavern Peach
W. 6—Palace Staircase Gray
W. 7—Governor's Office Yellow
W. 8—Palace Guard Room Green
W. 9—Powell-Hallam Blue
W-10—Apollo Room Blue
W-11—Palace Bed Chamber Blue
W-12—Raleigh Tavern Green
W-13—Governor's Dining Room Green
W-14—Governor's Office Red
W-15—Capitol Wainscot Brown
W-16—Palace Mulberry

EXTERIOR PAINTS

W-101—Raleigh Tavern Blinds Green
W-102—Davidson Shop Buff
W-103—Palace Southeast Outbuilding Brown
W-104—Raleigh Tavern Door Dark Brown
W-105—Charlton's Inn Light Gray
W-106—Captain Orr's Dwelling Warm Gray
W-107—Travis House Ivory
W-108—Lightfoot House White

APPROVED EXTERIOR COLORS

W—101
W—102
W—103
W—104
W—105
W—106
W—107
ALSO WHITE W—108

Colonial American oil and distemper paints (water-based, glue-bound, calcium carbonate paints that had a soft matte appearance) were made at the site and applied to wood trim and plaster walls and ceilings alike. Wood trim was always painted in oil. Distemper paints were always applied to plaster or to plain paper that was applied to plaster. These paints' characteristics include color, sheen, and surface texture as well as binder.

What the data makes evident is that no one color emerges as the most popular in colonial America. However, when separating exterior color usage from interior color usage, some patterns do become apparent. (This excludes decorative painting such as graining and marbling.)

Before 1750 the most widely used color on the exterior trim of masonry buildings was a moderate reddish brown color referred to at the time as Spanish brown. It was made with the pigment red iron oxide, also called red ocher. After 1750 the most widely used color on all types of buildings' exteriors was a white that was slightly yellowish in tone, made so because of the yellow cast of the linseed oil in which the white lead pigment was ground or dispersed. A guarded generalization might be that in the early or first half of the eighteenth century exteriors typically were painted in medium to dark tones such as reddish browns and grays and that in the second half of the eighteenth century building exteriors very frequently were painted with light colors such as whites, yellowish whites, very light grays, and sometimes pale blues. We have not yet been able to explain why this shift from dark to light occurred when it did, but it may be the result of political, economic, technological, or mercantile factors.

Dark green on exteriors, made primarily with verdigris dispersed in oil and varnish, generally did not come into use until the late 1790s to early 1800s, when it was used on louvered blinds (shutters), introduced at that time to American buildings. I often wonder if there is more than the superficial French connection between the use of verdigris green and louvered blinds.

With respect to interior colors one oil paint color that turns up in a vast majority of colonial homes and public buildings is a medium blue made with white lead and Prussian blue—

a pigment first made in Berlin in the late 1720s. I visualize this color as ubiquitous blue. I encounter it in such vernacular buildings as farmhouses on the remote eastern shore of Virginia as well as the large country homes and town houses in Philadelphia and Baltimore, rural homes in Deerfield, Massachusetts, and well-to-do churches in Boston and Newport.

From north to south the color that occurs next in frequency on diverse styles of buildings is green. However, with green there is an incredible range in the shades that were used—from light to dark and from blue-green to yellow-green. With both the blues and the greens the intensities seldom go to the extreme that I would consider bright. Instead I see them as very rich colors. The very richest and cleanest or purist of all the colonial colors was the dark blue-green made only with verdigris dispersed in a varnish and applied in multiple translucent layers to a gray or blue-gray base coat. This multiple coat application gave the paint a depth unobtainable by any other means.

The genuinely bright colors of the eighteenth century—the reds and the reddish oranges—were the most rarely used. These colors, made with vermilion and red lead respectively, were used principally for painting the interiors of cupboards.

Of all the colors used on both interiors and exteriors, only one—Spanish brown—could be construed to be a utilitarian or multipurpose shade. It was used as an interior and exterior paint as both a primer and a finish coating. No one of the paint colors appears to be the most expensive, the one used only by the most well-to-do, or the one used exclusively in the very best room of the house. The inclination to express one's affluence may have been reflected more through the use of fancy French or Chinese wallpapers (see fig. 1) and expensive textiles rather than through the use of paint colors. I am excluding of course the rare and exceptional use of gold leaf. Gilding was occasionally but not often used. The most frequent usage was in the churches—either on the altarpieces, such as at St. Francis Xavier Church (1730s) in St. Mary's County, Maryland, or on the pulpits, such as at Christ Church (1744) in Philadelphia. At Stratford Hall (1730) in Virginia, I found gold leaf on a lower portion of fluted pilaster in the Great Hall; it was obviously an experiment that was not continued. At the Miles Brewton House (1769) in Charleston, South Carolina, gilding was used on a fillet applied to medium blue painted wallpaper on the ceiling over the staircase landing.

What is conspicuous with respect to all the data on color I have amassed is that while the range of shades of colors is great, the palette itself is unbelievably similar from region to region throughout the colonies. Clearly, there was a routine or traditional way of communicating color in the eighteenth century from painter to painter and from homeowner to homeowner. There

Figure 3. *Colonial Williamsburg paint card, produced in 1967 by Martin Senour Paints, the third licensee for reproducing Colonial Williamsburg paints. Most of these colors were developed to enhance the marketability of the entire line of reproduction colors; only a few were based on colors found on buildings. Some of the dark colors reflect late Victorian paints rather than colonial paints. (Colonial Williamsburg Foundation)*

Figure 4. *Window and shutters, Peter Wentz House (1758), Worcester, Pa., an unusual use of black and white paint. The sash and the shutters' stiles, rails, and raised panels were painted white, while the frames and the shutters' panel molding, and sinkage were painted black. On the reverse, the stiles and rails were painted white and the entire flat panel was painted black. (H. Ross Watson, Jr.)*

was unquestionably an accepted eighteenth-century color palette, a reliable way of communicating it, and a common fashion of using that palette within a house.

THE COLORS, THE PIGMENTS, AND HOW THEY WERE USED

The following is a concise discussion of each color within the palette along with how each was typically used. The palette is illustrated with thirty-five representative colors that I selected from the more than one hundred hues that I have analyzed. They are illustrated in the accompanying charts at the end of this chapter.

BLACKS

Black paints typically were made either of lampblack or bone black. In the eighteenth century black was primarily used as a color on the vertical faces of baseboards, known as mop boards. Dark brown also was a popular color for baseboards. Depending on the region, the dark baseboard color often was painted as a band all around a room, running across the door trim and doors and across fireplace paneling and sometimes into the fireplace itself, all at the height of the baseboard. The reason was practicality: dirt was better hidden by dark paints. Some areas around door knobs were painted dark for the same reason. The popularity of black and dark brown baseboards declined after about 1800, and by 1815 it was probably considered an out-of-date painting practice in most areas.

Several unusual uses of black include a room at Waverly, ca.1755, in Howard County, Maryland, where all the wood trim was painted black. Another example is the South Square Room at Monticello, which uses black plaster. All the walls there were plastered with a very dark gray skim coat of lime plaster tinted heavily with lampblack. Also, in 1797 Benjamin Chew of Philadelphia noted in his account books that he had paid painter John Frank for an uncommon usage of black paint—"painting black the putty of the front windows of Cliveden." Another atypical use of black is on the exterior frames and shutters of the Peter Wentz House (1758), Worcester, Pennsylvania **(fig. 4)**.

BROWNS

The brown paints use a great variety of pigments. Usually they are made with red iron oxide and lampblack. As mentioned earlier, dark brown paint was frequently used as a baseboard color. Also it was frequently used on the cap moldings of chair rails, on window benches, and even on the cap moldings of staircase handrails—again for the practicality of disguising dirt.

A 1750s exterior medium brown paint from the original rusticated front clapboard on the Redwood Library in Newport, Rhode Island, was made of eight different pigments: white lead, calcium carbonate, yellow ocher, raw sienna, raw umber, charcoal black, bone black, and red iron oxide. Occasionally dark brown was used for painting all wood trim in a room, as in the winter kitchen of the Peter Wentz House.

MODERATE REDDISH BROWN

This is the color that in the eighteenth century was referred to as Spanish brown. It is red iron oxide. It was very often used as a prime coat as described by John Smith in *The Art of Painting in Oyl* (4th ed., 1705). In America, however, it was often used as a finish-coat color too. At Independence Hall in Philadelphia, for instance, all the exterior trim was painted with Spanish brown for the first twenty years. A mid-eighteenth century shutter found at Wyck House, an early Quaker home in Germantown, Philadelphia, was finish painted with the same color, suggesting that the associated exterior window trim was also the same moderate reddish brown.

At Colonial Williamsburg, an area-wide study for repainting the interior and exterior of the court house found that many eighteenth-century Tidewater Virginia buildings were originally finish painted with this color on both the inside and the outside.

Historical documents also mention the painting of roofing shingles with this paint color.

GRAYS

Light gray was a very popular color. Shades of it often were made with a simple combination of white lead and charcoal black, as on the interior wood trim at Trinity Church in Newport, Rhode Island, in the 1770s to 1780s. Or they were created with combinations of white lead, charcoal black, and iron earth pigments, as at Gunston Hall in the 1750s, in Lorton, Virginia. Most examples of light grays that I have studied come from interior wood trim. The one exterior use that I researched is at the late eighteenth-century Morris-Jummel Mansion in New York City. All evidence indicates that this frame building was originally painted with a light gray on the clapboards, cornice, and windows, although no original shutters survive to sample and analyze.

Shades of medium gray were made with the same pigments as the light grays, but the percentage of lampblack or charcoal black and the iron earth pigments increased in order to darken the color. Medium gray was used for the chair rail, staircase elements, door face, and window trim of the slave quarters, Pottsgrove Manor (1754), Pottstown, Pennsylvania (fig. 5).

The dark grays used considerably more tinting pigments by volume in combination with the white lead and calcium carbonate pigments. From my data it appears that all uses except one are for early and mid-eighteenth-century color schemes only. The first of two interesting exterior uses of dark gray is on the exterior window trim of Trinity Church in Newport. The

Figure 5. *Slave quarters, Pottsgrove Manor (1754), Pottstown, Pa. When analyzed, the medium gray paint was found to contain white lead, calcium carbonate, and lampblack.*
(Frank S. Welsh)

other is on an original roofing shingle from the late eighteenth-century house, Battersea, in Petersburg, Virginia.

YELLOWISH WHITES

Shades of off-white or yellowish white were extremely popular. The earliest example in my data is about 1720 at the William Trent House in Trenton, New Jersey. Another mid-eighteenth-century example is on the wood trim in the back parlor at the Carter House (ca. 1746) in Williamsburg. A late Federal usage (ca. 1815) is at a private residence in Alexandria, where all the trim in the house was originally yellowish white. The sheen or gloss of the finish was enhanced by glazing with a clear and very thin, oily, slightly resinous glaze. The walls were papered.

The yellowish whites can be distinguished readily from the yellowed pure whites only by a thorough polarized light microscopical pigment analysis. From the buildings I have studied, it is apparent that the yellowish whites vary in color. All basically had the same pigment composition but differed of course in the proportions of pigments.

WHITE

White was probably the most popular and ubiquitous exterior paint color used in America in the second half of the eighteenth century. On building exteriors it was usually created with white lead and linseed oil alone, but sometimes it was made with a small amount of calcium carbonate. If the white is slightly shaded, the paint film generally contains trace amounts of red iron oxide and charcoal black or lampblack. This was true for samples taken from the late eighteenth-century exterior cornice of Ash Lawn (1799) in Charlottesville, Virginia, and on the early interior wood trim at the Nathaniel Russell House (1808) in Charleston, South Carolina.

At Independence Hall the early exterior paint films now are severely yellowed from their original appearance. However, polarized light and scanning electron microscopical analyses of the original and early white paint layers show only white lead and calcium carbonate. There are no tinting pigments to effect the overall white color of the paint.

Additional insight concerning interior treatments using white comes from William Seale's book on the White House. In the fall of 1800 whitewash was used on walls in utilitarian spaces and the associated wood trim was painted white. Wallpaper was used in the best rooms, and the trim there was also painted with tinted lead-in-oil paints:

The basement was whitewashed, its wood trim painted white; against this flat and gloss white were orange brick pavers nine inches square that covered the floors of rooms and halls. [1]

On the principal floor the best rooms were to be wallpapered. The commissioners had discussed "the fitness of the pattern," preferring French papers or, second best, those made in England. Two tons of white lead were acquired for making the paint for the woodwork, along with the tinting pigments yellow ocher, Prussian blue, and red lead. [2]

GREENS

This group probably presents the most variety among all the colors. I have found pale blue green, light blue green, very pale green, pale green, light green, light grayish green, grayish green, medium yellowish green, and light grayish olive primarily on interiors. Perhaps the variety is a product of popularity. Likewise, the varieties of pigments and pigment combinations are extensive.

For the light and medium shades of green, white lead and calcium carbonate are the white pigments. The typical coloring pigments I find are Prussian blue, verdigris, lampblack, yellow ocher, and red iron oxide. (Indigo, a blue pigment, is used only in the distemper or water-based paints I have analyzed; it is not typically used in oil paints.)

The dark green paints contain primarily verdigris, one of the most fugitive of all paint pigments. It often was used in combination with white lead and Prussian blue in an oil medium. It also was used by itself, usually in a varnish medium. Early American painters knew how fugitive it was, and they tried to arrest its quick color change by mixing it with varnish. Since one coat of verdigris mixed with varnish has no opacity, it was often applied in multiple coats or glazes to achieve a strong, rich blue-green color. Often it was applied over an opaque blue-gray base coat. Many times I have found a two-hundred-year-old layer of verdigris green that looks just like a dark brown paint because it has degraded and discolored so much. Only polarized light microscopical analysis confirms the presence of the verdigris.

A dark green was used at Monticello, and it is instructive to see how a color was referred to and how it was communicated from painter to homeowner to builder. On June 8, 1805, Jefferson wrote to his carpenter, the builder at Monticello, James Dinsmore:

After writing to you yeasterday, I was at the painting room of mr Stewart (the celebrated portrait painter) who had first suggested to me the painting a floor green, which he had himself tried with fine effect. he observed that care should be taken to hit the true *grass*-green, & as he had his pallet & colors in his hand, I asked him to give me a specimen of the colour, which he instantly mixed up to his mind, and I spread it with a knife on the inclosed paper. be so good there fore as to give it to mr Barry as a model of the colour I wish to have the hall floor painted of. the painters here talk of putting a japan varnish over the painted floor and floor-cloth after the paint is dry, which they say will prevent its being sticky and will bear washing. as I have not seen it I cannot say what it is. mr Barry is probably the best judge of it. accept my good wishes.

P.S. the floor should be painted the instant you have it ready, and all other work should give way to getting that ready.

I found evidence of this grass green in both the entrance hall and the dome room. It had been stripped years ago from the flooring. In the entrance hall the evidence was behind doors in the jamb areas and also in the middle of the floor. In the dome room evidence was found only in the middle of the floor area. This paint color was recently restored in the entrance hall (fig. 6). The green was made with white lead, calcium carbonate, verdigris, Prussian blue, yellow ocher, and bone black.

YELLOWS

The most popular of the yellows is a moderate orange-yellow made primarily with yellow ocher, white lead, and calcium carbonate. This yellow varies in shade from pale to light to

Figure 6. *Entrance hall, Monticello (1805), Charlottesville, Va. All painted finishes have been restored to the original colors on the basis of the author's stereo- and polarized light microscopical analyses.*

(Robert C. Lautman)

medium. I have never found a dark yellow. The darkest and the reddest was the orange-yellow on the trim in the Supreme Court Chamber at Independence Hall in Philadelphia. This shade of yellow was tinted with yellow ocher, red lead and haematite, which explains its darker and more orange tone.

Popular not only as an oil paint for trim, yellow also was made in distemper for use on walls. Thomas Jefferson used it in two rooms—on the dado of the entrance hall and on the dome room walls.

The color appeared in private and in public spaces alike, both formal and informal, grand and utilitarian. In the eighteenth and early nineteenth centuries a medium yellow was always used as the ground coat for mahogany graining. It allowed the grainer to wipe off the graining glaze in a thin line if he wanted to imitate a boxwood inlay, because the color tone of finished boxwood is close to the medium yellow paint color.

Other yellow pigments used in this period but found only infrequently in architectural paints include orpiment, lead tin yellow, patent yellow, and massicot.

It is interesting to see how a yellow color was referred to in correspondence from the early 1800s. For example, at Thomas Jefferson's Monticello, in 1808, Ellen Wayles Randolph wrote: "…. went over to Monticello; I think the hall, with its gravel colored border is the most beautiful room I ever was in, without excepting the Drawing rooms at Washington." [3]

During my paint analysis in the 1970s and again in the early 1990s samples were found of this gravel color, which turns out to be a moderate orange yellow. The paint was a distemper (calcimine) and had been washed off the plaster dado. Only tiny fragments of evidence survived behind a metal plaque indicating the day of the week (Friday) attached to a wood block on the face of the chair rail. This paint color was recently restored and is also illustrated in figure 6.

RED AND REDDISH ORANGE

The brightest and the least used colors in the colonial period are the reds and the reddish oranges. The reds are made with vermilion and have been found only on cupboard interiors. I know of only two examples—at the Cornelius Low House (1741) in Highland Park, New Jersey, and at the Governor Belcher Mansion (1750s), Elizabeth, New Jersey, found by Penelope Hartshorne Batcheler and Frederick B. Hanson in 1960.

Vermilion is sometimes impossible to distinguish from the haematite form of red iron oxide. Only a microchemical test can confirm the difference. I use a sodium azide-iodine test at present.

Figure 8. *Parlor; Wickham House (1813), Richmond, Va. Three old painting schemes have been uncovered; the section on the far left shows the original one that has been copied in the new painting on the surrounding walls. The one on the right dates from the ca. 1850's. The original light pink is made with white lead, calcium carbonate, vermilion, and yellow ocher. (Frank S. Welsh)*

The reddish orange color comes from red lead. Like vermilion, the reddish orange paints are used to paint cupboard interiors. The color may have been selected to allow china to be shown off more easily, as becomes clear when one studies the colors used in the Chinese export porcelain of the period. The cupboard interior and window seat in the parlor of Washington's Headquarters at Valley Forge were originally painted a strong reddish orange **(fig. 7)**.

PINKS

Pinks were more often used than one might expect. They were made with white lead and calcium carbonate tinted with either vermilion, haematite, or red iron oxide and shaded with charcoal black, yellow ocher, and umber. The earliest example I know of is on the interior wood trim of the unrestored cottage (1720s) at Belmont Mansion in Fairmount Park, Philadelphia. A light pink was also used on the 1760s exterior window trim of the main block of the mansion. Pink was also used in the Wickham House (1813), Richmond, Virginia **(fig. 8)**.

BLUES

There is as much variation in the light blues as there is in the light to medium greens. The blue pigment used is almost always Prussian blue. The most interesting uses of light blue are the vertical faces of the baseboards at Monticello and the exterior clapboards, windows, and

Figure 9. *Cross-sectional photomicrograph of window shutters from the southeast room, second floor, Cliveden (1763–67), Philadelphia. The various layers of this sample (201-7) represent, from bottom to top, the wood, the original red oxide primer coat, the original yellowish white intermediate coat, the original grayish green finish coat, late eighteenth-century greens, late eighteenth-century blues, and later yellowish whites and whites. (Frank S. Welsh)*

doors at the Wells Thorn House (1750s) in Deerfield, Massachusetts. At Wells Thorn the blue was not the original paint color; it was applied about 1800.

Perhaps medium blue is the most talked-about color of our recent past. That shade of medium blue was most often achieved by mixing white lead, calcium carbonate, and Prussian blue.[4] Shading was done with small amounts of yellow ocher or charcoal black. Typical eighteenth-century blues can be seen in the cross-sectional photomicrograph of a paint sample from Cliveden (1763–67), Philadelphia (**fig. 9**).

The color was very popular in almost all homes and all types of public buildings. For example, it is the predominant color of the master bedroom of the Hampton Mansion (1790), Towson, Maryland (**fig. 10**). The color was usually more on the red side of medium blue, not on the green side. The yellowing of the oil medium tends to make the old paint samples look greener than the original color actually was. Bleaching this color with sunlight or a black light (ultraviolet radiation) can sometimes be helpful in reversing a small portion of the yellowing. But again, the original color is never achieved by bleaching the highly yellowed samples. Thick globs of original paint are essential for evaluating original color and achieving an accurate color match. When they are unavailable, sometimes it seems tempting to overextrapolate the color into a stronger, brighter color than it ever was. Prussian blue was used with small amounts of yellow ocher and red iron oxide to color white lead and calcium carbonate, making a pale blue-green paint (**fig. 11**).

Indigo is the other widely used eighteenth-century blue pigment. It was used only in distemper or water-based paints—not oil paints, which discolor it. The best blue distemper example I know of is that used by Thomas Jefferson at Monticello in the South Square Room.

INTERIOR AND EXTERIOR COLORS DOCUMENTED IN A 1798 PAINTING SPECIFICATION

Probably one of the most important documents already published concerning exterior and interior paints, paint materials, and costs is a detailed painting specification of the St. George Tucker House, Williamsburg, Virginia. It dates from August 1798 and sheds much light on how colors were named and how they were placed in and on this frame structure, which still survives in Williamsburg.

Agreement between St. George Tucker and Jeremiah Satterwhite of Williamsburg on 30, August, 1798.[5]

The said Jeremiah Satterwhite agrees and undertakes to paint the Outside of the dwelling house, & part of the inside together With the Kitchen & Dairy, belonging to the said St. George Tucker in the City of Williamsburg as herein after mentioned, & in the most compleat & workmanlike manner; taking Care never to paint but in dry Weather, nor at any time when the part to be painted is not perfectly dry. The tops of the House, Kitchen & dairy are to be painted with Fish oil mixt in the paint, the oil to be well boiled before it is mixed with the Paint. St. George Tucker hath imported boiled Linseed Oil, but if it should not be sufficiently boiled, it is to be boiled to a proper consistency. Every part that is to be

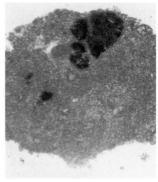

Figure 10. *Master bedroom, Hampton Mansion (1790), Towson, Md. The colors in this room —a total of eight colors or decorative finishes, of which medium blue predominates —represent the most popular colors in use in the colonial period. The overmantel is highly stylized. (H. Ross Watson, Jr.)*

Figure 11. *Pale blue-green paint sample from fireplace paneling, parlor, Woodford Mansion (ca. 1756), Philadelphia. The pigments are typical eighteenth-century pigments (chart color no. 15). (Frank S. Welsh)*

painted is to have two good Coats well laid on, in the best Manner. St. George Tucker hath provided about 240 pounds of best white Lead, half an hundred weight of Spanish brown, and the like Quantity of Yellow Ochre, all ground in oil and about sixteen Gallons of boiled Linseed Oil, he is further to provide as much fish-oil as will be sufficient to paint the roofs, & sheds, as hereafter mentioned. He has also provided eleven bottles of Spirits of Turpentine and a sufficient Quantity of Tar and the said Satterwhite agrees to keep an exact Account of the Quantity of each of these article s that he may expend in painting the House. The said Satterwhite is to find his own Brushes and a pot to boil the oil, and paint. St. George Tucker will provide ladders & furnish every necessary Assistance to him. "The top of the House, the roof of the Shed, and of the covered Way are to be painted with Spanish brown, somewhat enlivened, if necessary, with red Lead, or other proper paint. "The sides of the House, and of the covered way, & the Ends of the house are to be painted of a pure White. The outer doors a chocolate colour—the brick underpinning and the other parts of the house below the floor of a dark brick Colour, nearly approaching to a Chocolate colour. The Chair boards, picture slips, Window, & other parts of the front & back passage (except the doors & door Cases, which are to be of Chocolate Colour) are to be of a pale Stone colour, or straw Colour. The two small side passages of a Mahogany Colour, except the part leading to

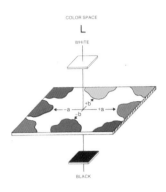

Figure 12. *CIE LAB color space. The CIE LAB system identifies colors mathematically rather than using color samples in specific arrangements, as other color systems do. LAB (represented as L*a*b) is an opponent color system that is linked with the use of the spectrophotometer and that references colors with respect to whiteness-blackness, redness-greenness, and yellowness-blueness. (Courtesy of Macbeth®; H. Ross Watson, Jr.)*

the dining room, which is to be of a stone colour. The platform for the Steps, in front of the house, when finished, is also to be painted of a light stone colour.

The top of the Kitchen, and of the shed leading from the Cellar to the Kitchen yard, are to be painted with Spanish brown, mixed with Tar, & fish oil, & well boiled together. The sides of the Kitchen of yellow Ochre, with a very small mixture of White Lead: the window frames & Sashes of straw-colour, or white: the sliders to the windows in Imitation of the Sashes.

The dairy is to be painted as the kitchen; the open work under the Eaves white.

When the work is compleated, St. George Tucker agrees to pay fifty dollars for the same; but in Case he should conceive the work not to be well done, or in Case of disagreement on any other subject; he is to chuse one person & the said Satterwhite another, who, or in Case of disagreement (torn and illegible) them, any third person by them to be chosen shall determine whether any, or what abatement ought to be made, by reason of the work not being compleatly finished, in a masterly workmanlike manner, pursuant to the true Intent & meaning of this Agreement.

In witness whereof the parties aforesaid have subscribed their names to this present instrument of writing the day & year above—

Witness Jeremiah Sattywhite E.H. Dunbar St G Tucker

NB. The boiled Linseed Oil is not to be used for the Kitchen, the Dairy, or the top of the House.

THE COLOR PALETTE OF THE EIGHTEENTH CENTURY: A DATABASE OF COLORS AND PIGMENTS

The following chart presents for the first time a comprehensive look at the actual paint colors used on the interior and exterior of colonial homes. The data document the pigments used to make those colors and also specify how colonial Americans used and placed colors on a building and within a room.

These data begin to answer the fundamental questions about paints and pigments that researchers and restorationists continually ask about colonial America: What are the authentic colors? What pigments were used to make them? How were the colors used? The chart (pages 81–85) provides this information at a glance.

The majority of the sites I have studied over the past twenty years are concentrated in the Middle Atlantic states. Even so, I believe that by and large they and the colors I have chosen to illustrate are representative of all of colonial America.

The method of color measurement (column 6 in the chart) is the CIE LAB color-order system, a mathematical, opponent color-order system related to precise descriptions of light source, object, and a standard observer and linked to the spectrophotometer. The name derives from the international organization—Commission Internationale de l'Eclairage (CIE)—established to evaluate and set standards for the scientific community involved with color research and application. The CIE LAB color space is easy to visualize **(fig. 12)**.

As perceptions of color usage in America two hundred years ago gradually seep into the popular and scholarly consciousness, the results of this article should help direct further research and investigation into more buildings from more regions to find different colors and combinations of pigments. As analytical technology continues to advance, one can expect that further discoveries will continue to be made.

	Building	Paint Type	Color Name and Age of Layer	Pigments Identified	Features Painted	CIE LAB [Illum C[2]]		Color Sample*
1.	Independence Hall Philadelphia, Pa. 1732–48	Oil	Black 1730s–1750s	Lampblack	Interior: Baseboard height of wood trim; baseboards (below cap molding)	L* a* b*	4.89 0.00 0.00	
2.	Cliveden Philadelphia, Pa. 1763–67	Oil	Dark brown Ca. 1767	Red iron oxide Lampblack Calcium carbonate White lead	Exterior: Door (in association with white trim)	L* a* b*	21.05 +8.22 +7.08	
3.	George Wythe House Williamsburg, Va. 1750s	Oil	Dark brown 1760s–1770s	Red iron oxide Lampblack Calcium carbonate White lead	Interior: Baseboards; baseboard height of wood trim; doors (in association with pale orange-yellow trim)	L* a* b*	19.52 +11.51 +8.95	
4.	Cliveden Philadelphia, Pa. 1763–67	Oil	Moderate reddish brown Ca. 1767	Red iron oxide	Exterior: Door	L* a* b*	31.13 +20.72 +17.95	
5.	Redwood Library Newport, R.I. 1749	Oil	Medium brown 1750s	White lead Calcium carbonate Yellow ocher Raw sienna Raw umber Charcoal black Bone black Red iron oxide	Exterior: Wood rustication	L* a* b*	41.50 +6.56 +10.14	
6.	Trinity Church Newport, R.I. 1726, 1769	Oil	Light gray 1770s–1780s	White lead Charcoal black	Interior: Wood trim (throughout sanctuary)	L* a* b*	81.27 −1.44 −1.25	
7.	Prestwould Clarkesville, Va. 1790s	Oil	Medium gray 1790s	Not analyzed	Interior: Wood trim (in association with light gray trim and white window sashes)	L* a* b*	71.65 −0.01 −0.01	
8.	Stratford Hall Stratford, Va. 1730	Oil	Medium gray 1730s	White lead Calcium carbonate Lampblack	Interior: Wood trim (Great Hall)	L* a* b*	56.84 −1.11 −2.61	

* See the note on page 85 describing the effect of the printing process on reproduction of these color samples.

	Building	Paint Type	Color Name and Age of Layer	Pigments Identified	Features Painted	CIE LAB [Illum C²]		Color Sample*
9.	Gunston Hall Lorton, Va. 1750s	Oil	Dark gray 1750s	White lead Calcium carbonate Bone black Yellow ocher	Interior: Wood trim	L* 46.66 a* 0.00 b* −0.01		
10.	Independence Hall Philadelphia, Pa. 1732–48	Oil	Yellowish white Ca.1760s	White lead Calcium carbonate Yellow ocher Charcoal black Red iron oxide	Interior: Wood trim (in association with black baseboards)	L* 79.35 a* +0.64 b* +8.21		
11.	Miles Brewton House Charleston, S.C. 1769	Oil	Yellowish white 1770s	White lead Calcium carbonate Yellow ocher Red iron oxide Burnt umber Charcoal black	Interior: All wood trim (including baseboards)	L* 86.05 a* −0.34 b* +15.02		
12.	Monticello Charlottesville, Va. 1805	Oil	Yellowish white 1805	White lead Calcium carbonate Yellow ocher Raw umber Charcoal black	Interior: Wood trim (in association with light blue baseboards and mahogany grained doors)	L* 90.84 a* −1.31 b* +8.20		
13.	William Trent House Trenton, N.J. 1719	Oil	Yellowish white 1720s	White lead Calcium carbonate Yellow ocher Raw sienna Red iron oxide Bone black (trace)	Interior: All wood trim (in association with black baseboards)	L* 86.05 a* −0.30 b* +11.29		
14.	Independence Hall Philadelphia, Pa. 1732–48	Oil	White 1755	White lead Calcium carbonate	Exterior: All wood trim	L* 87.97 a* −0.60 b* +6.29		
15.	Woodford Philadelphia, Pa Ca. 1756	Oil	Pale blue green Mid-18th century	White lead Calcium carbonate Prussian blue Yellow ocher Red iron oxide	Interior: Wood trim (in association with dark brown chair rail cap and black baseboards)	L* 90.84 a* −6.60 b* +2.71		

* See the note on page 85 describing the effect of the printing process on reproduction of these color samples.

Building	Paint Type	Color Name and Age of Layer	Pigments Identified	Features Painted	CIE LAB [Illum C²]	Color Sample*
16. William Trent House Trenton, N.J. 1719	Oil	Light green 1750s–1760s	White lead Calcium carbonate Verdigris Bone black	Interior: Wood trim (excluding baseboards)	L* 71.65 a* −15.28 b* +13.06	
17. Ellsworth House Windsor, Conn. 1760s	Oil	Light green Ca. 1788	White lead Calcium carbonate Prussian blue Yellow ocher Charcoal black Red iron oxide	Interior: Wood trim, including baseboards (in association with yellowish white window sash)	L* 81.27 a* −7.48 b* +9.06	
18. Trinity Church Newport, R.I. 1726, 1769	Oil	Pale green Mid- to late 18th century	White lead Prussian blue Verdigris	Interior: Pulpit interior	L* 61.84 a* −11.28 b* +4.18	
19. Monticello Charlottesville, Va. 1805	Distemper	Very pale green Early 19th century	Calcium carbonate Indigo Yellow ocher	Interior: Plaster walls (in association with yellowish white trim and mahogany grained doors)	L* 76.47 a* −10.96 b* +9.26	
20. Meason House Connellesville, Pa. 1802	Oil	Dark green Ca. 1802	Verdigris White lead	Exterior: Fixed louvered shutter	L* 47.06 a* −31.49 b* +14.56	
21. Gunston Hall Lorton, Va. 1750s	Oil	Dark olive Mid-18th century	White lead Calcium carbonate Verdigris Yellow ocher Raw sienna Red iron oxide Charcoal black	Interior: Wood trim (salvaged)	L* 41.50 a* −0.75 b* +14.32	
22. Independence Hall Philadelphia, Pa. 1732–48	Oil	Light yellowish brown 1760s	White lead Calcium carbonate Yellow ocher Red lead Red iron oxide (haematite)	Interior: Wood trim (in association with dark brown window sills and caps of chair rails)	L* 64.81 a* +10.01 b* +31.22	

* See the note on page 85 describing the effect of the printing process on reproduction of these color samples.

Building	Paint Type	Color Name and Age of Layer	Pigments Identified	Features Painted	CIE LAB [Illum C²]	Color Sample*
23. William Trent House Trenton, N.J. 1719	Oil	Moderate orange-yellow Mid-18th century	White lead Calcium carbonate Yellow ocher Burnt umber Charcoal black	Interior: Wood trim (excluding baseboards)	L* 78.40 a* +4.66 b* +24.99	
24. St. Francis Xavier Church St. Mary's Co., Md. 1730s	Oil	Light yellowish brown 1750s	White lead Calcium carbonate Raw sienna Yellow ocher Red iron oxide	Exterior: Clapboard siding (in association with white bargeboard)	L* 74.55 a* +6.63 b* +32.89	
25. Hampton Mansion Towson, Md. 1790	Oil	Brownish pink 1790s	White lead Calcium carbonate Red iron oxide Burnt umber Yellow ocher Charcoal black	Interior: Wood trim (used in a polychrome scheme)	L* 76.47 a* +7.97 b* +22.17	
26. Peter Wentz House Worcester, Pa. 1758	Oil	Reddish orange 1750s	Red lead Calcium carbonate	Interior: Inside of cupboards (in association with medium-blue wood trim)	L* 51.78 a* +42.50 b* +36.06	
27. Cornelius Low House Highland Park, N.J. 1741	Oil	Strong red 1760s	Vermilion White lead (trace) Calcium carbonate	Interior: Cupboard interior	L* 41.50 a* +47.97 b* +34.94	
28. Brice House Annapolis, Md. 1773	Oil	Medium pink 1770s	White lead Calcium carbonate Vermilion	Interior: Wood trim (in association with dark brown doors and baseboards)	L* 81.27 a* +13.25 b* +14.90	
29. Belmont Mansion Philadelphia, Pa. 1720s (cottage)	Oil	Light pink 1730s	White lead Calcium carbonate Haematite Yellow ocher	Interior: Wood trim	L* 81.27 a* +8.67 b* +12.26	
30. Wells Thorn House Deerfield, Mass. 1750s	Oil	Light blue 1800	White lead Prussian blue	Exterior: Wood trim and siding	L* 81.27 a* −13.48 b* −11.10	

* See the note on page 85 describing the effect of the printing process on reproduction of these color samples.

Building	Paint Type	Color Name and Age of Layer	Pigments Identified	Features Painted	CIE LAB [Illum C²]	Color Sample*
31. Independence Hall Philadelphia, Pa. 1732–48	Oil	Light greenish blue 1760s	White lead Calcium carbonate Prussian blue Charcoal black (large) Red iron oxide Yellow ocher	Interior: Wood trim	L* 73.58 a* −6.01 b* −6.15	
32. George Wythe House Williamsburg, Va. 1750s	Oil	Light blue-green 1750s–1760s	White lead Calcium carbonate (trace) Prussian blue Yellow ocher Raw sienna Red iron oxide	Interior: All wood trim (excluding baseboards, which may have been black)	L* 76.47 a* −9.98 b* −2.30	
33. Trinity Church Newport, R.I. 1726, 1769	Oil	Medium blue Mid-18th century	White lead Calcium carbonate Prussian blue Smalt	Interior: Pulpit interior	L* 66.77 a* −10.05 b* −12.64	
34. Independence Hall Philadelphia, Pa. 1732–48	Oil	Medium blue 1760s	White lead Calcium carbonate Prussian blue Charcoal black	Interior: Wood trim (in association with black baseboards and dark brown window sills and cap moldings of chair rails)	L* 63.82 a* −6.42 b* −17.05	
35. Charles Carroll House Annapolis, Md. 1730s	Distemper	Medium blue Late 18th century	Calcium carbonate Indigo	Interior: Plaster walls	L* 68.73 a* −6.30 b* −9.58	

* **Note:** Many colors cannot be reproduced exactly in four-color process inks (cyan, magenta, yellow, and black), in which this book is printed. All of the color samples shown in these charts thus vary from the precise paint colors used in the historic buildings noted. The L*a*b* reference values can provide an accurate color match when used by technical laboratories of paint companies operating with spectrophotometry and computer formulation software. Exact color chip samples are available from the author at P.O.Box 767, Bryn Mawr, PA 19010

Colonial Williamsburg Colors

A CHANGING SPECTRUM

THOMAS H. TAYLOR, JR., AND NICHOLAS A. PAPPAS

Since the late 1920s the restoration of Williamsburg has had a profound influence on American architecture. Thousands of buildings have been patterned after the restored and reconstructed structures of Virginia's colonial capital. The manifestations of this influence can be seen in every state and almost every city in this country.

THE WILLIAMSBURG REVIVAL

The initiative for the restoration came from the Rev. W.A.R. Goodwin, a local Episcopal minister with a dream of preserving not just one or two buildings but an entire town. Years after the restoration began Goodwin stated that "the compelling reasons for [the] restoration lie in the historic background of the city, and in the intrinsic simplicity and alluring beauty of its architectural form."[1] Through his fund-raising activities for the College of William and Mary, Goodwin met and persuaded John D. Rockefeller, Jr., to underwrite that dream. Rockefeller, after carefully considering the project and consulting with authorities on colonial architecture, including Fiske Kimball, Thomas E. Tallmadge, Ralph Adams Crams, and others, agreed on a limited program of restoration. He placed the project in the hands of two of his closest advisers, Col. Arthur Woods and Kenneth Chorley.

In the late 1920s and early 1930s a curious public watched as Rockefeller provided personal guidance, a management team, and the funds for the mammoth job of restoring Williamsburg's historic center. According to his biographer, Rockefeller was more deeply interested and more personally involved in the project than in any other of his many charitable undertakings.[2] Rockefeller's philosophy from the beginning centered on the creation of authentic restorations and reconstructions based on exhaustive historical, archaeological, and architectural research regardless of the cost in time, money, or effort. He continued to oversee every step of the project's development and frequently visited the town to observe the restoration and reconstruction of individual structures.[3] As the organization became self-sustaining, Rockefeller gradually withdrew his direct support of the operating costs but not before his total contribution amounted to nearly $68 million.

Figure 1. *Stair passage after restoration, Dr. Barraud House, showing the base color carried around the door architrave and frame. Although no inventory of Dr. Barraud's occupancy exists, the furnishings reflect items typically found in inventories of the period. (Colonial Williamsburg Foundation)*

Figure 2. *Pierce Middleton and Lester Cappon examining Galt family papers in the basement of the Goodwin Building, 1951. (Colonial Williamsburg Foundation)*

From the beginning of the restoration nearly six hundred structures have been restored or reconstructed in the approximately 170 acres that constitute the Historic Area. Of these, nearly one hundred contain sufficient amounts of eighteenth- or early nineteenth-century architectural fabric to be considered original structures. The rest, many of which have some original material, such as foundations and chimneys, are reconstructions.

Public response to this activity was immediate and favorable, creating a flood of requests for information and a rapidly growing tourist business. Every year during its first fifteen years the number of visitors to Williamsburg increased dramatically; before World War II nearly one million people had visited the town.

The use of eighteenth-century paint colors on the restored and newly reconstructed structures in particular attracted public interest. As part of the investigation of surviving structures, original paint layers were uncovered, matched, and applied to the buildings within the Historic Area of Williamsburg. As the first structures were completed, people requested samples of the paint and specific paint formulas. The inquiries grew to such numbers that early in 1932 a suggestion was made in a staff meeting that the foundation make and sell its own paint or arrange for a paint manufacturer to do so.[4]

The physical work of restoring the principal structures began in April 1928, when the architects and general contractors arrived in Williamsburg.[5] The Boston architectural firm of Perry, Shaw and Hepburn was selected by Goodwin to serve as the principal architects for the restoration from 1928 to 1934. After 1934, when the foundation established its own architectural department, Perry, Shaw and Hepburn continued to provide consulting services until the death of the last surviving partner, William Graves Perry (b.1883) in 1975. The other partners, Thomas Mott Shaw (1878–1965) and Andrew Hopewell Hepburn (1880–1967), established a small practice in Boston after World War I. When Perry joined the firm in 1923, it consisted of no more than five professionals and was involved in the design of residences and an occasional schoolhouse or small college building.

A historical research team was assembled by Goodwin to collect information on the buildings in Williamsburg from all parts of Virginia, North America, and Europe. As the volume of work increased, it was agreed that a separate department under the supervision of the architects should be created. On March 29, 1930, the architects hired Harold R. Shurtleff (d.1938) to head the research activities, which were intended to provide them with information that would be useful to the restoration or reconstruction of the structures within the Historic Area. Helen Duprey Bullock (b.1904), the principal researcher on the subject of paints, examined numerous eighteenth-century household inventories, wills, diaries, journals, merchants' records, and newspaper advertisements to locate descriptions and formulas for finishes used on the buildings in Williamsburg during the eighteenth century (fig. 2).[6] In some cases eighteenth-century household inventories were used to assist with the selection of interior paint colors. Occasionally, these inventories included a description of patterns and designs of fabrics or painted furnishings, such as blue Venetian blinds or Delft tiles, from which architectural finishes that would harmonize with these objects were derived. Where the original paint colors could not be determined, either through physical evidence or historical research, paints were prepared from ingredients mentioned in the early advertisements of Williamsburg merchants and apothecaries and found on other eighteenth-century buildings in Williamsburg or in Tidewater Virginia.[7] In a few cases the original colors were not used because of the wishes of the life tenants.[8]

PIONEERING PAINT COLOR RESEARCH

The first attempts to identify an original paint color on a specific structure occurred late in 1929, when Susan Higginson Nash, an interior designer hired by the architects to assist with the interior furnishing of Raleigh Tavern, observed and reproduced original paint colors found in historic houses in eastern Virginia.[9] Although this was her first paid commission, she had done considerable interior design work for family and friends. It was on one of these jobs that she first met Perry, Shaw and Hepburn. Later, when asked about her interest in house paints, she stated, "Paint does interest me tremendously, and I worked on it with anybody and everybody that I felt knew about it from the chemical angle and who could assist me with the formulas. They were my formulas that were used for the first ten years and more in Williamsburg."[10]

Immediately after her arrival, she embarked on a five-day tour of historic properties in eastern Virginia in the company of Goodwin and Perry.[11] The tour, the first of many for Nash, was arranged by George Coleman, former mayor of Williamsburg, and began on October 14, 1929. Other members of the group included Elizabeth Hayes (Goodwin's secretary), Andrew Hepburn, Walter Macomber, an architect that Perry, Shaw and Hepburn placed in charge of their Williamsburg office, and Robert Lee, the driver. Nash later recalled: "I found that many of the houses had original color in them and that almost everybody was perfectly willing that I should look and paint in watercolor any imitation I wished."[12] She chose watercolor as a medium to match paint films because the colors could be easily and quickly mixed and were fast drying. It is not known whether she went on the tour with the intention of matching paint colors or whether the idea came to her as she observed the architects sketching architectural details and taking molding profiles. The tour included a visit to more than twenty-nine buildings in four days, and there was no time to conduct a more careful investigation of the paint history of each building. Nevertheless, it was the first recorded attempt to locate and match original house paint colors as part of a restoration project.

Nash quickly realized the limitations of this medium. Watercolors are not permanent and easily run if they get wet. Watercolors did not stand up well to the frequent handling they received. On her return she recommended that a paint "colorist" accompany her on future trips to assist with mixing and matching original paint films with alkyd paints.[13] On her recommendation Edward K. Perry and Company, a Boston paint contracting firm, was consulted in the spring of 1930.[14] Nels Ehrenborg was sent to Williamsburg to assist Nash with the paint investigations.[15] Ehrenborg accompanied Nash on many of her early visits to historic structures in the region for the purpose of scraping and matching the finishes. They also revisited some of the buildings Nash saw on her first tour and were able to obtain better matches in oil than those she had previously obtained with watercolors.[16] In some cases property owners permitted them to remove small slivers or pieces of the woodwork to obtain a permanent record. These architectural fragments were labeled and later examined for evidence of early paint films. Years later Nash recalled:

Well, we went on these trips, you know, so that the descriptions given us in the various inventories and descriptions of the buildings could be verified by actual paint colors, wherever we could find them, and we did find them. I worked with the Masury Paint Company a little bit, too, with their chemists, on grinding paint colors and learning what I could about them.[17]

Nash's interest in paints was not new in 1929.[18] Before her work in Williamsburg, she spent several years with Dodge McKnight, a Boston painter, whom she credited with teaching her all she knew about color.[19] She also worked briefly for Charles Hopkinson, another Boston painter who was later commissioned to paint the portrait of Perry, Shaw and Hepburn that now hangs in the foundation's board room.

Initially, most of the architectural painting was done by local painters hired and supervised by the general contractors Rockefeller employed for the restoration, Todd and Brown of New York. The paint crews hired by Todd and Brown were supervised by C. M. Sandridge, who was hired in 1931.[20] One document mentions that he was assisting Nash with the preparation of colors in April and preparing general samples of paint colors in July.[21] Perry refers to him as a colorist.[22] Todd and Brown first set up their paint shop in an old kitchen behind the Raleigh Tavern. (The kitchen, originally located in Merchants Square, was later moved to Franklin Street.) Early in 1931 the paint shop was relocated to several tin garages behind the Grissell Hay Lodging.[23]

The first full-time painter hired by the foundation was Bruno Rissansen, who was recommended by Edward K. Perry in 1933.[24] Nash first interviewed him in Boston during the first week of June 1933.[25] Within a few years several other painters were hired and a local painter, Perry O. Thrall, became the first paint foreman.[26] He too did some paint investigation. By the mid-1930s the foundation had decided to establish its own paint shop and hired a crew of painters, which did most of the painting in the Historic Area.

Robert Webb, Jr., became the first paint superintendent on May 5, 1940.[27] Shortly thereafter the paint shop moved from the Grissell Hay property to a newly constructed addition to one of the foundation warehouses located outside the historic district (**fig. 3**). In 1955 a specially designed facility was constructed at the corner of North Botetourt and East Scotland streets.[28] The number of painters continued to increase until the early 1950s, when thirty painters worked for the foundation.[29]

The painters maintained both wet samples in the form of small cans of leftover paint for both the historic structures and the modern buildings maintained by the foundation. They also prepared dry samples in the form of small ($2\frac{7}{8}$ by $5\frac{1}{2}$ inches) wood panels painted on one side that hung on a board in the paint shop. The ingredients for each color were printed on the back of the panels. Within a few years many of the wet samples were either used up or dried up, and on several occasions the maintenance department expressed concern that the wood panels, which were in constant use, were becoming too soiled and faded to serve as a color standard. One of Sandridge's responsibilities was to ensure that both wet and dry samples were maintained.[30]

Nash advised the architects to use Edward K. Perry and Company for painting two of the foundation's largest reconstructions—the Capitol and the Governor's Palace. These buildings called for special skills such as marbleizing and graining that the architects thought were beyond the ability of the local painters. Little is known of Ehrenborg or the other painters whom Edward K. Perry sent to Williamsburg in spring 1932 to work on the Capitol and Palace. They were all of Scandinavian descent, including their foreman, Morris Casperson.[31] Ehrenborg did most of the marbleizing in the Capitol.[32] Rissansen was assigned to replace Ehrenborg as Nash's assistant with the paint investigations. On one of his trips to Williamsburg to check on the work his painters, Perry recommended that Rissansen produce several new sets of paint color sample cards to replace the wood panels. A thorough inventory of colors was undertaken, and it was discovered that some of the wood panels had disappeared. Nash decided that for

Figure 3. *The Colonial Williamsburg Foundation paint shop, 1952. (Colonial Williamsburg Foundation)*

those colors for which information was lacking, she would match the paint on the buildings rather than conduct new paint investigations.[33] Branch Bocock, the foundation's director of maintenance, arranged for Nash and Rissansen to go into more than forty residences to make new samples of the interior colors.[34] Rissansen made several sets of sample color cards. Each color card was placed in a separate protective envelope and filed.[35] They were periodically brought out and compared to the wood panels.[36] The maintenance department decided to keep the wood panels, replaced the missing ones, and made new ones as new colors were introduced. Wet samples of the historic colors were also kept. In most cases when a structure had to be touched up or repainted the small painted wood panels were used as the standard for mixing new batches of paint. The wood panels were used by the painters until the late 1950s and are still housed in the foundation's paint shop, which contains more than a thousand panels. The new paint-color sample card collection prepared by Nash and Rissansen was kept in the architect's office. There is little reference to its having been used after World War II.

Between 1930 and 1942 Nash was the sole judge of the match between the original and the prepared sample. The sample was taken back to the paint shop, where larger quantities were prepared. She kept careful records of the ingredients used to establish a match at the site. The matched sample was brought back to the paint shop, where larger quantities were prepared. When Nash, who was commuting from Boston, returned to Williamsburg, she would check and approve the new samples.[37] The architects examined and approved each color and sent them to the foundation's president for final approval. After all approvals had been obtained, wood panels were prepared and sent to the general contractor, the architects, and the foundation's offices in New York and Williamsburg. Before a color was applied to a building, Nash compared a sample of the newly mixed paint with the original wood panel. In some cases she would return to the structure to verify the match.[38]

Only a few references describe Nash's method of paint investigation. She scraped the paint films with a knife, exposing each layer until she reached the raw wood.[39] The range of layers thus exposed served as evidence for original colors. In most cases, if the first or second paint film was Spanish brown, it was assumed that it was a primer and the color selected was usually the next pigmented color.[40] Nash never mentioned using a magnifying glass or microscope during her investigations. If all comparisons were done by eye without the aid of magnification, it must have been extremely difficult, if not impossible, to distinguish primers from finish coats.[41] After Nash matched original colors with the use of watercolors, she and the colorist used only those ingredients identified by the researchers as having been available in Williamsburg during the eighteenth century in mixing colors to match original paint layers. During many of her visits to Williamsburg she spent time in the paint shop grinding pigments in oil and testing some of the new pigments identified by the research department . On several occasions she sent letters to the maintenance department requesting that *her* supplies of pigments be replenished and in some cases that new pigments be added. Nash never described the process of matching the original paint film with a sample. We do not know whether the sample was prepared on a card or wood panel. It is likely that the sample was prepared on a card and taken back to the paint shop, where larger quantities were mixed. The wood sample panel was probably not prepared until all the approvals had been obtained. If this assumption is correct, then all the painted cards must have been discarded after the wood sample panel was approved, as none has survived.

Nash was aware of the changes that could affect paint colors and tried to compensate for them in preparing new samples:

Allowance for change is perhaps as important a consideration as any other and one which demands a tax upon one's judgment. Firstly, in examining existing color it has been found that the color must have greatly changed since its application. Soil, cleaning, oxidation and overpainting can alter a tone very greatly. Secondly, reproduction of the color must be done with an estimate in mind of the change that will take place in it as the years go by.[42]

The only noticeable change in the analysis process that occurred in the 1950s and 1960s was the introduction of solvents to assist in removing each layer of paint.[43]

Nash found little paint evidence on building exteriors because many of the buildings went for extended periods without repainting. Prerestoration photographs indicate that there was little if any paint on some of the structures when the foundation acquired them. Nash stated:

Whenever we have repainted old houses, we have used the color found on the clapboards, and in almost every case this has been white. Also I find that certain of the tenants refused to allow me to paint their houses other than white, as they say that the white looks so much cooler. For example Mrs. Tilledge objected to the brown color which I selected for her house, and at Mr. Bocock's request I canceled my schedule. The request for white paint has been made to me in regard to quite a number of the houses and by numerous Williamsburg residents. Of course, white is cooler looking than any other color which can be used. Also in the case of small houses such as the houses on Francis Street, it makes them appear larger. I have not found any old green paint on the exterior of any house in the Tidewater, nor are there many old red or brown houses in that locality though I have seen quite a number of them near Charlottesville and through the valley.[44]

Consequently, nearly all the early paint investigations were done on interior woodwork.

The architects in the Williamsburg office were frequently involved in paint investigations, and occasionally they disagreed with Nash's findings for exterior colors. One example concerned the

James Geddy House and Shop. The original exterior body color of the house was a light gray with dark gray trim. The paint investigation was done by Walter M. Macomber, the person Perry, Shaw and Hepburn had placed in charge of its Williamsburg office. He disliked the two-tone gray scheme he found and tried to use brighter colors. Although Rockefeller rejected the use of the brighter colors, he did agree not to match the original colors and use another scheme based on eighteenth-century colors found on the Brush-Everard House, which dated from the same period as the James Geddy House and Shop. A recent paint investigation revealed evidence that the two-tone gray scheme Macomber disliked was actually a nineteenth-century color scheme. The house was recently painted white, its original eighteenth-century color.

During the early 1930s Goodwin and Macomber believed that the exteriors of structures in the Historic Area were originally painted brighter colors.[45] However, Nash was convinced that most of the eighteenth-century buildings in Williamsburg were painted white, a belief supported by Bullock's research, which revealed that white lead and linseed oil were the most frequently ordered paint materials from England.[46] Goodwin and Macomber believed that the buildings, particularly those constructed in the first half of the eighteenth century, were painted with brighter colors, such as pink and chocolate brown.[47] On the basis of the discovery of brighter colors on structures in other areas of Virginia, they conjectured that the earliest pigmented colors had probably worn off before the buildings were repainted. They acknowledged that white paint was a popular exterior finish in Williamsburg, particularly during the late eighteenth century and early nineteenth century, but did not think it was a typical exterior finish during most of the colonial period. Although both men expressed their feelings through friendly written protests, Rockefeller and the architects continued to accept Nash's recommendations for exterior colors—usually white but in a few cases ocher or Spanish brown. To resolve the issue Macomber wrote to Hepburn in 1932 recommending that

the architectural force be relieved of any connection with obtaining final colors, because there is a possibility of such a variation in opinion on what these shades should be, and I really feel it would be much more satisfactory if Mrs. Nash would visit the various buildings with Mr. Thrall, the painting foreman, and make samples of the original existing paint colors that are found on the woodwork.[48]

COLOR MATCHING AFTER WORLD WAR II

Before World War II all matching—whether by Nash, the colorist, or one of the architects—was done without the aid of microscopic or chemical analysis. During this period most of the paint schemes were developed. Only a few paint investigations were undertaken after the war, and these were done by the foundation's painters under the supervision of the paint superintendent and the resident architect.[49]

The foundation appears to have devoted more attention to retaining the paint colors Nash obtained than improving the precision of the paint identifications. As early as spring 1932 William Perry sought expert advice concerning the preservation of the paint colors on the wood panels.[50] One organization he wrote to was the National Bureau of Standards, which recommended retaining wet samples placed in sealed, opaque containers. Although the painters maintained two-ounce wet samples of all colors until 1935, when the sample size was increased to one quart, the painters relied on the painted wood panels as the standard for the colors on the restored and reconstructed structures. They often complained to the architects that the wet samples did not last more than six months. The National Bureau of Standards also offered to conduct spectrophotometric analysis of the paint samples, for a fee, if the samples were sent to them on 29-by-39-millimeter rectangular chips. The foundation was neither ready to submit the samples for analysis nor prepared to spend between twenty and thirty dollars for each sample analyzed.[51]

The need to develop better methods of preserving the paint colors continued to increase, particularly after the war. The problem of maintaining accurate records of the colors and periodically checking the colors on the buildings with the paint color samples became so acute that in 1948 Singleton Moorehead, director of architecture, wrote to the National Bureau of Standards for assistance in developing a permanent method of recording paint colors. The response to this inquiry has not survived, only a letter of thanks addressed to Deane B. Judd that mentioned receipt of descriptive reports and literature on permanent methods of recording paint colors.[52] Judd must have referred to the *Munsell Book of Color* in the reports because within a few months the foundation corresponded with Blanche R. Bellamy, office manager for the Munsell Color Company, and requested a copy of the *Munsell Book of Color,* both the library edition and the pocket edition. However, after a trial period the foundation decided that the Munsell Color System was not suitable for its needs and returned the books.

The architects' intention was to maintain a permanent record of the location of the paint investigations by leaving the sample test sites exposed, particularly those in the exhibition buildings. Gradually, most of these sites have been concealed with subsequent repaintings.[53] A few survive at the James Geddy House and the Brush-Everard House. In most cases the general location is noted in the architectural reports, but with the increasing number of overpaintings it is becoming more difficult to locate them even with raking light.

Because of the deteriorating condition of the reference collection, Moorehead wrote to several large museums in the early 1950s to locate someone to analyze the paint films on the architectural fragments that the architects had collected.[54] In a letter to Richard D. Buck, conservator at the Fogg Art Museum, he noted that "we have collected a rather large series of original examples of such eighteenth century paint colors" and asked for assistance in having the paint on these pieces analyzed.[55] Buck, who was in the process of establishing a new laboratory at Oberlin College, suggested he contact Rutherford J. Gettens, who was working at the Freer Gallery in Washington, D.C.[56] Gettens agreed to analyze a sample taken from a second-floor door frame at the Benjamin Powell House that had been concealed when the house was enlarged in the eighteenth century; it was believed to date from the earliest portion of the house.[57] Gettens's report has been lost. However, in acknowledging receipt of the report Moorehead stated:

We were all surprised that you discovered 2 layers of paint under what we surely thought was a red priming coat and thus the first coat of paint upon the surface of the bare wood. For years we have considered that this red color was used chiefly as a priming coat and as a base for the final color. Now your discovery may well change our thinking and therefore opens up a new avenue of investigation since the use of this color was so extremely common—perhaps more so than any other on interior woodwork surfaces.[58]

Gettens was too busy to analyze all the fragments in the collection, and the foundation continued to search for someone to do the paint analysis. Alexander Stewart, director of research of the National Lead Company, agreed to analyze five additional samples.[59] They were sent on February 16, 1954, and consisted of a piece of the crown molding from an unidentified structure in Princess Anne County, a portion of an architrave in the Benjamin Waller House, a piece from the chair rail of the Taliaferro-Cole House, and a portion of a newel and a piece of wall sheathing from the Benjamin Waller House. The foundation requested that the National Lead Company identify "the composition or formula of each of the paint coats, particularly the coat next to the wood."[60] The analysis was not completed until October. The detailed report prepared by E. J. Dunn, Jr., has also been lost, and only Bullock's letter of appreciation confirms that the analysis was done.[61] During the following years the architects' interests once again focused on accurately and permanently recording the existing colors. In 1959 A. Edwin Kendrew, resident architect, contacted several museums using spectrophotometers to see if they would recommend its use at Williamsburg. In a letter to Sheldon Keck, Kendrew stated:

We have reviewed this situation repeatedly with various paint manufacturers and other experts in the field. We have attempted to develop chemical analyses of established colors to form a permanent record; we have consulted with the U.S. Bureau of Standards in an effort to develop a color record, and have studied the possible use of the Munsell color process. Attempts have been made to record the colors on metal panels with colors baked on, etc. In spite of all these efforts, we find ourselves still quite unsatisfied with any such methods of establishing permanent accurate records of colors.[62]

As a result of the strong endorsement from all the museums contacted, the foundation acquired a Color Eye spectrophotometer during summer 1960.[63] It was obtained to measure the color reflectance spectra of each of the master color samples.[64] Between 1961 and 1973 reflectance curves were obtained for most of the colors on the master paint color reference board.

The Color Eye was used to establish a permanent color measurement for each of the approved colors. It continued to be used until a problem developed with the prisms. By 1968 the original set of color samples on wood panels had changed so much that the paint shop prepared a new set of master color samples on 8-by-10-inch archival-quality cards. These were cut into 4-by-5-inch cards and placed in sealed envelopes and stored in a refrigerator in the paint shop. A Du-Color colorimeter from Neotec Instruments was acquired in 1975, replacing the spectrophotometer as the primary instrument used to ensure a close match between one of the refrigerated color sample cards and a newly mixed batch of paint.[65] Each time a card was removed from the refrigerator and used to match a newly mixed batch of paint, it was discarded. When the last card was removed, new cards were made from the most recent batch of paint.

Very little new paint investigation was done in the 1960s and 1970s. Although the master color samples in the paint shop had already begun to soil and fade after many years of use, new paint investigations were not undertaken, and the colors selected by Nash thirty years earlier continued to be the standard.

While the paint investigation techniques described earlier were state-of-the-art for the 1930s, the past fifteen to twenty years have seen such great strides in paint analysis that those methods seem totally primitive by today's standards. In 1987 Colonial Williamsburg undertook its first modern scientific paint analysis, conducted by Frank S. Welsh. Although Williamsburg was the first historical museum to attempt the replication of period colors on a large scale, reexamination of the extant paint history in the Historic Area by current scientific methods has been long overdue. It is hoped that these first efforts are only the prologue in determining exactly what paint colors were used in eighteenth-century Williamsburg.

INTERPRETING MODERN PAINT RESEARCH

What happens after the paint analysis—after one has in hand the analyst's report on the paint layer history, the Munsell color chips, and some dates or time spans? How does one use this information, and what does it actually tell us? Paint analysis answers many questions but does not address them all. Often, many new issues, as well as the paint film itself, must be analyzed.

Two buildings in the Williamsburg Historic Area on which modern paint analysis was first conducted have revealed complex paint histories in the early stages of their existence, including paint color changes in the eighteenth century. When presented with the results of the analysis, interpretive choices had to be made as to which colors were the most relevant to the structure and the period in which it was to be interpreted.

THE DR. BARRAUD HOUSE

The first building analyzed was the Dr. Philip Barraud House. To understand the problems that arose with the interpretation of this property, a brief history of the site and the house is necessary.

An original eighteenth-century structure of one and a half stories, it is located on colonial lot 19 south, at the northwest corner of Francis and Botetourt streets. The house is one of the best preserved residences in the Historic Area and retains much of its original fabric. Colonial Williamsburg acquired the property in 1940 and restored the house shortly thereafter. In 1987 a generous grant from Mr. and Mrs. William Kimball allowed for a complete refurbishing of the house for its new use as guest quarters for members of the Raleigh Tavern Society, an organization of major donors to the foundation. Included in the grant were funds for dendrochronology as well as for paint analysis.

The early history of this site, as well as several others in the Historic Area, is sketchy. The eighteenth-century court records of both the city of Williamsburg and James City County were sent to Richmond for safekeeping during the Civil War and were destroyed in the conflagration that engulfed that city toward the end of the fighting. The earliest surviving record describing the lot is from 1761, when William Withers, a local merchant, sold lots 19 and 18 to Williamsburg apothecary William Carter. William Holt, who had later acquired the property, sold lot 18 and the south part of lot 19 to blacksmith James Anderson in 1770. Exactly when the lot left Anderson's possession is unknown, but tax records show that a Susannah Riddell (or Riddle), who had moved to Williamsburg after her house in Yorktown was razed by General Cornwallis during the Revolution,[66] was taxed for the lot from 1782 until her death in 1785. Dr. Philip Barraud purchased the property from her estate in 1786 and lived in the house until he moved to Norfolk in 1799. He had come to Williamsburg in 1783 and set up his medical practice with James Galt, a local apothecary. They later became joint visiting physicians at the Public Hospital, Williamsburg's asylum for the insane, the first building constructed in this country for that purpose.

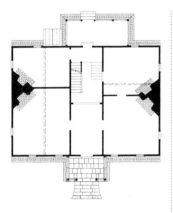

Figure 4. *First-floor plan, Dr. Barraud House, annotated by the author from a plan in Marcus Whiffen's* The Eighteenth-Century Houses of Williamsburg *(1960). Dashed lines indicate the first-phase west exterior wall and the original location of the partition between the east rooms. (Colonial Williamsburg Foundation)*

96

In 1801 Dr. Barraud sold the property to Anna M. Byrd, and it passed in turn to a succession of nineteenth- and early twentieth-century owners until it was bought by Mr. and Mrs. Archie G. Ryland in 1924. In 1940 Mr. and Mrs. Ryland conveyed the property to Colonial Williamsburg, retaining a life tenancy, which lasted until Mrs. Ryland's death in 1983.

The house was built in two phases, first as a modest frame structure, 37 feet wide and 33 feet deep, that consisted of four rooms on the first floor and three or four rooms on the second. Exact locations of the stair and chimneys of this early house are unknown. It is relatively certain that the house was built before 1782; however, it is not known which owner carried out this construction. The Frenchman's Map of 1782, a map showing all the buildings in Williamsburg that was probably drawn by one of Count Rochambeau's troops as a billeting map during the Revolution, clearly shows two structures on this lot—a squarish building on the corner and a smaller rectangular outbuilding to the rear, most likely the early house and its kitchen. Archaeology undertaken in the 1940s revealed foundations of an outbuilding behind the house with similar proportions to that on the Frenchman's Map. It was reconstructed when the house was restored.

The second phase of construction consisted of an expansion of ten feet to the west, creating a rectangular plan with a symmetrical facade (fig. 4). The additional width allowed the insertion of a central stair passage with independent access to all four rooms on each floor. The chimneys were relocated to the ends of the house, and a corner fireplace was provided in each room. Floorboards were taken up and relaid and the sizes of the two original eastern rooms were changed by moving the dividing partition approximately three feet to the south. Existing wainscot paneling in one of the old western rooms was refitted into the northwest room, and new wainscoting was installed in the southwest room.

Frank Welsh's paint analysis revealed that all the woodwork in the earlier house had been painted gray. In the second phase the new stair passage and the enlarged western rooms on both floors were painted a yellowish white followed by a clear oil glaze, while doors, baseboards, and door surrounds at the height of the baseboards were painted dark brown (fig. 1).[67] The analysis also revealed that some of the trim and doors from the earlier phase were reused in the enlarged portion of the house. The eastern rooms seem to have retained their gray color for a period of one to five years before being repainted a medium greenish blue followed by a clear glaze. The next layer of paint, a light green followed by a pigmented glaze, was applied to all the woodwork during the nineteenth century.

The question then arose as to which color to use in the refurbished eastern rooms—the dark gray or the medium greenish blue? The dendrochronology, performed by J. H. Heikkenen of Dendrochronology, Inc., in Blacksburg, Virginia, is inconclusive until further research on key year patterns of Williamsburg area pine has been done. Consequently, the exact dates of both phases of construction remain elusive. As stated earlier, the house in its first phase was in existence by 1782, as clearly shown on the Frenchman's Map. An insurance policy taken out by Dr. Barraud in 1796 lists a wooden structure 46 feet by 33 feet, almost the exact dimensions of the house in its present configuration. Therefore, it must have been enlarged between 1782 and 1796, either by Mrs. Byrd or Dr. Barraud. Because Mrs. Byrd was neither young nor affluent, it seems more likely that Dr. Barraud enlarged the house to accommodate his growing family. And, because the Barrauds lived there for thirteen years, it is most probable that they further

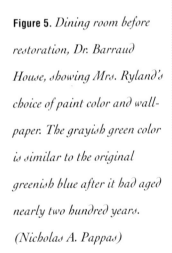

Figure 5. *Dining room before restoration, Dr. Barraud House, showing Mrs. Ryland's choice of paint color and wallpaper. The grayish green color is similar to the original greenish blue after it had aged nearly two hundred years.* (Nicholas A. Pappas)

Figure 6. *Dining room after restoration, Dr. Barraud House. The greenish blue color displays its original brilliance. (Colonial Williamsburg Foundation)*

embellished the interior by repainting some of the rooms a stylish greenish blue fairly early during their occupancy. Consequently, this color was replicated for the restoration (figs. 5 and 6).

The paint investigations during the 1940s restoration seem to parallel Welsh's findings in some ways. However, in many cases some layers of paint were undetected, finish coats were misidentified as prime coats, nineteenth-century paints were thought to be of the eighteenth century, and in all cases the colors noted are more subdued than those of the recent paint analysis. The architectural report noted, for instance, that in the southwest room the first coat was a "buff primer" and the second coat a "grey-green."[68] This can be read as relating to Welsh's analysis if one takes into consideration that the yellowish white had darkened with age (its two coats being read as one) and that the fugitive blue pigment of the light green had turned gray. The glazes were completely undetected.

None of the interior colors found was used in the early restoration. As this house had a life tenancy, the tenant was free to choose her own colors. Apparently Mrs. Ryland did not care for those uncovered during the paint investigation and chose other colors from the Williamsburg palette. A dark brown, however, was replicated on the interior doors and baseboards, although it was darker and less lively than the one that Welsh found and was not extended across the door surrounds.

Another interpretive decision to be made was the color for the exterior doors and shutters. One exterior door—the north passage door—had survived, but no original shutters remained. The original color for this door was the same dark brown used on the interior doors and baseboards. Thus, because the Barrauds' use of paint colors on the interior was rather economical (only three were used) and because the same brown color was used on the surviving exterior door, it seemed logical that the other exterior doors and the shutters should be painted the same shade of brown.

Figure 7. *Dr. Barraud House after restoration in 1941, showing the replicated nineteenth-century green trim color mistaken for the eighteenth-century color. (Colonial Williamsburg Foundation)*

Figure 8. *Dr. Barraud House after restoration in 1988, showing the revised colors. The brown color on the front doors and shutters is conjectural but is based on the color found on the original rear door. (Nicholas A. Pappas)*

As in the interior, some early findings on the exterior parallel Welsh's analysis. The discovery in the 1940s of eighteenth-century weatherboards hidden in a shed addition on the rear of the house confirmed that they were painted white. All the other weatherboards had been replaced in the nineteenth century. Welsh's analysis of surviving original exterior fabric showed white as the first finish coat. The exterior doors had also been painted brown in the early restoration. The two reports varied the most in the green exterior trim color. The early investigation noted that the first coat on the south cornice was white and the second green. It was assumed that the cornice was painted white in the first construction phase of the house and accented with green in the second. On the basis of this assumption, the cornice, shutters, and other architectural features were painted green. Welsh's analysis uncovered the fact that the green trim color contained zinc white, a pigment not in common use until the mid-nineteenth century. This proved conclusively that the trim could not have been painted green in the eighteenth century **(figs. 7 and 8)**.

THE LUDWELL-PARADISE HOUSE

The second building on which paint analysis was done is the Ludwell-Paradise House, another original eighteenth-century building. It was the first structure acquired for the restoration of Colonial Williamsburg in 1926, for a sum of eight thousand dollars.

As with the Dr. Barraud House, records for this building are also rather sketchy and little is known of its early history. Dendrochronology performed on the house in 1985 by Heikkenen revealed that the trees from which the first-floor structural members were fashioned were felled in 1752 and those for the roof in 1753. The property, colonial lot 45, was then in the ownership of Philip Ludwell III, owner of several Tidewater plantations, who presumably built the house. Ludwell inherited the site from his father, Philip Ludwell II, in 1727.

A 1700 deed states that the city of Williamsburg sold lots 43, 44, and 45 to Philip Ludwell II "for the consideration of 1 shilling."[69] Ludwell was a trustee of the city and a member of the Governor's council. The usual stipulation required by the city at that time was that the buyer should "within the space of 24 months build and furnish upon Each Lott one good dwelling house or houses. . . . "[70] It is assumed that lots 43 and 44 escheated to the city because houses had not been built on them within the stated time span, yet lot 45 was held by Ludwell and his descendants for many years.

Because this lot did not escheat to the city, Ludwell could very likely have built a house on the site within twenty-four months. In a letter dated July 1, 1718, Governor Spotswood mentions that "Ludwell's house (wch. is close to mine) was the common rendezvous of the disaffected Burgesses. . . . "[71] Whether this letter refers to the house on lot 45 or to a wooden tenement Ludwell built on a back street lot he had purchased in 1715 cannot be ascertained for certain. However, it seems more likely that the house mentioned in Spotswood's letter was located on the more prominent main street lot.

Our theory is that Philip Ludwell II had erected a frame dwelling of at least the required size (20 by 30 feet) on lot 45 by 1702, the year when the twenty-four-month period would have expired. Possible support for this theory is the recent discovery of a considerable quantity of reused timbers in the attic of the one-story rear portion of the house. During further examination of the main attic of the front portion, more reused timbers were found. Eighteenth-century Williamsburg was very practical, and usable materials were not often discarded. Philip

Figure 10. *Ludwell-Paradise House, showing the postanalysis darker trim. (Nicholas A. Pappas)*

Ludwell III probably pulled down the house that his father had built to erect a more impressive house or because the earlier house was in an advanced stage of disrepair. Unfortunately, no samples from the reused timbers were taken for the dendrochronology study, so the theory simply remains a theory until further research can be done on these members.

The present house was probably completed in 1755, for in the October 17 issue of the *Virginia Gazette* of that year Ludwell advertised the house for rent, describing it as a "very good Dwelling-House, well accommodated with Out-Houses, Garden, Well, Fine large Stable and Coach-House, & c. situate on the main street, the lower side of the Market Place."[72] That the present house is the one advertised is almost certain. However, the two-year time span between the 1753 date of the roof timbers and the 1755 advertisement represents a long construction period for a relatively simple although large house. But there are indications of a stay in construction and cutting down on cost. The brick on the second story differs from the brick on the first story in size, color, and workmanship, all of lesser quality than that of the first. The rear wall of the one-story portion is frame, and interior finishes were minimal. There was no interior paneling, although nailing blocks were found under the original plaster to support such paneling, or interior shutters or architraves for the windows. Floor boards were the least expensive by eighteenth-century standards,[73] and the reuse of timbers might also have been a cost-saving move. The fact that Ludwell's wife died in 1753 could well have given him reason to stop construction, cause him to change his mind about constructing a town house for his family, and complete the building as a rental property with the least amount of expenditure. There is no record that Ludwell occupied the house. It was used as a tavern, which George Washington frequented, and as a printing office for the *Virginia Gazette,* operated by Clementina Rind, Virginia's first woman publisher. The only family member known to have lived there was Ludwell's eccentric daughter, Lucy Ludwell Paradise, who occupied the premises from 1805 to 1812.

While the roof was being repaired in 1988, advantage was taken of the scaffolding to examine the cornice, the only original exterior woodwork to survive. Paint samples were taken and sent to Frank Welsh for analysis. He found that the first two paint layers were Spanish brown, with a coating of dirt over the second layer.[74] Spanish brown, an inexpensive paint composed of iron oxide pigment and oil, was commonly used as a prime coat in eighteenth-century

Williamsburg. However, Welsh's discovery of *two* layers and the dirt coating proved conclusively that this was not a prime coat but the finish coat. The situation was complicated by his finding that eight to twelve years later the cornice was painted a cream color. This led to considerable discussion as to which color to restore since both were eighteenth century and either was a defensible choice. In the end Spanish brown was selected because it was the color that Ludwell must have specified and because it seemed to conform to the theory that Ludwell finished his house as cheaply as possible. Because of the use of Spanish brown on the cornice, the indications of cost cutting, and the lack of documentation for any other colors, Spanish brown was used on all the exterior woodwork **(figs. 9 and 10)**. The 1930s paint investigation noted Spanish brown as the first paint layer and the cream color as the second. It was obviously assumed that Spanish brown was the prime coat and that the cream color was the finish coat. Thus, the cream color was used for the trim in the 1932 restoration. The doors and shutters were painted dark green and the rear weatherboards were pained a blue-green color.

PAST AND FUTURE FINDINGS

The Ludwell-Paradise House and the Dr. Barraud House underline the pressing need to investigate the paint history of all the original buildings in the Williamsburg Historic Area. Because these findings differ from the early paint investigations, there will undoubtedly be other examples of the early architects being misled by the primitive paint-scraping methods of the past. Given that most of the paint investigations were undertaken by one person—Susan Higginson Nash—who knew a great deal about paints and took great care to locate and match early paint films, it is likely that a great many of the current paint colors are indeed close to those found on the buildings during the early investigations. It is highly likely, however, that Nash and the architects may have been misled in one or more of the following ways:

1. On the basis of what is known of the paint investigation methods used by Nash and the colorist, it would be difficult if not impossible for them to distinguish a primer from a finish coat. Several references in the archives indicate that if the first coat was an ocher or Spanish brown, they assumed it was a primer.

2. The original color match sample made by Nash and the colorist was discarded after the matching paint sample on wood was prepared, thus precluding any further comparisons.

3. Thirty years had elapsed between the time when many of the painted wood sample panels were made and when the colors were recorded spectrophotometrically. During this period the sample colors had faded and had became soiled.

However, the two cases noted here also show that these pioneers—Nash, the architects, and the colorist—had reached what can only be considered as logical conclusions for their time, at least on these two houses. They did not have the advantage of high-powered microscopes and other current analytical methods to isolate the nineteenth-century pigment in the Dr. Barraud House green or determine that the Spanish brown they found on the Ludwell-Paradise House was a finish coat, not a primer.

But there still remains the question of the reconstructed buildings and some original buildings where no eighteenth-century paint history has survived. Once all the extant paint history has been analyzed, we hope to combine that knowledge with documentary evidence, such as the eighteenth-century St. George Tucker painting specification,[75] and perhaps be able to determine a paint color pattern in Williamsburg that might serve as a guide for repainting these buildings.

We have already begun this process with the outbuildings. An eight-year research and recording project of all the known extant eighteenth-century agricultural buildings in Virginia and adjacent portions of North Carolina and Maryland has revealed that little, if any, tinted paint was used on outbuildings. The only coatings found were whitewash and earth pigments, such as Spanish brown, mixed in oil. Consequently, all the polychrome outbuildings in the Williamsburg Historic Area are gradually being changed to whitewash or Spanish brown.

For the recent reconstruction of the interior of the courthouse,[76] Welsh conducted a paint research project of comparable public buildings in Williamsburg and the Tidewater area. Our goal was to determine whether the interior woodwork might have been painted and, if so, what color would be appropriate for this as well as for the exterior. The interior finishes (and nonfinishes) found were too varied to draw direct conclusions, but the exterior paints seem to indicate an interesting pattern. The woodwork of the brick buildings studied that were constructed in the mid-eighteenth century and earlier (including the first two stages of Bruton Parish Church, Prentis Store, and the Public Records Office in the Historic Area) was originally painted Spanish brown. In the latter part of the eighteenth century, the woodwork of newly constructed brick buildings was painted white and that of the earlier buildings was repainted white. This seems to suggest that Spanish brown was at least as much an aesthetic choice as an economical one in the first half of the century and that white became the more accepted color in the latter half.

This recent analysis raises the question of what is to become of the well-known Williamsburg palette of reproduction paints. Although these are the result of the early paint investigations, they rather faithfully reproduce the actual colors found during the scrapings—as they appeared two hundred years later. The colors were subject to considerable interest by the American public, and repeated requests for samples led to their reproduction. They became popular and were widely distributed throughout the country. As such, they are now an integral part of the history of the Colonial Revival movement in America. It is hoped that they will continue to be reproduced as historic documents of the twentieth century, with an explanation of how they were uncovered and of their historical importance, and that the colors found in the recent analyses will be reproduced and marketed in a separate palette.

We plan to continue with this research of original colors as funds become available. It will not only change the spectrum of Williamsburg colors but also will expand our knowledge of the use of color in the eighteenth century and lead to a more authentic interpretation of the buildings in Colonial Williamsburg.

Paint Decoration at Mount Vernon

THE REVIVAL OF EIGHTEENTH-CENTURY TECHNIQUES

MATTHEW J. MOSCA

With its copious documentation and its distinctive architecture, George Washington's Mount Vernon is a restoration challenge. Because Washington was so famous in his own lifetime, extensive records about him or by him have survived. Yet, despite the wealth of documentation, placing Washington and Mount Vernon in the context of the second half of the eighteenth century nevertheless is somewhat difficult, as so much of that world has disappeared. An important part of the most recent restoration of Mount Vernon included microscopic examination and chemical analysis of eighteenth-century paint finishes, which involved the collection and examination of more than twenty-five hundred paint samples from the interior of the building over a ten-month period during 1979–80. The restoration of the interior has provided a picture of the late eighteenth century that may be quite representative of its time, not only at Mount Vernon but at other sites, many now vanished, as well.

Restoration of the painted finishes involved replicating the techniques of the eighteenth century. The finish paints were ground by hand and were applied with round brushes of eighteenth-century design, a process carried out over a period of six years. The characteristics of handmade paints, including the uneven colors and textures, were replicated as exactly as possible. The results were startling: the eighteenth century colors proved to be brighter than had been anticipated and evidenced the subtle variations of handmade finishes. Although some other eighteenth-century houses have been similarly restored, the changes at Mount Vernon—seen by an average of one million visitors a year—prompted a rethinking about decorating in eighteenth-century America.

Philosophical questions were duly considered in the decision to use handmade materials. The interpretation of Mount Vernon depicts the property as George Washington left it at the time of his death in December 1799. Most of the paint finishes in the house were fifteen years old at that time. Thus, the natural process of the paints' aging needed to be addressed. Rather than induce an artificial aging or attempt to eliminate the process of aging, the choice was made to use materials as close to the originals as possible, thus ensuring that the paint films would gradually age and change in a manner consistent with the original eighteenth-century finishes. In addition, by confining modern artisans to the limitations of eighteenth-century technology,

Figure 1. *The large dining room, Washington's grandest and most public achievement at Mount Vernon, restored to the eighteenth-century color scheme. The "Venetian Window" derives from a design taken from Batty Langley's* City and Country Workman's Treasury of Designs *(1756). Pigment identification using polarized light microscopy and microchemical testing has permitted the alterations caused by time to be reversed. (Mount Vernon Ladies' Association of the Union, Office of the Curator)*

it was hoped that the problems that might arise would have been those faced by their eighteenth-century counterparts.

The evolution of Mount Vernon spans the tumultuous period of the American Revolution. Begun about 1757–60, the house attained its final form during the 1780s. In completing the interior, Washington insisted on the "new style"—that of Robert Adam, which provided the classical, symbolic framework of the New Republic. From the standpoint of paint materials, the changes are important. The decade of the 1780s was a period of increased use of bright blue and green colors and evinced an extensive use of painted graining. To understand the paints of this era one must know the pigments of which they were composed. Physical evidence is greatly enhanced by period documents that discuss pigments and paint media.

In his library Washington had a copy of the second edition (1764) of Robert Dossie's *Handmaid to the Arts*. While it is not certain that Washington followed Dossie in painting his house, this book was consulted during the course of the restoration. It proved to be an important source of information on paint making and other forms of decoration in the eighteenth century. Dossie describes not only the use of the pigments and other decorative materials but also their known characteristics, both positive and negative. His book is an excellent guide to understanding what was desirable in paints and pigments in the eighteenth century.

The principal qualities in colours, considered with regard to their perfection or faultiness are two, purity of colour and durableness: purity of colour is, by the painters called brightness, and the defect of it foulness, or sometimes the breaking the colour: durableness is called standing, and the negation or want of it flying or flying off....

The most considerable of colours after ... *brightness* and *standing well* are transparency and opacity; for according to their condition with respect to these qualities, they are fitted to answer very different kinds of purposes. Colours which become transparent in oil such as Prussian blue and brown pink are frequently used without the admixture of white by which means the tine of the ground on which they are laid retains in some degree its force; and the real colour, produced in the painting is the combined effect of both. This is called glazing, and the pigments indued *[sic]* with such property of becoming transparent in oil are called *glazing colours*.... When colours have no degree of such transparency in the vehicle in which they are used, as vermilion, King's yellow and several others, they are said to have a body and to cover. [1]

Here Dossie is discussing painting in general—the fine arts as well as the decorative arts. The principles for both are largely the same; however, many materials used in decorative house painting were not of the same quality as those used in fine arts. Glazing, the application of a transparent layer over an opaque layer, commonly used in the fine arts to create an illusion of depth or transparency, was also a technique frequently used in house painting. Examples of glazing were found at Mount Vernon.

Painting and construction continued throughout the entire forty-year span of George Washington's life at Mount Vernon, from about 1759 until his death in 1799. In these decades three general periods of activity in painting and decoration can be discerned: (1) from about 1759 to 1761, at the time of Washington's marriage to Martha Custis, when the first enlargement of the mansion took place; (2) during the 1780s, after the Revolutionary War and before his first term as president; and (3) from 1797, following his second term as president, until his death in December 1799.

THE FIRST ERA OF DECORATION

Washington's marriage to Martha Custis prompted the first enlargement and enrichment of Mount Vernon about 1759. The house was increased to two and a half stories, the full paneling of the west parlor and passage was completed, and the present walnut staircase was installed. By late 1759 painting was under way. The paints prepared from materials ordered by Washington at this time were covered over during the major redecoration of Mount Vernon that occurred when it was further enlarged in the 1770s and 1780s. The pigments from this period, however, introduce the reader to paint materials generally available at the time.

Pigments had been ordered in August 1757, and one of the orders to Richard Washington survives[2]:

50 lbs common red paint at 3d.

50 lbs fine Stone colored ... ditto at 4 1/2

50 lb white ... ditto at 4 d

20 lbs yellow ground ... ditto at 8

25 lbs Ash ... ditto at 5

15 lbs pearle ... ditto at 4 1/2

12 lbs green at 2

15 lbs Putty

Additional orders for paint materials followed:

1759

June

200 lbs Red led ground up in Oyl

100 lbs white ditto ground in ditto[3]

August

25 lbs whiting

1 Rundlet[4] white lead ground

1 Rundlet red paint ditto[5]

20 September Invoice of Sundries to be sent by Robert Cary

and Company to George Washington ...

4 lbs Ivory black 1 dozn painter's Brushes[6]

1760

9 February 6 barr'ls tar, 6 of Turpentine ...[7]

March 9 large painting brushes 4/6 3 small ditto 5−3

4 lbs Ivory Black

1761

March 1 rundlet Spanish brown ground

1 Rundlet white lead ground

October 500 lbs white lead ground in oil

100 lbs Spanish brown ditto

1762

April 2 rundlets white lead ground

1 rundlet Spanish brown ground

15 November 1 keg white lead ground in oil

1763

13 April 1 Keg white lead

27 September 100 wt white lead ground in oil

1764

10 August 6 painters brushes[8]

1768

20 June 2 qts Spirit of Turpentine[9]

Some of the pigments cited here were observed in the microscopic examination of samples collected. The common red paint and the stone-colored paint were used to make the first finishes in the west parlor. The "yellow ground [paint]" probably was the yellow ocher used in the passage and the "green" paint may be the common verdigris used in the southeast bedroom of the second floor.

PIGMENTS AND MATERIALS

The pigments and materials described in the orders are generally among those more commonly available in the American colonies and were probably used extensively there.

COMMON RED PAINT

Generic notations such as this preclude specific identification; however, on the basis of pricing and the term *common*, this is probably an iron oxide red, similar to Venetian red, Indian red, and Spanish brown. Iron oxide was usually a natural pigment, one of the ochers that derived its color from anhydrous iron oxide. This paint may have been the ground coat for the mahogany graining (ca. 1760) used in the west parlor.

STONE-COLORED PAINT

This paint was used for the paneled walls of the west parlor, fragments of which were discovered in 1980. The preparation of this specific example of stone color involved white lead with ochers. This was certainly one of the more frequently mentioned paint finishes and is cited in William Salmon's *Palladio Londinensis or the London Art of Building* (1734), and Hezekiah Reynolds's *Directions for House and Ship Painting* (1812), among others.[10]

WHITE PAINT

This is probably white lead, of which enormous quantities were used at Mount Vernon for exterior painting, as the figures recorded indicate. One of the most important pigments in the history of painting, white lead was known in ancient times and was mentioned by Vitruvius. Numerous preparations for it are given in different sources.

Among the most interesting descriptions of the preparation of pigments is the Dutch system for the preparation of white lead. This involved hanging lead panels or pieces in vats with vinegar at the bottom. These vats were set in tiers in a large shed and packed with manure and other organic matter. The building was then closed for about three months. The combined action of the ascetic acid vapors, heat, and carbon dioxide from the fermentation of the organic materials, oxygen, and water vapor eventually turned the lead into lead carbonate. Ultimately the lead carbonate was washed, dried, processed, and ground with linseed oil.[11]

White lead is also a drying agent and provided an opaque, fast- drying, and impervious paint film. Despite its poisonous nature, known since at least the seventeenth century, it was the white pigment most widely used for architectural purposes.[12]

Dossie describes two related white-lead pigments. White flake is explained as "lead corroded by the pressing of the grape ... brought here from Italy and [which] far surpasses both in regard to purity and whiteness and the certainty of its standing, all the cerruss, or white lead made here in common." This was probably used for easel painting rather than architectural finishes. For architectural paints the common white lead was apparently used, as Dossie notes: "White lead is the common corrosion or rust of lead formed by means of vinegar.... It is, however, the white employed for all common purposes in oil painting and also the body or solid basis of the paint in many mixed colours...." Dossie notes that white lead is often adulterated with the addition of chalk or powdered talc, "the cheapest ingredients with which it can be mixed without changing too much its appearance."[13] The term *ceruss*, or *ceruse*, was synonymous with white lead by the eighteenth century[14] but had been used earlier to describe other whites such as chalk whites.

YELLOW PAINT

While it is not known specifically what type of yellow was ordered, it is probable that Washington received a yellow ocher paint ground, as cited, in linseed oil. Such a paint was used in the passage in 1759. This is the first dated indication of an order for paint ground in oil rather than in powder form.

ASH PAINT

This is a term too general to ascertain exactly what was ordered. Cennino d'Andrea Cennini, author of the fifteenth-century work *Il libro dell'Arte* (ca.1437), cites an ash gray that was prepared from lime white and black.[15] More recent references indicate that the ash color was a combination of white with a carbonous black, usually lampblack. One such reference is in the second volume of *The Artist's Repository*, entitled *A Compendium of Colors and other Materials used in the Arts of Drawing, Painting, Engraving, &c ...*, which points out the various grays that can be achieved with different blacks. Lampblack and indigo yield cool grays whereas ivory black yields a warm gray. Physical evidence from numerous eighteenth-century sites points out to the use of white lead and carbonous black paint finishes, primarily in less important rooms.[16]

PEARL

Two "pearle" colors are noted in the early literature. Dossie describes pearl white as "the powder of pearls, or the finer parts of oyster shells," although because of their cost it is unlikely pearls were ever used for painting. The preparation involved using "oysters as they are found on the sea coast calcined by the sun or fresh ones by the fire till they will powder easily ... scrape off ... all the outward or other parts that may not be of the most perfect whiteness; levigate them well with water on the stone and wash the powder well over till thoroughly fine."[17] Since oyster shells were abundant, such a paint could have been made inexpensively enough. Another pearl color, however, mentioned by Reynolds, involves combining one pint of white lead with a teaspoon of Prussian blue and a teaspoon of spruce yellow, a form of yellow ocher.[18]

GREEN PAINT

The survival of an early, common verdigris green on woodwork from the second-floor southeast bedroom suggests that this may be the paint referred to in the order. Verdigris green was one of the most important pigments of the eighteenth century and was used throughout the history of Mount Vernon. Two forms of verdigris green were used—the common form and the distilled. This early order, based on the surviving physical evidence, was the less pure common form. During the 1780s the distilled form was used.

Dossie's description of verdigris provides an abundance of information on the character of this pigment: "Verdigrise is a rust or corrosion of copper formed by the action of [vinegar] it is ... used in most kinds of painting where green is required. It is bright when good; but very soon flies when used in oil: but when used in water painting it is dissolved previously in vinegar; which indeed, changing it to another substance renders it more durable. Crystals of verdigrise, called distilled verdigrise, is the salt produced by the solution of copper or common verdigris in vinegar. The crystals thus formed are of an extremely bright green colour, and in varnish, where they stand perfectly well, they have a very fine effect. In oil they hold their color well enough to answer many purposes, where colours are not required to be greatly durable, but in paintings of consequence they cannot be depended upon being apt to turn black with time."[19]

The discoloration of verdigris green was an important factor in early paint examination at Mount Vernon, which was based on the attempted exposure of early finish surfaces. The greens had blackened sufficiently to eliminate all trace of their original color, appearing in their aged form as dark grays and blacks. Dossie's notation on the greater durability of verdigris in water media is confirmed by the many examples of early wallpapers where verdigris green was used in the preparation. Later, in the 1780s, it is probable that Washington again referred to Dossie for directions in painting the small dining room with a varnish-medium paint.

PUTTY

While this is not exactly paint, it is a paintlike material. Putties in the eighteenth century generally consisted of linseed oil combined with whiting or white lead (or combinations) into a thick paste or "beaten together to form a dough"[20] used to fill in the seams and nail holes of joinery.

RED LEAD

A bright red-orange pigment commonly made by roasting white lead until it changed color. As Dossie states, "The bright orange colour of red lead might render it valuable in painting, if it would stand with certainty in either oil or water; but it is so subject to turn black when used with oil ... that it is by no means to be trusted ... except in hard varnishes, indeed which, locking up the pigments from the air and moisture renders their colour durable in almost all instances.... The goodness of red lead may be distinguished by the brightness of its color."[21] It is possible that this pigment was to be used for exterior painting or priming, or as a drying agent, for which purpose it was frequently added to oils.

IVORY BLACK

The order for ivory black is interesting, because at first it was the more expensive black pigment. Ivory black, made from "the coal of ivory or bone,"[22] was indeed at first made from ivory, which gave the deepest black. The wide-scale manufacture from bone and the poor quality of production, plus the adulteration of the final product with charcoal dust, made it an inexpensive pigment by the mid-eighteenth century.

TURPENTINE

This would have been the resinous oleoresin or balsam from various pine trees. It was the basic material from which oil of turpentine and spirit of turpentine were extracted. Turpentine was commonly used with drying oils in paint preparation to make a stable paint film that retained some flexibility and extended the period of gloss to the surface of the film. Spirit of turpentine is the clear volatile thinner distilled from the basic turpentine.[23]

SPANISH BROWN

At Mount Vernon this red oxide was used extensively as a primer and for finish paint for exterior surfaces, particularly roofs. Because it had good drying properties and was inexpensive, it was frequently suggested as the primer for woodwork, both interior and exterior. The low cost also recommended its use as a finish paint for subsidiary buildings.[24] Dossie describes it as a "native earth, found in the state and of the colour in which it is used: it is nearly the same colour as Venetian red, but fouler ... it is used for grounds and priming for coarse work by house painters and by colourmen in preparation of cloths for pictures and other coarse work.... "[25] Dossie continues to note that it is an absolutely stable pigment and may be rendered finer by careful washing. Certainly, inexpensiveness and stability made Spanish brown a frequently used pigment.

THE WEST PARLOR

The west parlor has perhaps the best examples of the interior woodwork of 1757–60, and the history of the room illuminates some interesting aspects of Mount Vernon. This fully paneled room is enriched with three major elements: a chimney with carved mantel and overmantel and two door frames in the Ionic order. The design for the chimney piece was derived, with certain liberties, from Abraham Swan's *British Architect* of 1745 (pls. 50, 51), and the doorways were copied exactly from Batty Langley's *Ancient Masonry* of 1736 (pl. 349).

The south door was added in 1776 to provide access to the north addition. The Palladian detailing of the door frames posed few problems for the woodcarvers, but the intricate rococo ornamentation of the chimney piece was evidently beyond their capabilities. The final design of the overmantel is influenced by plate 51 of Swan, which would later be the source for the chimney piece of the small dining room: the broken swan-neck pediment of the overmantel in the west parlor is taken from plate 50 and superimposed on an adaptation of the overmantel from the plate 51 design. The proportions of the overmantel may have been determined by the "neat landskip after Claude" that Washington ordered in 1757.[26] The allusion to Claude Lorraine is significant, for it was his views of the Roman campagna that greatly influenced landscape architecture in England during the mid-eighteenth century, providing the ideal for all Whig gentry, whether in England or its colonies.

The examination of the paint finishes that remained in this room illuminated the problems and costs involved in painting in the eighteenth century. The first finishes, applied around 1759, were stone color for the paneled walls and mahogany graining to emphasize the chimney piece and the door frames. The "Stone color" was no doubt the "fine Stone colored [paint]" ordered in August 1757.

The major architectural elements—the doorways and the chimney piece—appear to have been finished in a red mahogany graining, which survives today only in fragments because of a nineteenth-century paint removal process. The fragments indicate a red-ocher ground coat with a dark brown (it appears to be a burnt umber) in a glazelike layer applied over the red ocher.[27] Despite the removal of the original paints in 1885, there is some surviving information on this graining, and the grainer is known—one "convict servant" named John Winter, according to the June 26, 1760, issue of the *Maryland Gazette:*

House painter—ran away from the subscriber, a convict servant man named John Winter, a very complete House Painter, he can imitate marble or mahogany exactly and can paint Floor Cloths as neat as any imported from Britain.... The last work he did was a house for Col. Washington near Alexandria.[28]

Of the nearly three hundred paint samples examined, only about one-quarter proved to have eighteenth-century paint finishes remaining, and most of these were but fragments of the early finishes. Nonetheless, these paint samples indicated that the south door frame, which was added to the west parlor in 1776 to provide access to the north addition, was painted to match the existing finishes of the room, despite the fact that these existing finishes dated to 1759. Rather than incur the cost of repainting the entire room, only the new elements were painted. The same type of mahogany graining found on the door frame and chimney piece that date to 1757–60 was found on the new door of 1776.

ENLARGEMENTS OF MOUNT VERNON

Washington planned to enlarge Mount Vernon in the 1770s with additions to the south and north of the central block. The south wing, which included the study, pantry, closets, and back staircase on the first floor, with Washington's bedchamber and closets above, was built in 1775. In addition, the small dining room was completely redecorated: the superb plaster and woodwork of this room date to about 1775. In 1776 the north wing was raised but remained unfinished for eleven years.

Fewer orders for paint materials originate in this era:

1773

6 Oct. A cask of whiting, 400 wt of white lead ground

in oil over and above the last Order

30 lb red lead

100 lb yellow ocher

2 lbs lamp black

10 lbs umber

20 gallons best British Linseed oil for inside painting[29]

1773

Bill of Materials for Additions to the Mansion

"the outside may be done with Country Oil,

the above white lead to be ground in oil

1774

26 April 1 Barrl of Turpentine

1775

August TO Saml Moles for Bring sand from Norfolk[30]

PIGMENTS AND MATERIALS

Although fewer paint materials are indicated during the 1770s, the materials themselves are particularly interesting. The references to the "best British Linseed oil," the "Country Oil" for the exterior painting, and the "Barrl of Turpentine" are three materials that further our knowledge of painting practices. The sand from Norfolk was to be used for the exterior replication of stone: the practice of throwing sand onto the surface of wet paint to imitate the appearance of stone. This is still done at Mount Vernon.[31]

YELLOW OCHER

This is a natural earth pigment composed of various hydrated forms of iron oxide. As noted by Dossie, when pure it provides a "true yellow of moderate brightness"[32] that is completely durable. Since yellow ochers are primarily natural deposits, the purity of the pigment varies greatly. The variations in composition of trace elements can result in a vast range of colors produced with yellow ochers, from tannish yellows to the true yellow that Dossie mentions.

LAMPBLACK

Among the most ancient of colors, lampblack is the soot created in the burning of oily materials. It forms cool grays when mixed with white and dries well in oil media. Dossie cites it as the "principal black at present used in all nicer kinds of painting."[33] The woodwork of the study was painted in a gray made of white lead and lampblack when first finished, about 1775.

UMBER

Umber is a natural earth pigment named for the Italian city of Umbria, near which the best quality of pigment was found. Burnt umber is a deep, rich brown pigment made by roasting natural, or raw, umber. This gives burnt umber a very warm brown shade, since the yellow hydrous oxides of the raw umber are changed to reddish anhydrous oxides. Because they mixed readily with oil media, umbers were used to make translucent glazes and as such were ideal for graining. At Mount Vernon burnt umber was used for graining and as an opaque finish paint on doors and baseboard fascia in 1775, particularly in the south addition of the house.

"BEST BRITISH LINSEED OIL"

This interesting reference to the medium for the paints used on the woodwork of the south wing points out an important aspect of painting—oil media and the process of drying. Certain oils, such as linseed oil, were known to have natural drying properties. However, shortening the drying time of oil paints was a major concern. Thus, a variety of additives was suggested to improve the drying of oils. The most common for house painting, however, were litharge and red lead. In each case the pigment was added to the oil and boiled.[34] The modern term *boiled oil* is a result of this traditional practice, despite the fact that most modern boiled oil contains a chemical additive to improve drying time.

THE 1780S: MOUNT VERNON REALIZED

This decade saw the most dramatic changes in the decoration of Mount Vernon. A number of rooms were improved or completed. Nearly the entire house was repainted. Both the large and small dining rooms were finished in verdigris greens, and more than a dozen rooms were painted in Prussian blue of varying intensity. Large quantities of paint and supplies were ordered during this decade.[35]

While there was great painting activity at Mount Vernon in these years, few orders expand the list of pigments given earlier. However, one significant record dated May 13, 1785, indicates extensive paint materials, intended mostly for use in the large dining room:

1 dozen painters brushes

6 bottles of Linseed oil; 5 gallons to 30 gallons

6 Kegs ground white lead

2 kegs of fine ground yellow ochre

6 kegs of Red paint

10 lbs Lampblack

10 lbs Red lead

10 lbs of powder Spanish brown

12 lbs of ground Verdigris

10 lbs of best glue

1b of Fine Prussian blue[36]

PIGMENTS AND MATERIALS

The preceding order of materials suggests that the exterior of the building was also to be re-painted, in part if not entirely. The six kegs of white lead would certainly have been necessary to paint the exterior ashlar boards. Since Washington had more time to devote to the completion of Mount Vernon, the maintenance of the entire plantation as well as the redecoration of the interior had to be attended to. The one pigment mentioned for the first time in this order is Prussian blue, among the most important pigments in the history of paints.

PRUSSIAN BLUE

Discovered by accident in Berlin about 1710, Prussian blue (potassium ferric ferrocyanide) was the product of an elaborate formula, beginning with organic materials, usually pig's blood; a complex formula for the pigment takes up several pages in the 1791 *Encyclopedia Britannica*. What is significant is that Prussian blue provided a strong blue pigment at relatively reasonable cost, thus opening up an entirely new range of blue tones for exploitation. Because Prussian blue was still somewhat expensive, its use had the appeal of status. In addition, various grades were made, and much adulteration of the pigment took place.

The deficiencies of the pigment did not prevent its wide use. Characteristically, Dossie notes all the salient aspects:

It is used in all kinds of painting, except enamel; and is prepared of many different degrees of brightness and strength; as well as of different tints: some parcels being, though rarely, of a true blue, but the far greatest part of a purple hue.... With respect to standing, Prussian blue can neither be esteemed the most perfect nor the most faulty colour. When it is very dark [i.e., when the proportion of Prussian blue in paint mixture is very high], it will sometimes stand extremely well ... when it is light, it is more frequently bright and cool ... but extremely subject to fly, or turn to a greyish green. This is not however universal ... for I have seen some that has been light which would stand perfectly well. The common Prussian blue, however, found in the shops, which is prepared almost wholly at present by ignorant and sordid people, and sold at very low prices, can be very little depended upon in paintings of consequence ... prepared in the proper and true manner and ... considering the high price of ultramarine, and the foulness of indigo, it may be deemed an acquisition to the art of painting.[37]

The 1791 *Encyclopedia Britannica* adds: "Prussian blue is to be accounted the best quality when it is deep, bright and not inclined to purple. It ought to be tried by mixture with white lead as the brightness of the color will appear much more when diluted than when concentrated in lumps of the blue itself."[38] Reynolds alludes to another characteristic of this pigment: "Prussian blue color: To five pounds of white lead, add one ounce of Prussian blue 'best quality;' if the quality be inferior the quantity must be increased. In laying this paint, use a half worn brush; and press the brush harder than in laying other colors"[39]

The reason for the use of a half-worn brush and the increased pressure is that Prussian blue, when ground by hand, continues to disperse within the paint films. This problem had considerable impact on eighteenth-century paints and is dealt with at length in the following section on the preparation of paints.

With the inclusion of Prussian blue, all the major pigments that were important in the evolution of Mount Vernon have been documented. It should be noted that Dossie makes prominent mention of the tendency of light Prussian blue colors to turn grayish green. This is particularly

meaningful in view of the seemingly countless rooms of historic houses painted in grayish greens from the 1920s through the 1960s to match the modern condition of exposed historic finishes.

PAINT PREPARATION AND RESTORATION

Consideration of the paint finishes of the 1780s introduces the problems of paint preparation in the eighteenth century and the issues raised by attempts to replicate those finishes. In each of the following rooms the paints of the 1780s survived until long after George Washington's death; thus, reproduction of each of these finishes was central to the restoration. Moreover, the various uses of paint and wallpaper at Mount Vernon during the 1780s are as interesting as the historic pigments themselves. In that decade painting in oil and in varnish and the use of plain wallpaper all contributed to the house's mature appearance.

THE WEST PARLOR

Along with developing the large dining room, Washington decided to alter the west parlor in an attempt to make the room somewhat more in keeping with the new neoclassical style. The ceiling was decorated with a large central rosette of Adamesque design and further elaborated by a foliated border. The paneled woodwork was painted entirely in Prussian blue color: a mixture of Prussian blue, white lead, and a very small quantity of yellow ocher (figs. 2 and 3).[40] The use of Prussian blue in the west parlor demonstrates the frequent eighteenth-century problem of insufficient grinding of the pigment. The surviving paint samples in the room indicated uneven dispersion patterns of the Prussian blue in the white lead–based paint. This character in cross section translated to a slightly uneven finish, where the variability of the brush pressure was observed as a darker or lighter blue finish. Certainly, the problem of insufficient grinding was not new in the eighteenth century, as indeed the following passage from Cennini's *Il Libro dell'Arte* indicates: "Then take some clear ... water and grind this black for the space of half and hour, or an hour, or as long as you like; but know that if you were to work it up for a year it would be so much the blacker and better a color."[41]

It is possible that the painters working in the west parlor at Mount Vernon were somewhat inexperienced with this quality of the pigment, as the problem was rectified in the other rooms later painted with Prussian blue. That Washington was dissatisfied with the results in the west parlor seems clear from a letter of July 15, 1787, written to his nephew, George Augustine Washington. He was overseeing the work at Mount Vernon at the time, when the painting of the large dining room was about to begin.

I do not recollect how I expressed myself with respect to the painting of the New Room, that is whether when speaking of this business, you would understand that it was to be done by a proper and good painter ... I advise you to try Peales nephew [believed to be Charles Peale Polk (1767–1822)] or some one more knowing, both in the mixture and laying on of Paint than Morrison (I think his name was).... [42]

It is evident that Washington wanted the painting of the large dining room to be of a higher standard than he had been able to obtain earlier. A challenge of twentieth-century restoration was preparing a paint that would behave like that less-than-perfect Prussian blue color of the eighteenth century. To do this required materials and tools as close to those of the eighteenth century as feasible. Dry pigments, linseed oil—and patience—were the most important ingredients.

The preparation of paint in the eighteenth century was largely the same as it had been in the fifteenth century, when Cennini was writing. The need to thoroughly moisten the dry pigment with the liquid vehicle was solved with a muller and slab (fig. 4). The muller is a large stone, flat on one side, used in a circular motion on a stone slab. This action grinds the pigment and the vehicle into a paint. Cennini notes that porphyry is the best stone for grinding paints, but various types of marbles also were common. He continues to describe the muller as " ... a stone to hold in your hand, also of porphyry, flat underneath and rounded on top ... shaped so that your hand may be able to guide it readily, and move it this way and that, at will. ... "[43]

The modern equivalent of the stone muller and slab are heavy glass implements. A smooth or ground-glass slab may be used; the muller is made with a ground-glass flat surface and a protruding handle. Both implements were used for the paint preparation at Mount Vernon. For the west parlor, each of the three pigments was ground with "strong oil"—linseed oil that has been prepared with a drying agent.

The preparation of linseed oil is explained by Dossie. While linseed oil has a natural ability

Figure 3. *Panel from the west parlor showing variation in the color of the paint finish, a result of the hand grinding of Prussian blue and the somewhat uneven pigment distribution. The pressure of the individual brush strokes can be observed. (Mount Vernon Ladies' Association of the Union, Office of the Curator)*

Figure 4. *Stone mullers, slab, and stone scraper, ca. 1830, used to grind dry pigment powder with the liquid medium, thoroughly moisten all the dry pigment powder, and thus create a usable paint. Grinding paint was very laborious process. Many early paint samples show uneven distribution of pigment particles, indicating less than adequate grinding. (Paul Rocheleau; courtesy of Donald Carpentier)*

to dry through oxidation, various elements were often added to the oil to shorten the drying time. Dossie provides an extensive list but indicates that the cost of most of the drying agents prohibited their use in most cases. For architectural finishes, red lead and litharge were used as dryers.

Dossie recommends: "Take linseed oil one gallon, red lead one pound and a half. Boil them so long as the colour will bear it."[44] The process darkens the oil; thus, subsequent names for this type of drying oil were "black oil" and, of course, boiled oil. Reynolds provides two recipes for boiled oil—one for inside work and one for outside work. These vary by the proportion of red lead used and the addition of copal varnish, or spirits of turpentine, to the interior oil.[45] Black, or boiled, oil is still available from special art supply sources. It is not suggested that making boiled oil be undertaken, as boiling red lead is a dangerous process.

Many of the materials used in historic paints are poisonous and must be treated with the utmost care. Throughout the restoration at Mount Vernon, safety was of primary concern. In grinding the paints, workers wore rubber gloves, lead respirators, and goggles. Proper ventilation had to be assured at all times. Paints used in areas where the public might come in contact with them are completely lead free. Titanium-dioxide white, zinc oxide white, and modern dryers were used in place of lead-based materials. The problem of toxicity of historic materials may mean that historic pigments will not be used at a majority of sites. The use of these pigments is limited by federal and local law and by the increasing difficulty of procuring them.

The three pigments for the west parlor were ground up separately in a boiled oil, to which approximately one-half cup (one gill) of a natural copal varnish was added. This was based on Reynolds's description of a method for the preparation of oil and Washington's own notations on paint making.[46] The process of mixing the three pigments was governed by the pigment-dispersion patterns of the original samples and the color observed under the microscope. Several samples were prepared. A variety of Prussian blues was used; the variations were results of differences in the lengths of time that the pigment was ground—from ten minutes to thirty minutes. The samples prepared with the Prussian blue that had been hand ground for approximately fifteen minutes produced paints that in cross section approximated the pigment dispersion pattern of the original. It was clear that the original could be closely approximated but not replicated exactly because of the difference in the pigment particle size of the modern materials. As expected, the particle size of the contemporary pigments was finer and more even than the historic pigments. Thus, the pigment-dispersion pattern had to be rectified with the color observed from the original exposures and samples.

During the preparation of the finishes the texture of the paint also became an issue. Generally, eighteenth-century paints were heavier bodied, having much higher pigment content, thus they retained brush marks in the paint, giving the paint a "ropiness." The proportion of pigment to medium, which governed paint texture, varies at different sites, however, and is also influenced by the characteristics of the pigment. At Mount Vernon the survival of painted surfaces from the 1770s and 1780s greatly aided in determining the required texture. The general rule is noted in *The Builder's Dictionary* of 1734. In discussing exterior finishes, this important contemporary source says that the paint should be stiff but not too stiff, "for the better Body will be laid on, and the longer it will last...."[47]

The brushes used for painting in the eighteenth century were round in cross section, and the largest examples are forty-nine millimeters in diameter. The round brush works well with the heavier textured paint, for it holds more paint than a flat brush. Indeed, flat brushes were known in the eighteenth century but were used for varnishing and graining. The domed ends of the round brush also leave a characteristic mark in the paint finish. With practice the restoration painters at Mount Vernon became adept at using the round brushes, finding that they were good for cutting in edges. The traditional process of painting woodwork, which persists to this day, is to follow the grain of the wood. This was strictly adhered to in the eighteenth century, and because the paint retained the brush marks, a pattern of vertical and horizontal marks resulted.

The application of the Prussian blue with round bristle brushes resulted in the variable finish seen today. When the restoration painting was competed in 1982, the paint finish had a glossy surface. This gloss level was not completely uniform. Since then the gloss level has largely declined, resulting in a gloss approximating a modern eggshell finish. This reduction of gloss has been noticed in all the paints made at Mount Vernon and has been caused by pigment particles breaking through the surface of the paint film, a process resulting from factors that cannot be addressed here. Suffice it to say that this decline in gloss level was often counteracted by the use of glazes on the surface of paints. The glaze may have been prepared with a drying oil, often combined with a natural varnish, and at times a small quantity of pigment was added to eliminate the color of the oil-varnish mixture. The applied glaze protected the paint finish and created a more uniformly glossy surface. However, at Mount Vernon glazes were, surprisingly, rarely used.

THE STUDY

George Washington's study, the major room of the south addition of 1775, was the first space to be examined and restored; work was begun in 1980 (fig. 5). The study yielded extensive historic finish information and firm dating for certain finishes, as the bookpress, Washington's term for the bookcase, of the east wall was known to have been added in 1786. No other room at Mount Vernon is as closely associated with Washington: from here he directed the management of the estate and wrote the letters that would help establish the federal government following the Revolutionary War.

Before the bookpress wall was installed, the room was dominated by the fully paneled fireplace wall. The decoration of the fireplace mantel and overmantel is the earliest surviving example of "composition" ornament at Mount Vernon. Composition, an inexpensive molded form of decoration made from a variety of materials but usually including a hide glue, linseed

oil, and whiting, was to become enormously popular in the late eighteenth century, virtually eliminating woodcarving. The study's other walls and dadoes of plaster were detailed by millwork—an elaborate cornice, a plain chair rail, and a baseboard.

The room's initial finish, applied in 1775, was quite plain. Woodwork was painted a blue-gray color made of white lead tinted with lampblack. Doors were painted with a dark burnt-umber brown, and plaster surfaces were whitewashed. These early finishes remain exposed in the back closet. The fireplace smoked badly, however, and the room required repainting, probably around 1780. The color chosen was a stone color, a combination of white lead and a natural yellow ocher. This finish can be seen behind the bookpress addition of 1786. The area behind the bookpress also indicated the natural

Figure 5. *George Washington's study, the first room restored at Mount Vernon. The dated addition of the bookpress, known to have been constructed in June 1786, allowed specific dating of the graining, its first finish. (Mount Vernon Ladies' Association of the Union, Office of the Curator)*

unfinished condition of the pine flooring at Mount Vernon. As part of the restoration, all stain, varnish, and wax first applied in the nineteenth century was removed, reestablishing the natural color of the floors.

The fireplace continued to smoke despite attempts to remedy the poor draft. Its opening was again reduced in size, and the room was altered when the bookpress was installed. In his diary entry for June 16, 1786, Washington remarked, "Began about 10 O clock to put up the Book press in my Study."[48] The installation of the bookpress and the improved fireplace warranted a repainting. The woodwork was finished in a walnut-type graining, intended to look like a light English walnut. That this graining was the first finish on the bookpress made it possible to pinpoint the date of the graining to 1786. The eighteenth-century painter of the study probably did the graining from memory, for it is a somewhat abstract rendition of walnut, complete with panels suggesting "oyster grain" on the cabinets of the bookpress.

All the grained bookpress panels were exposed during the restoration, photographed, and studied. Additional wall panels were also exposed. The condition of the graining indicated that it was worn by the time it was repainted (estimated to be around 1820). The graining layers were severely crazed, and the later gray paint had flowed into the cracks of the graining.

Several reproduction test panels were produced. The exposure of grained panels from the study had indicated that the ground coat of the graining was essentially without texture. Surfaces were made smooth so as not to disrupt the grain layers with the ropiness of the ground coat. Handmade ground coats were applied to the test panels, allowed to dry completely, and were rubbed down with pumice. The results confirmed the surface texture of the historic panels.

Because the study is one of the rooms that visitors pass through, the paint used in restoration was a modern, lead-free, titanium-based material. This proved to provide the necessary base for the graining layers. The 1980 regraining was executed by Malcolm Robson, who meticulously reproduced the surviving examples of the original. The graining glaze was prepared with natural earth pigments to match the historic materials and recreate their effect. Because of public access to the room, however, the glaze medium had to be lead-free, and thus modern driers were used. Three coats of varnish were applied to the surface of the graining to protect it from wear.

The impact of nearly a million visitors annually is strikingly demonstrated by the fact that the protective coats of varnish cannot be adequately maintained for long periods in areas that can be touched or rubbed against. In these locations wear has demanded that the graining be redone annually.

THE SMALL DINING ROOM

One room in which a glazelike finish was used is the small dining room. The original finish used a varnish-medium paint, which has a translucency approaching that of a glaze. The painting of the room was completed about 1785, even though the room had been completely redecorated a decade earlier, in 1775, in the rococo manner seen today (fig. 6).

Examination of the painted finishes indicated that the woodwork of the small dining room, such as the paneled dado, dates to about 1757–60. Information on the decoration of this room as it appeared from 1757 to 1775 is gained only from written documents, as in the following, dated April 15, 1757.

… also a paper of a very good kind and colour for a Dining Room 18 by 16. Above the Chair Boards the pitch of the room is 11 feet. Papier Machee [sic] for the Ceiling of two Rooms, one of them 18 feet square, the other 18 by 16 with Cr. Chimneys. … "[49]

This invoice also indicated that a marble mantel was ordered for this room; however, it is not known whether it arrived or was installed.

The 1775 redecoration may have been caused by a change in the room's configuration resulting from the addition of the study and possible alterations to the fireplace at this time. When a design was chosen for the mantel and overmantel, Washington returned to the same source he used for the mantel of the west parlor, Swan's *The British Architect* (London, 1745). He employed two extraordinary craftsmen to ensure that the design would be replicated faithfully with all its splendid rococo ornament. The mantel carver was Bernard Sears, who was also responsible for the initial painting of the woodwork and provided some of the sources for the plaster decoration. A fascinating series of letters from Lund Washington, a distant relative who was the estate manager, to General Washington conveys a sense of the work taking place in the small dining room:

The stucco man is still about the Dining Room and will I fear be some time. Sears is here about the chimney piece. I suppose he will finish it next week. You no doubt think him long about it, so do I, but I can assure you he is constantly at work (September 29).

The stucco man thinks he shall be 4 weeks about the Dining room. The ceiling is not clumsy. I think it light and handsome. It is altogether worked by hand which makes it tedious (October 15).

Figure 6. *The small dining room, showing the the simulation of the verdigris finish in a varnish-enriched medium. The pigment was prepared by hand with a modern nonyellowing acrylic gloss medium. (Mount Vernon Ladies' Association of the Union, Office of the Curator)*

The Dining room will I expect be finished this week now come in. It is, I think, very pretty. The stucco man agrees the ceiling is a handsomer one than any of Colonel Lewis' although not half the work in it. It has a plan recommended by Sears (November 12).[50]

The plaster decoration was done by the same man who was working for Fielding Lewis, Washington's brother-in-law, at his home, Kenmore (early 1770s), in Fredericksburg, Virginia. He is known only as "the Frenchman." The plaster decoration in the small dining room of Mount Vernon—the overmantel, cornice, and ceiling—is remarkable for its skillful execution and its excellent state of preservation. Much of the work is formed-in-place decoration, although some repeated motifs were cast and applied. Many of the same cast-plaster decorative elements are seen in the more elaborate ceilings at Kenmore.

The small dining room was not fully painted until 1785, however, for as in the study, the chimney smoked for a long period after construction. As a consequence, the room was at first whitewashed, rather than painted. Surviving documents indicate that the room was whitewashed as late as 1782. Following the arrival of "12 lbs of Verdigris" green pigment, the room was entirely repainted. From the cornice to the floor, the room was given an undercoat of white lead with small amounts of yellow ocher, verdigris, and lampblack, making a light gray-green finish. This was coated with a resin-varnish paint of verdigris green, to which a small quantity of white lead was added.

George Washington himself gave instructions to paint the small dining room entirely in a varnish-medium paint made with distilled verdigris. The use of the varnish paint might have been a result of the smoking chimney and a desire to have a surface that could be kept clean. It is also perhaps the clearest example of Washington's reliance on Dossie's *Handmaid to the Arts* for information. Dossie strongly recommends using a varnish medium for verdigris green finishes to preserve the green coloration of the pigment. The result was glazelike in its translucency, and the verdigris varnish paint provided the most intense green that could be produced. The effect is similar to the intensity and translucence of stained glass. Yet Washington was not entirely pleased with the outcome in the small dining room. It is clear from microscopic examination that the Mount Vernon painters had difficulty grinding the pigment sufficiently to achieve the optimum effect.

The restoration of this room called for a special approach, for the room had been overpainted with twenty-four layers of paint. Plaster surfaces, particularly the overmantel, had greatly deteriorated. The tension created by the cupping action of the shrinking paint layers had gradually caused the plaster surface to delaminate. Under the direction of Morgan Phillips, architectural conservator for the Society for the Preservation of New England Antiquities, the overmantel plaster was relieved of the accumulated paint layers and stabilized with injections of acryloid resins.

The delicate nature of the plaster demanded a restoration paint that would age as slowly as possible, thus postponing the need for repainting. It was evident that any additional paint should be made with a vehicle that could be relatively easily removed yet could be made to appear like the oil-varnish paint of the eighteenth century. In addition, it had to be a material that was available in northern Virginia and that could be manipulated by the painters. The results of tests indicated that a glazelike paint could be prepared using Liquitex Acrylic gloss medium. The pigments were first carefully ground with a gum-arabic solution, to which the Liquitex medium was added. This produced a paint with the required texture. Furthermore, when dry it retained the gloss level of an early varnish-based paint. An additional coat of the Liquitex gloss medium was applied over the glaze to protect the pigment. At the present time the modern paint has not discolored, the medium has not yellowed, and the pigment has retained its bright green finish.

The paint used for finishing the overmantel had to be reversible in a solvent that would not affect the acryloid resin used to stabilize the plaster. A series of tests was done using an alcohol-soluble thermoplastic varnish: Polyvinyl Butyral B-98, which is used as a picture varnish. This provided a clear, flexible film resistant to heat and sunlight. An exact match to the wall finish was made entirely with modern solvent-based materials: titanium-dioxide white and a viridian green (Guignet green transparent). The overmantel finish has proved to be stable and to date has not altered in color or gloss level. It has also provided an excellent benchmark for comparison with the finish of the rest of the room. The two finishes have remained stable, and both give the appearance of oil-varnish finishes of the eighteenth century.

By the time the small dining room was painted in glazed verdigris, its rococo style had already been succeeded in other rooms at Mount Vernon by the neoclassicism exemplified by the work of Robert Adam. The Adam style found its fullest expression in the so-called new room, or large dining room, that Washington spent eleven years completing.

THE LARGE DINING ROOM

Washington conceived of his new room as a grand public space on a scale unprecedented at Mount Vernon. The entire north addition first raised in 1776 is devoted to this single large room **(fig. 1)**.

Shortly after his return to Mount Vernon on Christmas Eve 1783, Washington began planning for the new room. On January 14, 1784, he wrote to Samuel Vaughan, an English admirer, about features of the latest style in England. The style that Robert Adam had brought back to England from Italy was by 1784 firmly established in Britain. Adam's tour of Roman sites greatly enriched the vocabulary of classical design with newly discovered sources of Roman decoration—notably, of course, at Pompeii. Adam's style used this expanded variety of classical forms and extensive use of color derived from Roman prototypes. This new style could be executed almost entirely in cast ornament—either in plaster or composition—thus making it considerably less expensive than the earlier Palladian and rococo styles, which required skilled woodcarvers and plaster workers.

Nevertheless, Washington's writings indicate that the completion of the new room was hampered by difficulties in getting the materials he needed. He wrote on January 17, 1784:

I have seen rooms with gilded borders; made of I believe papier mache fastened on with Brads or Cement round the Doors and window casings, surbase &ca; and which gives a plain blew or green paper a rich and handsome look. Is there any to be had in Philadelphia? and at what price? is there any plain blew and green Paper to be had also? ... [51]

It would take two years to obtain the "plain green paper." And finding the skilled craftsmen to undertake the project proved difficult. A Mr. Turner was hired in April 1784. Turner was responsible for some plastering and probably setting the marble mantel, a gift from Samuel Vaughan, in February 1785. Washington wrote to Vaughan a famous response: "Dr. Sir: I have the honor to inform you that the Chimney piece is arrived and by the number of cases (ten) too elegant and costly by far I fear for my room and my republican stile of living."[52]

Fears of apparent ostentation were put aside, and the beautiful mantelpiece was set as the centerpiece of the south wall in the new room **(fig. 7)**. Mr. Turner proved to be unsatisfactory, and one Richard Boulton was hired to finish the room in May 1785. Boulton preferred drinking to working and by August 1785 was dismissed. By that date Washington was writing to John Rawlins:

I have a room 32 by 24 feet and 16 feet pitch which I want to finish in stucco; it is my intention to do it in a plain neat style; which independently of its being the present taste (as I am informed) is my choice. The chimney is in the center of the longest side, for which I have a very elegent mantel piece directly opposite thereto is a Venetian window, of equal breadth and pitch of the room, on each side of the chimney is a door, leading into other rooms, and on each of the short sides is a door and a window."[53]

Washington had finally found the man capable of completing the large dining room to his satisfaction. John Rawlins was clearly knowledgeable about the Adamesque style and had advertised this knowledge in February 1771:

Rawlins and Barnes, Plasterers and Stucco Workers late from London, Take this method of informing the Gentlemen that they intend carrying on with care and Diligence the said Business. Those Gentlemen who please to favor then with Commands may depend on their work being done as neat as in London.... [54]

To execute the large dining room diverse decorative techniques were used: cast and plain plaster work, composition ornamentation, wood fretwork and running moldings, paint, wallpaper, and printed borders. Rawlins, with his firsthand knowledge of London decoration, was probably responsible for the room's design, but Washington took a special interest in planning and executing the decoration. The marble mantel, with its decorative motif of agricultural emblems, may have suggested the theme of the room's decoration. Washington had considered himself first and foremost a farmer; thus the use of agricultural symbols in the decoration—such as on the ceiling—was certainly characteristic. The vocabulary of the decoration is directly from the Adam style as it developed in the 1760s and 1770s.

Work on the large dining room progressed slowly. By July 1787, however, painting was under way, while plasterwork on the cornice continued. The room was probably completed by 1788. By April of that year John Rawlins had died.

Washington was directly involved in the finishing of the room, as is indicated by his written instructions to his overseer, George Augustine Washington:

Figure 7. *Mantel, large dining room, a gift from Samuel Vaughan, an English admirer. The room's color scheme was relatively simple, requiring few pigments, but provided contrast and visual interest. (Mount Vernon Ladies' Association of the Union, Office of the Curator)*

The wood part of the New Room may be painted of any tolerably fashionable color; so as to serve present purposes; and this might be a buff. Tis more than probable it will receive a finishing color hereafter. The buff should be the lightest kind, inclining to white.... [55]

The execution of the painting was of great importance to him, as indicated by this important letter of July 15, 1787, also addressed to his overseer:

I do not recollect how I expressed myself with respect to the painting of the New Room, that is whether when speaking of this business, you would understand that it was to be done by a proper and good painter.... I advise you to try Peales nephew, or some one more knowing, both in the mixture and laying on of Paint than Morrison (I think his name was). It will require Small brushes and considerable attention to paint the carved mouldings *[sic]*, to prevent their filling too much with the paint. None but the wood work and the Ornaments annexed to them, are to be painted. I mean that the stucco walls are not to be touched."[56]

The surviving physical evidence indicates that a more skilled painter was used in the new room than elsewhere. It is evident that the colors of the wallpaper and the printed border at Mount Vernon in 1786 were matched by the paint colors used for the architectural detailing. The painter used white lead, yellow ocher, yellow lead (litharge), and verdigris green to prepare the green, buff, and white colors used in the finish painting. These paint finishes deteriorated through discoloration and yellowing of the oil medium. The verdigris green, mixed in an oil medium with white lead, had turned gray after years of exposure, just as Dossie had mentioned was typical of verdigris. The original paint exhibits more even pigment dispersion than in other early finishes elsewhere at Mount Vernon, indicating that the painter of the large dining room was indeed more skillful in the preparation of the paint. The paint layers used for the composition ornament also appeared to be thinner-bodied, suggesting that the finishes had less texture than those used elsewhere in the house. It is probable that Rawlins was either personally involved in painting the large dining room or may have instructed the painters who executed the work, for the entire project has a more sophisticated appearance than the painting and decoration in other rooms.

Subsequent repaintings of the room had, unfortunately, filled in the delicate composition ornamentation to such a degree that paint accumulation had to be removed to expose the original character of the ornamentation. Portions of the southeast wall that extends from the chimney breast to the east wall retained the greatest amount of original paint materials. To provide a field for future examination, it was not disturbed. In other areas commercial semipaste paint removers, toothbrushes, and toothpicks were used to gently remove the overcoating paints, a process that occupied four workers for approximately four months. During this process Naptha was used to neutralize the active chemicals on the surface. The reproduction finishes were made with titanium-dioxide–based modern paints, as these surfaces were within the reach of visitors.

The use of the printed architectural border in the large dining room may be one of the earliest such examples in the United States. Such borders were relatively new in the mid-1780s. A piece of that original wallpaper and border was found behind the west window frame in 1902. The discovered paper preserved a small area of the original green finish. This finish was prepared with a distemper base of whiting and water-soluble glues, the glues generally having been made from rabbit skin or fish (isinglass). The preservation of the green color of the verdigris in this water-soluble medium suggests that the pigment may have undergone the process outlined in the 1797 *Encyclopedia Britannica*: "A more durable water color is made by dissolving the verdigris in cream of tartar or rather pure tartaric acid...."[57]

The replication of the wallpaper involved not only finding a paper of fiber content and structure similar to the original but also a problem of scale. Eighteenth-century wallpaper was made from individual sheets smaller than those made today. By about 1770 the assemblage of wallpaper sheets into a piece twenty-one inches wide and twelve yards long had become an established standard in England. The modern paper used in the Mount Vernon restoration had to be cut into pieces and rejoined to provide historically characteristic horizontal joint lines. Because of logistical problems, the paper was hung and then the coating was applied, not the typical procedure in the eighteenth century. Historically, the paper was coated in the shop while laid out horizontally on tables. The horizontal position of the paper assisted the quick spreading of the water-soluble coating on the surface, ensuring a wet edge and the most even application of the color coating. In the large dining room the coating was applied after the paper was hung. Great care had to be taken not to overlap the vertical joint lines to give the impression of the plain green paper. Because this room is one in which visitors are allowed, the wallpaper coating had to be more durable than the historic water-soluble gouache. An acrylic binder, Liquitex matte medium, was used. This accomplished two important tasks: (1) it made a water-miscible coating that was stable when dry and not water soluble, and (2) it held a wet edge for a sufficient period to allow painters to replicate the generally even texture of the the original coating. The border paper had been reproduced in France with gouache paints and the traditional wood-block print techniques.

The completed large dining room was certainly a well-known room in the late eighteenth century and was frequently described by visitors. This was Washington's last and most important design addition to the mansion. The large dining room played a significant historic role: in 1781 Washington met with the French generals in the unfinished room to discuss the coming battle at Yorktown. In 1789 he received word there that he had been elected the first president of the nation. And in 1799 he lay in state in his new room for three days before burial.

In the large dining room Washington expressed his national and agrarian aspirations within the framework of classical decoration: the ceiling depicts oak leaves, symbolizing national strength, olive branches, symbolizing peace, and grape vines, the harvest. Compotes of fruit symbolize the abundance of the earth, and farming tools our most noble employment. The room is dominated by paintings of American landscapes, views of the Hudson and Potomac rivers that relate to the scenes "After Claude," which would have dominated a comparable English interior. Indeed, the symbolism and decoration of this room provide a basis for the development of a national aesthetic, filled with an iconography suitable for the new republic.

The Color of Change

A NINETEENTH-CENTURY MASSACHUSETTS HOUSE

MYRON O. STACHIW

In the decades between the end of the American Revolution and the middle of the nineteenth century, New England's society, culture, and economy underwent a series of changes that swept through every aspect of public and private life. These not only altered the social landscape of the countryside; they radically reshaped the physical landscape and the material basis of life in New England. These changes found strong expression in the home, where the organization and use of space as well as the tools, furnishings, and settings of everyday life were transformed.[1]

SOCIAL AND ECONOMIC CHANGES

Writing in 1793, the Rev. Peter Whitney characterized the rural central New England pattern of dispersed agricultural settlement with this statement about the town of Harvard in Worcester County, Massachusetts: " ... here are two hundred dwelling houses, which, like those of most country towns in this State, are scattered over the place without much order." Two decades later this description of the rural Windham County town of Columbia in northeastern Connecticut was probably still representative of the appearance of many inland towns: " ... the dwelling houses were mostly in a dilapidated condition, weather-worn and mostly unpainted; such as were painted were a dingy red. I can recall to mind but two in the town at that time that were painted white."[2]

But in other parts of New England these seemingly unordered and unimproved landscapes were beginning to show the effects of a growing attitude of improvement and a rapidly quickening commercial pace. The construction of turnpikes, establishment of factory villages, and access to and adoption of new ideas and information, occupations, and economic relations began to transform both the appearance and manners of rural life. By 1835 Englishman Patrick Shirreff, traveling from Northampton to Boston, could write that "the villages through which we passed presented the same characters—white wooden houses with green Venetian blinds, and everything wearing the appearance of cleanliness, order, and comfort."[3]

This traveler's image of a transformed countryside bears up equally well in historical data. In the 1830s cleared acreage, total farm output, and agricultural production of farms and farm

Figure 1. *Reconstruction of the original color scheme in the best room, Bixby House, Barre Four Corners, Mass., ca. 1807. (Drawing by Charles Pelletier after Christopher Mundy; painting by author)*

Figure 2. *Reconstruction of the color scheme of the best room, Bixby House, ca. 1840. (Drawing by Charles Pelletier after Christopher Mundy; painting by author)*

households changed. Across New England one had to search far and wide for a town that did not have at least one factory village. In addition, most rural families became part of the extensive home-manufacturing networks established by storekeepers, merchants, and manufacturers. Farm families carried on in their homes such diverse hand-manufacturing processes as weaving, braiding straw, binding shoes, or making palm-leaf hats. And, as Shirreff observed, in nearly every town in New England, neat commercial villages bustling with artisans, travelers, merchants, and farmers had grown up around transportation nodes and isolated eighteenth-century rural centers, once the site of little more than meetinghouses and taverns.[4]

The architectural, archaeological, and documentary study of the Bixby House and the rural neighborhood of Barre Four Corners, Massachusetts, in which it was located, has provided an extraordinary opportunity to document the expression of these social and economic transformations within one neighborhood, house and house lot, and family. In addition to the excellent preservation of the Bixby House with all its layers of paint and wallpaper and the evidence of its architectural changes intact and readable, the grounds remained virtually undisturbed for the past century. Four years of archaeological excavation around the house yielded evidence of changes in site use, traffic patterns, and patterns of household refuse disposal. Documentation, in the form of Emerson Bixby's surviving daybook and ledger, allowed careful study and reconstruction of the economic life of a rural blacksmith and his family from 1824 to 1855. Finally, extensive archaeological, architectural, and documentary research in the neighborhood established a larger context in which the social and economic changes experienced by neighborhood residents and by the members of the Bixby household could be linked to the structural and ornamental changes of the Bixby House and lot **(fig. 3)**.[5]

EARLY YEARS, CA. 1807-24

The Bixby House, erected about 1807, was located in an outlying rural neighborhood of the central Massachusetts town of Barre. The neighborhood, known as Barre Four Corners, flourished for a brief period in the first half of the nineteenth century around the intersection of two county roads. At its peak, in the early 1830s, the neighborhood contained a district school, carriage maker's shop, two sawmills, a gristmill, triphammer shop, blacksmith shop, and fourteen households of farmers and artisans.[6]

The house was built by members of the Hemenway family, who boasted four generations of housewrights by the early nineteenth century. Physical and documentary evidence suggests that a decade may have elapsed between the beginning of construction of the house by Nathan Hemenway and the clapboarding and trimming of the exterior by his younger brother Rufus. Another decade or more elapsed before the interior was completed and all the ceilings plastered.[7]

As originally constructed, the one-story house measured twenty-six feet square. Three rooms and a small passage were arranged around an off-center, interior chimney. A kitchen occupied the entire north side of the house, which faced the road, with the best room—the only room with plastered walls and an applied Federal-style mantel—and a smaller sitting room located across the south side of the house. The walls of the kitchen, sitting room, and passage were covered with planed, horizontal sheathing. Entry to the house was possible through three doors, all opening directly into the living quarters with no mediating space of a hall or entry lobby.

Shortly after Rufus Hemenway's marriage in 1815, the house underwent its first major alteration. Hemenway moved his barn back on the lot and added a wing to the east gable end of the house. This enclosed the well and added a floored room and a woodshed, extending the work spaces but not altering the interior arrangement of rooms. Careful examination of the architectural evidence and detailed paint analyses allowed the reconstruction of the interior and exterior finishes of the house at this and subsequent stages. What emerged was a striking vernacular expression of a relatively familiar late eighteenth- and early nineteenth-century rural color scheme (fig. 4).[8]

Like most other houses in the New England countryside of the early nineteenth century, the unpainted clapboards and trim presented a weathered brown color to passers-by. The rear of the woodshed, facing away from the road, was not even clapboarded, covered only by the hand-planed sheathing boards. The only exterior application of color was found on the doors, painted red. The interior of the house, however, presented a very different image as nearly every surface was painted, papered, or plastered.[9]

The horizontal wooden sheathing of kitchen walls and the built-in cupboards were painted with an oil-based, red oxide-pigmented paint. The discovery of red pigment on the ceiling lath in the kitchen and sitting room and of blue pigment on the lath in the best room indicated that the painting of the walls, chimney breasts, and wainscoting was done before the ceiling and walls were plastered. Painted at the base of the walls in the kitchen and carried across the cupboard base and bottom of the doors was a brown band simulating a baseboard; the same brown was painted on the kitchen chimney-breast panels. Microscopic examination and infrared spectroscopy of paint samples from the chimney-breast panels revealed that the reddish brown iron oxide pigments were carried not by an oil-based binder, but in a resin or varnish, possibly a copal resin. The floors of the kitchen were painted with the same red-oxide paint as the walls.[10]

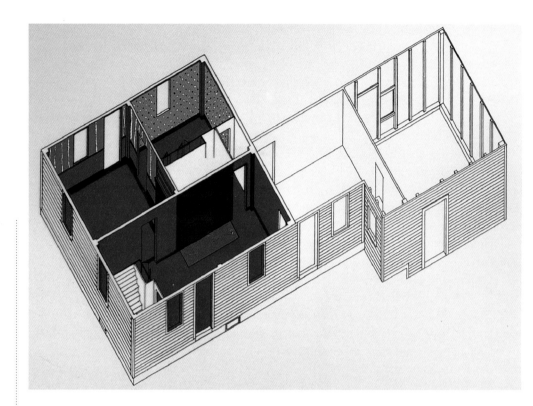

Figure 4. *Reconstruction of the original color scheme of the Bixby House, ca. 1807–26. (Drawing by author and Charles Pelletier after Christopher Mundy; painting by author)*

Figure 5. *Reconstruction of the decorative scheme of the house with the second wallpaper in the sitting room, ca. 1827–37. (Drawing by Charles Pelletier after Christopher Mundy; painting by author)*

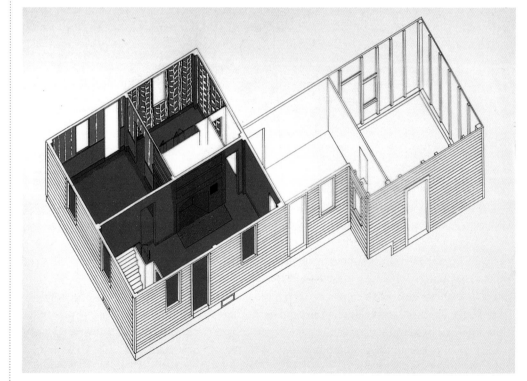

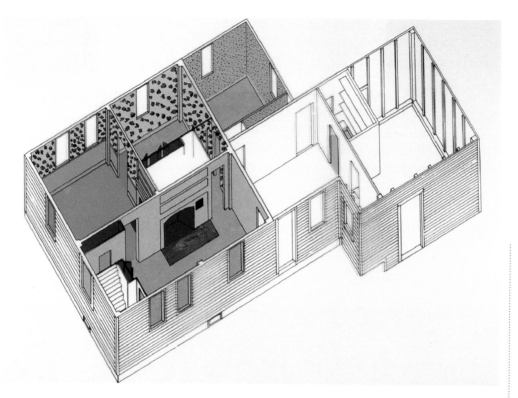

Figure 6. *Reconstruction of the color scheme of the Bixby House, ca. 1850. (Drawing by author and Charles Pelletier after Christopher Mundy; painting by author)*

In the best room, which served as a sleeping room, dining room, and parlor, the wainscoting, chair rail, doors, and chimney-breast panels were painted a Prussian blue **(fig. 1)**. The mantelpiece face was painted brown, while the top of the mantel shelf was painted red. The floor of this room was also painted red but with a brown band around the perimeter of the floor and with the brown color carried up onto the applied baseboards and across the base of the doors. Above the chair rail an ungrounded blue wallpaper was applied. The surviving fragments of this paper were too small to reveal the actual pattern, but they do show at least three colors on the blue paper: white, pink, and green. This wallpaper, together with the red, brown, and blue of the floors, walls, and mantelpiece, must have presented a striking image. With polychrome bedhangings and painted furniture in the room, the impression was even stronger.[11]

The sitting room provided the most unusual decorative scheme in the house. As in the other rooms, the floor was painted red and a brown band was painted at the base of the walls to simulate a baseboard. The earliest wallpaper in this room, placed directly over the sheathing, appears to have been a black-and-white geometric pattern on an ocher ground. This paper stopped several inches below the ceiling to reveal a red frieze painted on the wall and also stopped at the top of the painted baseboard. The chimney-breast paneling, cupboard door, and doors to the best room and passage were also painted red, but a rectangular portion of the paneled wall surrounding the fireplace opening was painted brown. The purpose of this brown-painted surround was obviously to suggest, at least visually, the presence of a mantelpiece like the one in the best room. Like the brown paint on the kitchen chimney breast, the painted fireplace surround in the sitting room was composed of reddish brown iron-oxide pigment in a resin binder.[12]

The only unpainted and unpapered space in the house was the narrow passage between the kitchen and the sitting room. No evidence of either red or brown paint was found on any of the walls or doors of this unlighted space.

LATER CHANGES BY THE BIXBYS

The color scheme of the sitting room, probably created within the first decade of the house's history, was completed before the ceiling was plastered. It appears to have been renewed after the plaster was applied; an unpainted portion of the plaster ceiling above a tall, freestanding cupboard retained evidence of the repainting of the frieze. But within a few years—perhaps in 1824 or 1825, following a transfer of ownership, or after 1826, when the small house and one acre of land was transferred again, this time to Emerson and Laura Bixby—a change occurred in this room (fig. 5). A new wallpaper was applied, this time extending all the way to the ceiling and covering the red-painted frieze. This paper consisted of a large drapery and vine pattern, block printed in black and white on coarse, ungrounded blue paper. The pattern is identical to one produced by Moses Grant and Company of Boston from 1811 to 1817. Because most of Grant's papers were on finer paper with painted grounds, it is likely that this was a less expensive copy.[13]

Surviving evidence of the application of this wallpaper reinforces the idea that the residents probably did the papering themselves and that they were not overly concerned with minor dissonance in the overall symmetry and visual effect of the paper. It was applied with little forethought to the most efficient manner of laying out and applying the paper. As a result, in two places a full repeat would not fit. In one instance, over a door, the pattern was compressed and part of it turned upside-down so that the backgrounds matched—almost. This acceptance of visual imbalance in the wallpaper is echoed in the lack of symmetry in the house's facade, in the interior arrangement of the rooms, in the off-balance construction of the best room's chimney-breast paneling, and in the application of the mantelpiece over the panels.

By the early nineteenth century the use of red and brown iron-oxide paints in the houses of rural New England had been common for almost a century and the use of blue-pigmented paints for almost half a century. In nearly all the houses surveyed in the Four Corners neighborhood, red, brown, and blue were found to be the original colors, with red in the kitchens and secondary rooms and blue in the best rooms. What was surprising in the Bixby House was the extent of the painting and the use of resin as a binder for the pigments on some of the architectural elements. Given the difficulty of preparing the resin and mixing in the pigments, the owners went to considerable trouble to achieve the desired effects. The depth and translucent quality of the resin-based brown paint must have created quite a contrast against the duller red and blue of the walls and floors.[14]

Although painting of floors is known to have occurred in rural New England by the third quarter of the eighteenth century, it appears to have been found only in the homes of the wealthier or more pretentious rural residents. Londoner Edward Parry, a Loyalist functionary of the Crown interned in 1775 in Sturbridge, Massachusetts, in the modest, four-room house of Timothy Parker, the town's representative to the General Court, described the floor of the

best room as painted in squares of "Spanish brown and oker." But it does not appear that painting floors was a common practice among a large proportion of the rural populace until the late 1790s and early decades of the nineteenth century. In the mid- to late nineteenth-century reminiscences of aged rural residents about their childhood homes, descriptions of unpainted and uncarpeted floors abound. So it may be a bit surprising, if not entirely unusual, that the floors and walls of the Bixby House received such attention and full paint coverage as early as the end of the first decade of the nineteenth century.[15]

The Bixby House underwent little or no change during the next decade and a half, as Emerson and Laura Bixby raised their three daughters and Emerson's blacksmithing business flourished. However, in the late 1830s the family undertook a number of changes that significantly altered the appearance and configuration of the house, both inside and out, and of the surrounding house lot.

The first change was the installation of windows to replace the outside doors leading into the best room and kitchen. This was soon followed by major changes in the decorative scheme of the interior (fig. 6). All the walls and floors in the kitchen were painted a uniform light gray. In the best room the floor was painted yellow-orange, and the wainscoting, baseboards, doors, window frames, mantelpiece, and paneling received a coat of pale greenish gray paint. The plastered walls were repapered with a bouquet-and-wreath pattern in black, green, and silver on a gray ground (fig. 2). In the sitting room this same wallpaper was used on the walls, and the chimney breast wall and floor, as in the kitchen, were painted a uniform light gray. This painting obscured the strongly contrasting polychrome decorative schemes of the original finishes in the three rooms, replacing them with more fashionable, lighter, harmonizing colors. The passage was also papered with the gray wallpaper, and its floor and other woodwork were painted gray.

Not long after these interior changes the Bixbys began another series of improvements to the house and house lot that were completed in 1845. These included removing the old barn, renovating a former wheelwright's shop into a new barn, adding a new room to the ground floor of the house, adding a dairy room in the wing, and finishing a room in the garret to serve as a bedroom for the daughters. At this time the exterior of the house was reclapboarded and given its first coat of paint. The clapboards and trim were painted white and the doors and shutters a bright green, bringing the house into conformity, at least visually, with the neat white houses in the center village and the neighborhood.[16]

As in the sitting room and kitchen, the floor, baseboards, doors, windows, trim, and floors of the new rooms on the ground floor and in the garret were painted a light gray. Within a few years the plastered walls of the ground-floor room were papered; the pattern consisted of roller printed lozenges, ovals, and dots in white, blue, and orange on a glazed tan ground.[17]

PHYSICAL EXPRESSIONS OF CHANGE

The importance of the structural and decorative changes to the house and lot are far greater than the fact of their survival, reconstruction, and tight dating. Their real significance lies in our ability to understand them as physical expressions of the important transformations that occurred in the social and economic relations within the household, neighborhood, and region during the first half of the nineteenth century.

Like much of New England and the nation in the mid-1830s, Barre Four Corners was experiencing the benefits of two decades of prosperity. With the establishment of textile and woodworking manufactories and villages throughout the countryside and the growth of cities such as Boston, Providence, and Worcester, the markets for agricultural products and locally manufactured goods were steadily expanding. Dairying for the market was increasing, and Barre became a major supplier of cheese in the Boston market. The storekeepers in Barre's center village established extensive networks of homeworkers for the weaving of palm-leaf hats and became the largest dealers in New England.[18]

In Barre Four Corners the steadily growing volume of Emerson Bixby's blacksmithing trade and work with a neighboring carriage maker through the mid-1830s was a reflection of the region's prosperity and economic optimism. Bixby was providing his services to nearly eighty customers, many of whom were his long-standing neighbors and trading partners.

But things began to change rapidly, especially after the economic upheavals of the Panic of 1837 and the ensuing depression. Up to this time most of Bixby's economic relations were mediated through the traditional account book system. However, following the panic, increasing numbers of his trading partners chose to settle their obligations with cash, and the value and volume of work recorded in the account book began to shrink dramatically. The effects of the panic and depression on the Four Corners neighborhood were felt in other ways, as several local artisans suffered financial difficulties and were forced to close their shops. The neighborhood then fell into a long, steady decline in population and economic vitality; as the range of services and opportunities available in the neighborhood continued to dwindle, the young people married out of the community, and many moved away.[19]

The prosperity preceding the panic undoubtedly prompted Bixby to increase his one-acre land holdings with the purchase of thirty-two acres of farmland and begin the improvements to the house and lot. It is likely that the major stimuli to the timing and nature of the changes implemented over the next eight years were the new social and economic roles of his daughters and wife. As the girls entered their teenage years, they could begin to contribute their labor to the household economy by binding shoe uppers, braiding straw, and weaving palm-leaf hats and the strenuous and exacting tasks of making cheese and butter. All these activities provided either cash or credit at the center village store. As they became more active socially and aware of the new social as well as economic patterns of behavior and their new material accouterments, they probably became increasingly sensitive to the "old-fashioned" nature of their own house and furnishings. It is no coincidence that this new involvement beyond the immediate neighborhood occurred at a time when the traditional values and bonds of neighborhood cohesion—kinship and social and economic cooperation—were under serious stress. The Bixbys and their neighbors began to turn to the new social values and standards of the culture of improvement and gentility that had begun to challenge the traditional order.[20]

One of the first things the family did, even before repainting and repapering the interior of the house, was begin to change the pattern of refuse disposal around their house. While formerly household trash and scraps had been strewn freely in the front, side, and rear yards, creating what one reformer called "an inlaid pavement of bones and broken bottles, the relics of departed earthenware, or the fragments of abandoned domestic utensils," the Bixbys now began to dispose of their trash in discreet deposits out of the sight of passers-by.[21]

Replacing the doors into the kitchen and best room with windows achieved two things. First, it allowed 40 percent more light into the two rooms; this, along with the fashionable, lighter-toned walls and floors, made the house seem more spacious and certainly much brighter than it had been with the dark blue-, brown- and red-painted surfaces. Second, it restricted entry into the house to only one door, located in the wing and opening into the kitchen. This gave the occupants more control over access into the house and provided at least a little more privacy for Emerson and Laura, whose bed was located in the best room. But this apparently was not enough, for several years later a ground-floor room was added. This room, now the most private room of the house, probably served as their new bedroom. The best room could then serve as a more formal parlor, a place where the new rituals of social entertaining could be staged and performed. Equally as important, the young women received a neatly plastered room of their own in the garret, a marked improvement over the unfinished garret space they occupied until this time.[22]

The changes in the paint colors and wallpaper described here have been linked to structural changes in the building, the use of both interior and exterior space, the dynamics of the family, and the social and economic organization of the neighborhood. Together, they provide an important case study of the complex processes of social and economic change that occurred in thousands of households throughout New England during the first half of the nineteenth century. Cumulatively, these changes not only marked a shift in tastes or fashion, reflected in teacups, wallpaper, paint colors, and the way one dressed or wore one's hair. They also embodied a significant shift in ideology, a shift expressed in nearly every aspect of life, from material culture to economic life, from changing patterns of marriage, childbearing, and child rearing to the rules of social interaction and religious practice.[23]

An Early Colonial Mural

THE CONSERVATION OF WALL PAINTINGS

CHRISTY CUNNINGHAM-ADAMS

CHRISTY CUNNINGHAM-ADAMS

The wall paintings in the historic Warner House in Portsmouth, New Hampshire, are among the oldest colonial wall paintings on the East Coast surviving at their original site. The elegant Georgian mansion was built by Capt. Archibald Macpheadris in 1716, and it appears that the paintings on the walls around the central staircase were part of the original decoration completed that year. The murals have long been considered important and interesting simply because they are so old, but their dark, murky surfaces permitted only a dim view of what seemed to be some primitive pictures. The scenes appeared disconnected and curiously incompatible with the fashionable high style of the house and the rest of its decor.

Concerned about their continued preservation and hoping that cleaning them might brighten up their rather grim appearance, the officers of the Warner House Association arranged for their conservation treatment in 1988. As the treatment progressed over the months and the original surfaces emerged from under layers of dirt, darkened varnishes, and past restorations, unexpected qualities appeared that provided an astonishing new look at American art history. A technique and spirit not generally associated with early American art were uncovered, along with an abundance of technical and art history information.

Three aspects of this project make the experience of preserving and conserving the Warner House wall paintings an especially worthy case study: careful planning, innovative conservation methodology, and new discoveries recorded for the benefit of art history study in the United States.

THE WALL PAINTINGS

The wall paintings cover more than five hundred square feet and are immediately visible to the visitor entering the house. Beginning at the foot of the central staircase in the front hall, the paintings decorate the walls above the paneled dado all the way up the staircase, around the landing, and to the second floor.

The pictures present four scenes that reflect social and religious interests of the period. The first scene, which begins at the foot of the staircase, shows a woman in a simple domestic farm

Figure 1. *View of the upper section of the Warner House murals, Portsmouth, N. H., seen from the second floor, after treatment. The scene of the colonial officer on horseback is on the right, and the portraits of the Mohawk Indians flank the window. (Lars Christensen)*

dress, seated at a spinning wheel. A spotted dog at her feet barks and leaps at a large eagle with a chicken in its talons. Further up the stairs, the dramatic image of Abraham's sacrifice of Isaac echoes that biblical scene's immense popularity in the early colonies. On the two walls flanking the tall arched windows at the landing are the extraordinary images of two Indians (fig. 1). They are larger-than-life portraits of two of the four Mohawk Indian sachems taken to England and presented to Queen Anne in 1710 as diplomats from this country. The Indians' visit caused a sensation in England. Their portraits were painted by John Verelst, from which mezzotints were engraved by John Simon and widely circulated. The portraits at the Warner House are inspired copies of those well-known mezzotints, which must have reached the colonies shortly after the Indians' visit.[1] The two Indians represented here are king of the River Nation, Turtle Tribe, and king of the Generethgarich, Wolf Tribe. The scene that follows the images of the Indians and fills the wall between the landing and the second floor is a life-size portrait of a colonial officer on horseback. His identity is still not certain, but the letter *P* appears on his saddlebag.

The difficulty of seeing the paintings through heavy layers of overpaint and darkened varnishes and the diversity of scenes and subject matter has led art historians in the past to suppose that the unsigned murals were painted at different times and by different painters. But the conservation treatment provided an unexpected view of consistency in style, compositional structure, technique, and execution of particular details, indicating that all the paintings were executed by the same artist.

PLANNING THE CONSERVATION PROJECT

The significance of this group of wall paintings in American art history made a well-planned conservation project imperative. Two years went into planning the appropriate treatment, which was carried out between January and July 1988. Art historian Mary Black did the preliminary art history research and was the driving force behind the organization of the entire project. Her commitment to the realization of the conservation project led the Warner House Association through planning, fund raising, and collaboration with the conservator.

That collaboration began with a review of historical information about the house and the paintings and discussion of the theoretical and practical techniques the conservator considers in planning a treatment. From the outset the treatment was regarded by the conservator, art historian, and owner as a necessary intervention in the life of the wall paintings that would stabilize them, recover their original aesthetic character, and secure their continued preservation. Throughout the treatment, close collaboration with the art historian and owners continued and was extended to include the architectural conservator, structural engineer, conservation scientist, ornithologist, and participating assistants and conservators.

PRETREATMENT EXAMINATION AND DOCUMENTATION

To plan the treatment, I carried out a complete conditions examination and analysis of the paintings a year before treatment was scheduled. The purpose of the examination was to become as familiar as possible with how the paintings were made, what conservation problems they had suffered in the past, what alterations past restorations and conditions had caused, what the present condition of each painting was, and what had caused any present deterioration. This order of inquiry in examining works of art is critical to understanding both what the work of art requires and what kind of treatment is possible.

The examination and analysis was made layer by layer, addressing the conditions present in each layer individually. Like most paintings, the Warner House murals consist of three layers: the support (the structure on which the painting is executed); the preparation (whatever is done or applied to the surface of the support to make it smooth, porous, or otherwise favorable for the application of the paint); and the paint layer. With the aid of solubility testing, ultraviolet fluorescence, and laboratory analysis of samples, the analysis of each layer was conducted and documented in a detailed written report identifying the information in the following order: the original materials and execution technique; previous restoration treatments; the state of conservation; the cause of deterioration; and the required conservation treatment.

Because the surface of the murals was so obscured, conditions examination, testing, and analysis continued throughout the treatment phase in which the paintings were cleaned. Pictorial graphics with acetate overlays were made to indicate the location of various conditions, and a grid system outlining every square foot of the wall paintings was followed in photographing each square foot from the same angle and distance to document conditions before, during, and after treatment, in addition to overviews and particular details of significance.

THE ORIGINAL MATERIALS AND EXECUTION TECHNIQUE

The wall paintings' support layer was identified as a traditional lime and sand mortar keyed into a wooden lath substructure. The mortar from all three walls was compared and found to be the same. Examination of the wall surfaces under raking light revealed frequent trowel marks and other irregularities created during the original application of the mortar to the wooden lath. Some of the sand present in the mortar was grainy enough to show through the preparation layer and cause numerous small peaks in the paint layer.

Although the sequence of mortar application to the side interior walls could not be determined, mortar overlapping the painted surface indicated that the images on the outside wall—those of the Indians—was applied last. This was a surprise because art historians had believed that the Indians were the first images painted and that the side walls were painted afterward, possibly even somewhat later. The reasons for assuming that the Indians were painted first were their prominence on the wall facing the front door, their importance historically and politically, and the lack of compositional, pictorial, or stylistic reference to the two other painted walls, which share a similar landscape background. It became evident in the conditions examination, however, that the three walls were all prepared and painted at about the same time and that the Indians were painted last.

The preparation layer consisted of a one-sixteenth-inch water-soluble layer of calcium sulfate and protein-based glue, applied to provide a smooth surface to the wall. Analyzed by Richard Newman in the analytical laboratory of the conservation department of the Museum of Fine Arts, Boston, the preparation layer was discovered to have been sealed with a single coat of sizing, presumably to prevent the paint layer from being absorbed into the preparation.

The original paint layer had surface qualities and cracking patterns characteristic of oil paint, but the possibility of its having been executed in tempera, casein, or lime wash was not excluded until laboratory tests could be carried out. Microsamples of the paint layer were also analyzed in the Museum of Fine Arts laboratory, where the results of gas chromatography analysis confirmed that the binding medium was oil.

Paint losses in the colonial officer's face revealed an underdrawing of the facial features executed in blue pencil on the surface of the preparation. Several pentimenti found during the cleaning process, however, suggested that for the most part the paintings were executed by freehand and without the aid of preliminary sketches or cartoons. The difficulty of painting in a large scale has led many artists in the past to use cartoons—that is, large drawings hung on the wall to guide the artist in laying out the picture. The number and location of pentimenti in the Warner House murals, however, indicate that the artist continued to work out the strengths of the compositions as he or she worked directly on the wall. Pentimento is an Italian word meaning "second thought," or change of mind. In painting it refers to an artist's second version or correction of an image, seen on a painting alongside the first version. The artist may cover up the first version with overpaint, but as the overpaint ages it can become transparent enough to allow the first version to show through. The conservator should always respect the artist's decision to alter the image and not remove the artist's own overpaint that covers the first version.

Pentimenti were found in two parts of the horse's mane, where on second thought the artist decided to show the hair being blown up with the wind rather than down. A pentimento in the outline of the officer's back made him appear slimmer, and his lapel was modified to give more open space around the horse's head. All these changes represent significant compositional alterations. An especially interesting pentimento occurs in the detail of the chicken clutched in the flying eagle's talons. The first chicken painted by the artist was shown alive and much fatter than the artist's second version, in which the chicken is dead.

Cleaning tests for the purpose of studying the original execution technique of the paint layer and the character of overlaying materials were conducted in saliva-moistened swabs to remove surface dirt, ethyl alcohol to remove varnishes, acetone and dimethylformamide to dissolve old retouching, and a mixture of water, alcohol, acetone, and ammonia in equal parts to clean some areas of the original surface. As the original paint layer was exposed, a surprisingly lively technique of fluid brushwork and a palette of bright colors were revealed.

The colors used in all scenes are yellow, brown, red, green, blue, white, and black. A reddish brown was used to paint the Indians' skin, the colonial officer's saddle blanket and saddlebag, and the hair of both the angel and Isaac. Laboratory analysis conducted by Eugene Farrell at the Center for Conservation and Technical Studies, Harvard University Art Museums, identified the materials making up the colors as yellow ocher for yellow; brown ocher for brown; red lead and vermilion for the reds; a mixture of lead white, yellow ocher, and carbon black for green; a mixture of calcite, natural ocher, and chunks of bone black for blue; lead white and calcite for white; and carbon black and bone black for black.

Paint was usually applied with a loaded brush, and resulting impasto and bristle impressions are distinct where the paint is well preserved. All paint was the same consistency and was applied in one or two and in some areas as many as three layers. The rapid strokes that characterize the brushwork are effectively succinct throughout the murals. The strength and vitality of the horse's head in the mural of the colonial officer, for example, is represented by about fifteen brush strokes that sum up the horse's flaring nostrils, flashing eyes, and strong mouth and nose. The limited number of strokes used in the trees, lifted curtains, flying birds, and clothing are all painted in similar fluidity. Treatment of drapery was found distinctly similar in the Indians' cloaks, the colonial officer's coat, and Abraham's clothing. Thin, wiggly lines are used to animate the faces of Abraham, Isaac, the spinner, and the colonial officer. The faces of the Indians are executed with the same bold, simple brushwork found in the horse's head.

Consistency in both palette and paint application techniques throughout the group of wall paintings indicated the predominance of the same hand in all the paintings. It appears that if the artist did not work alone, he or she did most of the actual painting. Moreover, the murals all share a lighthearted, whimsical spirit—an attitude expressed with playful boldness in the overall scheme and in details such as the facial expressions and the birds flitting throughout.

PREVIOUS RESTORATION TREATMENTS

The only documentation regarding previous treatment of the murals was a brief, handwritten report by M. T. Beck about the restoration he did in 1953 on the "two Indian Chiefs."[2] In it he stated that he consolidated plaster with a solution of sulfate of iron, readhered loose paint "by heating process and pressure," filled cracks with Swedish putty, removed dirt and dust with cleaning fluid and pumice stone, painted over faulty previous restoration to resemble the original, painted exposed plaster to resemble the original, and applied a protective finish of a wax and starch mixture. He did not mention what type of paints he used to retouch the paint losses and previous restoration work but stated that the "basic materials used [were] the kind which were manufactured about 50 or more years ago." The Warner House Association has records that the other murals were restored by Beck in 1954, but no specific documentation could be found for that treatment, nor any record or memory that restoration work had been done on the murals since then.

Although it was not mentioned in Beck's report, I found that the last treatment had included the use of a varnish tinted brown applied to much of the surfaces of the murals and that what appeared to be synthetic paints were used in retouching. The retouching materials seemed to be synthetic because they became stringy and dissolved readily in ethyl alcohol. Extensive retouching and overpainting in that material were found, particularly in the murals of the Indians, in the trees of the murals on either side of the Indians, in the background landscapes of the two side murals, and in the figure of the colonial officer. The tinted varnish applied over the painting of the Indians and the landscapes in the other two murals may have been applied to obscure the diminished condition of the paintings or to make them appear old.

In addition to the 1953–54 restoration treatments, diverse restoration materials were found that suggested two other previous treatments. The Warner House Association also had notes indicating that during the mid-nineteenth century wallpaper was removed from the two side interior walls to reveal the murals that had been hidden under it for an unknown amount of time. Both the restorations before 1953–54 appeared to have taken place after removal of the wallpaper. I came to this conclusion because the earliest restoration materials found appeared to have been applied to correct alterations caused by removal of the paper, and traces of the wallpaper were found on surfaces whose quality resembled the best-preserved surfaces located elsewhere.

In the first treatment after the removal of the wallpaper, the murals appear to have been cleaned, retouched in oil paint, and varnished. The restoration work may have been done immediately after removal of the paper. Oil paint had been used to compensate for a reduction in original paint apparently associated with removal of the paper and rubbing and solvent action. Areas measuring up to five by twelve inches, particularly in the skies around the colonial officer in the right painting and around the figures of Abraham and the angel in the left painting, had been generously overpainted to correct the loss of impasto and color intensity. Considerable dark staining, possibly a result of the tannin in the wallpaper or the wallpaper glue, had created patchiness in the landscape backgrounds and skies of the two side paintings, which had also been retouched in oil in places. Because these restoration materials were still present, it was evident that in the subsequent two treatments the murals were not thoroughly cleaned.

A different quality of restoration materials and techniques was identified as having come from a subsequent, second treatment, apparently undertaken after considerable flaking had occurred in all the wall paintings. No documentation dating the treatment was found, but it appeared to have taken place around the beginning of the century, approximately fifty years after the former treatment and fifty years before the next big restoration project of 1953–54. In the second restoration it appears that losses in the preparation and paint layers were filled with gesso and retouched with pigments ground in varnish, the shapes of some figures were reinforced by being outlined, and all the paintings were varnished. No adhesive for reattaching flaking was discernible. Areas of preparation and paint loss around the feet of both Indians, caused by the infiltration of water from the window, were treated, and a three-by-six-foot loss of preparation and paint at the lower edge of the painting of the colonial officer, also caused by infiltration of water from the window, was similarly filled with gesso and retouched. A great number of small paint losses caused by flaking throughout the murals were carefully filled and retouched. Possibly because the paintings were not cleaned at the time, it was considered desirable to bring out the figures by reinforcing their outlines with overpaint.

In his 1953 account of the treatment of the Indian murals, Beck reported cleaning the paintings of "dirt and dust." A thorough cleaning and removal of all previously applied retouching and varnishes was apparently not undertaken then.

THE STATE OF CONSERVATION

The wall paintings were examined layer by layer for failures in their condition. Different types of failure were recorded on separate acetate overlays of the graphic documentation. Once the areas of instability were recorded in this way, patterns of deterioration could be analyzed. Crack patterns all radiating from a door jamb, for example, suggested disturbance in the wall's stability resulting from door closing.

In determining the stability of the support, resonance sounding by finger tapping and manual pressure to the surface were used to locate fracturing in the wooden lath substructure and areas of cohesion breakdown in the wall mortar (for example, crumbling or cracking). Only two serious breakdowns of contact between the mortar and the wooden lath were found, both of them in the support of the mural of the colonial officer near the door jamb. Although the mortar had cracked in many places throughout the group of murals, it remained securely keyed into the system of wooden laths. The cracks in the mortar had broken through the preparation and paint layer as well and were apparently the result of the settling of the architectural structure.

Attachment of the preparation to the support was generally good, and for the most part the preparation was found stable. Severe deterioration of the preparation did exist, however, in the lower half of the paintings of the Indians on the exterior wall, where water had evidently infiltrated and caused the hygroscopic preparation to crumble, as it had in the past, necessitating previous restoration work.

Flaking of the paint layer was the most serious instability found throughout the wall paintings. This breakdown in the adhesion between the paint layer and preparation had apparently long been a recurring problem because most of the extensive past restoration work was done to cover losses from flaking. The flaking had occurred in random patterns. The robust pink paint layer in the faces of Abraham, Isaac, and the angel, for example, had few losses, but the same materials used in the face of the colonial officer had flaked off in more than thirty places. The sky behind the colonial officer was found in good condition, as was the sky behind Abraham and Isaac. But the sky behind the spinner, made of the same materials, suffered as many as ten losses per square foot. General areas with the highest concentration of losses from flaking were the lower half of the mural of the spinner and most of the wall with the paintings of the Indians.

The best-preserved limited areas of paint throughout all the murals were the Indians' heads and shoulders and the background immediately around their heads **(figs. 2, 3, 4, and 5)**. The paint layer there was found almost completely intact, although the surfaces are bumpy with peaked protrusions caused by swelling of the preparation beneath. Despite this and a two-by-four-inch vertical loss located in the middle of the face of the Indian on the right, the paint in the upper portion of the figures was found in such extraordinary condition as to almost appear painted only a year ago. The impasto in the feathers and flowers behind the Indians' ears is high, glossy, and completely undamaged by flaking.

The interruption of the paint layer that flaking causes can reduce the adhesion of surrounding paint as well. Tenuous adhesion of this kind was noted, and the general condition of complete bonding between the paint layer and the preparation throughout the paintings was found questionable.

The removal of the wallpaper had caused some additional loss of a particular character in the paint layer on the interior walls. It appeared that when the paper was pulled off the surface quality was slightly altered and some impasto reduced. This explains why the Indians' heads were in the condition best representative of the original, even though they are on the exterior wall that had suffered such extensive deterioration. It may be that use of excessive water in the removal of the wallpaper also contributed to subsequent flaking. Staining, possibly because of tannin in the wallpaper or the wallpaper glue, caused a patchiness particularly in the sky around the angel and in the rolling green hills of the landscapes in the murals that had been covered with wallpaper.

Figure 2. *Detail of portrait of the Mohawk Indian, King of the River Nation, during removal of dirt, overpaint, and discolored varnishes from the surface. (Christy Cunningham-Adams)*

Figure 3. *Detail of portrait of the Mohawk Indian, King of the River Nation after treatment. (Christy Cunningham-Adams)*

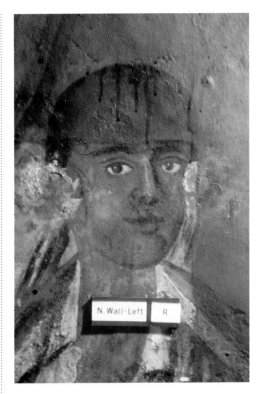

Figure 4. *Detail of portrait of the Mohawk Indian, King of the Generethgarich, before treatment. (Christy Cunningham-Adams)*

Figure 5. *Detail of portrait of the Mohawk Indian, King of the Generethgarich, after completion of treatment. (Christy Cunningham-Adams)*

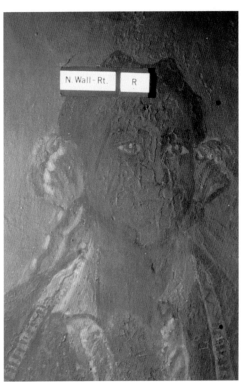

In areas around the images of the angel, Abraham, and the colonial officer, thinning and smearing of the paint layer was evidently the result of previous cleaning attempts with excessively aggressive solvents and rubbing.

The extensive previous restoration work, aging of restoration materials, and accumulation of dirt had given the murals a very dark appearance. The tinted varnish apparently applied in the last restoration camouflaged a multitude of unfilled, unretouched losses in areas such as the landscape background, the trees, the Indians' cloaks, and the eagle's wings. In other areas, such as the colonial officer's face, a natural resin varnish turned yellow with age covered retouching from all three previous restoration treatments. In addition to being dark, the murals had a primitive aspect because of the extensiveness and quality of the old retouching and the attempt to strengthen and renew the paintings by reinforcing shapes of figures with outlines during the second treatment. The effect of this restoration work was to make the figures look like primitive cardboard cutouts. Moreover, the paintings' details, original lively brushwork, and spirited palette were buried and the depth of each scene flattened.

THE CAUSE OF DETERIORATION

The most serious instability and deterioration in the Warner House wall paintings were widespread flaking of the paint layer and crumbling of the preparation around the window. It was evident that both the deterioration of the preparation in the murals of the Indians, and the large three-by-six-foot loss at the bottom of the mural of the colonial officer stemmed from water infiltration and migration from the window and exterior wall.

The flaking in the paint layer throughout the murals appeared to be the result of unfavorable environmental conditions rather than faulty execution technique. Most problems in an artwork's stability have to do with how well its layers are sticking together, and a common threat to that adhesion is changes in the relative humidity in the environment surrounding the object. As the support, preparation, and paint layer are all made of different materials, they all respond to humidity at different rates. Swelling and contracting at different rates, in response to fluctuations in the surrounding atmosphere, the layers can pull away from each other, causing flaking.

It is quite probable that for the first 150 years of their life the wall paintings at the Warner House were able to stand up to the gradual temperature and relative humidity fluctuations associated with seasonal changes. Most of the rooms in the house have fireplaces, but the paintings around the central staircase would not have been exposed to the drying effect of local heating and resulting low humidities in the winter until the mid- to late 1800s, when central heating was introduced in the house. There was no indication that the paintings on the side interior walls had suffered flaking before they were covered over with wallpaper.

CONSERVATION TREATMENT

Structural examination of the house was carried out by a consulting architectural conservator to determine its required treatment. To improve environmental conditions the window was treated to make it watertight, and the bricks were repointed and coated with a silicone sealant. The Warner House Association began a climate stabilization program within the house: removable partitions were made to isolate the stairwell for better winter control of the environment; moderate heat was introduced in the winter; and humidity and temperature fluctuations were recorded with a thermohygrometer to study patterns. Members learned to use the thermohygrograph and share responsibility for changing and collecting the graphs.

The shutters were fixed to stay only one-third open, which greatly reduced the amount of light and glare on the paintings but allowed some natural raking light to dramatize their surface quality. The artificial area lighting in the stairway was reduced and low-wattage tungsten light installed to subtly suggest any artificial light that might have been used originally on a dark day.

The conservation conditions examination and analysis clearly indicated the wall paintings' requirements: (1) stabilizing the mortar-lath contact, preparation crumbling, and paint layer flaking; (2) cleaning the original paint layer, including removal of dirt, disfiguring layers of darkened varnishes, overpainting, and retouching; (3) filling selected losses in the preparation and paint layer; (4) retouching to integrate filled losses and diminish visibility of abrasions and unfilled losses; and (5) surface protection.

STABILIZATION

Although stabilization is performed before cleaning when possible, in this case it was carried out concurrently with the cleaning because the heavy blanket of dirt, varnishes, and old retouching sometimes held lifting paint in place, impeded penetration of our consolidants, and hid from view areas requiring special attention.

Because the paint layer was in such delicate condition, it was treated before the preparation and support layers. Lifting paint throughout the group of murals was reattached to the underlying preparation layer with a synthetic adhesive (polyvinyl alcohol), introduced in drops with a syringe between the lifting paint and the preparation. Gentle pressure was then applied with the fingers over a piece of silicone-treated mylar to ensure proper contact during penetration and drying of the adhesive.

In addition to the lifting and flaking paint, contact between the preparation and paint layer was tenuous in a number of places where no flaking existed yet. I wanted to devise a method for introducing the adhesive to every square foot of the wall paintings to reinforce existing contact and consolidate any hidden separation between the layers. Consulting engineer George W. Adams agreed to help me develop a procedure for facilitating penetration of the adhesive through all existing cracks and other interruptions in the surface. We did not attempt to develop a universal method for all wall paintings but only to remedy the problem at the Warner House. We wanted a system that would not eliminate the need for operator skill, patience, and judgment but would permit observation and control.

In practical terms we did not need or want particularly deep penetration of the consolidant into the preparation. We wanted to avoid any procedure such as the introduction of large quantities of consolidant at the paint surface that might displace the flakes before they were adhered.

The machine we developed to achieve this task was named the pneumatic consolidation device (PCD). It consists of a pair of stacked rings with a membrane loosely clamped between, connected by a tube to a vacuum pump. In operation, the consolidant (polyvinyl alcohol) is applied with a brush to a circular area of approximately one square foot, and the PCD is placed over the area and turned on. The outside air pressure forces the consolidant into the wall and the flakes and membrane onto the wall, first at the center of the disk and then, slowly, over an increasing area. The vacuum and the device are removed after five minutes, and excess consolidant is removed from the surface with swabs. The device was used throughout the walls and enabled us to firmly readhere the paint in relatively short time (fig. 6).

Crumbling preparation around the feet of the Indians was also consolidated with polyvinyl alcohol by brush where paint had fallen away and by injection elsewhere. Polyvinyl acetate in emulsion was injected into the areas of detachment from the lath substructure, and supports pressed against the wall over silicone-treated mylar and a compliant foam-applied pressure required to keep the mortar in contact with the lath for four days while the consolidant dried.

CLEANING

Four Italian conservators who specialize in wall paintings came from Rome to Portsmouth to assist in the stabilization, cleaning, and aesthetic treatment of the murals. The visiting conservators were as surprised and delighted as I was by each inch of the original painting revealed by our painstaking efforts to remove the layers of dirt, varnishes, and old retouching.

Cleaning tests had indicated that the dirt deposited on the surfaces could be removed along with the uppermost layer of varnish. Ethyl alcohol was used to put the upper layers of varnish into solution, and loosely made swabs were used to remove the dirt and dissolved varnish. Swabs were rolled rather than pushed across the surface to avoid disturbing any lifting paint. In some areas where a thick layer of tinted varnish existed, ethyl alcohol was introduced to the surface by a large swab and allowed to run down the surface for about four inches to bathe and soften the varnish. Swabs moistened in acetone were then used to pick up the softened varnish and increase visibility of remaining varnish and any lifting paint.

Most of the more recent retouching also came up with ethyl alcohol. Acetone was used to remove retouching from the second treatment and dimethylformamide to dissolve oil retouching from the earliest restoration work. Once exposed, the original surface showed some patchy brown staining and imbedded dirt, which was cleaned with a mixture of water, alcohol, acetone, and ammonia in equal parts.

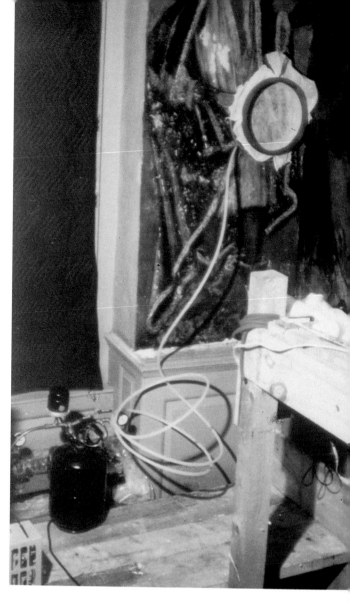

Figure 6. *Pneumatic consolidation device in operation at the Warner House during consolidation of one of the Mohawk Indian portraits. (Christy Cunningham-Adams)*

FILLING SELECTED LOSSES

Losses were filled with a mixture of natural gesso and rabbit-skin glue to match the quality of the original preparation. Filling every loss in the paint layer for the purpose of reconstructing the fabric and color of all missing paint would have given the murals a stiff appearance because of the dispersion and extraordinary quantity of losses throughout the surfaces. Therefore, only losses whose filling and in-painting would substantially enhance legibility of the murals' iconography, composition, and balance were filled. In recovering overall legibility but preserving the painting's character, we did not want to hide the fact that many areas had been altered by time and simply were not what they used to be.

Approximately one-third of the losses were filled in preparation for in-painting to match the original color surrounding each loss so that they were no longer visible as losses. The other two-thirds were left unfilled; the exposed preparation would be toned in optical value rather than color-matched to the missing original. This combination of treatments was undertaken to reduce visibility of distracting losses without disguising the paintings' age and general state of conservation.

Losses that were filled usually represented the only interruption in well-preserved areas measuring anywhere from five square inches to two square feet. Filling the only interruption in such an area greatly improved appearance and legibility of the painting in that section because the surrounding paint was in such good condition and the area would now appear completely intact.

In most cases numerous small losses within a square foot were not filled simply to make that area look better preserved. Instead, we tried to diminish the striking contrast between well-preserved and severely deteriorated areas, by treating areas of transition, or creating transition. Such a transition was created, for example, in the torsos of the Indians, where numerous small losses within a small area were filled to diminish the striking disparity between the well-preserved area of the head and shoulders and the poor condition of the lower portions of their bodies. Exceptions to this general rule included treatment of the colonial officer's face. The deteriorated state of the face contrasted so sharply with the rest of his figure that it created a distracting imbalance to the whole painting and significantly diminished legibility of the whole figure. Most losses in the face, therefore, were filled (figs. 7 and 8).

The decision about which losses to fill for reconstruction of the original paint layer should be reserved until the actual condition of the whole painting is understood. The number, size, and location of the losses influence the decision of which ones should be reconstructed. If a painting is in good condition and suffers only a few losses, it may be that they can all be reconstructed. However, a painting with a great number of losses can acquire an unnatural appearance if the restorer's work, however skillful, is too prominent. In addition to risking the painting's authenticity, questions also arise as to falsification when more than approximately one-third of a painting is reconstructed by a restorer.

RETOUCHING

The retouching of the wall paintings was done with watercolors over a thin layer of methylacrelate resin that isolated the original surface from the retouching. There are four important reasons for using watercolors rather than other materials: watercolors are stable, readily reversible, discernible from the original at close range, and effective in matching the transparent quality of aged paint.

Our aesthetic treatment of the murals at the Warner House reflected our concern about filling losses. We wanted to diminish visibility of the losses and distortions without disguising the quality of the paintings' original materials or the murals' age, general condition, and original aesthetic character.

Many aspects of an artwork define its original aesthetic character. The artist's own feeling, technique, and the type of materials used are important elements. In recovering the original aesthetic character, however, it is also important not to obscure the

Figure 7. *Portrait of the colonial officer during cleaning. (Christy Cunningham-Adams)*

Figure 8. *Portrait of the colonial officer after treatment. (Christy Cunningham-Adams)*

painting's age and the indications of the life it has lived, both of which contribute to the painting's acquired character. The painting's proper place in art history can be confused by the conservator's cosmetically hiding all the signs of age, which help the observer place the painting in time. An old painting is different from a new painting; and although its cracks, losses, faded colors, and other distortions may alter what we may consider the artist's intent, they are as much a part of the painting as are wrinkles in an aged face.

With this philosophy and an awareness of the Warner House murals' considerable age, difficult life, and unusual technique, spirit, and iconography, we concentrated on recovering balance in color value and composition. Imbalances in the compositions and disunity between the murals were primarily a result of the disruption of the value caused by color losses. The uneven state of conservation throughout the group of murals added to the imbalance. Our objective, then, was to reestablish the values of color—and therefore proper relationships—in each composition without replicating all lost color.

Where losses were filled, original colors were matched by in-painting the gesso and rabbitskin fills. The majority of losses (approximately two-thirds), however, were left unfilled and toned with a neutral color to match the value of the original color. By retouching the off-white of the exposed preparation with a neutral color made up of a mixture of raw umber and black, the optical value of the missing color was reestablished and the proper relationships within and between the scenes were recovered. The eagle's great weight and size and the relationship between the eagle and the earth were recovered by darkening the numerous small losses in the figure of the eagle itself and throughout the rolling hills around him. Around the Indians' feet, where the light-colored preparation was predominant, darkening each loss to or slightly below the color value of the surrounding paint helped unify the feet with each other and with the bodies. Recovering the proper weight of the lower half of the two sections with the figures of the Indians helped recover their original relationship to the staircase landing and the surrounding wall.

The excellent condition of the paint in the Indians' faces and the unfortunate prominent large loss in the middle of the face of the Indian on the right persuaded us to fill in that loss and reconstruct the nose **(see figs. 4 and 5)**. This was the only place in the paintings where reconstruction of an unknown detail was done. Creation of an unknown detail without a guide, such as a photograph of the original before it was damaged, is not generally advisable because it does not represent the artist's work. However, the high visibility of this important focal point in the murals recommended compensation for the pictorial void as the best course. In recreating the nose to guarantee its detectability from a close range I used the Italian technique *trateggio*, a method of reconstructing detail with a series of vertical lines, or hatching, that does not resemble brush strokes but blends in from a distance of approximately five feet.

SURFACE PROTECTION

A thin, protective layer of an acrylic solution varnish in a mineral spirit base was sprayed on all surfaces to integrate the retouching and isolate the surfaces from deteriorating factors in the environment. A matte varnish was chosen to best simulate the natural reflective quality of the wall paintings, given their age. Light, pollution, and humidity are all buffered slightly by the surface protection. Future removal of dust and other accumulated surface dirt is greatly facilitated by the presence of such a surface layer, and the layer can be removed and replaced without disturbing other conservation materials present because it is soluble in naptha. Like all materials used in the treatment, however, the varnish is stable and should not require attention for at least one hundred years.

ART HISTORY CONSIDERATIONS

The conservation treatment carried out at the Warner House has given us a series of paintings exciting to look at because of their bold technique, bright colors, and exotic iconography. In addition, the treatment revealed surprising historical aspects, including the unexpected whimsical and dramatic spirit with which they were painted, the single authorship of the group of paintings, and the implicit indication that similar paintings existed in colonial America.

The murals' unexpected boldness and fluidity reflect a taste for sophisticated decorative drama associated with contemporary European tendencies but not so readily associated with colonial American art. This discovery illuminates significant indications about colonial artistic and social attitudes concerning the natural connection between the contemporary European culture and the colonists. The contemporary European taste for stage sets and masquerade is reflected in the theatrical positioning of the exotic Indians at center stage under lifted curtains, the bold presence of Abraham and the colonial officer pulling the observer up the staircase, and the sense of active participation in the drama that the observer feels when surveying the scenes from the second floor at the railing. Together, the whole group strongly reflects a local taste for drama and an inspiring backdrop for daily life and entertaining.

The consistency of spirit, skill, and especially technique, despite the diversity of subject matter, clearly indicates that the murals were all painted by the same person. Now that the original brushwork can be seen and all can be attributed to a single hand, the former impression that the work was done by several artists was evidently based on the diversity of subject matter. The subject selection was most likely determined by the homeowner who commissioned the work, however, and reflects a variety of images popular and available at the time. Each of the scenes may, in fact, have been adopted for the wall decoration from other sources. We know that the Indians were copied from well-known mezzotints and that the popular scene of the sacrifice of Isaac was almost a requisite image in the home at the time. Both the colonial officer and the farm woman spinning may also have been inspired by other contemporary illustrations.

The artist's sense of design, flowing composition, fluid brushwork, and ease in working in large scale with a light hand further inspire us to imagine that he or she painted large-scale paintings frequently and with confidence. The technique was clearly well tested and sound. The painting is simple but effective, and the drama of each scene is well expressed. The compositions fill the wall spaces well and relate to one another. The proportions of the figures and all details are successful in relation to the overall composition and the architectural elements of the house. All these aspects suggest that the artist was accustomed to painting on walls.

Furthermore, Captain Macpheadris had the house built and decorated to support his success and rising social position, and it is reasonable to assume that he would demonstrate his social acceptability by having his elegant house decorated in the most acceptable fashion and taste. The implication is surprising: this group of wall paintings was clearly not an isolated phenomenon but must have already had some precedents. We can therefore conclude that there must have been other similarly stylish wall paintings decorating the fashionable houses of the day and possibly painted by the same artist whose work can now be enjoyed at the Warner House.

A Victorian Trompe l'Oeil

THE RESTORATION OF DISTEMPER PAINTS

MORGAN W. PHILLIPS

Tradition has it that the First Unitarian Church in Hampton Falls, New Hampshire, was built in 1838, although the present Victorian scheme of trompe l'oeil architectural features dates possibly from the 1850s. Everything that appears as a molding, panel, or projecting plaster medallion or window casing is entirely illusionistic; all are painted on perfectly flat plaster. The work is laid over a plain, bright yellow wall paint and a white ceiling paint, both water soluble and probably original. The two surviving trompe l'oeil medallions at the center of the ceiling and in the rear apse are painted with supreme skill (fig. 1), and even the plain moldings and panels, consisting of simple lines, are the work of a hand that moved with great ease, showing years of facility with a medium that can be temperamental in handling.

Painted with glue distemper paints (also known as calcimines), the trompe l'oeil work has been conserved and partially replicated. The investigation, test treatments, and actual treatment took place during the period 1984–87. The major phase of treatment, in summer 1987, was carried out by the firm of Biltmore, Campbell, Smith Restorations. Conservation decisions were primarily mine, although some were advantageously modified during 1987 by the firm's painting conservator, Tom Rut. Steven Weems was the firm's decorative painter.

The result of the work was a great improvement in the condition and appearance of the paintings. Moreover, some lessons were learned about the restoration of decorative schemes in distemper paints, which are bound by animal glue. The project also served to focus some problems requiring further study and treatments requiring testing in the conservation of distempers.

This chapter summarizes information gleaned from readings and discussions with thirty-six conservators and several decorative painters, including one who had made glue distempers in the early years of his career. Some of the conservators were painting conservators who had worked on distemper paintings on canvas. Some were paper conservators experienced in treating wallpapers (and thus distemper paints). Others were object conservators who had treated items of all ages that had been decorated with distempers or similar powdery matte paints. One or two conservators had experience with large decorative schemes in distempers directly on the woodwork or plaster of buildings.

Figure 1. *Rear wall and portion of ceiling, First Unitarian Church, Hampton Falls, N. H., after conservation. The central medallion and all the panels and moldings of the ceiling and walls are illusionistic. (Morgan W. Phillips)*

Thus, besides being a project from which much was learned, Hampton Falls has led to further inquiry. Without claiming to have done an exhaustive literature search or conducted a broad survey of practitioners, I can outline a wide variety of treatments that various conservators have favored (strongly or hesitantly) for the problems that typically affect distempers. Some conservators expressed doubt that thoroughly satisfactory solutions exist for certain problems.

A point emerging clearly from these readings and inquiries is that preferences for various treatments of glue distempers vary widely among conservators. Some disparities of opinion are surely due to differing conditions found on the variety of artworks on which conservators had worked. The Hampton Falls church, for example, presented its own special problems. If all the conservators who were consulted had been gathered in the Hampton Falls church, there might have been more unanimity of opinion on suitable treatments in this case. But it is clear that there still would have been major differences. Some conservators have made certain materials work for them that other conservators have found unsatisfactory, even when the problems—flaking paint on early wallpapers, for example—have probably been similar. There must be differences between the techniques (or habits) of different conservators, as well as differences between the exact types of similar materials used, that account for varying experiences and preferences. Although no one treatment will work in every case, it would seem that someday a smaller number of treatments should emerge as generally preferable for each of the conditions commonly encountered.

GLUE DISTEMPER PAINTS

The term *distemper* is imprecise unless the type of distemper is specified. Although in American house painting *distemper* has tended to be restricted in meaning to glue distempers, in England the term has been applied broadly to many other types of water-based paints, including those bound by casein.[1] Here *distemper* will be understood to mean glue distemper. (The chapter "A Survey of Paint Technology" in this volume contains a summary description of the composition and properties of such paints and of animal glue.)

The term *calcimine* also requires clarification. As indicated clearly in nineteenth-century painters' guides, its oldest—and perhaps most proper—meaning is commercially prepared glue distemper paint. Mainly in this century, however, this term has referred to both glue distemper paints and paints containing casein as all or part of the binder.[2, 3]

Similar semantic confusion surrounds the term *tempera*. Like the term *distemper, tempera* has both a narrower and a broader meaning. Its narrower meaning is paint bound by a medium prepared from the yolk or white of egg (or both), which is properly called "egg tempera." However, it has been applied broadly to many kinds of water-based paint, including glue distemper.

Animal glue has been known as an adhesive and paint binder since the time of the ancient Egyptians.[4] It was an important paint binder in Japanese art as early as the eighth century.[5] In medieval Europe it was used as a paint binder for manuscripts and even for murals.[6, 7] In the late sixteenth and early seventeenth centuries, most interior decorative painting in Scotland was carried out in glue distemper.[8, 9] With chalk or gypsum as filler, glue has been used for centuries in making painted ground layers (gesso) for gilding or painting.

As a paint for general-purpose interior work in buildings, glue distemper can be documented in England to at least 1603, when aspects of its use were regulated by an act of Parliament.[10] Recent analyses of interior woodwork paint of the late seventeenth century or around 1700 in the Gedney House in Salem, Massachusetts, have produced physical proof of the first-period American use of glue distemper house paints (see Abbott Lowell Cummings and Richard M. Candee, "Colonial and Federal America: Accounts of Early Painting Practices," in this volume). Glue distemper has been described as a paint for building interiors in English publications since at least 1725, and recipes are found in the works of many well-known eighteenth- and early nineteenth-century writers.[11] Nineteenth- and twentieth-century references to glue distempers, both recipes for the painter to follow and descriptions of the increasingly common prepared calcimines, are numerous, and a large number of the actual films survive, at least in fragmentary form. Glue distempers and, to a lesser extent, gouaches were the most common colorants for wallpapers during the eighteenth and nineteenth centuries.[12, 13]

Although widely used on woodwork before about 1720, distempers and other water-based paints, such as whitewashes, soon gave way to oil paints for durable painting on interior woodwork. With their high content of resilient binder, oil paints simply adhere much better to woodwork than do the water-based paints widely available in early America. The need for good adhesion on wood is especially important in view of the fact that woodwork, more than plaster, is what takes a beating in buildings: doors are slammed; wainscoting is bumped by furniture. Also, woodwork expands and contracts more than plaster in response to changing levels of temperature and relative humidity. Therefore, since the early eighteenth century glue distempers have been used mainly either on wallpapers or directly on plaster walls and ceilings. An important exception is their use in the graining of woodwork, as noted, for example, in the publications of T. H. Vanherman (1829), Anson Gilman (1871), and William E. Wall.[14, 15, 16] It is clear from such books that the sort of distemper used for graining was quite different from the typical opaque coatings with which this chapter is concerned. Glue-bound paints used in graining were only slightly pigmented and thus, although tinted, translucent if not transparent. The high content of glue in relation to pigment must have rendered the films far more adhesive and tougher than typical highly pigmented (and porous) opaque distemper paints.

With respect to ordinary opaque distempers, one can cite two traditions in their use as paints for plaster: plain and decorative. Cummings has shown that decorative painting was popular in even the earliest New England buildings.[17] However, this early work was simple and usually crude in comparison with the lush, sophisticated decorative painting of the Victorian age. Splendid examples of this later work, apparently in distemper and in oil, survive on walls and ceilings of the Victoria Mansion (Morse-Libby House) in Portland, Maine.[18] The much simpler decorative painting of the First Unitarian Church at Hampton Falls is in this Victorian tradition. Inexpensive, fast drying, and thus convenient to apply in multilayered schemes, capable of hiding well in one coat, and (to judge by the quality of surviving old artwork) easily handled by those who had learned the paints' sometimes temperamental behavior, distempers provided a relatively expedient way to achieve opulent effects of line and color and of trompe l'oeil architecture. Although often presenting conservation problems today, these decorative treatments were entirely permanent from the building owner's point of view. Decorative treatments in distemper and in oil were called frescoes in Victorian literature and documents, although true fresco (pigments worked into wet plaster) was virtually unknown in America.

Plain-colored distempers for walls and ceilings were common in the eighteenth century and continued to be applied through the nineteenth century and the first half of the twentieth century, long after the taste and the money for decorative painting had diminished. Besides the extensive literature of all periods referring to glue distempers, or calcimines, the unbroken record of physical evidence of the paints survives. In the Gardner-Pingree House (1804) in Salem, Massachusetts (McIntyre-designed elegance at its best), original or very early distempers in bright green and peach were found on the walls of the stair hall and double parlors, respectively, and in the parlors a bright yellow soon followed.[19] At the Hampton Falls church can be found another plain, bright yellow wall color in distemper and a white ceiling paint that predate the present Victorian "frescoes."

The long history of plain-colored distempers, especially white or off-white ceiling paints, extends to the personal experience of many of us. Prepared calcimines bound solely by animal glue were made in America until as recently as about 1985, and indeed some little-known brands may still be in production for specialized uses. They were popular for ceilings because of their low cost, speed of application, and good hiding power. Also, they could be washed off before repainting, restoring a perfect plaster surface free of the peeling and permanent filling of molded details associated with the use of oil paints. Unfortunately, instead of being washed off, calcimines have often wrongly been recoated with oil or latex paints, the result being a strong-over-weak situation that produces severe peeling. It is only through this improper overcoating that glue-bound calcimines have earned a bad name.

The fact that distempers are meant to be washed off before recoating or papering makes it quite a task to find samples that have escaped this and especially to date those samples (see "A Survey of Paint Technology). A factor that greatly complicates our interpretation of stratigraphic evidence is that two traditions exist for interposing distemper paints and oils in one paint job. An inexpensive type of eighteenth-century paint application in England and perhaps America consisted of a layer of oil paint over a layer of distemper.[20] Sometimes distemper was used first as a temporary layer while the plaster dried and cured, the oil coat following perhaps a year later.[21] Conversely, oil primers for distempers were common practice in fine work of both early and late periods.[22, 23]

CONDITIONS AND TREATMENTS AT HAMPTON FALLS

Battered through the years by roof leaks and other sources of damage, the decorative paints at the Hampton Falls church had repeatedly been touched up. Many broad field areas (flat areas of panels, stiles, and rails in the trompe l'oeil design) had been overpainted in oil one or more times and badly matched to the original. In 1951 Allyn Cox, a prolific restorer of wall paintings, repainted some of the fields and details in a water-soluble medium, not copying very well the technique or capturing the feeling of the original. Although Cox entirely repainted the front apse, which has always been subject to the worst roof leaks, he did not touch the fine medallions of the ceiling or rear apse. Finally, probably in the 1960s, some of the fields were again repainted in oil or latex. This last paint was badly matched and on the ceiling was peeling extensively. Besides the two medallions, one wall panel had entirely escaped any retouching. In some of these repaintings, shellac or some other penetrating consolidant had been used to convert weak, water-soluble old paint into a firmer although utterly discolored base for new paint.

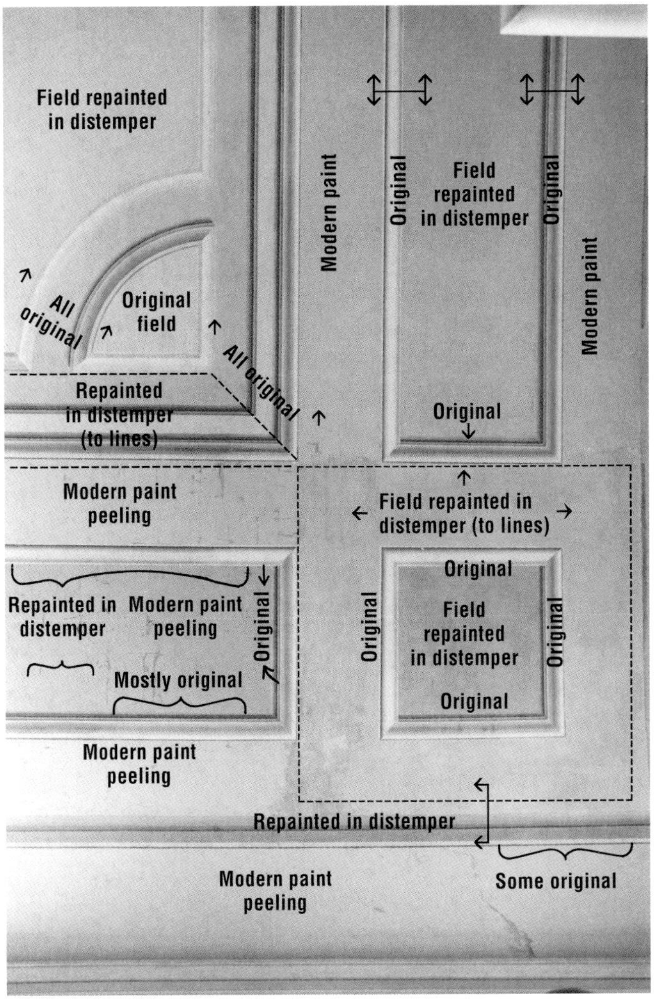

DOCUMENTATION

Original and later paints as well as paint and plaster conditions were recorded in detail on drawings and marked photographs (fig. 2). I prepared a report of conditions and recommendations and provided specifications outlining the steps to be taken in conserving or renewing the work, according to the varying antiquity and condition of the existing paint. The binder, in several representative paints of the decorative scheme, has been identified as animal glue by means of fluorescence staining with a confirmation check using ninhydrin.[24]

PLASTER

Loose areas of ceiling plaster were adhered to the lath using acrylic emulsions.[25] A few small loose areas of wall plaster were adhered with poly(vinyl acetate) emulsion (PVA). The largest plaster cracks were filled with new gypsum plaster bonded to the lath with a conventional PVA emulsion bonding agent, and smaller but still objectionable cracks were filled with a water-based synthetic resin joint compound. Fortunately, the plaster was not internally crumbly and thus did not require consolidation.

Figure 2. *One of six marked photographs of the ceiling before treatment, indicating original paint, later paint, and conditions. (Morgan W. Phillips)*

ENVIRONMENTAL CONDITIONS

The church is a small wooden structure lacking any form of heat or environmental control. It is five miles from the Atlantic Ocean and sits on granite blocks over a low but dry crawl space. Besides repairing one or two roof leaks and opening a few chinks in the foundation to ensure air flow beneath the church, no environmental controls could be afforded.

Many areas had flaked where the paint had been built up thickly. The paint is bound by a hygroscopic material (glue) that expands and contracts in response to changes in humidity.[26] Thus, it is a safe assumption that wide variations in relative humidity, especially the high levels that must occur at some times, have exacerbated the flaking and deterioration of the early paint. Wary of the cost and operating problems of full-fledged environmental control systems in old buildings not constructed with such systems in mind and not closely monitored, I suggested that some simpler system of dehumidification—slight heating in damp, cool weather and ventilation under certain circumstances—would at least remove the worst peaks and valleys from the relative humidity curve. However, both the costs of equipment and energy and the lack of simplified systems of proven design prevented taking even these measures. One element that should be developed for such situations is a small device to control a forced-air ventilator in response to weather conditions: either steady ventilation or the steady lack thereof can lead to condensation, depending on weather changes. Thus, the environment remains uncontrolled. However, recent important advances have been made in designing limited, cost-effective environmental control systems that would have been appropriate at Hampton Falls.[27]

FUNGICIDAL PROTECTION

Although mildew was not a severe problem in the case of the original paints, Allyn Cox's water-soluble paints were heavily mildewed, mainly in the perennially leaking front apse. Mildew protection seemed like a good idea even though Cox's paint in the apse was to be removed entirely. A computerized search of the conservation literature was generously performed by the Conservation Analytical Laboratory of the Smithsonian Institution but failed to turn up clear evidence that any fungicide would meet the following four criteria: effectiveness against a broad range of fungi under adverse circumstances; long-lasting residual effect; acceptably low human toxicity; and absence of any possible color development.

Recently Frank Preusser has told me of his long-term excellent results protecting glue-based paints with copper sulfate. In very dilute solutions it meets all four criteria, including freedom from any visible color.[28] This clearly appears to be the answer to this problem.

Producers of fungicides were contacted, some of whom suggested much newer materials than those cited in the conservation literature search. However, these materials have not been tested as long-term conservation materials. No guarantee could be given against long-term failure, such as the possible deactivation of quaternary ammonium salt fungicides by the protein binder of the paint. Some crude tests revealed a risk of color development with some materials. Thus, although orthophenylphenol is eventually lost to the air through sublimation, a solution of this widely used material seemed like the safest choice for those few areas where a fungicide appeared needed.[29] Fungi have not returned in the six years since the work was done.

For new distemper paint to be applied, zinc oxide, a safe fungistat, was considered as the white pigment. This pigment sometimes was used historically instead of whiting (calcium carbonate) in fine-quality distemper work.[30, 31] Because of possible unforeseen problems and because it would do nothing to protect the old paint, it was not used.

CLEANING

The church had not been heated often, so the walls and ceiling were not too heavily soiled with dirt or smoke. (Heating, besides often supplying soot, drives dirt onto the colder wall and ceiling surfaces through the phenomenon of "pattern staining."[32])

The materials tested for removal of dirt represent a fair sampling of those that appear in conservation literature or were much the same as those suggested (after the project) by conservators.

All were dry materials. While the literature mentions organic solvents in the successful cleaning of distempers, as well as water, steam, and solutions of ammonia and ammonium carbonate, only the more popular dry methods were attempted.[33] These included various erasers, eraser powder used by drafters, slightly moist wallpaper cleaners, and various fine abrasive powders dusted on and off again with a soft squirrel-hair brush. Laboratory-grade finely powdered gum arabic worked better than other powders, matched only by a powdered Union Carbide water-soluble resin, Polyox® WSR 205, a nontoxic poly(ethylene oxide). A follow-up with Talas's kneadable "molecular trap" rolled over the surface produced decent results. The powdered resin and "molecular trap" were used for part of the work until Constance Silver made us a gift of the German "Wishab" sponge sold by Talas. This sponge, which was rubbed dry over the paint, was by far the most effective and least damaging cleaning material and was used for the remainder of the work.

No doubt some minute amount of the weak paint was removed in cleaning; perhaps this is a more common occurrence in many kinds of paint cleaning than conservators like to think. Dirt was removed only to the point where paint removal began to be observable.

REMOVAL OF OVERPAINT

Funds did not permit the painstaking work of removing later paints down to the distemper. Later paints, if mechanically sound, were left in place and either overpainted again or, if acceptable in appearance, allowed to show. Where multiple layers of repaints on the field areas had produced peeling, all the layers were stripped down to bare plaster, which was then smoothed with joint compound troweled on and off so as to just fill the low spots between projecting sand grains in the rough plaster. Bare plaster was sized with a dilute shellac solution, an effective and historic method.

The removal of overpaints from distempers recalls a personal experience of several years earlier in a church where the distemper scheme of the 1840s had first been fully overpainted in distemper (quite different in color and design) and then, over a period of years, three times in oil. Ordinary paint stripper (methylene chloride/methanol/toluol) readily removed the oils and revealed the upper distemper in a stained but readable state suitable for guiding a recreation. Nothing was found, however, that would remove the upper distemper from the lower except a slightly moist aqueous gel gently rolled over the surface. This procedure was so slow that it was impractical for the large areas that needed to be exposed. Several conservators were unable to suggest better methods. Infrared scanning might have produced the desired information, but there was no more time for study. Sometimes, an unwanted upper layer of distemper may be more water soluble than the desired layer beneath.

CONSOLIDATION AND READHESION OF PAINT

Before, during, and since the project the greatest amount of reading, inquiry, and testing was directed toward the problems of consolidating powdery paint and readhering flaking paint (**figs. 3 and 4**). The two problems are considered together because in the case of a building interior they may have to be solved simultaneously by one treatment.

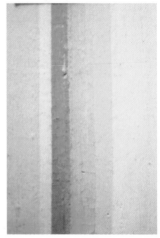

Figure 3. *A particularly badly peeling area of wall panel "molding" before treatment. (Morgan W. Phillips)*

Figure 4. *An area of flaking paint after treatment with Acryloid® B-72. Flakes are somewhat flattened but not strongly adhered. (Morgan W. Phillips)*

In many situations, as when trying to remove overpaints, the architectural conservator usually must work within a maximum per-square-foot cost that is low in comparison with a museum conservator's treatment of, say, illuminated manuscripts. Thus, introducing adhesive individually behind each flake of loose paint, using a syringe or tiny brush, is usually not an option. If a flaking distemper must be laid down, economics generally will dictate that the adhesive be broadly applied to the paint surface and pass through the pores in the paint as well as behind open edges. Such an adhesive will automatically function as a consolidant for powdery paint. The great problem is how to introduce enough adhesive in this broad-brushed manner to bond loose flakes without excessively filling the open pores on which distemper paints depend for opacity and color. Filling pores leads to drastic darkening and the loss of opacity (see "A Survey of Paint Technology"). Feller and Kunz have explained the nature of the darkening effect often observed in consolidating porous paints.[34]

Where paint is not flaking but only powdering, our experience at Hampton Falls taught us how much more easily the powdering problem can be solved. Only a small amount of binder need be added, not enough to alter the optics of the film.

The list of materials cited in the literature and mentioned by conservators for consolidating and setting down distempers and similar porous paints is long, and consensus has not been reached. The following list is arranged roughly in order from the most traditional to the most nontraditional.[35]

WATER

Applied warm or cold. Relaxes curled flakes of paint containing water-soluble binders so that they can be pushed flat. May reform microscopically fractured original glue binder in distemper paint to consolidate and readhere without adding any new pore-filling material.

GELATIN

A purified form of animal glue. Also parchment size and sturgeon glue, particularly pure and strong animal glues. These are customarily applied as dilute, well-warmed aqueous solutions. Gelatin has been used with lasting success by some conservators, including in architectural situations where environmental controls are lacking. In other cases, gelatin has been found to fail after time. It is advantageous, as an aqueous solution, in relaxing and perhaps reforming the original glue. It is a powerful binder and can be effective in low proportions (2 or 3 percent solutions). It is disadvantageous in that it increases the glue content in the paint, which has long been known to increase the risk of flaking through cyclical dimensional change with changing humidity. It is subject to biological attack.

STARCHES

Carbohydrates extracted from corn, wheat, and other plants. Applied as aqueous solutions. Starches were not encountered in other references (see note 35).

VEGETABLE GUMS, SUCH AS GUM ARABIC

Polysaccharides, of plant origin. Applied as aqueous solutions. These are useful in relaxing and perhaps reforming the original glue; they deserve more study. Probably, being weaker than gelatin, they are required in larger (more pore-filling) proportions.

CELLULOSE ETHERS

A family of polymers, which are derivatives of cellulose, in which the hydroxyl groups have been converted to ether groups. Include methyl cellulose, hydroxypropyl cellulose. Applied as aqueous solutions; some are used in solution in alcohol or in alcohol/water mixtures. As aqueous solutions, cellulose ethers may serve to relax and perhaps reform the original glue in the paint. They are believed by some conservators to be too weak to secure strong curled flakes such as existed at Hampton Falls. Thomas Edmondson of Heugh-Edmondson, Kansas City, Missouri, has permitted me to note that he has achieved consistent success in using a high-molecular weight (thus relatively strong) grade of methyl cellulose to secure loose flakes of glue distemper on wallpapers—a 1 or 2 percent solution applied broadly through the paint. He cites the advantage of freedom from the shrinkage and embrittlement that he has observed when using gelatin. Feller and Wilt have just completed a major study of the stability of various cellulose ethers, through the Getty Conservation Institute. [36]

SOLVENT-SOLUBLE SYNTHETIC RESINS

Synthetic polymers soluble in organic solvents, such as toluene. Applied as a solution in organic solvents. Cellulose acetate, poly(vinyl acetate), poly(vinyl butyral), and acrylic resins are among the solvent-soluble synthetic resins that have been used as consolidants for powdery matte paints and in some cases as adhesives for setting down loose paint flakes on wallpapers. Several advantages are often cited over proteins, starches, and gums. These include comparative freedom from dimensional change under changing conditions of humidity, resistance to biological attack, and, in the case of certain well-tested resins, great chemical stability and resistance to color change. However, some conservators have found that a sufficient quantity of solvent-borne resin to adhere loose flakes often produces unacceptable darkening. Also, because these systems contain no water, they are of little value in softening and setting down curled flakes of paint.

SYNTHETIC RESIN EMULSIONS

Synthetic polymers dispersed as particles in water. Often applied after dilution with water and perhaps the addition of an alcohol or wetting agent. Although the large size of particles in a dispersion might be expected to reduce penetration through a powdery paint, success in setting down loose flakes of distemper with PVA dispersion is reported by Olin and Riddleberger in the treatment of a painting by Vuillard.[37] The water in the dispersion relaxed the flakes. Finer, particle-size colloidal dispersions deserve more study. The high molecular weight of dispersions should permit small amounts to serve effectively as adhesives.

CROSS-LINKING AGENTS

A wide variety of materials capable of reacting with protein molecules to form chemical cross links between them. In widespread use for hardening photographic gelatin emulsions.[38]

Gelatin, the main ingredient of animal glue, contains chemical groups with which various materials can react that will form cross links between the gelatin chains. In this manner great improvements in strength and moisture resistance can be achieved. Two traditional materials used for this purpose, in treating old distempers or making new ones, are formaldehyde and alum. Richard Wolbers is currently studying yet another: dimethyl suberimidate dihydrochloride. Ethyl silicate and organosilanes may function as cross-linking agents for gelatin.

Formaldehyde is a cross-linking agent for gelatin but was shunned because of its toxicity and newly understood damaging effects to various materials.[39] Other cross-linking agents surely merit testing as consolidants for glue distemper paints, but this could not be done within the context of the Hampton Falls project.

ETHYL SILICATE (CONSERVARE® OH)

A compound consisting of a silicon atom bonded, via oxygen atoms, to four ethyl groups. Normally used as a strengthener for deteriorated stone. Applied as a solution in organic solvent; reacts with atmospheric moisture to form essentially a network of silica (SiO_2). Ethyl silicate could strengthen a distemper paint not only through the reinforcing effect of the silica network but also by a chemical reaction that would cross link gelatin molecules.

That the plaster at Hampton Falls was not internally crumbly was fortunate, as an amount of any of these listed consolidants sufficient to strengthen the plaster would almost surely infuse and darken the paint. Constance Silver related to me that she had dealt successfully with this problem in a similar case by applying an ethyl silicate solution through the painted face and into the plaster. The product was the well-known German stone consolidant Conservare® OH. In that the silica network formed by Conservare OH may tend to be deposited in a physically open, light-scattering form, it may have a limited darkening effect even when used in quantity. Silver was able first to compact a powdery paint layer by moistening it with vapor and pressing through Japanese paper. The water having dried out, she applied the solvent-borne consolidant. Her success raises the possibility of using fully organic resins that through skillful formulation of solvent systems are deposited in a light-scattering form.

Organosilanes, closely related to ethyl silicate, have been investigated for use as consolidants for flaking photographic gelatin emulsions on historic glass-plate negatives.[40]

Two types of consolidant were used at Hampton Falls, and some details of our experiences are worth reporting. In an early test area—the tops of two panels on the rear wall of the church **(see fig. 1, left)**— we applied a 4 percent solution of Silver Label gelatin, a brand sold to gilders and known to have respectable adhesive strength. The solution was kept well warmed (to lower its viscosity) and copiously brushed on. First, with the use of a soft, squirrel-hair brush, it was flooded directly into the spaces behind the most prominently protruding curled flakes. Then 24-by-36-inch sheets of a long-fiber tea-bag-like Aldine® brand paper (Aldine AE 204) were placed against the wall and the solution brushed liberally onto the whole surface. The paper prevented the partially dissolved paints from being smudged by the action of the brush. The paper was then peeled away and excess solution mopped off with the same paper.

An observation well worth reporting was the vast improvement in speed and depth of penetration when a potent wetting agent was used in the solution: Fluorad® FC-120, a fluorocarbon[41] from 3M. Following the manufacturer's product literature, the material was diluted to a 1 percent aqueous solution, and on the verbal recommendation of a technical representative, 1 milliliter of that 1 percent solution was used for each liter of the total formulation. (This was the starting formulation suggested for nonpigmented systems.) At this level, a hundred-thousandth of the whole formulation, the product caused the gelatin solution to race into the old paint and plaster.

While wetted, the curled flakes were easily pushed flat by pressing against the Aldine paper. The paper could be peeled away without transfer of pigment from the paint. Several weeks later I tested the dried product. Darkening of the paints had been slight. The surface of the paint was no longer powdery. Formerly loose flakes, which included the earlier yellow layer, were strongly adhered and could be pried off with a knife point only with some effort.

Unfortunately, when the main part of the project was to be done two years later, the very flakes that had been well secured by the gelatin were beginning to loosen again. Perhaps in drying gelatin had migrated toward the face of the paint, making the surface too strong in relation to the rearward part in contact with the plaster. If this did occur, it might have been avoided by covering the face to force drying to occur through the back side of the plaster. In addition, to get really good bonding behind thick, curled flakes, the strongest gelatin solution that would not discolor the paint noticeably was used. I resolved that if I continued to use gelatin, I would use perhaps 2 rather than 4 percent and mop it off the surface with something more absorbent than Aldine paper, such as Bounty paper towels.

In any event, we faced the onset of the main body of work with no proven adhesive system. Tom Rut proved to me that a 4 percent solution of Rohm and Haas Acryloid® B-72 in toluene, expertly sprayed onto the paint surface, consolidated the powdery paint surface well with no darkening (fig. 5). Although loose flakes were not strongly readhered in this way, wetting with the B-72 solution did have a slight softening effect on the flakes, and through the use of soft rubber rollers (brayers) the flakes could be pushed back into a much flatter position and seemed more secure after treatment (see figs. 3 and 4). This was the method used for the bulk of the work. Fortunately, flaking of original paint was confined to areas of illusionistic wall moldings, which can be easily reached again for further treatment. The ceiling did not suffer from flaking. There has been no loss of paint in the six years since the work was done.

Readings and discussions have raised the point several times that a resin dissolved in organic solvent will not fully relax or at all reform original glue present in a distemper paint and that a two-stage treatment could be used to advantage. First, water or a greatly diluted aqueous consolidant could be applied to relax loose flakes and allow them to be pushed back into contact with the substrate. This having dried, a solvent-borne resin then could be applied through the paint and into the substrate.

Figure 5. *Central trompe l'oeil "medallion" of ceiling. The paint of the medallion is original, treated with Acryloid® B-72. The surrounding field is repainted in distemper made by the traditional wet-mix method. (Morgan W. Phillips)*

Another matter relevant to treatment with Acryloid® B-72 is worth mentioning. In an important study in 1980, Elizabeth Welsh found that the use of diethylbenzene as a solvent for Acryloid® B-72 gave better results in consolidating powdery matte paint than did toluene, xylene, or acetone.[42] The diethylbenzene she used was made by the Dow Chemical Company.[43] Since then B-72 in diethylbenzene, generally the Dow product, has been used with varying degrees of success by different conservators. A major objection by some is the pungent odor. Eastman supplies diethylbenzene having much less odor, but it may consist of a different mixture of isomers and may not perform as well. Rut had success with B-72 in toluene and preferred not to use diethylbenzene.

In conjunction with the problem of consolidating powdery paints, the Getty Conservation Institute is studying the differences in the final (long-term) properties of synthetic resins deposited from different solvents.[44]

IN-PAINTING AND REPAINTING

When in-painting areas where paint has been lost, an established practice in museum conservation is to use paint that is chemically different from the original so that solvents can be used to remove it in the future without damage to the original paint. In architectural conservation this is not always possible at the present state of the art. Sometimes readily reversible paint would not meet the other criteria: smooth leveling over large areas, easy handling for striping and other decorative work, durability, and appearance acceptably matching the original. New reversible in-painting media for architectural work should be designed and tested. If reversible paints are not available, architectural in-painting should be confined as much as possible to areas of loss or areas that can be sacrificed (such as those that have already been overpainted).

To match the handling and distinctive soft appearance of the original glue distemper and partly for the instructive experience of using the historic material, I chose glue distemper itself for in-painting and for repainting the already repainted plain fields. Another major reason for choosing distemper was its weakness: it would not pull off underlying weak distempers at the inevitable overlaps. Where applied over old distemper that had been rendered somewhat water resistant by treatment with a hydrophobic resin, new distempers may be selectively removable with water.

What we learned about making glue distempers applies as much to complete replication of plain or decorative distempers as to in-painting or partial repainting. An important reason for making our own paint was that the ingredients would all be known and thus their properties and chemical stability predictable. For this reason various proprietary "temperas" used for stage scenery and like purposes were rejected. Recently, one painter has reported great satisfaction in using a casein paint to replicate distemper.[45]

MAKING THE NEW DISTEMPER PAINT

Two alternative methods were used in making the new distemper paint: the historic method and one of my own invention. Before describing these methods, it is important to note several general points observed in testing ingredients for the paint.

First, a good strong grade of glue must be used. A weak glue will not provide adequate binding of the pigment unless it is used in excessively high proportion in relation to water and pigment, which makes the paint gooey and hard to handle. Old manuals note that the least amount of glue that will bind the paint well should be used, as excessive glue leads to a risk of flaking. After some bad experiences with inferior glue, I successfully used the product C. M. Bond granular hide glue. It is said that good animal glue is almost impossible to find today and that formerly satisfactory brands may suddenly decline in quality.

Second, different pigments vary widely (by a factor of at least 400 percent) in the amount of glue needed to bind them. This, too, is noted in old painters' guides. (The fact that various pigments require differing quantities of any given binder, such as linseed oil, is well known.)

Third, the type of whiting (calcium carbonate) used is critical in making a paint that is not gooey. Old manuals merely specify "Paris white," "best quality bolted whiting," "extra gilder's" or "xxxx gilder's" whiting, or use some other term that refers to a commonly available good product. Bolted whiting was whiting that had been sifted through a fine silk bolting cloth.[46] Today a multitude of types of calcium carbonate are available, many of them not crushed limestone but precipitated synthetics. Particle size varies widely, which is probably a key factor. I tried a number of whitings unsuccessfully until I obtained a smooth-working paint using the gilder's whiting, B720–16005. Because gilders must have smooth-working, well-bound distempers (gesso) for their grounds, their suppliers might be expected to have suitable materials. James Bernstein recently reported that kaolin (a type of clay) in a proportion of about 5 percent of pigment content greatly enhances the working smoothness of distempers, and a recently made commercial calcimine contained clay (the Muralo Company, Bayonne, New Jersey, informed me in 1985 that its product Dutch Kalsomine consisted of chalk, clay, and "red stripe" animal glue plus modifiers).

As for the two methods used to make the paint, most of the paint was prepared following traditional instructions, which have remained essentially the same since eighteenth-century publications. Granular glue is soaked overnight in cold water to soften it and then heated the next day to make a thick syrup. Meanwhile, the whiting is separately soaked in water to become more or less well dispersed; colored pigments may either be soaked or ground in water or ground in a dilute glue solution, according to the source consulted. No doubt the particular pigment's ease of wetting affects the choice of method. Straining to remove undispersed agglomerates of pigment may be required.

The glue is diluted with hot water. To make paint of a certain color, pigments are then mixed by pouring off excess water from the now settled pigment-water slurries and combining them, sometimes before adding the glue. Samples are painted out and dried, usually with mild heat, to test for color. Glue is used in just sufficient amount to provide firm binding of dried test samples—an amount dependent on the combined total of the varying glue requirements of the different-colored pigments forming the paint.

Today many brands of dispersions of colored pigments in water are available; these are purchased by manufacturers of emulsion paints and could easily be mixed into distempers. The pigment composition is stated, and dispersions of lightfast pigments are widely available.

Rut and Weems, once shown the historic method, readily learned to make smooth, well-bound paint that matched the original colors well. Although traditional good practice has been to strain the paint, this was not done: the slight imperfection of dispersion of the pigments produced just enough unevenness of color to replicate the appearance of the surviving original paints, which had not been possible to clean back to the rather uniform colors that they would have had when first applied. Whereas the recently repainted fields, because they were too uniform, had stood out sorely, the new distempers blended perfectly. The paint was easy to handle when slightly warm; published sources recommend different application temperatures. Although well matched, the new is distinguishable from the old on close inspection.

I designed an alternative method of making the paints that circumvents several problems of the historic process. This method was successfully used to in-paint and partially repaint two panels in 1985, the same two on the tops of which I had used gelatin as a consolidant. The method was a variant on that often used in painting theater scenery, in which colorants are mixed and stored dry and diluted glue ("size water") is added just before use.

This method has at least two advantages. First, large batches of each color of paint could be made and stored indefinitely. (I have found that paint made up of several pigments in water—even without the size, which spoils after a day—changed in color after a few days.) Extended shelf life could prove an advantage when sections of a space are restored bit by bit and the same color is needed repeatedly on different days. It also meant that large containers of each paint in dry form could be kept indefinitely for touching up where future roof leaks might occur.

Besides storage, a second advantage is that the system was designed to substitute measurement for estimation in the addition of the glue—now and at any future time. This is made clear in the description given here.

The traditional objection to the dry-mixing method of white and colored pigments is that a good dispersion, and thus color uniformity and freedom from streaks, could not be obtained. This problem was circumvented by mixing each colored pigment with an equal volume of white and running the mixture in a small ball mill (a rotating canister charged with tumbling steel balls and the materials to be broken up and mixed together, in this case two pigments). Thus, "dry color concentrates" were obtained in which agglomerates (clumps) of colored particles had been broken down and mingled with white. With patience these would stir evenly together into large dry batches of final paint, using a mixing blade in a high-speed electric drill. The color was adjusted by removing small samples, mixing them with a dilute glue solution, and drying.

Once each dry-pigment batch was mixed, it was necessary only to determine the glue content required for its proper binding. Diluted glue solutions ("size waters") of known glue concentration were made up as shown in table 1. (The numerical system given is a small refinement on that actually used, which was based on a 32 percent stock solution.) Using the particular brand of glue noted, which had a certain density, particle size and shape, a stock solution of about 24 percent (weight) could be made up by adding three-parts-by volume glue to seven parts cold water. These are measured separately, as together the volume total does not equal 10. For each different brand and batch of glue, the volume-mixing ratio to achieve roughly a 24 percent solution (24 grams glue, 76 grams water) must be determined experimentally.

The 24 percent "stock" is soaked overnight, heated, and then diluted with hot water, by volume (table 1), to achieve any of the stated approximate solution strengths of glue size. It was determined experimentally which "strength" of size water worked best when added, to achieve brushing consistency, to each dry paint. The gray background colors worked best when mixed with 3 percent size. The pure white highlights needed only 2 percent size. Darker colors required 4 or 6 percent. Each dry-mixed paint was labeled with the "strength" of size it required. For future retouches, recalibration might be needed if stronger or weaker brands of glue are used.

The dry-mix system, using ball-milled pigment concentrates and patient power mixing of the dry colors, provided repeatable and highly uniform paints with no need for straining. However, considerable work in milling and mixing was needed. Given the choice of both systems and trying both at their shop, Rut and Weems preferred the historic method. To me, the dry-mix method retains the important appeal that exactly the right colorant mixture can be stored indefinitely. It will work conveniently, however, only if hydrophilic (readily wetted) pigments are used. Thus, for both the dry- and wet-mix methods, I used carbon black made by burning bones ("bone black"), rather than the more greasy and hydrophobic lampblack, made from oil. Carbon black made by burning plant material would also have worked. All three types are well precedented historically.[47] Fortunately, the other pigments needed (whiting, natural iron oxides) are all easily wetted by water. I have not yet had to select or learn to pretreat for easy wetting color-stable, high-chroma modern pigments for the dry-mix method, although I am confident that it could be done. An advantage of the wet-mix method, as stated earlier, is the availability of a wide range of quality pigments stably dispersed in water by means of chemical dispersing aids and mechanical milling equipment.

The project at the First Unitarian Church in Hampton Falls resulted in a great improvement in the stability and appearance of the painted decorations. Some useful techniques were developed, and we learned a great deal about making and applying distemper paint. The problems of conserving distempers were clarified and led to further inquiry, which has been summarized here. And further research on these issues is being conducted.[48]

Table 1. *Diluted Glue Solutions*

Solution strength desired (percent)	stock	water
12	1	1
8	1	2
6	1	3
4	1	5
3	1	7
2	1	11
1	1	23

Modern Paint Analysis and Restoration

Analyzing Paint Samples

INVESTIGATION AND INTERPRETATION

ANDREA M. GILMORE

*V*aluable information about the wide variety of historic American paint colors and materials, and their methods of application, comes from written documentation such as old painters' material supply lists and recipes as well as photographic documentation, particularly for elaborate decorative paint schemes. Actual paint samples, however, contain the most valid documentation of the color, physical composition, and method of application of historic architectural paints.

Locating and identifying early architectural paints is an evolving area of study in the field of architectural conservation. To date, no single comprehensive methodology for their identification has been developed. Rather, several factors—the significance of the paint finish being studied, whether the paints are to be conserved or recreated, the complexity of the paints with respect to their media and pigments, and, of course, the cost—combine to dictate the appropriate investigative procedures.

The method of early paint identification most commonly practiced by architectural conservators is to expose the desired paint layer by scraping down to its surface in situ or removing a paint sample with a scalpel and mounting it for microscopic examination. In conjunction with the microscopic examination of the paints, chemical testing and fluorescent staining are done to identify pigments and media. This methodology identifies restoration paint colors by matching the color of the exposed paint layers. It can also be used to date architectural elements relatively by comparing the number of paint layers on their surface.

This level of identification of historic paints is adequate for much of the paint restoration currently being done in America: interior and exterior architectural surfaces are repainted with modern paints, matched to a historic paint color. It does not, however, provide the information required for a highly precise replication of a historic paint nor the positive identification of a historic paint that may be required for its successful conservation. Both paint replication and the conservation of historic painted finishes can require more accurate identification of a paint's medium and pigments. The more complex procedures for obtaining this level of information include emission spectroscopy, x-ray diffraction, scanning electron microscopy with x-ray fluorescence, thin-layer gas chromatography. These analytical procedures are described by Eugene Farrell in his chapter "Pigments and Media: Techniques in Paint Analysis" (in this volume).

Figure 1. *A corner cupboard from the Jaffrey House (1720s), Portsmouth, N.H. The original color scheme of this architectural cabinetry was restored on the basis of research by the Conservation Center, Society for the Preservation of New England Antiquities. (Society for the Preservation of New England Antiquities)*

Figure 2. *Decorative painting exposed with solvents, main courtroom, Barnstable County Courthouse, Barnstable, Massachusetts. (Society for the Preservation of New England Antiquities)*

Figure 3. *Historic photograph of the secretary of state's office, Old Executive Office Building, showing decorative wall painting. This photograph was used to identify areas where overpainted decorative painting was exposed. (National Park Service, U.S. Department of the Interior)*

The equipment and training required for this level of analysis remain, for the most part, within the domain of the major fine arts conservation laboratories. These analytical procedures are costly and can be justified only for projects where the accurate identification of a paint's pigments and media are required for the success of a restoration or conservation treatment. Repainting a room with modern paint materials mixed to match a historic paint color does not merit this expenditure. Thus, the number of architectural paint studies that include complex pigment and binder identification is small.

The discussion that follows examines the investigative procedures for paint research based on the mechanical exposure of the historic paint layer for microscopic study, simple chemical testing, and fluorescent staining. It is intended to give a general overview of these procedures as a basis for understanding the scope, challenges, and limitations of this level of paint investigation.

RESEARCH PLAN AND OBJECTIVE

The architectural conservator's initial task in studying early architectural paints is to develop a research plan that clearly identifies the objective of the study. Most often, a study of early paint is undertaken to recreate an earlier paint color scheme or document alterations to building fabric. Conservation of original decorative finishes is another possible goal, as is the scholarly study of the materials of architectural paints. Studies often have overlapping objectives (fig. 1).

DOCUMENTARY SEARCH

Once the objective of a paint study has been determined, photographic and written documentation of a building is assembled. Historic structure reports can provide invaluable information about alterations that may have covered over original or datable color schemes. Of course, the best sample of a historic paint is one that has not been overpainted. Unfortunately, the architectural history of many buildings has not been documented thoroughly, and architectural conservators must attempt to assemble this information as they study the paints. Historic photographs are indispensable for identifying areas of decorative painting (figs. 2 and 3). They

may also be used to identify polychromatic paint schemes because they reveal differences in color, although not actual paint colors. In addition, letters, bills of sale, and painters' materials lists are potential sources of useful information.

ON-SITE INVESTIGATION

On completion of the documentary research, on-site investigation of architectural paints begins with a thorough examination of the surfaces to be studied (fig. 4). Differences in the profile of molded woodwork (fig. 5) and clearly delineated plaster cracks may be indicative of building fabric alterations; irregularities in a plaster wall surface revealed with raking light can sometimes identify the location of decorative painting, and variations in the character of the painted surface—such as circular sanding marks or lines marking areas of reduced paint buildup—identify areas where paints may have been removed.

In addition to the visible clues that may be found in a room, knowledge of period painting practices also suggests areas that should be sampled. During the eighteenth century paint was used to simulate chair rails and baseboards on plaster and wood-paneled walls; in the early nineteenth century overmantel painting was common.

Figure 4. On-site examination with a field microscope, conducted by Brian Powell, to identify locations for paint sampling. (Society for the Preservation of New England Antiquities)

SAMPLING TECHNIQUES

A sampling plan for historic paint research is devised from the information generated by the project objective, written and photographic documentation, and on-site investigation. This plan identifies the appropriate sampling techniques and locations to be sampled. There are four basic techniques for sampling architectural paints.

CRATERING

In cratering a scalpel is used to make a circular cut in a painted surface. The sides of the circle are sanded to expose the paint layers in a craterlike configuration. Cratering is usually done on site and is an efficient method for checking paint-layering sequences and documenting alterations to building elements. Craters can be studied with a hand lens or a portable microscope. Architectural conservators at the Society for the Preservation of New England Antiquities study paint craters with a Zeiss binocular microscope.

SCRAPING

A scalpel is used to remove later paint layers, exposing the paint layer to be studied. Scraping is usually done on site. It is an efficient sampling procedure if a fracture line occurs at the paint layer to be studied (the term *fracture line* is used here to identify weakly bonded paint layers whose separation can be induced easily by cutting or scraping with a scalpel). It may be the best sampling procedure for exposing glazes. Glazed finishes are thin and can be difficult to identify in cross section, particularly their surface texture and gloss. The bond of glazed finishes to adjoining paint layers, either under or on top of the glazed finish, often is weak and vulnerable to separation by scraping.

SOLVENT EXPOSURE

Solvents too are used to remove later paint layers and expose the paint layer to be studied. Solvent exposure is usually an in situ method of sampling but may also be used on architectural elements that have been removed to the laboratory for study. It is frequently the only investigative technique that successfully uncovers decorative paint finishes that have been over-painted. Solvents must be identified that will remove overpainting without damaging the decorative paint finish. Identifying the correct solvent requires testing and is time consuming. SPNEA conservators have assembled a solvent kit for this work and recommend recording the solvents that successfully remove specific paints. This information provides a useful basis for selecting appropriate solvents for future exposure projects.

EXTRACTION

Full layering sequences of paint and the substrate are removed for microscopic examination in the laboratory. Samples are removed mechanically, most commonly with a scalpel or microdrill, such as a dentist's drill or Dremel tool (figs. 6 and 7). A scalpel produces a sample with irregular edges and may cause fracturing between the layers of a poorly bonded paint sample. A microdrill produces samples with uniform edges and causes minimal impact vibration. The microdrill is especially useful for plaster sampling and for samples for polished cross section. Extracted paint samples are used for determining paint layering sequences, for microchemical testing, and for color matching.

Paint samples are removed for two primary research objectives: to identify the color of early paints and to comparatively date architectural changes. If a decorative paint scheme is to be documented, sampling for color identification may have to follow exposure of the painted pattern.

For color identification, particularly of original painted finishes, the best location of samples is in cracks or joints into which the paint has flowed. Paint found in these locations is thicker than on smooth surfaces; it has been less subject to discoloration from exposure to light. Paint drips, at the corners of window and door casings, are also good sources of samples for color matching.

For identifying architectural changes or dating intermediary paint layers, samples containing full layering sequences are required. These samples are found on surfaces that were covered with each repainting and have not been damaged by abrasion. The upper portions of window and door casings, mantelpieces, and door stiles are often suitable locations. Within the paint layering sequences, overlapping paint layers may also be informative for identifying the chronology of paint color schemes—the wall, ceiling, and woodwork paint colors. Wall paint was frequently applied to the top several inches of a baseboard before the final paint finish was applied to the baseboard. Similarly, there may be an informative overlap at the junction of exterior window sash and casings and exterior doors and casings, as they were often painted contrasting colors.

Figure 5. *Carved wood trim showing a well-preserved paint sample behind a missing dentil. (Society for the Preservation of New England Antiquities)*

Of course, the situations encountered in the field often reveal that even the most thorough sampling plan may not readily provide the information needed. A basic difficulty encountered in sampling is ensuring that the samples taken reveal the layer being studied. Identifying the finish layer of a decorative paint scheme, particularly if it has been created by multiple thin layers of similarly colored paint, can be problematic. Ideally a fracture line will occur at the surface paint layer; however, when it does not, cross sections have to be relied on to study this paint layer. Three rooms in the senate president's suite in the Massachusetts State House demonstrate different variations that can be encountered when attempting to identify a finish paint layer.

In the senate president's office, formerly the senate reading room, an extremely weak paint bond on the surface of the original finish paint layer on the walls and ceiling enabled the ready identification of their decorative pattern. This weak bond existed because the surface of the decorative painting had been finished with several glazes that prevented adequate penetration by the overpaint. Scalpels were successfully used to chip away the overpaint on the decorative painting on the walls and ceiling in this room.

In contrast, in the Coolidge Room, formerly the senate president's office, a thin layer of metallic spray paint had been used to overpaint the original wall finish. Cross sections revealed that the original wall finish, which had been applied over an uneven coat of plaster, was created by a layer of silver leaf and several colored glazes. Identifying the surface character of this finish, however, was difficult because the overpaint was thin and well bonded. It could not be removed mechanically with a scalpel. Solvents that removed the overpaint penetrated the layer below, leaving it muddied. Accurate documentation for this finish was found only when a patch of joint compound, which had been applied before the spray painting, was removed, exposing the original finish.

In the clerk's office, the original finish on the wall surfaces was created by multiple layers of similarly colored green paint. A rough fracture line appeared to occur at the original finish layer; however, because the paint layer above the fracture line was also green the evidence was confusing. In this instance, cross sections were prepared of the full layering sequence and of the layers below and above the fracture line. The finish layers were identified—slightly different shades of green above and below the chair rail—and paint colors matched.

The accuracy of the colors was verified when the removal of a built-in cabinet uncovered the original paint color scheme for the room. The paint samples from the walls had afforded good color documentation, but they had not identified fine chalklike particles dispersed throughout the surface paint layer. These particles, which were randomly dispersed, were not found in the limited number of small samples studied but were readily apparent when the original finish was exposed. In this instance, the uneven dispersion of the particles meant that multiple samples could be studied that did not contain a key ingredient in creating the surface character of this finish.

Another sampling problem often encountered by architectural conservators is the difficulty of detecting early distemper paints on plaster walls. Frequently these paints were washed off before repainting. They were also used alternately with wallpapers, making efforts to date a distemper paint layer difficult. The best hope for identifying distemper paints on plaster walls is at the overlap with the woodwork paint. At the overlap they may be covered with oil-base woodwork paints that protected them from being washed off and whose layering sequence provides

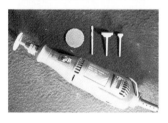

Figure 6. *Scalpels used for extracting paint samples. (Society for the Preservation of New England Antiquities)*

Figure 7. *Dremel tool used for extracting paint samples. (Society for the Preservation of New England Antiquities)*

a relative means for dating the distemper paint layer. Deep pores in a plaster surface and corners are other possible locations where distemper paints may have survived removal efforts.

SAMPLE REMOVAL

Architectural paint samples are most commonly removed from a building with a scalpel or microdrill. The majority of paint samples taken range in size from one-sixteenth to three-quarters of an inch, although in some instances whole elements, such as a bracket or door casing, may be removed for study. Samples should be taken to include a portion of the substrate to ensure that a full paint-layering sequence is obtained. Once removed, paint samples may be stored in coin envelopes or glass vials for transport to the laboratory. Coin envelopes are well suited for large, intact samples, and they have the advantage that a detailed description of the location of the sample can be written directly on the envelope. Coin envelopes can be stored compactly and are not breakable. Plastic ziplock bags may also be used for sample storage. Samples are labeled with slips of paper placed inside the bag; permanent ink labeling on the outside of the bags tends to get rubbed off.

SAMPLE MOUNTING

Architectural paint samples may be mounted for microscopic study in several ways, depending on the sample type and the objective for which they are being studied. The majority of the architectural paint samples studied fall into two categories: finish paint layers that have been exposed for documentary study, usually for color identification; and cross sections, which illustrate the full chronology of paint layers on an architectural element.

Paint samples taken to study an exposed finish layer may be mounted in several ways. A good temporary mounting material is Silly Putty, which allows the samples to be moved around and can be reused. Petri dishes filled with white microcrystalline wax can also be used to mount these samples. Samples mounted in wax can be moved around, and the wax has good reflective qualities for photomicroscopy. A third technique for mounting samples of an exposed finish layer is with an acrylic emulsion on a glass slide. Such samples are not movable, unless they are broken out of the emulsion. Glass-slide mounting, however, has the advantage in that it affords compact, long-term storage. All these mounting techniques leave the surface of the paint sample fully exposed, a requirement for color identification and microchemical analysis.

These three mounting techniques are suitable as well for mounting cross-section samples. Cross sections mounted in any of these ways can be used for color identification, microchemical analysis, and comparative study of some paint-layering sequences. More precise and careful study of a cross section, however, requires embedding the sample in an acrylic, epoxy, or polyester "casting" resin and polishing to achieve a uniform surface. Polished cross sections are particularly good for the detection and analysis of thin finish coats and glazes in complex layering sequences. Samples mounted in a casting resin, however, are not especially suitable for microchemical analysis, as the resin may interfere with the penetration of the chemical. Nor are resin-mounted samples recommended for color matching because paint colors can sometimes be affected by contact with the resin.

MICROSCOPIC EXAMINATION

Microscopy provides the basis for all laboratory study of architectural paint samples. It is used to identify the chronology of a sample's paint layers, for microchemical analysis of paint media and pigments, and for color matching.

The microscopes most commonly used for architectural paint research are binocular stereoscopes, with a magnification of ten to eighty power. Samples are illuminated for examination with these microscopes with fiber-optic halogen lamps. Polarizing microscopes are also used by architectural conservators for examining resin-cast cross sections, identifying pigments, and fluorescent staining for media identification. At the SPNEA Conservation Center we use an Olympus BHT Series 2 polarizing and ultraviolet light microscope with magnifications of 125, 250, and 500 power.

PAINT LAYER IDENTIFICATION

Nearly all architectural paint research requires that the chronology of the paint layers on a particular element be established. This chronology may be used to identify restoration paint colors, comparatively date building elements, and determine paint layers requiring further study.

Chronologies begin with the identification of the substrate, wood, plaster, masonry, or metal. Substrate identification can provide information about the original surface finish and alterations to the building fabric. For example, discolored and weathered exterior wood substrates are indicative of unfinished surfaces, most often found on early clapboards and vertical sheathing. A dirt layer on an interior plaster substrate indicates that it was originally unfinished. Differences in wood species may provide documentation for architectural alterations. In the Old State House in Boston, the 1909 alterations were made with poplar, a green-colored wood that was clearly distinguishable from the yellow tone of the pine used for the original interior woodwork.

Paint layers are identified, beginning with the layer immediately above the substrate, usually by color. Not all finish layers are identifiable by color. Varnishes, shellacs, and other resinous finishes do not fall into an obvious color category. These finishes are identified by their material name. In addition, dirt layers, wallpaper, and wallpaper paste residue are listed separately in the layering sequence.

Once all the paint layers have been identified, paint layers are categorized as primers or finish coats. The most obvious means of determining a finish coat is in the distinct color change between paint layers. Fracture lines and dirt layers also indicate finish paint layers, as do identifiable textured surfaces, such as sand.

Paint-layering chronologies are usually established for several elements in an interior room or on the exterior of a building, even if the objective of the paint study is only to document accurate restoration paint colors. Within these samples, variations will occur in the paint-layering sequences. The most obvious explanation for significant differences in the number of paint layers found on samples is that the building elements date from different periods of construction. However, this is not the only logical explanation. Other reasons may be that portions of the painted surfaces were originally unpainted, areas of high use received more than one coat of paint, areas of high abrasion (human contact) or intense weathering may have lost paint layers, or portions of the painted surfaces may have been deliberately removed. Scraping before repainting often leaves significant gaps in paint-layering sequences, while stripping with chemicals or rotary sanders may obliterate all evidence of early paint layers.

In addition, different samples may have different paint-layering sequences because of deterioration (alligatoring) of paint layers. Such deterioration allows recently applied paint to penetrate beneath earlier paint layers.

MICROCHEMICAL ANALYSIS

Microchemical analysis of architectural paints is undertaken to identify paint media and pigments. Their identification enables the accurate reproduction of historic paints (with closely matching materials), the determination of appropriate conservation treatments for intact historic paint schemes, and the dating of some paint layers (fig. 8).

As indicated earlier, complex media and pigment identification is seldom done for architectural paints; if it is undertaken, it is done by fine arts research scientists. The microchemical tests described here are those that are within the capabilities of architectural conservators. These tests will provide relatively accurate identification of the materials being studied; however, test findings should be verified by more precise means if identification of the material is critical for successfully meeting the objectives of the paint research.

The microchemical analysis of paint samples has been guided by several publications, most notably Rutherford J. Gettens and George L. Stout's *Painting Materials: A Short Encyclopedia* and Joyce Plesters's "Cross-Sections and Chemical Analysis of Paint Samples." *Painting Materials* is a standard reference that identifies paint media and pigments. Plesters's article describes a series of microchemical tests for pigment identification.

PIGMENT IDENTIFICATION

The most commonly used and readily identifiable pigment found in architectural paints is white lead. It can be identified by applying sodium sulfide (Na_2S) solution to a paint layer. If the paint contains white lead, it turns black on contact. Because white lead was so universally used in architectural paints until the late 1950s, identifying its presence in a paint is not overly informative in and of itself. In isolation, this information can be used only to date a recent paint layer to pre-1960, when laws prohibiting the use of lead-based paint were passed, and to generate appropriate safety procedures if work is undertaken that will disturb the lead-containing paint layer.

The absence of white lead in an early paint layer suggests that the paint may be non–oil based (a whitewash or distemper) or that the white pigment used is zinc oxide, rather than white lead. Zinc oxide was first used for white architectural paints in the mid-nineteenth century, and its positive identification can provide a useful dating reference in a layering sequence.

Another pigment that can be identified with simple microchemical tests is Prussian blue, a synthetic pigment invented by Dusbach in 1704 and commonly used in early architectural paints. Prussian blue particles, which have been isolated either by crushing the sample or by dissolving the medium, are treated with sodium hydroxide ($NaOH$), which causes the pigment to go into solution with the precipitation of orange-brown ferric hydroxide. The precipitate

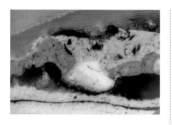

Figure 8. *Cross section of corner cupboard, Jaffrey House. (Society for the Preservation of New England Antiquities)*

is dissolved in hydrochloric acid (HCl) and a few drops of ammonium thiocyanate added to the solution. This produces a red color.[1]

Microchemical tests for pigment identification, while they can be informative, have been used by architectural conservators only on a limited basis. They often involve treating the pigment sample with a combination of different chemicals, frequently destroy the pigment sample being studied, and produce results that provide less than positive identification.

Increasingly, architectural conservators are using polarizing light microscopy to identify paint pigments with greater precision. With a polarizing microscope, pigment particles are characterized and reasonably well identified by comparing their color, crystal shape, size, refractive index, and polarization colors with those of known pigment particles that are mounted and identified on standard reference slides.

Pigment identification is especially important for fugitive pigments, as their color usually has changed significantly over time. Reproduction of an early paint color made with fugitive pigments, even if it is to be done with modern materials, requires their accurate identification. For example, the reproduction of an early blue paint made with a Prussian blue pigment that now appears green requires that the original pigment color be identified for correct coloration. Otherwise, it might be assumed that the original pigment used to color the paint was green rather than blue.

MEDIA IDENTIFICATION

Identification of paint media in both architecture and fine arts is the most complex task encountered. Analytical procedures required for highly accurate media identification—thin-layer gas chromatography—requires training and equipment that exceed the capabilities of most architectural conservators. However, some paint media can be generally characterized with simple solubility tests and more accurately identified with fluorescent staining and ultraviolet light microscopy.

The most commonly used solubility test is for distemper paints. Viewed under a microscope, distemper paints slowly absorb the water, swell, and then begin to break down. Distemper paints also darken when wet. Whitewashes and oil-based paints are not water soluble.

Fluorescent staining can identify many more media than simple solubility tests and with far greater accuracy. The following biological stains are used to identify architectural paint media: (1) TTC (triphenyl tetrazolium chloride)—4 percent in methanol to identify the presence of carbohydrate (starch paste, gum arabic, sugars, cellulosics); positive reaction color is dark red to dark brown; (2) FITC (fluorescein isothiocyanate)—0.2 percent in acetone to identify the presence of proteins (typically hide glue, casein, gelatin); positive reaction color is bright yellow-green; and (3) DCF (2, 7 dichlorofluorscein)—0.2 percent in ethanol to identify the presence of saturated and unsaturated lipids (oils); positive reaction color is bright yellow for unsaturated lipids and bright pink for saturated lipids (**figs. 9 and 10**).

Ultraviolet light microscopy is also used to identify architectural paint media. Illumination of different materials with ultraviolet light causes them to autofluoresce (glow) with characteristic colors. For example, shellac fluoresces orange or yellow-orange when exposed to ultraviolet light; plant resins (amber, copal, sandaria, and mastic) fluoresce bright white.

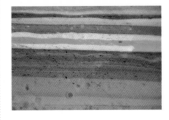

Figure 9. *Cross section of paint sample from the U.S. Treasury Building, Washington, D.C., in natural light. (Society for the Preservation of New England Antiquities)*

Figure 10. *Cross section of paint sample from the U.S. Treasury Building, stained with dichlorofluorescein (DCF). The bright yellow layers are unsaturated lipids (oils); the bright pink layers are saturated lipids (oils). (Society for the Preservation of New England Antiquities)*

Identification of paint media is seldom required for the replication of an architectural paint with modern materials. It is, however, critical information if an early painted finish is to be cleaned or conserved. Incorrect identification of a medium that is to be cleaned can result in irreparable damage to a decorative paint scheme. Areas of painted pattern can be quickly washed away, subtle shading effects obliterated, and colors changed by running together. Most paint failure is attributable to the breakdown of the binder; therefore, treatments to reestablish the bond of the paint to the substrate require the identification of the media so that its interaction with the new bonding material will be acceptable.

PAINT COLOR IDENTIFICATION

Paint color identification is the area of architectural paint research that remains the most problematic for architectural conservators. Not only must the hue of a layer in the sample be identified; possible changes in the surface color and appearance also must be evaluated.

As discussed earlier, the successful identification of an early paint color is contingent on obtaining a good sample for study. Thick paint samples, which have had limited exposure to light, retain their truest color. These samples are found in cracks or joints into which the paint originally flowed or in drips where excessive paint was applied. Even in the best paint samples, however, discoloration occurs, and this unstable nature of architectural paints complicates the identification of original color.

Studies of architectural paints, principally by Morgan Phillips, indicate that the most unstable component of architectural paints is the oil medium. The most commonly used paint medium, linseed oil, turns yellow-brown, especially when placed in darkness. Therefore, paint discoloration frequently is encountered behind large pieces of furniture, such as pictures, mirrors, and bookshelves. If overpainted, the entire old paint layer is subject to discoloration because it is no longer exposed to light. Fortunately, it appears that the longer a painted surface has been exposed to normal light, the less it darkens when overpainted.[2] The length of time a paint layer has been exposed before overpainting, however, is not easily measurable. Hence, it is difficult to evaluate levels of discoloration.

Oil media also discolor by physical deterioration, a process known as blanching. Oxidation and exposure to light degrade the oil, reducing its glossiness and causing diffuse reflections of incident white light.[3] This deterioration causes paints to appear dull and faded. Paint layers that have been exposed for long periods of time are especially susceptible to discoloration by blanching.

In addition to changes in the oil media, the presence of fugitive pigments is another source of discoloration. Pigments can discolor because of exposure to light, heat, and atmospheric pollutants. Verdigris and Prussian blue are two pigments used in early architectural paints and glazes that are subject to radical color change. Prussian blue turns green over time, particularly when mixed in an oil medium; verdigris turns brown.

The particle size and dispersion of the pigments in early architectural paints further affects paint color. A pigment's coloring power varies in direct relation to its particle size. The larger the particle, the less coloring strength it will have. If a pigment is coarsely ground, much of its coloring power remains concealed within the pigment particles. An equal amount of pigment, finely ground, has far greater tinting strength.

In addition to particle size, the dispersion of pigments in early architectural paints further affects their color. Early paints were hand mixed so that particle dispersion is not uniform. This may result in subtle color variations throughout a paint layer, especially if several pigments have combined to create a paint color. Thus, it is necessary not only to identify the amount of pigment used to color an early architectural paint but also to identify its particle size and dispersion.

While physical characteristics of architectural paints make the identification of their original color difficult, the task is further complicated by the phenomenon, known as metamerism, that enables paint colors to match in one light and appear noticeably different in another. It also explains why two researchers sometimes will match a paint color differently.

Metamerism also complicates the ability to reproduce historic paint colors with modern materials. While the color of a modern and historic paint may match well in daylight, in fluorescent light differences in their material composition may cause their colors to look noticeably different.

Identifying the original color of an architectural paint requires that the effects of medium discoloration and blanching, pigment discoloration and dispersion, and metamerism be taken into consideration, sometimes compensated for, or even reversed. There are no clear formulas for accomplishing this task; rather, there are some commonly practiced procedures that are relatively subjective.

The discoloration of oil media can usually be reduced by exposing the paint layer to long-wave ultraviolet light. This procedure is called bleaching. The length of exposure required varies with different paints and is difficult to measure. One technique of measurement, providing the paint sample is of adequate size, is to cover portions of the sample with an opaque material, revealing more and more of the paint surface at twelve- to twenty-four-hour intervals until the color change between exposures is negligible. For some paints, natural daylight will produce significant reversal of medium discoloration. It has been suggested that for paints with particularly fugitive pigments, such as Prussian blue, daylight may reduce the discoloration of the medium adequately while affecting the pigment less adversely than ultraviolet light.[4]

Discoloration caused by blanching is rarely entirely reversible, although its effects can sometimes be diminished by the application of propylene glycol to the paint layer during color matching. The propylene glycol temporarily recreates the glossiness of the paint layer, smoothing the surface and thus reducing the diffusion of color.

Reversing the color change that occurs in fugitive pigments is rarely, if ever, possible. Prussian blues that have turned green because of discoloration of the medium do become more blue when exposed to natural light but never return to their original brilliance. Modern samples of the pigments found in early architectural paints can be used to identify the actual pigment color, but the translation of pigment color to a particular paint color becomes more difficult because of particle size, dispersion, and interaction with the medium.

Metamerism is partially compensated for in color identification by viewing the paint sample with a blue filter on the microscope and full illumination with quartz halogen lamps. This filtering of the light and the level of illumination are designed to reproduce natural day lighting, in which most architectural paints are viewed.

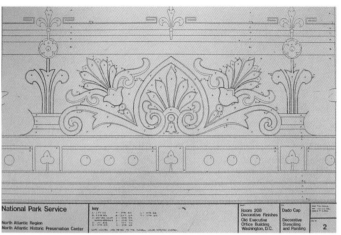

After a historic paint color is identified, it is matched to a color standard. The three most frequently used standards are commercial paint colors; color reference systems, such as Munsell, Plochere, and CIE; and custom color reference cards. Commercial paint colors are used for projects with limited budgets. For some colors, good commercial paint color matches are available. These paint colors have two advan-

Figure 11. *Drawing for a report showing a decorative pattern to be recreated and keyed with Munsell Colors. (National Park Service, U.S. Department of the Interior)*

Figure 12. *Munsell Colors keyed to the drawing shown in figure 11. (National Park Service, U.S. Department of the Interior)*

tages: they are easily given to a painting contractor and no custom mixing is required. However, commercial paint colors also have two significant disadvantages: their system of identification, whether numerical or verbal, frequently changes; and paint colors are periodically added and deleted from the product line. Consequently, reproducing a commercial paint color, short of custom mixing to a sample of its original color, may not prove possible.

Color reference systems, such as Munsell, Plochere, and CIE, are most often used to specify architectural paint colors because they have a permanent nomenclature for color. For example, Munsell 4.5Y will always be the same hue, and both matte and glossy samples of the color can be obtained. Munsell 4.5Y, however, is not an existing paint color but a standard to which a paint must be matched by custom mixing. The difficulty is that there is a margin for error inherent in all color mixing. Paint colors must be checked and adjusted to ensure that an accurate color match has been achieved. In addition, color reference systems were not developed especially for architectural paints, and therefore exact and nonmetameric color matches often are not possible. One frequently finds that a historic paint color falls between two color reference standards.

Custom color reference cards can be made by architectural conservators for major architectural paint studies that require highly accurate paint color documentation. Color reference cards are made by mixing a small amount of paint that exactly matches the color of the early paint **(figs. 11 and 12)**. Acrylic polymer emulsions are used as the medium for these paints; pigments premixed in acrylic polymer emulsion are used for color. Titanium white (titanium dioxide) is used as a substitute base for white lead. Paint colors are mixed, painted onto test cards, dried with the assistance of a hair dryer, and compared to the historic paint color. Pigment combinations are adjusted until an exact match is achieved. Once the correct color has been obtained, it is mixed in a formula: ten parts paint, two parts propylene glycol, one part water. The addition of the propylene glycol and water allows the paint to be brushed smoothly onto the cards. Once mixed, the paint is brushed onto eight-by-ten-inch cards—four-ply, acid-free, rag, illustration board. Usually, four cards are made for each paint color. Two samples are given to the client, and two samples are retained by the researcher.

Custom color reference cards have the distinct advantage of enabling a researcher to obtain an exact match to an early architectural paint. The materials used to make the paint colors are stable and do not change over time. Color reference cards do require custom mixing for restoration paint colors, and they are time consuming and costly to make. However, because the ultimate objective of identifying historic architectural paint colors is usually their accurate reproduction and the long-term stability of the paint color reproduced, custom color reference cards should be made whenever possible.

SAMPLE STORAGE

Once laboratory study of architectural paint samples is complete, the samples are prepared for storage. They are numbered and labeled with the name of the building and the sample location. Samples mounted on slides can be stored in standard slide boxes, samples mounted in Petri dishes in wooden racks, and resin-mounted samples in plastic containers. Paint samples are usually retained by the researcher.

Samples must be stored for verification of study findings and for future research. Because the physical characteristics of a paint, particularly its color, can vary within a room, verification of a study's findings, at a later date, necessitates viewing the same samples previously examined. In addition, the field of architectural paint investigation is evolving and new methodologies for analysis continue to be developed. Future study of the same paint samples may produce more accurate identification of the composition of the paints, as well as of their original color.

In addition to retaining extracted samples, it is imperative that complete in situ paint samples be preserved. In general, stripping early architectural paints is not recommended; however, bond failure or excessive paint buildup may leave no alternative. If stripping is to be done, it is important that areas with full paint layering sequences be identified and preserved. These areas should be as large as possible, so that the variation occurring on architectural paint surfaces is retained.

RESEARCH REPORTS

At the conclusion of an architectural paint study a report is prepared. An architectural paint study report typically includes a brief architectural description of the structure whose paints are being studied; a statement of the objective of the paint study; an outline of the procedures used to study the paints; a summary of the information derived from the specific paint samples studied; detailed descriptions, including layering chronologies, of samples documenting the study's findings; and color reference cards of historic paint colors. An architectural paint study may stand alone or be integrated into a historic structure report.

Architectural conservators are compiling an extensive database of early architectural paints. These data are being used to reproduce historic paint colors with modern materials and to comparatively date architectural alterations. Architectural conservators must continue to collaborate with fine arts laboratory scientists, refine their investigative techniques, thoroughly record the findings of their research, and ensure that good samples of architectural paints are preserved for future study.

Pigments and Media

TECHNIQUES IN PAINT ANALYSIS

EUGENE FARRELL

The essential problem in paint analysis is to identify pigments and binding media. Consequently, paint analyses are resolved into two separate steps: (1) analysis of the pigments and (2) analysis of the binding media. Pigment analysis may require techniques adapted from inorganic or organic analyses, depending on the nature of the pigment. Media analysis, however, is often an organic analysis, although lime and potassium silicate binders are common in architectural paint, as shown by Morgan Phillips in "A Survey of Paint Technology: The Composition and Nature of Paints" (in this volume).

Modern analyses are almost always instrumental, and although microchemical techniques and spot tests should not be ignored, they are best used, with some exceptions, as supplementary and confirming techniques and not as a substitute for more reliable instrumental methods.

Paint in an architectural context is usually decorative or protective wall, ceiling, or floor paint. However, many old houses contain mural paintings that because of the limited amount of painted surface require a different approach toward sampling. Only very small samples can be taken from a painting. Samples from architectural surfaces can, however, be larger.

Aging introduces problems, as pigments and especially media change with time—that is, they react with oxygen in the atmosphere and as oxidation proceeds, they cross link and lose volatiles. Consequently, an aged oil, resin, or proteinaceous medium is decidedly different after fifty to a hundred years than when it was applied fresh.

PIGMENT ANALYSIS

Often the problem in architectural paint analysis is to determine original paint layers. A visual overall survey of the painted surface is necessary in deciding the best place to sample. This is equally true for mural and easel paintings. The importance of a careful visual examination to locate sampling sites and to determine repaint, fills, losses, and even forgeries cannot be overemphasized. Andrea M. Gilmore ("Analyzing Paint Samples: Investigation and Interpretation" in this volume) has covered methods of examination on architectural samples.

Figure 1. *Detail of* The Trout Brook, *by Albert Bierstadt, 1859. This painting, which was analyzed in 1990 by Marlene Werhach under the author's direction, contains many of the pigments used by artists and house painters in the mid-nineteenth century, including chrome yellow, Prussian blue, cadmium yellow, Naples yellow, zinc white, and lead white. (Courtesy of the Fogg Art Museum, Harvard University Art Museums, Gift of G. M. Leonard)*

Once the visual survey is complete, magnification is required to confirm and extend the visual observations. Modern binocular microscopes have zoom capacity, which allows magnification change at the turn of a dial. Maximum magnification in the range of five to fifty times is adequate. Illumination with fiber optics presents further advantages. Samples may be in the form of powders or cross sections. Cross sections usually require a greater volume of pigment but also yield the most information. From a wall painting, powder may be obtained with a microneedle by carefully scraping the paint surface. This can often be done so that the sample site is invisible to the unaided eye and even invisible under the binocular microscope. If a varnish layer is present and interferes, it may be removed locally by scraping or using solvents. Cross sections can be taken with a chisel-shaped microneedle or a pointed scalpel; both tools can be shaped to suit the occasion. Slight moistening of the site helps keep sections and powders from flying off under the pressure of needle and scalpel. Once secured, the sample can be transferred to a cup slide and sealed with a cover glass taped down to the slide; then the slide must be labeled. If the samples are to be transferred any distance, they can be stored in gelatin capsules. Larger architectural paint samples can be stored and transported in polyethylene bags. Careful documentation of the sample site is vital. Reference to the lower left corner as the zero point with Cartesian coordinates x, y (width by height) to locate the sample site is important for paintings. For buildings, architectural drawings can be used.

Paint analysis proceeds from the macroscopic to the microscopic to the submicroscopic and atomic level. Rather than depend on one technique alone, it should be supported by additional complementary methods such as those discussed below.

POLARIZED LIGHT MICROSCOPY

The examination of a pigment or medium by polarizing microscopy may be divided into two separate operations. The first is the mounting of the sample, the second is the actual examination in polarized light under magnification.

The method of sample preparation depends on whether a dispersed pigment sample or a cross section is to be examined. The term *dispersed pigment* refers to a powder sample dispersed on the surface of a microscope slide so that individual particles can be observed. Pigment should be transferred from the well of the cup slide while being viewed under a binocular microscope to ensure proper transfer and dispersal. Only a few grains are necessary. The sample is covered with a cover glass and a mounting medium of appropriate index of refraction is added along the edge of the cover glass to be drawn into the sample by capillarity.

In many cases an oil of specified index of refraction may be used. If a permanent slide is needed, a medium requiring low heat to melt the solid should be used. Cargille melt mount with an index of refraction of 1.662 at 25 degrees (mp 60 to 70 degrees) Centigrade is a PCB-free substitute for Aroclor 5442, a polychloryl-biphenyl thought to be carcinogenic. The latter was in common use for many years before being withdrawn from the market because of toxic problems. Lakeside no. 70 cement ($n = 1.54$, mp 140 degrees Centigrade), a product commonly used to fix petrographic slides and considered a substitute for Aroclor 5442, is available from suppliers of Petrographic equipment.

Cross sections—pigment samples having two or more layers—provide information regarding pigment identification, single particle chemistry, media analyses, pigment stratigraphy, and the artist's technique.

There are several references on the preparation of cross sections depending on the purpose of the section—for example, whether it is intended for pigment or binding media analysis.[1] Andrea Gilmore discusses cross sections with reference to architectural samples (see "Analyzing Paint Samples").

Cold-setting resins are in general use, as heat will cause the resin to alter or even react with pigments and binding media. Bio-plast is recommended by Wolbers for use with sections intended for fluorescent stain analysis and is used at the Center for Conservation and Technical Studies at Harvard for sections to be examined by microscopy and scanning electron microscopy.

Most paint sections are now mounted in anticipation of fluorescent staining. In general the technique involves casting one layer of resin in the bottom of a mold, placing the sample with paint layers horizontally oriented so that the difference between the ground and top layer can be distinguished, and then covering the sample with more resin and allowing the resin to harden. Once solidified, the sample can be sanded to expose the layers and then sawed to size, roughly a half-centimeter cube or less. The sanding and polishing phase of the cross-section preparation should be done while the sample can still be held without difficulty. Particular care must be exercised if polishing is to be done, as fine polishing grit can contaminate the sample. Oil-based diamond paste can be used only if fluorescent staining is not to be done. Micro-mesh abrasive cloths work well with Bio-plast mounting medium.

Several excellent references on polarizing microscopy are available, and these should be referred to for further details; however, a summary of the components of the microscope and their functions follows.[2, 3, 4]

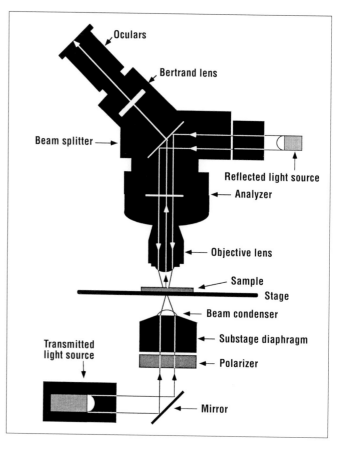

Figure 2. *A polarizing micro-scope, which exploits the optical properties of materials. Its distinguishing features include polarizers above and below the stage, the ability of the stage itself to rotate, and the optical analyzing characteristics of the Bertrand lens and retardation plates. (Eugene Farrell)*

MICROSCOPIC EXAMINATION

Briefly, microscope components may be listed by following a light beam from the base up along the axis of the microscope (fig. 2). The first component is the substage illuminator, or light source; in modern microscopes it is a bulb set into the base whose light reflects off a mirror, passes through an adjustable diaphragm, and proceeds along the optical axis of the microscope to the polarizer. In older microscopes this was a Nicols prism, consisting of two pieces of crystalline calcite ($CaCO_3$), cut and rejoined in such a way that one of the two principal vibration directions, the extraordinary, or e-ray, is allowed to pass through the prism to be a source of polarized light while the ordinary, or o-ray, is totally reflected. The same feat is now achieved with polaroid plates that produce polarization by absorbing light in all directions except one, which becomes the plane of polarization. The polarizer can be rotated so that the plane of polarization can be changed in relation to the plane of polarization of the analyzer. Light from the polarizer passes to the beam condenser, which can be rotated out of the light path. A diaphragm between the polarizer and beam condenser narrows the beam as required. When the condenser is out, the light maintains its vibration directions without change. In the condition of plane-polarized light, with the beam condenser in, polarized light is focused at the base of the sample located on the stage in such a way as to form a cone of polarized light rays. The microscope in this condition is said to be in the conoscopic arrangement. Light then passes through the sample, whether in the conoscopic or plane polarized mode.

What occurs in the sample will be discussed later, but it is in the sample that optical effects occur, allowing several kinds of analyses to be performed and making the polarizing microscope an analytical instrument and not just a magnification device.

Light from the sample passes into the objective lens, where it is magnified for the first time. All polarizing microscopes are provided with a set of objective lenses of various magnifications. The magnification is inscribed on the barrel of the lens, along with the numerical aperture (N.A.).

The amount of light entering the lens and consequently the brightness and quality of the image is a function of the numerical aperture. The larger the numerical aperture, the brighter the image and the better the resolving power. For lenses used without oil, the numerical aperture depends on the index of refraction of air between the lens and the object or cover glass. Oil immersion lenses are used where greater magnification and better resolution are needed.

Once light passes from the objective lens, it enters the analyzer, which is a second polarizing prism or plate whose plane of polarization is normally 90 degrees to that of the polarizer. If light remains vibrating parallel to the plane of the polarizer, total extinction will occur— that is, no light will pass through the analyzer. Only when an optically active material is placed on the stage in the optical light path will light pass through the analyzer.

Light continues along the optical path and enters the oculars or eyepieces, where the final magnification occurs. The magnification of the image is simply the product of the power of the objective lens times the power of the ocular: $M = ob \times oc$.

A retractable lens called the Bertrand lens can be placed between the analyzer and the ocular. The Bertrand lens is used at high magnification when the substage condenser is in place to obtain inference figures from active materials being examined. Optical analysis can be further aided by retardation plates inserted into a slot located above the objective lens. The sharpness of the image throughout the optical system is controlled by a method of uniform field illumination, which depends on forming an image of the light source at the rear focal plane of the lamp condenser, the substage beam condenser, the objective lens, and the ocular. This is achieved by the use of aperture diaphragms and is referred to as Kohler illumination.

In addition to the transmitted light mode described above, a reflected light mode may be used and is combined with transmitted light in the same microscope in modern instruments. In this case the light source is located behind the microscope above the objective lenses. After passing through a polarizer or neutral-density optical filters and a dark field–light field device, it is reflected down onto the sample through the objective lenses. The reflected light then passes back through the objective lens through a mirror and up along the optical light through a polarizer to the ocular. Reflected light is used for opaque polished samples, although dispersed pigments and other particles may be examined in reflected light alone or in combination with transmitted light. The difference between the light-field and dark-field methods is a matter of illumination. The bright-field method relies on light passing directly through the objective lens in a straight-line path to be reflected perpendicularly back along the axis of the microscope. In the dark-field method, light emerges from specially constructed objective lenses at an angle, an effect produced by the dark-field device by blocking the light with a disk, which allows a cylinder of light to emerge to reflect down into the objective lens. This cylinder of light is reflected to one side in the objective lens and emerges at an angle to the light train.

On polished pigment cross sections, bright-field illumination produces an image of bright white and gray tones. The image is dramatically altered in dark field, where the off-perpendicular light produces a high-contrast, easily read colored image. Pigment cross sections are usually viewed in dark-field illumination.

EXAMINATION IN CROSSED AND PLANE POLARIZED LIGHT

It is rare in paint to find a sample of a single pigment. Inevitably, most samples consist of two or more pigments; therefore, a knowledge of how many separate phases are present is the first task of polarizing light examination. This is easily achieved by examining a dispersed sample mounted in a medium of known index of refraction in crossed polarized light (i.e., in light created when the polarizing plane of the polarizer and analyzer are at 90 degrees to each other). One method of separating and classifying pigments is to divide them into isotropic and anisotropic categories. Isotropic materials do not cause the plane of polarization from the polarizer to deviate in any way while passing through it; as a consequence, when light from an isotropic material reaches the analyzer, total extinction occurs and the field remains dark upon rotation of the stage. Prussian blue, ultramarine, Naples yellow, and the glass slide on which the sample is mounted are all examples of isotropic materials.

Anisotropic materials do cause a change in the direction of the plane of polarization, except in two perpendicular settings where the material behaves as if it were isotropic. As a result, when the stage is rotated anisotropic materials go extinct four times in a rotation of 360 degrees. Lead white, chrome yellow, hematite, and vermilion are all examples. However, it is important to emphasize that single crystals must be examined, because aggregates will give conflicting results. Once the various phases have been accounted for they can be further classified by index of refraction (n). If a permanent mount is made with Cargille, the pigments present on the slide may be separated into those having an index of refraction greater than 1.67 and those with a lesser index of refraction. This is done by examining a single crystal in plane polarized light and using the Becke line to establish whether n pigment is greater or lesser than 1.67. The Becke line method is well described elsewhere.[5]

Oils of known index of refraction can be used in place of a permanent mounting medium and the exact index of refraction can be obtained. In general the measurement of n is done only as a supplementary means of identification, since chemical and physical methods are quicker and demand less skill from the microscopist.

Further observations to be made on the pigments in a dispersed sample include color, crystal shape, fracture, grain size, and cleavage. Compensating plates can also be used to check on the sign of elongation of acicular crystals. However, because of the fine grain size of many modern pigments, such measurements can be difficult to perform.

Anisotropic crystalline pigment particles can be further characterized by obtaining an interference figure with the Bertrand lens using high magnification (400 times) with the substage beam condenser in place. Crystals can be classified into uniaxial and biaxial groups, depending on whether uniaxial or biaxial interference figures are seen. The optic sign—positive or negative—may be determined with the use of compensating plates. The use of interference figures depends on the orientation of the crystal grain in relation to the axis of the microscope, and knowledge of off-axis interference figures is necessary to make use of the technique. Consequently a thorough knowledge of the optical indicatrix is required to make practical use of interference figures. The indicatrix is best understood as being a three-dimensional model representing the numerical values of the index of refraction oriented in relation to the optical crystallographic axes of the crystal. There are uniaxial and biaxial indicatrices.[6]

In pragmatic terms there are only a relatively few choices when it comes to identifying the majority of pigments. Getting a relative value of index of refraction and measuring particle size and shape and the color of individual particles therefore carry the analysis a long way. More advanced optical methods can be used when the usual tests fail to pin down the identification.

MICROCHEMISTRY

Microchemistry, like optical microscopy, represents a relatively unappreciated triumph of nineteenth- and early twentieth-century science. It is a subject that has gone out of favor with the advent of modern instrumental analyses, but some practical knowledge of the subject remains important, as many microchemical tests are diagnostically efficient and can be used where instruments are not available.

Microchemistry developed from the application of chemical analytical methods to microsamples in the polarizing microscope and as a subject was perfected by T. H. Behrens.[7] His students P. D. C. Kley and Emile Chamot continued his work after his death in 1905. Chamot emigrated to Cornell University while Kley remained in Europe. The text on microchemistry by Chamot and Mason remains the standard inorganic reference, while Behrens and Kley wrote the definitive work on organic microchemical analyses.[8]

Pioneer work on pigment and media analyses was carried out by Alexander Eibner[9] and later extended by Rutherford J. Gettens.[10] Lyde Pratt describes in detail specific microchemical tests for organic pigments and dyes based on the crystal shapes seen when the colored substance is precipitated from a solution of sulfuric acid.[11]

If a sample is available that is small but larger than necessary for microchemistry, a spot test may be performed. Fritz Feigl was a pioneer in this field. Feigl's text on spot tests, a work based on fifty years of research, remains the basic treatise on the subject.[12]

One of the best references on the microchemistry of pigments used in paintings is Joyce Plesters's article and accompanying tables for *The Identification of Pigments*.[13] These tables give the basic descriptions of a sample along with its chemistry and appearance under low magnification, the effect of heat on the sample, and its solubilities in hydrochloric acid, sodium hydroxide, and nitric acid. Specific tests for elements are also indicated. The tables include all the common inorganic and organic pigments.

ORGANIC PIGMENT ANALYSIS

Plesters mentions tests for indigo, Prussian blue, verdigris, copper resinate (transparent copper green), dragon's blood, madder lake, alizarin crimson, brown madder, bitumen, and Van Dyke brown. This is a reasonable list for pigments found in paintings up to 1856, the date of William Perkins's invention of mauve. But after that came the synthetic organic dyes derived from coal tar, some of which were used as artist's pigments.

Pratt has given a microchemical method for identifying azo-dyes and organic pigments based on the fact that they give characteristic crystal precipitates from 93 percent concentrated sulfuric acid solutions. He published thirty-three photomicrographs and descriptions of common organic pigments.

Fred Billmeyer has given a spectrophotometric method for the analysis of modern organic and traditional plant dyes and pigments.[14] Paul Whitemore modified this scheme using the solubilities to identify several organic pigments from the Harvard murals of Mark Rothko.[15] The solvents recommended by Billmeyer are chloroform methanol, dimethyl formamide (DMF), and concentrated sulfuric acid. A particle is examined under the microscope while solvent is applied with a micropipette and the solubilities noted. The solvent is allowed to dry and the particle, if not dissolved, is moved to a clean spot and tested successively until dissolved. Standards are required for comparison. Once the range of pigments has been narrowed or the pigment identified, the sample can be confirmed by optical absorption curves if enough samples can be obtained.

Many organic pigments have inorganic components that can be detected by the methods described so far or with x-ray fluorescence elemental analyses, in the scanning electron microscope, or with and electron beam microprobe. Elemental inorganic analysis should then be a part of the analysis for any organic dyes and pigments. FTIR analysis is one of the more powerful methods of analyzing organic pigments and will be discussed in more detail.

As stated earlier, any method of analysis should be checked by a second method. The following discussion relates to methods that can stand alone or be used to supplement data from microscopy and microanalysis.

THIN-LAYER CHROMATOGRAPHY

A traditional method used to analyze organic pigments and dyes is thin-layer chromatography. It is also applicable to some media analyses. In either case the problem of small samples applies. There have been many articles on this subject; one of the most recent and most successful is that by Helmut Schweepe, which covers mostly dyes but also pigments. Schweepe has standardized the method and its materials to an easily workable routine.[16] Basically, the technique consists of taking a sample into solution and spotting a prepared sheet at one end with the solution, then "developing" the sheet by inserting it into a solvent. The spot advances up the sheet, leaving certain molecular groups along its path, depending on absorption, partition, and ion exchange processes. Once developed, the spots require some means of being visualized. Exposure to ultraviolet light reveals any fluorescent spots, while nonfluorescent spots require a chemical means of detection.

Unknowns must be matched with standards, preferably seen under the same conditions and at the same time. There are sample kits available commercially for thin-layer chromatography, but the choice of solvents, developers, and plate can be critical to make the scheme work satisfactorily.

Organic analyses can also be carried out by gas chromatography, high-performance liquid chromatography, and mass spectrometry (see section on media analysis).

EMISSION SPECTROSCOPY

Emission spectroscopy seems to have fallen from favor as newer analytical instruments become available. It does combine wide applicability, economy, and sensitivity in a single instrument and is still useful.[17]

Even if other methods are to be used, emission spectroscopy is a good place to start to survey the inorganic components of a paint. Induction-coupled plasma mass spectroscopy is the logical replacement for emission spectroscopy, but because of costs will not be widely available for a few years. The sample required by emission spectroscopy, however, is larger than that used in x-ray fluorescence or scanning electron microscopy but more sensitive for low-level components. Emission spectroscopy is especially useful for architectural pigments.

Single layers of cross sections from architectural paint samples can be scraped away until the desired pigment layer is exposed and a sample of as little as .01 milligram may be used to qualitatively identify its components.[18] The sample size for architectural samples can be much larger and may be removed in powdered form, as Gilmore notes ("Analyzing Paint Samples").

The paint sample to be analyzed is mixed with powdered graphite or a similar matrix in a graphite electrode and burned by passing a high-voltage current through the electrode across an air gap to a counter electrode. Other emission spectrograph models use laser microprobes to vaporize the sample directly from a paint layer. The spectral energy generated in the sample passes through a slit or one or two filters and then its wavelengths are separated by a prism or diffraction grating and recorded on light-sensitive glass plates or film. The film may be read on a projector. Rough quantitative estimates, such as major, minor, and trace levels, may be made visually or made more accurate with densitometer traces across significant lines.

X-RAY DIFFRACTION

Diffraction is a method that can stand alone, although it certainly can supplement other analytical methods.[19, 20, 21, 22, 23] It is used only to analyze crystalline materials of inorganic or organic origin. Amorphous materials simply scatter the x-rays to form a diffuse background.

When architectural samples of several milligrams are available, diffractometer strip chart recordings are ideal. The diffractometer consists of an x-ray source, a set of primary collimating slits, a sample holder, a diffraction-beam slit, a filter, and a detector mounted on a moving platform.

Monochromatic radiation is used to interact with the sample, which is either packed in a special holder or adhered to a one-by-three-inch glass microscope slide with collodion.

The detector is attached to the platform, which is horizontal or vertical depending on specific instrumental design. The platform with detector is set in motion at twice the angular velocity of the sample. The detector sweeps through the entire angular range, close to 180 degrees · 2θ picking up radiation diffracted from the sample and recording the spectrum on a strip chart recorder that is correlated with the angular sweep of the detector.

The strip chart gives a spectrum of peaks representing diffracted energy from specific crystal planes in the pigment versus 2θ, the angular displacement of the peaks. The 2θ values of the peak positions can be converted into crystal lattice spacings using the Bragg equation

$$n\lambda = 2d\sin\theta \text{ solved for } d; \ d = n\lambda \ /2 \sin\theta \text{ where } \lambda \text{ is the wavelength of the x-rays}$$

That value is 1.54Å for copper K alpha (CuK_a) radiation, the common target used for general x-ray diffraction work and n is a whole number. Tables of d spacings that solve the Bragg equation are also available for a variety of target wavelengths.

Measurements of intensities either from the peak height or the integrated area under the peak are also needed. A list of d (lattice spacings) and intensities are made up and the task of identification undertaken by matching standard x-ray patterns from the literature to the unknown. The search may be conducted manually or by a computer search program.

When only small samples are available the powder camera may be used. Standard cameras are available whose diameters are designed to make reading the film a matter of reading a millimeter scale. The geometry of the camera is cylindrical and wide enough to accept a strip of 35-millimeter, x-ray–sensitive film—for example, Kodak DEF 392. Probably the most useful for pigment identification designs are the Debye-Scherrer and Gandolfi cameras, the Gandolfi being a variation of the Debye-Scherrer.

These cameras consist of a cylindrical shape whose diameter in millimeters is based on one radian or two radians—that is, 57.3 millimeters or 114.6 millimeters. They use 7.0- and 14.0-inch strips of 35-millimeter film respectively. Angle 2θ measurements (Bragg equation) can be read on a millimeter scale; on the small camera 1 millimeter equals 2 degrees 2θ, while on the larger 1 millimeter equals 1 degree 2θ. Holes for the x-rays to enter and exit are fitted with a collimator and an x-ray beam catcher located 90 or 180 degrees from each other, which on a millimeter scale is 90 or 180 millimeters respectively. The sample can be very small, typically a volume equal to about one-fourth to one-half the size of the head of a common pin.

Exposure times commonly vary from twelve to eighteen hours at 35 to 40 kilovolts and 10 to 15 milliamps. Exposures are conveniently made overnight. The sample is mounted to a tiny rotating shaft that usually mounts a glass rod (.1–.2 millimeter in diameter). The sample is glued to the glass rod with collodion. The Gandolfi motion adds a second motion to the rotation seen on Debye-Scherrer. During the exposure x-rays enter the camera along the collimator, strike the sample, and diffract in a group of nested cones according to the Bragg equation. When the x-ray cones intersect the film, which is pressed against the inside diameter of the camera, a series of symmetrical arcs are formed around the hole of the beam catcher and

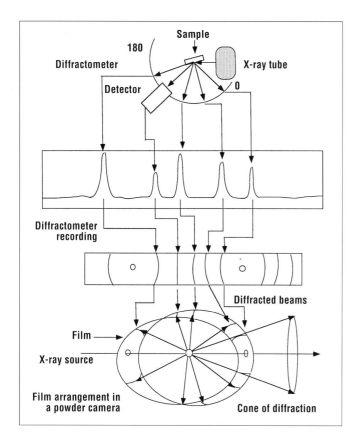

Figure 3. *Diffraction. Crystalline materials, including many pigments, scatter x-rays in a consistent, unique, and identifiable pattern, a process known as x-ray diffraction. The camera and diffractometer are two means of recording this pattern. In this figure both the diffractometer and the camera give identical results, the first on a strip chart and the second on film.*

collimator. The information provided by the powder camera is identical to that provided by the diffractometer **(fig.3)**.

Several devices described in the literature are designed to measure x-ray diffraction powder camera film. For routine identification where lattice parameters or precise *d* spacings are not required, plastic rulers that measure *d* spacings directly are commercially available. They are designed for large- and small-diameter cameras (57.3 and 114.6 millimeters) and for all the common wavelengths. They have the additional advantage in that each ruler has five separate scales and each scale is contracted in relation to the preceding scale, so that film shrinkage can be taken into account without calculations. The main disadvantage of these scales is their lack of accuracy for large *d* spacings. We find that the most consistent set-up uses the 114.6mm Gandolfi camera with CuK_a radiation with the appropriate scale to read the film. Any spacing greater than around 8.0Å should be checked by a second method. For most pigments, however, this is not a problem, since most pigments are inorganic substances and their lattices are smaller than around 8.0Å.

Lattice spacings need to be read from the zero end and listed in increasing order of magnitude. A set of corresponding intensities relative to the most intense are recorded. The list of the spacings and intensities are enough to identify most common substances by doing a systematic search in the Joint Committee on Powder Diffraction Standards manuals. The most common search method is to list the three strongest lines and use the Inorganic Hanawalt Index to identify the material from these three lines (JCPDS, Hanawalt, Search Manual, International Centre for Diffraction Data, Swarthmore, Pennsylvania.). A second method uses the Fink index, in which the largest spacings are catalogued (JCPDS, Fink Powder Diffraction Data File Retrieval Index, International Centre for Diffraction Data, Swarthmore, Pennsylvania.). The search may and often does require chemical analysis to aid in identification.

X-ray diffraction is one of the most definitive methods available to the analyst and its use is strongly recommended.

X-RAY FLUORESCENCE ANALYSIS

Several instruments make use of x-ray fluorescence. The two most commonly used in conservation are scanning electron microscopy and the x-ray fluorescence unit, which operates in the open air.

X-RAY FLUORESCENCE IN AIR

X-ray fluorescence in air consists of a source, either x-ray or radioactive, which stimulates x-ray fluorescence in an object or sample. The fluorescence is an x-ray whose energy is characteristic of the element producing the signal in the object. The characteristic energy is detected by a Li drifted silicon detector kept at liquid nitrogen temperature.[24, 25, 26] The signal is amplified and processed by a multichannel analyzer and displayed on a cathode ray tube (CRT) screen (**fig. 4**). Identification of the peaks can be done automatically or semiautomatically if the system has a computer. They may also be easily identified by the use of a cursor or moving indicator that can be manually operated on the panel of the multichannel analyzer. A stimulating energy of 40 to 50 kilovolts and a few milliamps are sufficient to stimulate fluorescence in most art-related materials. The main advantage of such an instrument is that an object may be analyzed in the open air and need not be sampled. It is ideal for surveying large art objects such as paintings and metal statuary. The great disadvantage lies in the fact that because air absorbs and scatters x-rays from the lighter elements, only those objects having elements heavier than potassium or calcium can be detected.

This restriction leaves out elements critical to the identification of many pigments. In these cases the object can be surveyed for all the elements detectable and then sampled to pick up missing elements. The method is invaluable for locating problem areas on art works.

X-ray fluorescence in air can also be used on architectural samples. The sample consisting of a board or an architectural element needs to be brought to the instrument, although eventually such instruments could be made portable. The value of a few hours' survey by x-ray fluorescence cannot be overestimated. Its application to architecture is only in the beginning stages.

SCANNING ELECTRON MICROSCOPY AND ELECTRON-BEAM MICROPROBE

Both these instruments enable analyses to be done using the principle of x-ray fluorescence.[27, 28, 29] Scanning electron microscopy (SEM) uses an electron beam that scans across the sample under vacuum, producing a variety of electronic phenomena, including the release of secondary and back-scattered electrons as well as x-rays characteristic of the elements in the sample. Early electron-beam microprobes (EBMs) used a nonscanning point source electron beam a few microns wide to do point analyses on homogeneous samples, while later instruments used a scanning beam. The SEM uses solid-state or energy-dispersive Si crystal detectors as do EBMs equipped to scan a sample. The EBM's main function is quantitative analysis, which is carried out using a set of diffracting crystals to disperse the fluorescent energy. This is the method of wavelength dispersion.

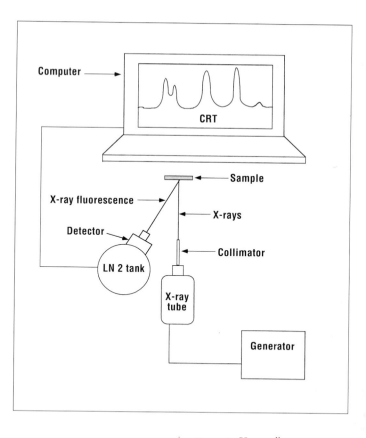

Figure 4. *X-ray fluorescence. In this figure the x-ray tube is the stimulating source. The stimulated sample gives off radiation characteristic of the elements present in the sample. These x-rays are detected by a solid-state liquid nitrogen–cooled detector. The detector's signal is displayed on a computer screen, where the data can then be manipulated to give the most information.*

Calculations for the EBM are carried out by computer with programs specially designed to do atomic and weight percentage analyses from background-corrected intensity data from a flat polished sample. Corrections are made for atomic number, fluorescence, and absorption in the final calculations. Either instrument can be used to do pigment analysis, although quantitative data are rarely needed. Sample preparation is simple. Carbon planchettes with a grid can be purchased from SEM suppliers. Each square in the grid should be inscribed with a number so that the numbers can be read when the samples are in the SEM. One or two small pigment samples can be set in each square fixed in place with collodion. If amylacetate is added to the collodion, its drying time can be extended. Because the electron beam causes an electrostatic charge to develop on nonconducting samples (such as pigments), they must be sputter-coated with conducting carbon.

The actual details of the analysis are beyond the scope of this discussion. What is important is to note that the samples can be examined in the back-scattered as well as the secondary emission mode. Because the majority of pigment samples contain lead white, the back-scatter mode allows pigments having a lower atomic number than Pb to be readily seen. The view on the CRT screen is in tones of whites and grays, depending on atomic number. The highest atomic number pigments show up the brightest and in the secondary electron image (SEI) mode the gray tones representing pigment particles can easily be overlooked.

Cross sections present an equivalent challenge in locating colored pigments in a lead-white matrix. Careful sketches showing the shape of the section, all the layers, and the location of particles facilitate the analysis; otherwise much time can be lost in the search. Photographs can also be used but often require sketches or overlays to locate colored pigment particles.

INFRARED ANALYSIS

The technique of infrared analysis relies on the fact that in the infrared region of the electromagnetic spectrum between 2000 and 400 wavenumber (5 to 25 microns), a large number of compounds absorb infrared energy, giving rise to a set of peaks that are considered definitive enough to be fingerprints. Identification is usually based on direct comparisons of a standard and the unknown in the fingerprint region.

Pigment, media, and varnish infrared (IR) analyses can be carried out on small samples thanks to such devices as beam condensers and the more recent infrared microscope.[30, 31,] The traditional IR instruments disperse energy by means of prisms or gratings. As costs come down, Fourier Transform-infrared (FTIR) instruments are coming into wide use. Paints, however, have the complication of being mixtures sometimes of several pigments and even mixtures of media.

Lead white is virtually ubiquitous and hides many peaks characteristic of oils, glues, resins, and varnishes. Consequently, IR methods work best if a single pigment can be sampled from a paint or if a separation can be made. It is possible to leach out media from large samples and separate pigments by solubilities or by mechanical means but this does complicate the analysis. Standard spectra for a wide variety of materials are available in the literature.[32] The spectra of pigments are also widely available.[33, 34, 35]

The operating principle behind the FTIR involves the use of a Michelson interferometer, which generates the entire infrared spectrum in a single action and passes it through the sample to be detected. The sample spectrum is detected as an interferogram, which cannot be interpreted directly but must be transformed mathematically by the integrating formulas developed by the French mathematician Fourier. Computer technology permits this transformation to be done in a matter of seconds. The resulting spectrum is the conventional absorptance or transmittance spectrum versus energy in inverse centimeters (cm^{-1}).

A sample is required of nanogram to microgram size and is mounted in or on a material that transmits infrared energy without absorbing any portion of the spectrum and remains relatively flat throughout the infrared region. Potassium bromide (KBr) and diamond are the most widely used materials. KBr can be used in plate form or may be mixed with the sample in powder form. The plate may have the sample painted or otherwise deposited on it if the sample is large enough. Samples prepared in this manner may then be run without condensing the beam. Microgram and smaller samples require some form of beam condenser. This is usually achieved by a set of focusing mirrors that condense the infrared beam to a size small enough to pass through a holder one-half to several millimeters across. The sample is mixed with powdered and dried KBr, set in the center of the disc, and pressed in a die, often under vacuum. The resulting sample is used in a beam condenser.

Infrared microscopy operates by having infrared energy reflected out of the instrument sample chamber and through a microscope specially designed to transmit infrared energy. The microscope currently operates best in the transmission mode. Reflection spectra are complicated by interferences and multiple reflection and require much more care in preparation and interpretation. Computer programs are required to correct the raw data. The coupling of an FTIR spectrometer to an infrared microscope run by a microcomputer is a powerful technique for analyzing paint samples. Software currently available allows rapid identification and data manipulation.

While most spectra are identified by matching with standards, important details can be worked out from a knowledge of physical effects such as vibration and rotation on specific bands in the spectrum.

Inorganic as well as organic pigments can be studied and identified by infrared techniques. The spectra of dyes, organic pigments, and binding media may all be identified with infrared.

MEDIA ANALYSIS

The greatest challenge to the analyst remains the unequivocal identification of paint media including adhesives and varnishes—all of which are organic substances distinct from organic dyes and pigments. For large samples the problem may be solved by infrared spectra, stains, solubility, or spot tests. Paintings samples are almost always small and aged. The situation is much better for architectural samples because sample size is usually unrestricted. Once the sample has aged, it cross links, oxidizes, and loses volatile components, making the aged material less soluble and chemically distinct from its original composition.[36] Several references dating from the 1960s and after detail the analyses of media (see Richard Newman and Eugene Farrell, "House Paint Pigments: Composition and Use, 1600 to 1850," in this volume).

Liliane Masschelein-Kleiner et al. present a systematic approach to the analyses of media, adhesives, and varnishes in a 1968 article that summarizes all the techniques then available to the analyst.[37] In a 1986 article Masschelein-Kleiner updates these procedures, reviewing newer techniques such as high-performance liquid chromatography (HPLC), pyrolysis gas-chromatography, and mass spectrometry.[38] John Mills and Raymond White in 1987 review the most recent instrumental techniques in some detail and present an extensive discussion of the chemistry of oils and fats, waxes, bituminous materials, sugars and polysaccharides, proteins, natural resins, and lacquers as well as synthetic materials and dyestuffs.[39] Details of sample preparation are presented for gas chromatography and gas chromatography mass spectra analyses.[40]

Historically the first efforts at media analysis go back to Wilhelm Ostwald in a paper dating from 1905 in which he used histological methods to stain binding media.[41] Ostwald used methyl violet and methylene blue to identify drying oils. Watercolor binders were divided into nitrogenous and nonnitrogenous groups—the former, glue, albumen, and casein; the latter, gum arabic. Gum arabic was identified by its solubility in cold water and nonreaction to stains for nitrogenous substances. All the nitrogen-bearing compounds were found to stain equally and were not distinguishable but could be separated, because albumen is soluble in cold water and gelatin dissolves in warm water, while casein does not dissolve in acid water.

In 1914 Arthur Laurie described the use of methylene violet to stain egg and size.[42] The removal of pigments with and before staining is discussed, as well as the darkening of emulsions treated with sulfuric acid.

Rutherford Gettens in an unpublished sequence to *Painting Materials* (1941) compiled an extensive set of notes on the identification of pigments, chemical elements, and media.[43] Beginning with the identification of a substance as organic by burning or treating it with concentrated sulfuric acid, he then presents specific tests for nitrogen, proteins, phosphorus, sulfur, and specific mediums, including glue casein, egg white, egg yolk, gums, starch, honey, wax, resins, and oils. Gettens's tests are basically similar to those of Ostwald and Laurie and involve solubility, melting temperature, burning, and specific chemical tests including simple reactions with concentrated nitric and sulfuric acid.

In 1964 R. H. de Silva gave a useful summary of most of the binding medium tests.[44]

The Molish test for carbohydrate is described after Eibner (1932) in detecting honey. The Molish test can be used on gums that are polysaccharides, which can be hydrolyzed to simple sugars in the test. Milk and egg white were found to contain carbohydrate and tested positively. De Silva notes that acid green with a little hydrochloric acid stains glue and casein and that Iodeosin dissolved in ammonium salt in water stains glue but that casein goes into solution.

The paper continues by discussing the tests for drying oil, reviewing Ostwald's work, and pointing out that Joyce Plesters successfully stained oil with Nile blue. However, other compounds color with both these stains, and it is probably free fatty acid that is picking up the stain. A positive reaction can occur on egg yolks and egg white or milk as well as silica and silicates. De Silva continues listing many of the common microchemical tests for milk, egg tempera, and drying oils, pointing out the problems in their interpretation. He concludes by recommending paper chromatography as the preferred method of analysis.

Masschelein-Kleiner (1986) discusses all the most common stains used to date for proteins. These are thought to react with the NH_3^+ groups of the proteins in the presence of acid. Lipids (oils) were early detected by saponification with 10 percent potassium hydroxide (KOH).

Stains are not considered always successful because of aging. She lists the melting temperatures of wax, drying oils, and egg yolks. After a brief discussion of the topochemical identification of dried oils proposed by M. Matteini and others, she points out the bromocresol test proposed by Elisabeth Martin for resins. In conclusion, she states that interpretation of all such tests requires care and should be based on long-term experimentation with standards. Furthermore, she notes, black paint layers cannot be tested with the methods just reviewed and all such analyses should be confirmed by other techniques.

In discussing infrared analysis, Masschelein-Kleiner emphasizes that some method of purification is required because of the uncertainties that occur when analyzing complex mixtures of substances and that progress in instruments is encouraging; nonetheless, only general categories of natural media can be distinguished. Her discussion of thin-layer chromatography includes details of the absorbent layer, the solvent, and detection reagents for polysaccharides, proteins, lipids, and resins. Her review also covers the gas chromatography of sugars, proteins, lipids, and natural resins. Pyrolysis gas chromatography is covered in a few paragraphs followed by mass spectrometry and combined gas chromatography, mass spectrometry, liquid chromatography, and differential thermal analysis. Her conclusions are important, as she points out that art objects "present very special difficulties which cannot be surmounted by routine procedures." However, very expensive instruments such as gas chromatography–mass spectrometry (GC-MS) and high-pressure liquid chromatography (HPLC) do not solve the problems by themselves but require the skills of specialized chemists. She notes that more than one method of analysis should be used for each sample in conjunction with a permanent dialogue between chemist, conservator, and art historian.

A generalized scheme for the analyses of binding media, varnish, and ancient adhesives is given by Masschelein-Kleiner in her 1968 paper. It is a very useful scheme to follow since it starts with simple tests and progresses to the most sophisticated. It is clear from her paper that simple solubility tests in cold and hot water or chloroform can go a long way in characterizing a sample and infrared or spot tests can be applied to classify the sample into broad categories. To be certain, however, the infrared analysis or chromatography of high-performance liquid chromatography, thin-layer chromatography (TLC), gas-liquid chromatography, or gas chromatography-mass spectrometry must then be carried out. Nevertheless, in many cases where the need to know is not great or sufficient funding is not available for extensive analyses, the classification into broad groups is better than no information at all.

FLUORESCENT STAINING

One recent development in microscopic techniques used to characterize binding media is fluorescent staining. This technique, whose recent development and exploitation are largely the work of Richard Wolbers, has in fact a long background derived from histological stains referred to elsewhere in this paper.[45]

In a 1987 paper Wolbers and Gregory Landrey cover much of the history of the application of staining techniques discussed by Plesters (1956), Meryl Johnson and Elisabeth Packard (1971), and Martin (1977).[46, 47, 48] In 1982 R. Talbot, at the suggestion of Johnson and Packard,

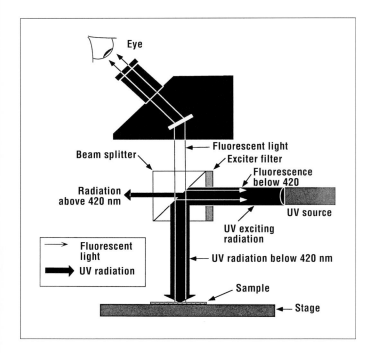

Figure 5. *Optical fluorescence. Ultraviolet energy, which peaks at 360 nanometers, passes through an exciter filter as it enters the beam splitter. Energy below 420 nanometers is reflected onto the sample. Fluorescent light is stimulated in the sample and passes along the optical axis of the microscope. It then goes directly through the beam splitter to the ocular and then to the observer.*

developed and used the fluorescent antibody technique in the identification of proteinaceous media.[49] Unfortunately, this later method depends greatly on the availability of specific antibodies and on the user's skill and interpretive ability. This method was superseded by Wolbers with the direct application of fluorescent stains to cross sections. The three most applicable stains that he recommends are rhodamine B 0.25 percent for solution in ethanol for the detection of lipids, lissamine rhodamine B sulfonyl chloride and 0.25 percent fluorescene isothrocyanate solution in acetone for proteins, and 0.25 percent solution in acetone and a 20 percent solution of antimony pentachloride in chloroform for the detection resins. The sample consisting of several layers is cast in Bio-Plast, and a cross section is made by sanding down to the paint cross section.

The method is simple and straightforward. A drop of the stain is applied to the mounted cross section. The excess is wiped away, and a drop of shell-solvent and a cover glass applied. The antimony-pentachloride should be applied under the hood because of its toxicity. The section is then examined under a fluorescent microscope. The details of the fluorescent microscope are beyond this discussion, but basically a high-energy light source such as mercury or xenon is passed through a filter; a band of wavelengths is selected for which dyes are most sensitive and will fluoresce the brightest (**fig. 5**). For the dyes under discussion, a broad-band ultraviolet filter works well, except for the FITC (Fluorescein Isothiocyanate) dye, which requires a filter that transmits in the blue. The response of these dyes in ultraviolet light is that rhodamine B fluoresces red-orange in the presence of lipids (oils), lissamine rhodamine B sulfonyl chloride fluoresces red-orange in the presence of proteins, and antimony-pentachloride fluoresces blue–white in the presence of resin varnishes.

These stains have proven their worth on sections from paintings and should work very well on architectural samples. The one drawback appears to be that they do not stain aged samples as well as the more recent samples and other stains are required for older samples (see Newman and Farrell, "House Paint Pigments: Composition and Use, 1600 to 1850").

CHROMATOGRAPHY

The principle behind chromatography is the separating of complex mixtures into simple recognizable components. Anyone who has spilled a stained liquid on a piece of paper notices that the stain spreads from its initial site and separates into variously colored or shaded bands. The controlled application of this simple observation gave rise to paper chromatography. Refinements use a solid in a thin layer applied to a glass plate to act as an absorbent for the sample material. The sample material is activated by a fluid. The fluid first dissolves molecular species in the sample and then deposits them on the solid along the path of the moving fluid. The first-column chromatography was described when plant pigment was separated along the length of a tube containing crystalline calcite ($CaCO_3$) powder as petroleum was passed through it.

GAS-LIQUID CHROMATOGRAPHY

Gas-liquid chromatography combines several features derived from column and thin-layer chromatography into one operation. The sample, after considerable preparation, is microsyringed into the entry port on the instrument, where it is mixed with a carrier gas (commonly helium, argon, or nitrogen gas) that carries it, the mobile phase, along a coiled column filled with some inert material in which a liquid has been absorbed, referred to as the stationary liquid phase. The coiled column is located in an oven where temperature can be increased in a linear ramp fashion according to a predetermined rate, driving off and separating various molecular species. These species are carried to a detector, converted to a current, amplified, then recorded on a strip chart recorder. Specific species may be recognized by their retention times or retention index.

The greatest problem in gas-liquid chromatography is the proper selection of a column to properly separate the sample constituents and the sample preparation. The samples must be broken down chemically into their various components, a process referred to as derivitization.

A successful analysis by gas-liquid chromatography depends on a proper derivitization or finding the appropriate coil and the correct interpretation of spectrum, simple in principle but difficult in practice.

Separation of species, especially those of low molecular weight, can be achieved by heating the sample rather than derivitizing it. This may be achieved by pyrolysis gas-chromatography. If the end product of the separation process of gas-liquid chromatography is fed into a mass spectrograph, the molecular species involved may be characterized with great accuracy with respect to mass.

To summarize, with regard to media analysis even the most expensive equipment is no substitute for an accumulated base of experience in the hands of a skilled analyst who knows the materials of art, who is willing to talk and collaborate with conservators and historians, and who is willing to run more than one test on a sample to cross-check results. No matter what method is used, media analysis remains the challenge of art materials analysis.

Painting Techniques

SURFACE PREPARATION AND APPLICATION

BRIAN POWELL

uccessful painting depends not only on the paint itself but also on how the surface is prepared, how the paint is applied, and the environmental conditions during drying. The number of specialized paints now available and the range of uses for which they have been formulated are enormous, as are the specialized means of application. Many are highly technical factory methods whose successful application is possible only with sophisticated equipment and under controlled conditions. Even field techniques are similarly demanding. Treated here is the more common range of paint types and applications on wood and masonry in the largely architectural uses most frequently encountered by building owners and contractors (**fig. 1**).

SUBSTRATES

The nature of the surface to be painted and its particular requirements are the first consideration in planning a paint job. Some surfaces are characterized by great porosity and if not properly treated can absorb large amounts of paint. The porosity of other substrates is such that they may selectively pull in some ingredients of a paint, leaving an altered material on the surface. Still other substrates are not at all porous, allowing the paint no surface penetration.

Some surfaces are more amenable than others to being wetted by a given material. The linseed oil of traditional oil paints tended to wet easily onto many surfaces. The water vehicle of latex paints has often had a much harder time wetting.

Another characteristic of surfaces is their texture. Rougher surfaces provide an opportunity for mechanical bonding of the paint. This quality is referred to as "tooth" and may be created or enhanced as necessary. Smoother surfaces provide less mechanical bonding and may require preparation to encourage more adhesive bonding.

Some substrates are dimensionally stable in conditions of varying temperature or humidity. These materials put fewer demands on paint layers than those whose dimensions vary. Proper preparation and painting take probable movement into consideration and in the case of wood may even mitigate its extremes.

Figure 1. *A high-style Victorian paint scheme recreated on an 1871 New England house. This elaborate treatment, which includes eight colors, was researched by the Conservation Center of the Society for the Preservation of New England Antiquities. (Society for the Preservation of New England Antiquities)*

Another factor that may affect the successful painting of a given substrate is its chemical nature or chemical activity within it. The nature of some materials may preclude adequate bonding of a given paint film or may attack the film itself. Some materials release "exudates" that will migrate through the film and cause unacceptable marking. In other cases salts within a substrate may move to its surface and detach an otherwise well-adhered paint. Alkaline substrates such as lime plaster, concrete, and galvanized steel may chemically react with a paint to cause binder deterioration.

WOOD

Wood is a fibrous, porous, organic material. As humidity varies it absorbs or emits water vapor and in the process swells or contracts. Wood will also absorb liquid water. Its greatest movement is perpendicular to the direction of the grain.

Any paint film on wood must be flexible enough to allow movement. A coating that is too brittle initially or that becomes embrittled will probably crack except in the most constant atmospheric conditions.

Before wood can be painted it must be seasoned. This is the process of drying by which its moisture content is reduced. Painting wood that holds an excess of water invites failure because trapped moisture will migrate outward and the wood itself will continue to shrink. It is generally agreed that exterior woodwork should not be painted if its moisture content exceeds 15 percent of its weight. Trapped moisture can result in severe blistering that may not be evident immediately. There is less consensus on the proper moisture content for interior woodwork. A level at or below 10 percent is generally considered best.

The percentage of moisture content of wood may be measured by a moisture meter, a device with two projecting nail-like probes. When these are driven a short distance into the wood the meter measures the electrical resistance between them and gives a reading calibrated to the wood's dampness. Readings below 6 percent are generally not reliable.

A major goal in painting exterior woodwork is to exclude as much water vapor and liquid water as possible. This necessitates a well-adhered priming coat. Because the end grain of the wood has by far the greatest ability to absorb water, end grains should be generously primed whenever possible. A further step to minimize water penetration, and one that has been shown to increase the service life of a paint significantly, is to apply a paintable water repellent to bare wood before the primer and top coats.

The best way to keep excessive moisture out of painted exterior wood is to maintain existing paint layers and repaint before failure occurs. A cracking paint layer will allow moisture into the substrate, which will in turn accelerate the cracking process. When allowed to proceed too long, the paint film may deteriorate to the point where extensive scraping or even removal may be necessary. Maintaining unbroken exterior paint layers can lead to significant savings over time.

The characteristics of wood vary from species to species. Each species has been rated for its ability to hold paint, determined in part by its porosity and growth patterns. Wood grows seasonally, showing differences in density and therefore porosity in its spring and summer growth. The fast-growing soft woods, whose seasonal rings are most pronounced, show distinct differences in paint-holding ability. Paint usually adheres well to "spring" wood but may not hold as well on the denser "summer" wood. The woods usually painted are softwood species, those with the least summer wood holding the paint best. Paint also tends to adhere better on the edge grain of boards than on the side with the broader grain. Some woods are known to present problems, such as species of southern yellow pine, whose wide summer rings may not hold paint well.

Some woods have characteristics that present special considerations for painting. Redwood and cedar are oily woods that hold paint well but may develop brown staining through the paint. The danger of this can be reduced through the use of stain-blocking primers.

New woods, clean, well seasoned and well chosen for paint-holding qualities, have few specific needs for preparation. Nails should be sunk and holes filled. If putty or spackle is used for filling, the wood should be primed first. Otherwise, the liquid ingredients of the fill may be absorbed into the substrate, causing poor setting and possible failure. Small patches and filled holes should be allowed to set at least forty-eight hours before painting. Larger patches may need up to three weeks. Some open-grained hard woods may also need a grain filler to give a uniform flat surface.

"Plastic" wood products are more expensive and more difficult to tool and sand but set much more rapidly, may be applied to bare wood, and may be painted more promptly. Other widely available filling materials also dry very quickly to a paintable surface.

It is important to paint as quickly as possible new wood or wood that has for any reason been newly exposed to sunlight. Research at the Department of Agriculture's Forest Products Laboratory has shown that wood's ability to hold paint may begin to be reduced after only two weeks of exposure.

Occasionally new wood has been so smoothly planed that it provides little tooth for good adhesion. It should be roughened with a fine grit sandpaper to increase its paint-holding ability.

Old wood may have much more demanding preparatory requirements than new wood. Exterior wood in northern areas may have been damaged by moisture entrapped during the freeze-thaw cycle. In humid areas wood may have been damaged by mildew or other fungus. Exterior wood that has been left unpainted long or lost its paint entirely may have been attacked by ultraviolet light, damaging its lignin connective tissue and significantly weakening its surface. It may be covered with dirt and oily grime. Furthermore, wood may have been split by nailing, damaged by too rough sanding or ill-advised blasting, or otherwise rendered amenable to water penetration and not ready for immediate painting.

Exterior wooden elements do wear out. Wood of little historical or artistic interest may be replaced, eliminating the need for special preparation. Wood with greater value may be revived by modern consolidation and filling methods beyond the scope of this chapter.

In the past, painters would coat with boiled linseed oil wood whose surfaces were weakened but otherwise sound. This process bound the fibers and enabled the wood to be painted. Some traditional painters use this method today. In recent years a number of paint manufacturers have offered a modern family of materials generically known as preprimers. They may be seen as surface wood consolidants, used in much the same way that boiled linseed oil was. While each product should be used in accordance with its specific instructions, a general procedure is common to most.

Any bits of surviving paint in the target area should be removed, and the wood should be allowed to dry thoroughly. The material should be applied generously, allowing as much to soak in as the wood will accept in one prolonged coating. Any excess should be wiped off, and the area should be left to dry. An area should be treated only once. The initial pass will seal the wood. Subsequent passes may stand on the surface, potentially forming a semismooth layer that may not allow good binding of the paints. After the single preprimer treatment the wood may be primed and painted normally. Degraded wood surfaces can also be prepared by sanding down to sound material.

PREPARATION OF PAINTED WOOD

If wood has been painted before, the necessary preparation will be determined by the condition of the existing paint. Coatings in good condition—those that show good substrate and intercoat adhesion (that is, the layers stick together) and no pronounced checking, cracking, or alligatoring—may be repainted with little special preparation.

Previously painted wood must have all dirt and oily materials washed off. This may be done with detergents and followed by a rinse of clean water or mineral spirits. Washing should precede any scraping or sanding to prevent spreading of the surface contaminants.

If damp conditions have allowed the growth of mildew it should be killed with a bleach solution (a one-to-one mixture of household bleach and water) before washing.

Dirty exterior paints may be cleaned by hand and hose or with mechanical help. In most cases a low-pressure detergent machine wash would be sufficient for washing wooden buildings. Washing must be followed by a clean water rinse. High-pressure water or detergent blasting and steam cleaning are effective techniques, often more associated with masonry buildings or with the degreasing of machinery. In fact, a high-pressure wash (up to 2,200 pounds per square inch) may be an acceptable method of preparation on any exterior surface except the most fragile or porous.

If existing painted surfaces are too smooth or glossy, they should be lightly sanded or otherwise roughened before repainting. The surfaces of interior enamel paints in particular may need to be abraded or etched to ensure the proper adhesion of subsequent coats. A family of materials that may substitute for surface sanding are deglossers. Deglossers both clean and chemically roughen a paint surface, providing mechanical tooth for the adherence of the next layer. In formulation they are related to solvent-based paint removers but have no additives to retard drying. Because their ingredients are chosen in part for quick evaporation, they attack the surface rapidly and are gone, leaving no surface contaminants to prevent good adhesion of the next paint layer. Deglossers have traditionally been used before oil- and alkyd-based coatings. They should be used with water-based coatings only on the manufacturer's recommendation.

Excessive surface gloss may be more an interior than an exterior problem. By both formulation and the nature of their materials, the surfaces of some exterior alkyd and oil paints incrementally degrade or chalk. Part of this process is the slow degradation of surface binding oils by ultraviolet light. The process serves several ends. To a degree it is a self-cleaning feature, with dirt and contaminants washing off with the surface of the paint layer. It also thins the coatings, preventing too thick a buildup and avoiding the consequent cracking and alligatoring. Finally, it dulls any surface glossiness so that new paints will adhere well.

While the chalking remains a characteristic of some modern alkyds, especially whites formulated with anatase instead of rutile titanium dioxide (check the label), modern paints are increasingly nonchalking and non–self cleaning. Of course, latexes do not chalk at all. As legislation increasingly removes volatile hydrocarbon solvents from paints, chalking may be relegated to a historic feature and its problems obviated.

Intact chalking paint surfaces may need little preparation before repainting with an oil or alkyd. Any loose material should be dusted off, and if necessary the surface should be given a light detergent wash and clean water rinse. Severely chalking paints may need a more thorough scrub or power wash. Oils and alkyds often have the ability to wet into and bind the chalking surface, guaranteeing a successful bonding of the new coating over the old. In the past latexes have not bonded well over chalky paint; they tended to sit on the surface rather than penetrate and bind. The best modern 100 percent acrylic latexes now may be applied over typical moderately chalky surfaces, although some painters still feel that the safest advice is to prime with an oil or alkyd primer, allow twenty-four to forty-eight hours for drying, then add a top coat of a latex.

The most sensible practice is to repaint painted surfaces when the paint has aged but before it has begun to degrade seriously. Deteriorating paint layers need much more labor-intensive preparation than intact ones. Many factors can lead to paint weakening or failure, causing problems between the paint and its substrate, between the paint layers, or within the paint film itself. No new paint should be applied over failing existing paints. It is important to realize that some paint adhesion problems do not originate in the paints themselves or their application but derive from other sources. The chief among these is faulty moisture management within the building.

PAINT-REMOVAL METHODS

If the paint is weakened to the point of detaching from the building, the loose material should be removed. If there is a weakness or cleavage at a certain level in the layers, the paint must be removed down to that level. And if there is serious widespread cracking, lifting, or alligatoring, the wood should be stripped before repainting.

The standard preparation for lifting paint from woodwork remains scraping (figs. 2, 3, and 4). This may be done by hand or machine, always in the direction of the wood grain. In either case the metal tool is a great deal harder than the wood and can easily damage its surface. In hand scraping the knife or scraper should not be too sharp and should be held at a low angle to the wood. Molded or other shaped woodwork must be scraped with great care. A variety of curving scrapers of differing sizes and radii to fit particular molding profiles should be kept on hand. For the best work on milled or carved surfaces fabricate custom shapes designed for the specific job. Machine scraping by rotary wire brush or other means may be helpful on flat areas. Workers should be aware of the probable presence of lead in the paints, protect themselves accordingly, and contain and dispose of wastes properly.

Edges of scraped areas can be feathered into remaining paints with sandpaper. Sandpaper may also be used to give tooth to smooth surfaces or clean up the final residue after paint removal. It is important not to allow sanding to blunt molding profiles or otherwise reshape woodwork.

Figure 2. *Scraping in preparation for repainting. (Society for the Preservation of New England Antiquities)*

Sandpapers are sold in a number of grit types and sizes. Most papers are graded for their abrasive quality, with low numbers indicating very rough paper and higher numbers indicating finer grades. Garnet papers work very well on wood. Aluminum oxide and silicon carbide are useful on wood and other surfaces as well. The widely available flint papers are effective on wood but dull quickly. Emery papers are used for metals.

If the paint to be sanded contains lead, the residue must be considered a toxic substance. It is most dangerous in an interior setting in which young children live. While some children may ingest whole chips of lead paint, the incremental ingestion of lead dust, usually through hand-to-mouth transmission, is thought to be the greater threat. The amount of physical and neurobiological damage to a child may be substantial and irreversible.

Any disturbance of lead-bearing surfaces in a building can produce lead dust. Once deposited it is extremely difficult to remove. In fact, studies suggest that it is almost impossible to clean up completely after abrasive removal of lead paints. Therefore it is important to contain residues whenever any removal work is done. In small, localized uses residues may be contained somewhat by wet sanding. For large jobs, especially if a large amount of paint removal is a goal, extensive masking is necessary. The entire room, including all doors, walls, and floor surfaces, should be masked, and even doubly masked. Any carpeting or upholstered furniture should be removed or masked especially well. Those doing the sanding should wear respirators, should change their clothing on leaving the area, and should avoid hand-to-mouth exposure. After the work is completed the lead residue should be carefully enclosed as the masking sheeting is removed—first the dust-rich inner layer and then the less-contaminated outer one. A final cleanup should be done with a solution of trisodium phosphate in water, changing the mix often to prevent recontamination. Typical vacuuming is not effective for lead dust removal.

When a paint layer presents adhesion or other problems that cannot be dealt with by standard scraping and sanding or when someone hopes to recapture detail or clarity of woodwork that has been obscured by too much paint, the paint must be removed entirely. This will give the opportunity for a new coating, well chosen and well applied, to bond without the danger that underlying layers will cause problems. This level of paint removal is, however, costly, time consuming, and not without risks that may arise from the removal itself.

In addition to removing loose paints, scraping and sanding may also be used for total paint removal but only with great care, as they may easily damage the wood. Scraping is most successful on broad, flat areas. It may not give acceptable results on other surfaces such as carving or rounded moldings.

Removing paint by machines is even more dangerous on complex surfaces and may also damage flat areas. These methods include a number of devices that come in a variety of shapes and sizes. Better or worse results will depend on the type of machine and the skill of the operator.

The widely available rotary wire wheels offer quick results but almost invariably cut through the surface of the wood.

Hand sanding is slow and laborious and is seldom used for total paint removal. Machine sanding may be quite efficient and may give acceptable results on flat surfaces. Of the three common types of electric sanders—orbital, belt, and disk—the

belt and disk types are the most useful in removal. Both must be handled with great care. If held too long on a given point or if not held parallel to the surface, the belt sander may cut dull ridges and the disk sander shallow scallops.

Caustic paint strippers, based on sodium or potassium hydroxide or carbonate, are inexpensive and fast. They may be used on or off site. Building parts can be removed and taken to large dip tanks, in which they are immersed, soaked, scrubbed down, and neutralized. Caustic strippers pose two serious risks to wooden substrates: they may damage the surface, and they may deposit in the wood salts that can cause subsequent adhesion problems.

If soaked too long in caustic material, the wood surface itself is apt to be attacked, darkened, and weakened. In the worst case, individual fibers separate, giving the wood a soft, feltlike appearance. A traditional remedy for this condition in interiors is to apply successive coats of alcohol-thinned shellac, sanding each coat when dry. In this way the surface may be restored but not without the loss of material and possibly detail. The modern equivalent would be substrate hardening with a preprimer.

The caustic stripping process requires thorough neutralization with an acidic wash. Unless this process is completely effective, soluble salts will be left, deposited within the wood. With changes in humidity or moisture content these salts can redissolve and migrate to the surface of the wood, where they can cause paints to detach, in effect pushing them off the surface. If this occurs, the only remedy is to remove all the existing paint and treat the wood to remove the salts, a laborious and expensive process. To be sure that the substrate has been adequately neutralized it is wise to test with pH paper after treatment.

Later adhesion problems are common when caustic strippers are used on exterior woodwork. Many feel that the safest practice is to avoid this approach. While adhesion problems often follow caustic stripping of interior woodwork, this is not quite so great a risk.

Solvent-based strippers are the other main group of chemical paint removers. Most are based on methylene chloride and methanol and include other ingredients such as toluene. Additives are usually included to increase viscosity and retard evaporation.

The term *solvent based* may be a bit misleading, for the effective solvent action does not actually dissolve the cross-linked film but chemically induces swelling in it. When sufficiently

Figure 3. *General surface preparation for repainting. (Society for the Preservation of New England Antiquities)*

Figure 4. *Detail of a scraped and sanded surface ready for painting. Well-bonded historic paints are left intact. (Society for the Preservation of New England Antiquities)*

weakened in this way the paints may be removed easily, usually with metal tools chosen for the particular surface. When the surface is clean, the area must be washed with denatured alcohol or mineral spirits to remove the residual wax present in these paint removers. Any raised grain must be lightly sanded.

Solvent-based strippers are effective but must be used with caution. Most contain methylene chloride, a carcinogen that may be inhaled or absorbed through the skin; in time it can pass through rubber gloves. Most also contain methanol and toluene, which are additional health threats.

Paint also may be removed by heating. The oldest method is using an open torch. This process is fast but cannot be recommended. It may release toxic lead-containing fumes, it may scorch the wood, and it may ignite wooden or partially wooden structures. Often ignited materials within a wall will smolder unobserved for hours before bursting into flame. Open flame removal must be considered too great a risk to wooden buildings for any but the most rare and controlled uses.

Removing paint by using a heating coil or hot-air gun may also release toxic gases. Workers may protect themselves by wearing a properly fitted inhaler mask with fresh organic vapor cartridges. These methods are less likely to cause scorching and are not thought likely to start fires if sensibly used. They are also useful in softening and removing old window putty. The coil or air gun is held over a small area until the paint begins to lift. The paint can then be removed with a putty knife or other tool. It is best to begin removal in the deepest or otherwise most difficult part of each area. If easier surface areas are cleared first the paints may begin to cool and deeper areas may not yield to the tool. On the subsequent reheating necessary to soften deep spots, previously cleared surface may scorch.

Paint-removal techniques using heat seldom clear a surface sufficiently well for immediate repainting and usually must be followed by a final pass of sandpaper or chemical remover.

Sand or grit blasting, because of its great speed and coverage, might be a temptation. Wood is much too soft for this process and can be seriously damaged.

As should be clear, no paint removal method is free of potential problems. In any given situation one should choose the method with the fewest defects.

A final consideration in removing paint from wood is the historic or artistic qualities of the object. In historic buildings it may be important to preserve intact samples of the full paint layering of representative elements to ensure that any future research or restoration will have remaining evidence of original or early paint schemes.

PAINTING ON WOOD

Painting on most new or exposed old wood begins with priming or, in extreme cases, prepriming (fig. 5). Woods are porous and will readily absorb low-viscosity liquids. If a paint formulated as a top coat is applied to unprimed wood, some materials from that paint will be selectively pulled into it. In oil and alkyd paints both the binder (nonvolatile vehicle) and the vehicle (volatile vehicle) may be absorbed, leaving a reformulated and unacceptable material on the surface. Such a layer may not have adequate internal cohesion and may cause both immediate and future problems. With latexes water may be pulled out of the paint and alter the intended rate of drying as well as the final film strength. Primers are formulated to bond well to the substrate and provide a firm base for subsequent coats.

In some cases primers should be used over aged exterior paints. As stated earlier, some exterior oil or alkyd paints may chalk. Badly chalking paints may provide a poor footing for subsequent coats. Exterior primers are designed to penetrate and bind these chalking surfaces.

Traditionally, an oil primer has been recommended as the transition layer between an aging oil paint and a latex. La-

texes have improved greatly since their introduction to a mass market in the late 1940s. While some consider the continued use of oils to be prudent in these cases, a growing body of opinion believes that the best latex primers available today are equally effective. To make sure that a latex primer does have this improved property, read the label; do not trust one that fails to mention specifically the ability to bind to oil films.

Another family of materials now widely used is the primer-sealers. These are related to knot sealers and often share their alcohol and polyvinyl butyryl composition. Primer-sealers, as the name implies, are intended to serve a dual purpose. Like a standard primer, they bond with the substrate, provide hiding, and serve as a base for subsequent layers. In addition they seal the surface from the penetration of nuisance materials. To prepare a surface that has extensive staining from past water seepage, for example, a standard primer might allow that staining to penetrate and discolor the finish layer. A primer-sealer will lessen this danger.

In the past builders avoided using boards with knots for exterior cladding or interior finish work. We now commonly find knots in wood that is to be painted. Wood knots are filled with resinous material that migrates. Because the direction of the wood fibers in knots is perpendicular to the wood's grain, a small movement can bring this exudate to the surface, where it causes distinct stains that will bleed through multiple paint layers. Simple repainting will not prevent renewed staining. Each knot must be individually sealed.

The historic materials for knot sealing were shellac, either pigmented or unpigmented, and aluminum paints. Both worked but have now been superseded by sealers based on polyvinyl butyryl, vinyl toluene, or special acrylics. These are widely available and effective. To reduce the possibility of knot staining on new wood, precede the sealing step with a mineral spirits wash to pull out an amount of the exudate beforehand. These sealing products are also recommended to prevent bleed-through of the worst substrate stains. In exterior applications it is best to limit their use to small areas as some knot sealers may be a bit brittle.

Any primer, primer-sealer, or knot sealer must be thoroughly dried before the next coat is applied. This is especially true of oils and alkyds. Latexes are somewhat more forgiving, having the ability to transmit amounts of moisture even when dry. Generally, latexes may be recoated much sooner than oils or alkyds.

To apply an oil top coat over a wet or tacky primer is to invite problems. This can lead to cracking or wrinkling, as a primer finally dries and shrinks under a quick-drying upper coat, to blistering, especially in direct sunlight as solvents try to escape, or to other problems. While there are times that a primer may need to be applied very generously to a very porous surface, the usual practice is to apply both primers and undercoats thinly. Top coats are usually applied more thickly to ensure good leveling and good handling if brushed.

When painting a top coat over a primer, the two must be compatible. This is true not only generally with respect to the type of paint but also in formulation. The classic rule of softer over harder coats and weaker over stronger coats always applies. If a stronger paint is applied over a weaker one, the stronger may pull up or otherwise damage the weaker layer below. This may cause lifting or peeling. The best way to avoid incompatibility of layers is to stay within a given product line. This way one can have confidence that the primer and top coat offered by a company have been formulated and tested to work well together (**fig. 6**).

PLASTER

Plaster is a porous, inorganic masonry material. Its surface may be rough, nubbly, or smooth. It is dimensionally stable and may be chemically active or inactive.

There are two main types of plaster: lime plaster (calcium carbonate) and gypsum plaster (calcium sulfate). Lime plaster is the more archaic of the two, having been used from the first period of American building. Although it continues in use today, it has largely been superseded by gypsum plasters or lime-gypsum plasters. Gypsum plaster (plaster of Paris) was used historically for cast decoration. With its increased availability beginning in the late nineteenth century, it also came to be used for flat plastering.

Lime plaster is initially and may long remain chemically active. It cures by a slow process of carbonation as moisture turns the slaked lime into calcium carbonate. Final carbonation to the full depth of the plaster coat may take up to nine months, a year, or even longer. (Remarkably, cases have been reported in which the interiors of lime plasters have remained uncured for more that one hundred years.) It remains alkaline throughout this period and has the ability to saponify paints. Saponification can be recognized by a marked softening of the paint layer and may be accompanied by a brown exudation.

Because of the danger of chemical attack, most sources now recommend the use of latex paints on lime plaster. Latexes are unaffected by the alkalinity of young lime plasters and may be applied as soon as the plaster is set and largely dry, often in about two weeks.

Lime plasters may be painted with oil paints if certain cautions are observed. The main guarantor of success is delay. Some sources suggest a wait of sixty to ninety days. Traditionally, many waited a year. While oil or alkyd painting of new lime plaster is always risky, a litmus paper test of pH may indicate when the material has reached a safe level. Wait for a neutral pH, keeping in mind that the pH of the interior of the plaster may remain much higher than that of the surface. Therefore the most reliable reading will be from the interior of the layer. Another test for the alkalinity of plaster is to wet the surface and apply a 1 percent solution of phenolphthalein in methanol or ethanol. If it turns purple, the plaster remains too alkaline for oil or alkyd painting.

Any plaster, even an aged one, must be adequately dry before painting in oil or alkyd. A moisture meter reading of 7.5 percent or below is considered safe. Extremes of humidity can affect the reading; as with moisture readings on wood, tests deeper in the layer are more reliable. If, as recommended, a final damp wipe of the surface is done to redissolve any surface alkali or reduce the risk of "hot spots," this too must also be allowed to dry thoroughly. Of course, this wetting should not be a soaking, penetrating only thinly and allowing quick drying.

Occupants of a building may find it unacceptable to live with raw, uncoated plaster walls in the interval between plastering and safe painting. In the past temporary painting with a water-soluble distemper was used as a strategy to mitigate the wall's appearance during this waiting period. When the walls were believed to be ready for their oil coats, the distemper was washed off, the wall was allowed to dry, and oils were applied.

Another past strategy that allowed quick oil painting of lime plaster was to coat the surface with a solution of zinc sulfate in water or with vinegar or acetic acid. This is no longer recommended.

New gypsum plasters present few special difficulties in preparation. They set quickly by reaction with water, crystallizing to form a chemically inactive substrate that may be painted with latex, oil, or alkyd paints. While they must be allowed to dry thoroughly before painting with an oil or alkyd, latexes will tolerate an amount of residual dampness and may be applied very soon. It is quite common to add an amount of lime to gypsum plasters to enhance their working properties. This will raise the alkalinity and invoke the cautions of painting lime plasters, although on a lesser scale. New plasters of either type should be primed before sanding.

OLD PLASTER

Excepting renewed chemical activity from the wetting of unreacted lime, old plaster surfaces are usually chemically stable. Especially if they have been painted before with paints that are intact, they may require little preparation save patching and the removal of any dirt or oily residue with a mild detergent or mineral spirits. Old plaster surfaces may, however, have a number of problems that must be addressed to ensure successful painting.

Some plasters contain soluble salts. These may be surviving contaminants in the original material, or they may have been deposited in the plaster by exterior agents. In either case they may threaten the adhesion of paint. When wetted these salts may be dissolved in water and may migrate to the surface of the material where they recrystallize. They form a powdery layer known as efflorescence. This process can loosen even well-adhered paint layers.

Whenever efflorescence is seen, it is important to identify the source of the moisture and seal it off. This is especially important if the offending salts are being introduced into the plaster with the water. Often more vigilant building maintenance will suffice. All traces of the efflorescence must be removed from the surface. Depending on the strength and characteristics of the plaster, this may be done by wiping with a rag, brushing with a stout bristle (or equivalent), gently brushing with wire, or by gently sanding. Efflorescence should always be removed dry so that the material will not be dissolved and redeposited in the plaster.

The surfaces of most plasters are adequately strong to hold a coat of paint. Occasionally, however, a plaster may be very weak, showing little cohesion either internally or on the surface. This problem is beyond the scope of simple painting preparation. Its best solution may be the replacement of dispensable plaster or the consolidation of plaster with historic or artistic interest. When this cannot be done, the painter needs to judge whether it is actually possible to paint the plaster successfully.

If plaster has been painted before and that paint is intact, it may be, as stated earlier, repainted after a thorough cleaning. If the paint is not intact, loose paint must be removed beforehand. Paint may be carefully scraped from plaster, but the surface may be damaged by too aggressive an approach. Because the plaster is much softer than the metal tools usually used in scraping, other methods may be more appropriate in a given case. Even where careful scraping is successful on flat plaster, decorative plasterwork is almost always threatened except by the most painstaking scraping with small specialized tools.

Paint may be removed from plaster by some but not all the methods by which it can be removed from wood. Heat techniques are not appropriate for work on plaster. Heat will not only dissipate into the plaster but also when used on gypsum plasters will drive water from their crystal structure and convert the gypsum into weak anhydride. Nor are machine abrasion or sanding recommended. Blasting, of course, is unacceptable. Chemical means, however, may be effective. Drawbacks of caustic removal are the danger of deposition of salts and inadequate neutralization, but solvent-based removers are effective on plaster. They may have a temporary softening effect on the surface that must be considered during removal.

Avoid thick buildups of oil paint on plaster. Oil paints continue to oxidize and cross link over time, causing a slight progressive shrinking. Thick oil-paint films are usually stronger than the plaster substrate. If they are well adhered to the surface they can, as they shrink, literally pull the plaster apart. This condition may be corrected only by complete removal of the paint, ideally before the plaster itself has been too damaged.

Latex paints shrink somewhat while drying but are dimensionally stable when dry. They do not threaten surface destruction of plaster but may, like oils, obscure the detail of cast decorative work. In the past glue-based distempers or calcimine paints were often used on plaster walls and were commonly used on plaster ceilings. Before recoating they were washed off, allowing any cast detail to remain crisp.

Those wishing to maintain good detail on plaster decoration or avoid further loss of detail may consider the use of such reversible water-soluble paints. The present bad reputation of these paints derives from incomplete removal before coating with other types of paint, which may lead to severe peeling and lifting. The only reliable cure for this condition is to entirely remove the later paints and wash off or seal the distemper with the traditional cut (alcohol-thinned) shellac, a modern primer-sealer, or a product specially formulated for the purpose.

To apply a new distemper paint, work quickly and use a large brush. The rate of setting can be slowed by keeping the humidity high in the room. All doors and windows should be kept closed while working.

Uncoated plaster presents a porous surface that will easily accept water, solvents, and oils. The accepted practice is to seal any new or newly stripped plaster surface with a plaster primer or primer-sealer before painting. Formerly plaster was prepared by sizing. This step sealed and to a degree bound the surface so that the oils of an oil paint or the water of a glue-based paint or wallpaper glue would not selectively penetrate the surface, leaving a reformulated and probably poorly bound material on the surface. Some sizes also had a stain-sealing effect.

Shellac and glue were the most commonly used sizing materials. Surviving period glue sizes may give problems today. Some have suffered decomposition. Most, unless rendered harder and more insoluble with alum, remain water soluble, and may detach with moisture. And because an accretion of oil paints above such a size may be much stronger than the size, the size may provide a cleavage layer that may encourage lifting as the oils shrink with progressive oxidation. When glue sizes are found, surfaces may have to be stripped, the glue size removed, and the surfaces resealed with a modern material.

SHEETROCK

Sheetrock is a masonry material lined with paper. Although it is possible to paint it with either latex or oil-alkyd materials, oil or alkyd primers run the danger of raising the nap of the paper. The commonly accepted approach to sheetrock is to start with a latex primer or a primer-sealer.

CONCRETE

Concrete is an inorganic cast masonry material with significant porosity, great dimensional stability, and potential chemical activity. Many of the same considerations that apply to plaster apply also to concrete.

Portland cement, a chief ingredient of most concrete, is naturally alkaline, producing calcium hydroxide as it cures. If painting with oil or alkyd materials, the best practice is to wait a long while before applying paint. A year is not too long, and some concrete surfaces remain quite alkaline for several years. In the past, to accelerate the painting of concrete surfaces with oil or alkyd paints, the concrete was sometimes treated with a solution of zinc sulfate. This treatment is no longer recommended. Another practice was to apply a dilute solution of zinc chloride and phosphoric acid in water. This treatment, too, has largely fallen out of use as acrylic latexes have emerged as the paint of choice for most concrete.

Latex paints, with their resistance to alkaline materials, may be applied when the concrete is set and dry to the point of slight dampness. Even with latexes, however, it is safest to wait for a month or more.

Cement paints, whose base is portland cement, may be applied directly on concrete surfaces once they have set. They may not, however, be used over other types of coatings.

Several synthetic resin paints with high degrees of alkali resistance perform well on concrete. Epoxy paints are extremely durable and adherent on concrete. They are especially serviceable on concrete floors where the wear from foot traffic is a major consideration. Polyurethanes, synthetic rubbers and polyesters may also be used. For all these materials the concrete must be dry, but it is not necessary to wait for extremely long periods before coating.

In all painting of new concrete it is important to remove any trace of form oil left on the surface by the molds. This may be done by weathering, with a dilute solution of trisodium phosphate or with a 5 to 10 percent solution of muriatic acid, rinsed with water, neutralized with trisodium phosphate or weak ammonia water, and rinsed again.

Some concrete, either old or new, may be too smooth to provide adequate tooth for proper bonding of paint. Such surfaces may be roughened mechanically with tools or blasting or may be etched chemically, also with a 5 to 10 percent solution of muriatic acid in water. The solution is left on until the desired degree of roughness is achieved; then it is rinsed off with clean water. Keep in mind that roughness alone is not an adequate condition to ensure proper adhesion and should not be considered a substitute for the practices described earlier.

Old concrete may be painted successfully with latex, oil, or alkyd when clean and dry. If using latex it is important to clean off any loose material. In cases of extreme powdering it may be necessary to use a penetrating conditioner to bind the loose surface material before painting.

Concrete block may be treated in a fashion similar to dry concrete if its mortar composition and degree of dryness permit. Because of concrete block's great porosity, block fillers have been developed. These materials, usually latexes, penetrate, fill some voids, and prepare the surface for priming.

BRICK AND STONE

Brick and stone are dimensionally stable inorganic materials that show a range of porosity. They are also chemically stable but may be affected by problems of soluble salts migrating within. Intact brick and stone present few problems for painting preparation, although the nature of their mortars may be complicating factors.

New brick and stonework with nonlime mortar may be primed and painted directly if clean and dry. Remember that even mortars referred to as cement mortars may have an amount of lime added. Masonry with new lime mortar is subject to the same considerations and delays described above for lime plaster. If latex paints are to be used, all surface dust and residue must be removed, usually by wire brushing or a water wash.

Intact old brick and stonework may be painted with little special preparation. Lime mortars will have had enough time to lose dangerous alkalinity. Deteriorating brick and stonework is sometimes painted, and painting may even have a minor preservative effect by consolidating surface material and restricting the entry of water and pollutants into the masonry pores. All dirt and oily material must be removed using a gentle detergent or solvent wash. Any efflorescence and surface dust and residue must be removed by brushing or other light abrasion, especially when using latexes.

Loose paint must be removed, usually by hand scraping or by machine abrasion. Many paint-removal methods recommended for woodwork may also be used on masonry, with the usual warnings about caustic strippers affecting later paints. While brick or softer stones may not be sandblasted or gritblasted, unpolished hard stones such as granite may be blasted if tests indicate that fine tool marks are not endangered.

Latexes will perform better that oils or alkyds on chronically damp masonry. Oils and alkyds may be used on brick, stone, or concrete if the material is and will remain dry. Synthetic rubber coatings also perform well on these surfaces.

METHODS OF APPLICATION

BRUSH

Brush application is the oldest method of applying paint. Egyptian brushes of reeds and palm stems have been found, and earlier cave paintings seem to have been done by brush. Well into historic times brushes for all uses were round and made entirely of natural materials. The flattened brushes with which we are familiar today were a nineteenth-century American invention.

In the past, the preferred material for brushes, except for artistic or other specialized uses, was hog's bristle. In fact, the term *bristle* properly refers only to the hair of hogs. This was taken from wild hogs, as the hair of domestic pigs does not have the same desirable traits. At one time natural bristle was available in a wide variety of types and colors including white, yellow, gray, and black; today most is white. Sources of supply have migrated as producing areas have successively eliminated large numbers of wild hogs in favor of more economically productive pigs. Today the largest producer is China.

Natural bristle has a number of desirable properties that enhance its paint-holding and paint-applying abilities. The fiber tapers a bit from root to tip and has small barbs that project from the tiny grooves along its length, thus promoting the holding of paint. The fiber's end is not blunt but rather fractures into many small divisions known as flag. As the bristle wears, new flag develops. These characteristics allow a smooth, even distribution of paint unavailable from other common fibers.

Other natural fibers are also used in brush making. Smaller brushes use hair from ox, badger, and sable, as well as squirrel, whose tail hair is commercially called camel. Tampico brushes, made from plant fibers, are used in instances where resistance to alkalis is important. Other fibers may be added to less expensive brushes as filling material. If a brush contains additional unnamed types of animal fiber it will be marked "all hair."

As more paints are water based the tendency of bristle to lose its springiness and shape in water has become a serious limitation. In recent years synthetic fibers have been developed to share some of natural bristles' desirable qualities and avoid its shortcomings.

In the early years synthetic fiber brushes were made of comparatively smooth, nontapering fibers whose ends remained blunt. Better synthetics are now given artificial flag to enhance application and roughened lengths to enhance paint-holding ability.

Synthetic brushes are made primarily of nylon or polyester. They perform well in a variety of paints, keeping their shape in water-based paints and also working well in oils and alkyds. As inherently harder materials than bristle or other hair, they last much longer than comparable natural fiber brushes.

Polyester brushes, somewhat more expensive than nylon ones, may be used with all commonly encountered coating materials. Nylon is not recommended for use in lacquers or alcohol.

A good brush is constructed with its fibers set into the ferule (the band that holds the fibers on the handle) with vulcanized rubber or synthetic cement. There should be some space allowed between rows of fibers. The best brushes are composed of fibers of varying lengths rather than a single uniform length. They should show a bit of spring and resistance when pressed against a surface and should fan out a bit but not too widely. A good brush will hold a large amount of paint and distribute it evenly.

A great variety of brushes intended for specific uses is available. Brushes intended for use on rough masonry will be wide and tough. At the other extreme, varnish brushes will be quite soft. Calcimine brushes have long, elastic fibers while stenciling brushes are made of short, stiff fibers. Even urethane foam brushes, intended to be used for a single application and thrown away, are available, although some, especially those of lower density, may trap bubbles and be poor choices for varnishing. Selecting the proper brush is, obviously, one key to efficient, high-quality work.

Any new brush needs to be broken in. Traditionally, new bristle brushes were soaked overnight, often in a one-to-one mixture of linseed oil and mineral spirits. New brushes may have an amount of loose fiber that may be readily deposited in a paint layer. Therefore any new brush should be considered a dirty brush. It is best to start one on a simple, noncritical job such as priming. Any loose material will emerge and the brush will be ready for application of the finish coat.

When painting by brush, dip the brush about one-third to one-half its length into the paint. To remove any excess tap the brush on the inside of the can. It is best not to draw the broad side of the brush against the lip of the can or pail because dust or other materials on the surface being painted may be transferred into the paint. Never draw the brush against its narrow side, either against the pail or on the wall. For cutting in and trim work, use a narrower brush rather than the side of a broader one. Use both sides of the brush, applying enough pressure to spread the paint evenly but not so much that the bottoms of the fibers touch the wall. Especially when painting with modern paints that may dry very quickly, wipe off the base of the fibers and the ferule often to prevent the brush from stiffening. Try to apply a layer that is even but not excessively thick, as overly thick layers may lead to a variety of problems. As a way of controlling thickness, always brush from dry areas to wet areas.

Alone among paint application methods brushes leave clear directional markings, with those of latex usually being a bit more pronounced than those of oils or alkyds. Quality brushwork regularizes these brush marks as a final step. This process is called laying off. When painting a broad surface, start by applying the paint in an irregular pattern against the direction of the final brushwork. After the given wall or ceiling area is covered with paint, lay off with even parallel strokes. On doors or paneling with many small wooden elements, each element is laid off in the direction of its grain. On a door, for example, the vertical stiles and panels are painted in up and down strokes while the horizontal rails are laid off crosswise. Areas missed by brushing are referred to by many regional names, including holidays.

As soon as the paint is applied it begins to dry. Latex tends to dry faster than oil, but even oil paint may begin to set up before all of a particular wall or ceiling is done. When a wet brush hits an area of drying paint it may raise an area along the edge. Such spots may take on a different level of gloss or a different texture than the surrounding paint. This is called flashing. To avoid flashing it is necessary to keep a wet edge—that is, paint in such a pattern and at such a rate that all areas adjacent to the work area remain adequately wet. This is especially important when painting large walls or ceilings with flat paints.

There are different strategies for keeping a wet edge. Some painters do brushwork on large surfaces in teams with one person following another in alternating fashion, guaranteeing that each edge will be joined into quickly. When painting alone you can divide a large surface into smaller portions, working from one end of the room to the other, completing a vertical column of squares before moving on to the next. This way no single area will sit too long before the neighboring area is done.

Some persons prescribe a precise order of painting, both of large features and of their composite elements. A typical general sequence would be as follows: exterior before interior, upper floors before lower floors, ceilings before walls, walls before woodwork, upper woodwork before lower, and floors last. The Painting and Decorating Contractors of America recommend the following sequence for doors: panels, center rail, top and bottom rails, vertical stiles, and finally edges.

Besides the difficulty of keeping a wet edge, the chief disadvantage of brush painting is its relative slowness. The two other major methods of application, roller and spray, share the advantage of speed. Roller application is acknowledged to be many times quicker than brush, and spray application is perhaps even ten times more rapid than that. Of the three, however, brush application is the most reminiscent of traditional craft work and is, therefore, in the opinion of some, the most desirable and the most indicative of quality practice and traditional taste. In those cases where recreating a historical finish treatment is the goal, as in a museum house, brush application is necessary. To achieve a brushed finish over a large area while saving time, the paint can be applied by roller or spray and then laid off by brush.

A great advantage of brush painting is its ability to force paint into the surface. When it is hoped that a primer will bind especially well with a substrate or when a top coat is being applied over existing paints that are well adhered, thorough brushing may improve long-term performance. This may be especially important in rough areas such as mortar joints.

Brushing also will pick up an amount of surface dirt and bind it into the paint layer. Therefore it is the method of choice if it is feared that surfaces have not been thoroughly cleaned.

The life of a brush may be extended by proper use and care. A good brush should never be used on an extremely rough surface. This is especially true for natural bristle brushes, which wear rapidly. Nor should a good brush be forced tip end first into a tight space. A brush should never be left long resting on its fiber ends, although it may be left soaking during the duration of a job if it is hung in its solvent from a small hole in the handle. Professional painters carry brush boxes constructed for this purpose.

Brushes used in oils or alkyds should be washed in turpentine or mineral spirits, keeping in mind the hazards of hydrocarbon solvents and avoiding breathing of fumes and excessive skin contact. Ideally brushes should be combed periodically during the process. For the most thorough cleaning the bristles should be manipulated along their length between the fingers. Special care should be taken that paint not be left to dry in the base of the brush. Not only does this reduce the brush's flexibility, but also it may lead to the separation of fibers into grouped bunches, a condition known as "fingering." Professional painters often spin the brush with a mechanical spinner to drive out excess solvent after cleaning.

Brushes used in latex should be washed in warm, soapy water. Brushes used in shellac, alcohol-based stains, or stain sealers should be washed in alcohol. Distemper brushes should be cleaned in soapy water.

Brushes that have been neglected and left uncleaned after use in oil or alkyd paints may often be revived by soaking in solvent-based paint strippers or in commercial solvents formulated specially for this purpose. Brushes encrusted with latex may sometimes be revived by soaking in removers or acetone. It is best not to use brushes revived in this way for top coats, as particles left at the base of the fibers may migrate into the next finish surface. In fact, imperfectly cleaned brushes may be the chief source of contaminants in a quality job.

ROLLERS

Paint rollers are efficient tools for painting large, flat areas. They are also good for painting some rough, irregular, or discontinuous surfaces such as chain-link fencing. The common hardware-store variety of roller has a width of nine inches and a diameter of one and one-fourth inches. Commercial painters may use a larger standard size having a width of eighteen inches and a diameter of two and one-fourth inches, although the increase in size requires a concomitant increase in effort. Several specialized rollers are available for specific uses. Narrow trim rollers allow a close approach to edges. Wedged and conical shapes cover inside corners.

Roller covers come in several materials and nap lengths. The earliest covers were of wool. They are still available and may be used for most paints, although they are not the best for latexes and are a poor choice for enamels, for which mohair gives the best results. Synthetic roller covers come in a wide variety of materials including nylon, acrylic, rayon, foam rubber, and urethane. Most may be used for most types of paints, with some limitations based on solvent types.

The length of the nap determines the texture of the finished surface. Short naps give a low, even orange-peel type texture, while progressively longer naps increase the surface relief. Longer naps also have the ability to coat very rough or irregular surfaces.

In the most usual method of roller work, the cover is coated by being rolled in a shallow tray of slightly greater width. To save labor costs commercial painters sometimes use pressure-feed rollers to which a constant supply of paint is fed.

Unless special corner and edging rollers are being used, it is usual to begin by painting these areas by brush, then overlapping them with the roller when the adjacent area is done. In this way the painted surface is more uniform in texture, rather than showing wide areas of corner and edge brushwork, as would be the case if the brushing followed the rolling.

When painting with a roller, start by rolling an area in random directions to apply the paint evenly over the surface. Follow this with a final pass of parallel strokes analogous to the laying off of brush work. As guidance, a full roller load of paint on three-eighths-inch nap roller should cover roughly twelve square feet.

If the same paint is to be roller applied the next day or sometime soon, the roller and cover can be kept from drying in a well-sealed plastic bag. Roller covers may be cleaned in the same solvents recommended for cleaning brushes. The excess paint should be rolled out first, and then the solvent should be worked into the nap. Prolonged solvent soaking should be avoided. When the cover is clean, it may be blotted to speed drying.

SPRAYING

Spraying is the most efficient way to paint large areas quickly. Spray is well suited for flat areas, trim, complex shapes, and even pipe and ductwork. Among the chief determinants of whether sprayers should be used on a given job is the difficulty of masking elements that will not be painted. If masking an area would be difficult, time-consuming, or costly, it may be more practical to use other means.

Unlike in brushing or even rolling, in which the paint is forced onto the surface, in spraying the paint is simply deposited on the surface. It is, therefore, especially important that the surfaces to be painted are clean and otherwise well prepared.

Two types of sprayers are commonly available: air spray and airless spray. Air spray is the older method. Two hoses are connected to the gun. One pulls the paint into the gun. The other provides pressurized air from a compressor. The two streams meet in the nozzle of the gun. The pressurized paint is shot out, atomized, and propelled by the blast of air from behind. The tiny paint droplets travel to the work in the plume of air.

Because the air rebounds from the surface to be painted, an amount of paint also rebounds, causing overspray. A similar rebound happens in inside corners. This can result in poor corner coverage. The spray can be controlled by manipulating the balance of the fluid and air pressures and by adjusting the spreader valve (usually at the rear of the gun).

Airless spraying expels the paint itself under great enough pressure that it atomizes without an additional air blast. The shape of the fan of atomized paint is controlled by the degree of pressure and the choice of nozzle tip. The paint is carried to the surface on its own propulsion without the turbulent eddy and rebound of air spraying. Therefore more of the sprayed paint stays on the surface, and overspray is minimized.

It is important to control the viscosity of the paint being applied. The paint must not be so viscous that it does not move easily through the gun, but it must not be overly thinned, which can lead to poor coverage, increased overspray, and runs. Problems of paint thickness can be helped by heating the paint. This in effect thins the paint without the addition of solvents.

When spraying with either type of equipment the gun must be kept parallel to and about six to ten inches from the surface as it moves, and the spray must be directed at a ninety-degree angle. There should be no arching, either from the arm as it moves or from the wrist; the action should be in a straight line, otherwise the paint application will be of uneven thickness, resulting in one of two extremes: inadequate coverage or runs. Spraying should begin along edges and corners and on any irregular features such as pipes, followed by open areas. The spray trigger should be pulled before the pass begins and held until just after the pass has been made.

It is essential that the spray equipment be cleaned promptly and well. After an initial solvent rinse, spray solvent through the system to ensure that all parts are thoroughly clean. The temptation to clean out nozzle openings with a wire or tool must be resisted. For optimum control of the spray they are designed to a tolerance of microns and can be damaged by reaming.

OTHER APPLICATION METHODS

Most field painting is done by one or a combination of the three methods described above, but other methods deserve mention.

Paint pads are flat applicators related to rollers in that the paint is held in a nap material glued to a rigid backing. Like rollers, they may be hand loaded or supplied with a continuous flow of paint from a reservoir. They are best for controlled edging and detail work and floors.

Paint mitts also hold paint in a fiber matting. The matting is attached to a flexible glove or mitten, allowing one to grip and coat pipes, the primary purpose of the mitts.

ALTERATION OF PAINTS

Most modern paints are formulated to be used as they are supplied. Whereas old paints may have had five or six ingredients, modern paints may number from twenty-five to thirty. In altering paint, one cannot expect uniform good results. And, of course, the manufacturer will not stand behind guarantees if the product has been changed. On occasion, however, there is a reason to alter a given property. A paint to be used in sprayers, for example, may have to be thinned to an optimum consistency, following the manufacturer's recommendations. Or perhaps the color or gloss level of a paint is a bit off the mark. Therefore, on rare occasions, a paint may be changed for specific needs.

Paints are available in a range of surface finishes. The usual categories are flat, eggshell, satin, semigloss, and gloss. Shiny oil or alkyd paints may be made less so by the addition of flatting oils, which add an amount of light-scattering silica. Similar materials are available for latexes. Theoretically a flat paint may be made more reflective by increasing the relative amount of its binder. More binder would engulf the pigment particles under a uniform, clear, and shiny surface layer. In practice this is seldom attempted. The best way to alter the gloss level of modern paints may be to purchase and mix differing sheens of the same color.

Surfaces may also be given a different gloss level by adding clear coatings to the desired finish. Such additions may somewhat alter the color of the paint, making latexes seem lighter and oils darker. Generally, clear oily or resinous materials are applied over oil and alkyd paints while synthetic acrylic finishes may be applied to oils, alkyds, and latexes. Modern acrylic varnishes resist the yellowing characteristic of oil varnishes, but because of their rapid drying do not offer the wide range of decorative possibilities available from the more traditional materials.

Occasionally a paint may fail to match an existing surface or an earlier mix of a nominally similar color. The color of a paint may be changed or lightened by the addition of pigmented material. Two main types of such material are widely available: colors in oil and universal colors. Colors in oil are just that—concentrated pigment dispersed in drying oil. Those containing driers may be used directly as a paint and may be used in any amount to tint any oil or alkyd.

Concentrated color dispersions that do not contain driers may be used in amounts up to three ounces per gallon. In higher concentrations they may retard drying. When unable to obtain colors in oil, Japan colors, marketed for sign painters, may be a substitute. Artists' oils could theoretically also be used, but they would be inordinately expensive and may contain lead.

Universal colors are pigments dispersed in propylene glycol. (Propylene glycol is compatible with either oil or latex systems, thus it is universal.) Such colors are the tinting materials used in commercial custom color paint lines. Not more than a given number of ounces may be used per gallon of paint. Depending on the base, a given amount of universal color will provide a greater or lesser degree of tinting. The tinting bases used for darker colors, for example, are actually more transparent than those used for lighter ones, allowing a greater proportion of the pigments to be seen. Some modern bases can take as much as fourteen ounces of universal tint per gallon. When working with an existing paint whose color must be altered, the allowable amount is no more than three ounces per gallon. Exceeding the recommended amount may lead to problems in drying and generally poor performance.

As supplied, a paint may not have the brushing or rolling characteristics desired by the painter. Oil and alkyd paints may be thinned with mineral spirits or paint thinner. A paint that has been thinned too much will suffer in hiding ability, may run, and may dry more slowly. These paints may also be altered with commercially available reinforcing oils, composed of drying oils and resins, which enhance penetration and binding. Most manufacturers caution against this.

Latex paints may also require thinning. Acrylic latexes in particular may develop hard brushing qualities in warm weather. However, many latexes flow readily under the high shear of a brush or roller while seeming too thick in the can. Water may be added to latexes but should never exceed one pint per gallon. Additional materials, analogous to the reinforcing oils mentioned earlier, are available to enhance penetration and bonding. These should not be necessary with the 100 percent acrylics that are now formulated to bond well, even to chalky surfaces.

In the past, catalysts in the form of driers were often added to oils and alkyds to accelerate their set. Basically, these materials aid in the oxidation by which these paints in part dry. Too much drier may lead to embrittlement or wrinkling. Those who add Japan driers in an attempt to paint late into the season risk a situation in which the paints will surface dry while the inner portions of the layer remain wet, inviting failure. Here again, the manufacturer's recommendations should be followed.

When materials have been added to a paint or when the paint's ingredients have settled, it must be well stirred from the bottom of the can before use. Blade mixing attachments on a drill may be useful when stirring a large volume. The upper blade forces material down while the lower one moves it up, ensuring an even mix. Automatic shakers are helpful when available.

The ingredients that may be added to a commercial paint with the strongest blessing from the manufacturer are mildewcides. The allowable concentration will be indicated on the bottle.

WHEN TO PAINT

Painting should not be done if conditions are too cool, humid, or rainy. The usual temperature guidelines are a surface temperature of not below forty degrees Fahrenheit and best above forty-five degrees for oils, not below fifty degrees Fahrenheit and best above fifty-five or even sixty degrees for latexes, and not above ninety degrees for either. In oil and alkyd paints the first stage of drying is solvent loss, or flash off. If this stage occurs in extremely high humidity and at low temperatures, uneven gloss levels can result. The second step of drying is oxidation within the film. Lower temperatures slow this process considerably. A film that would normally take eight hours to cure may take twenty-four. During that longer time it could rain or temperatures could fall even lower. For the same reasons it is best not to paint near dusk.

Whenever painting is done in conditions approaching the lower temperature limit and in high humidity, primers and undercoats should be allowed a longer drying time. With the old linseed oil primers a delay of several weeks between priming and top coating was recommended. A top coat should be applied to alkyd or latex primers within forty-eight hours, as they are not designed to be exposed to sunlight or weather.

Oil and alkyd paints should not be applied in extremely hot conditions, nor should they be put on surfaces in direct sun. The heating may cause the solvent to evaporate too fast, thus leading to blistering. The danger of this is increased for more darkly pigmented paints.

Although there is a range of permissible application temperatures for different latex paints, the general rule of not painting when the temperature is below fifty degrees holds. In low temperatures latex films will not coalesce properly. Although the paint may look hard and dry it may actually be poorly formed and have bad adhesion. As with oils and alkyds, it is best not to apply latexes in direct sun.

Latexes are more forgiving of high humidity than oils or alkyds, although they may be subject to spotting from condensation or rain in the first few hours after application.

CLIMATIC CONSIDERATIONS

Differences in climate make little difference in the formulation or choice of modern paints. Excepting variance for mildew control, national companies market similar and even identical paints for use in all regions of the country. Regional differences may matter most with regard to preparation for painting and weather conditions.

Arid regions where humidity remains constant and low are among the best environments for painting. There are no special considerations in preparation.

In humid areas where there may be wide ranges of both temperature and moisture levels precautions are necessary. In temperate northern regions low spring, fall, and winter temperatures may restrict the exterior painting seasons to less than half the year. Temperate southern regions have a longer painting season but must also observe the standard temperature rules.

Extremely humid areas may have few days dry enough for safe exterior painting. Ocean areas are particularly difficult and have their own considerations. Entrapped salt spray is very damaging to paint; it may prevent formation of a strong film and guarantee that it will always be especially sensitive to high humidity. Any salt spray residues must be thoroughly eliminated before painting. In years past painters in marine environments would sometimes add zinc oxide to their paints to increase their hardness. This is unnecessary today because modern alkyds are made to have a much higher inherent strength.

Humid southern areas are particularly prone to mildew and other fungal problems. The addition of mildewcides may be a wise step. The container label will indicate the permissible amount per gallon. The traditional advice for removal of fungal stains has been to wash the area with trisodium phosphate followed by dilute bleach. We are now aware that residual phosphates from the trisodium phosphate may provide food for future microorganisms. A better course is to scrub first with dilute bleach followed by a detergent and a clean water rinse. A one-to-one mix of household bleach and water will provide a 2.5 percent solution of sodium hypochlorite, which should be effective.

MOISTURE MANAGEMENT

In the past many paint adhesion problems were caused by faulty materials. Today most severe adhesion problems in nonarid regions are caused by moisture. This is especially true in older buildings. Some buildings seem plagued by an inability to hold a coat of paint. Repeated preparation and repainting using the best materials and following the best procedures does not solve the problem. In these cases it is likely that the problem is caused by moisture migrating out through the walls. Until the inner moisture problem is solved, the outer adhesion problem will continue.

Some buildings take in a large amount of moisture through the ground. Perhaps the local water table is high, perhaps faulty gutters and downspouts fail to channel runoff from the building, or perhaps the grading of the site encourages water to move toward the building. If there is no cellar floor or crawl space vapor barrier, this water will migrate inside. Often basement windows are kept shut all year without additional dehumidification, forcing the vapors to dissipate up into the building.

Modern standards of comfort surpass those of the past. Buildings are kept warmer in cold weather, and, as energy costs have risen, interiors have been insulated and sealed as never before. Humidity levels are kept higher for comfort and as a result of such activities as showering and clothes drying. Unless stopped by vapor barriers or controlled by venting or other measures, this humidity will migrate to the exterior, moving through walls if necessary and often causing paint failure in the process.

If moisture migration is causing paint adhesion problems in older buildings without vapor barriers, remedial vapor barriers may be added on the inside. A number of materials have been found effective including aluminum paint, polyvinyl wall sealers, rubber-based paint, and coated wall fabrics. It is important to coat all exterior walls and about two feet onto the interior walls as they meet exterior walls. On top floors the coating should also cover the ceiling.

A large part of the built environment in the United States is painted. With the wise choice of materials, proper surface preparation, and skillful application, we can enjoy the twin goals of painting—beauty and protection.

The Nature
of Paints

A Survey of Paint Technology

THE COMPOSITION AND PROPERTIES OF PAINTS

MORGAN W. PHILLIPS

he term *paint*, like *mortar* and *adhesive*, describes no particular material or class of materials but rather refers to the way in which a wide variety of materials are used. Any substance that can be applied to a surface as a liquid at or near room temperature and that then forms a solid, opaque, adherent film is a paint.

The vital property of being convertible from the fluid to the solid state is common not only to paints but also to many other materials used in construction and conservation, such as plasters, concretes, varnishes, and consolidants (strengtheners for deteriorated porous substances). In many cases the same or similar ingredients are used in products that serve these varied purposes. A slurry (fluid mixture) of lime and water, for example, applied to woodwork or a wall, is a paint (whitewash). The same slurry, mixed with sand and placed between bricks or stones, is a mortar. Applied with sand to the interior of a wall, or to a ceiling, it is a lime plaster. Applied with sand to a building exterior, it is called a lime stucco or parging. Formed into a mass with sand and large aggregate, it is a lime concrete. Another ingredient common to many construction materials is linseed oil. Historically the most common binder in oil paints, it also once served as the main binder in putties for glazing windows and filling nail holes, in linoleum and Lincrusta wall coverings, in some now-obsolete spackling compounds for patching plaster, and in countless other products. This survey of basic paint technology can thus be used as an overview of many materials that solidify at room temperature and that for this reason are used in construction and conservation.

INORGANIC-ORGANIC BINDER CLASSIFICATION

Paints are typically classified according to the type of material that holds them together after application and drying—the binder. Both historic and modern paints can be grouped into two categories: those with inorganic binders and those with organic binders. A comprehension of the fundamental difference between inorganic and organic compounds and of the related concepts of ionic and covalent bonding is vital in understanding the widely differing physical properties of calcium carbonate and dried linseed oil, for example, or portland cement and animal glue—all materials that serve as binders for paints and other building materials.

Figure 1. *Front wall of Newport Congregational Church (1850s), Newport, R.I. In 1880 John La Farge redecorated the entire interior in this modified encaustic (wax) paint. Traces of the church's original glue distemper wall paints, imperfectly washed off, remain beneath the encaustic. These caused localized peeling and led to some renewal of the encaustic, with design changes, as early as 1903. (Morgan W. Phillips)*

As a comparison of basic chemistry texts will reveal, the terms *organic* and *inorganic* have been defined in more than one way and some substances fall into a gray area in between. An interesting way of defining these major subdivisions of chemistry, which may allow fewer exceptions than some others, is that of Therald Moeller:

Organic chemistry [is] the chemistry of carbon compounds and their derivatives. Organic compounds that contain only the two elements, carbon and hydrogen, are called *hydrocarbons*. Almost all other organic compounds can be thought of as derivatives of hydrocarbons. *Inorganic chemistry* is the chemistry of all elements (including carbon) and their compounds, with the exception of hydrocarbons and hydrocarbon derivatives.[1]

Related to the concepts of inorganic and organic compounds are those of ionic and covalent bonding. When two atoms are bonded ionically, one or more electrons are transferred from one atom to the other; because the electron bears a negative charge, the donor atom becomes a positively charged ion and the receptor a negatively charged ion. An ion can be a single atom or a group of atoms. In an ionic compound, all the positively charged ions are attracted to all the negatively charged ions, and no specific bond is formed between individual ions. This tends to result in the formation of crystals, which represent a compact and regular packing of mutually attracted ions. Crystalline compounds are usually rigid.

By contrast, covalent bonds are formed when two atoms share electrons, and these bonds, which do not entail the formation of charged ions, specifically connect individual atoms. The result is a "molecule" that is essentially limited to a certain size and is often only weakly attracted to adjacent similar molecules. (As described later, however, primary chemical bonds, known as cross links, can form between the molecules of many organic paint binders.) Pronounced crystallinity is much less common among organic compounds, especially as they are seldom pure, of uniform molecular size, and of compact molecular structure. Although many chemical bonds are of partially ionic and partially covalent character, organic compounds tend to be more covalently bonded, and inorganic compounds more ionically bonded. Carbon atoms are particularly prone to bond covalently with each other, thus forming the carbon-to-carbon molecular backbones of most organic substances. A key property of many organic materials is that they are flexible, to a greater or lesser extent.

With these fundamental concepts in mind, the stonelike rigidity of calcium carbonate is understandable. It is an ionic, crystalline, inorganic compound. The contrasting flexibility of dried linseed oil, an organic material, results from its lack of pronounced crystallinity and the fact that it is based on interlocked but still somewhat flexible chains of covalently bonded carbon atoms, with many attached hydrogen atoms and some oxygen atoms.

The mechanisms by which materials solidify or, in the case of paints, form dry films are closely related to these fundamentals of chemical composition. This chapter is organized according to those mechanisms of film formation.

PAINTS WITH INORGANIC BINDERS

Inorganically bound paints, which solidify through crystal formation, include whitewashes and cement paints and a few other types that have had more limited use in America.

WHITEWASH

Whitewashes predate oil paints in American architectural painting and continued in widespread use as utility paints until the mid-twentieth century. As pointed out by Abbott Lowell Cummings and Richard M. Candee in this volume ("Colonial and Federal America: Accounts of Early Painting Practices"), early examples from the seventeenth and early eighteenth centuries often contain color pigments, most often earth colors but also greens and other interesting tints. No white pigment need ever be added, as the lime itself serves this purpose.

COMPOSITION AND SOLIDIFICATION MECHANISM

The most preferred and strictest definition of lime is calcium oxide. However, the definition can include other compounds, such as calcium hydroxide.[2] As actually used in building and in this chapter, the term *lime* refers collectively to the carbonates, oxides, or hydroxides of calcium or calcium and magnesium.[3] Lime is usually derived from limestone, a sedimentary rock formed from the skeletons of microscopic sea creatures. Certain grades of ground limestone are called chalk or whiting. Many types of calcium carbonate have been used as pigment in organically bound paint.

High-calcium lime is derived from limestone consisting of pure calcium carbonate, $CaCO_3$. Magnesian and dolomitic limes are derived from limestone consisting of dolomite, the double salt of calcium and magnesium, $CaMg(CO_3)_2$. The term *magnesian* implies about 5 to 20 percent $MgCO_3$ in the parent stone, and "dolomitic" about 20 to 44 percent.[4] The reactions given here are for high-calcium lime only.

Ground limestone cannot serve as a binder in paint (or mortar, plaster, or lime concrete) unless it has passed through a series of chemical changes. First, crushed limestone (calcium carbonate) is heated (calcined) in a kiln, decomposing to form carbon dioxide and calcium oxide, or "quicklime":

$$CaCO_3 \rightarrow CaO + CO_2$$

Typical calcining temperatures today range from 1725 to 2450 degrees Fahrenheit.[5]

In contact with water, quicklime becomes hydrated, or "slaked":

$$CaO + H_2O \rightarrow Ca(OH)_2$$

A great deal of heat is liberated in this reaction, the reverse of the uptake of heat energy in the kiln during calcination. For this reason quicklime, CaO, has also been known as hot lime. From historic times until fairly recently, quicklime was slaked by the builder, and the excess water not consumed in the hydration reaction served to make the material a wet putty. Today hydration is carried out in the production plant, using just enough water for hydration; the result is the dry powder typically available today as lime for masonry or plastering. Water is added before use to make a slurry of the powdered hydrated lime.

Hydration is a necessary intermediate step in preparing the lime for carbonation, the final reaction it undergoes after being applied to a building. In carbonation, the lime recombines with atmospheric carbon dioxide to form the original compound that had been dug from the lime pit—calcium carbonate. Water must be present for the recombination to occur:

$$Ca(OH)_2 + CO_2 \rightarrow CaCO_3 + H_2O$$

Although chemically one has circled back to the starting point, physically a great deal has been accomplished. During the carbonation reaction the lime develops a new interlocked structure of small calcium carbonate crystals in whatever position it has been placed and however it has been applied—as a paint, mortar, plaster, or concrete binder. Thus, through carbonating it develops strength as a coating or masonry product.

Wet hydrated lime will not carbonate if it is not exposed to atmospheric carbon dioxide. For this reason, lime putty was commonly stored for long periods in sealed containers, actually becoming more workable (plastic) with age. Conversely, if denied water but not air, lime will also fail to carbonate (or cure), because water is the necessary medium in which the carbonation reaction occurs. Thus, today dry lime hydrate is stored in plastic-lined bags that protect it from atmospheric moisture.

Precautions are taken to prevent a whitewash, lime mortar, or lime plaster from drying too quickly after application, lest the curing reaction either fails to occur or occurs when insufficient moisture is present to allow for proper crystal growth. Porous substrates to which whitewash is applied should be well wetted in advance, so as not to draw water out of the whitewash too rapidly. One modern practitioner also uses a humidifier to cure new whitewash in rooms.[6]

Pure lime whitewash does not bond well to organic substrates such as wood. Thus, milk, tallow, linseed oil, and other organic additives have long been used to enhance the adhesiveness of whitewashes, especially to organic substrates. Some such additives might also enhance the abrasion resistance of a whitewash that may not have been carbonated under ideal circumstances. Other historic additives to whitewashes have included alum, salt, and other substances that enhanced the formation of a cohesive and adherent film, sometimes probably through changes in the rate of carbonation. Quite complex old formulations are found in period literature.

PROPERTIES

A layer of an inorganic crystalline compound, such as lime, tends to be brittle. Thus, whitewashes do not easily follow the expansion and contraction movements of wood. This and their poor adhesion to wood account for the fact that where they survive on early woodwork they are usually found only as fragments. They endure much better on dimensionally stable substrates such as plaster, brick, or stone. Determination of the chronological order of numerous fragmentary layers of whitewash, some colored, in early buildings can be exasperating: a bit of one layer is found in one place; portions of another remain only at some other location.

Brittleness is one property by which whitewashes may be readily distinguished from organically bound paints. Another is insolubility in water or organic solvents, such as methylene chloride. Also, unlike organic paints, they will not soften when heated.

Whitewashes are porous and readily permeated by water, the pores being spaces that were at first occupied by the water of mixing and that were then largely preserved as the interlocked crystals were formed. Porous and brittle, whitewashes do not fit the typical description of durable films: they have poor adhesion to organic substrates, no flexibility, and in most cases poor abrasion resistance. On masonry their weather resistance seems to vary widely—and is surely decreased by acid rain. Added organic binders can promote mold growth.

However, many whitewashes, especially those used on interior surfaces, do display excellent color retention and some other forms of longevity. Those that contain no added organic binders are immune to the color changes associated with such binders: most important, they do not yellow like oil or alkyd resin paints. Calcium carbonate is normally stable in indoor environments, and the colored pigments most often used in old whitewashes are also highly stable: iron oxide yellows, reds, and browns (the earth pigments), and carbon blacks. Although Candee and Cummings demonstrated the color variety of early whitewashes, only a minority of the old whitewashes I have seen contain color pigments, such as verdigris green, that fade or discolor in other ways. Thus, in investigating old paint layers, one often finds pristine color in whitewashes, especially by cutting past the soiled surface.

CEMENT PAINTS

The nineteenth century saw the increasing use of materials called "cements" as binders for many building materials and for paints. Used by the Romans and later forgotten, cements were rediscovered in the late eighteenth century. Cement paints were widely used on masonry buildings or stucco-covered wooden buildings in roughly the period 1850–1950. Many were proprietary mixtures containing a variety of colored pigments and other ingredients.

COMPOSITION AND SOLIDIFICATION MECHANISM

The defining ingredient in cement paint is cement. Like the term *lime, cement* can mean a variety of things. Common cements as used in construction and paints are silicates, aluminates, or alumino-ferrites of calcium. They differ from lime in the important property of being able to solidify without exposure to atmospheric carbon dioxide. This accounts for their value, well known to the Romans, for underwater construction.

Today's cement is known as portland cement and is a ground and calcined product made from lime and clay or a limestone containing clay. The clay serves as the source of silica for the production of calcium silicate compounds, which are the major constituent of cements. Portland cement was patented and named in the 1820s. The cements used by the Romans had been naturally occurring products of related composition, and such "natural cements" were widely used in the nineteenth century until at the end of the century portland cement became more nearly universal.

The major compounds present in modern portland cement are tricalcium silicate, dicalcium silicate, tricalcium aluminate, and tetracalcium aluminoferrite.[7]

Whereas lime cures by carbonation—that is, by reaction with carbon dioxide—in the presence of water, cements cure by hydration—that is, by combining chemically with water. A new, strong crystal structure is formed during this hydration. For tricalcium silicate the hydration reaction is

$$2(3CaO \cdot SiO_2) + 6H_2O \longrightarrow 2(xCaO \cdot SiO_2 \cdot H_2O) + x(6-2x)\ Ca(OH)_2$$

where x lies between 1.3 and 1.7[8] As in the case of whitewashes, cements and cement paints should be kept moist while curing.

PROPERTIES

A properly cured cement, whether serving as a paint or in some other role, is much stronger than lime. The minerals formed (mainly hydrated calcium silicates) are simply harder and stronger than calcium carbonate. Also the pore structure is much less open than that of cured (carbonated) lime: because it is not necessary that atmospheric carbon dioxide be admitted into cement to effect a cure, cement can form a much denser structure in curing.

Cement paints are akin to whitewashes in that their principal and defining ingredients are inorganic, mostly ionic, crystalline substances that serve both to bind the paint and provide opacity and bulk. Thus, like whitewashes, cement paints are brittle. However, they are much stronger and harder than whitewashes and more resistant to abrasion, weathering, and acid rain.

Though cement paints are more rugged than whitewashes, it may be speculated that some cement paints, especially if based on portland cement, might not be as color stable in outdoor exposure. This speculation is based on the presence in typical portland cement of iron-containing impurities, generally compounds having a black color. Some of these change color when exposed to the weather. A typical color change of portland cement used in various structural or coating applications is from gray to yellow or tan. Where this has occurred, the original gray color can be observed by breaking away the yellowed surface. In making a portland cement product today that must retain color for many decades, it is often wise to use white cement, which is free of unstable iron compounds, and add stable colorants.

The addition of colorants to cement paints, as to other cement products, has been common since at least the mid-nineteenth century. If stable colorants have been chosen—iron oxide yellows, reds, and browns, for example—little color change should be expected in the paint, except as noted here. Like whitewashes, cement paints are free of the yellowing associated with organic binders, such as linseed oil.

OTHER INORGANIC MATERIALS USED AS BINDERS

Primitive paints, as well as plasters, mortars, unfired bricks, and other materials of architecture, have been bound by clay. On drying from a wet paste, clay solidifies through the development of weak forces of attraction between particles. Another inorganic binder, of far more widespread usage in American construction, is plaster of Paris. Plaster of Paris is calcium sulfate hemihydrate and is made by calcining (dehydrating) gypsum rock (a dihydrate). Like common cements, plaster of Paris cures by hydration (reaction with water); it thus reforms dihydrate:

$$(CaSO_4)_2 \cdot H_2O + 3H_2O \rightarrow 2(CaSO_4 \cdot 2H_2O)$$
$$\text{hemihydrate} \qquad\qquad \text{dihydrate}$$

Plaster of Paris is mentioned here mainly because of its great importance and long history paralleling lime and cement as an inorganic material that forms a solid at room temperature. It has not been much used in paints, although the discovery of the dihydrate in early paint samples from several paint jobs 1665-ca. 1700 in Salem, Massachusetts, reported in the chapter by Candee and Cummings, suggests that gypsum or plaster of Paris may have been used in more early paints than has been appreciated. Whether it was used as binder (hemihydrate) or merely as pigment (crushed gypsum rock in an organic binder) in the Gedney paints has not been determined. A Victorian-period painter's guide refers to calcined plaster of Paris (which would serve as an inorganic binder) as a "very valuable article" for painting the interiors of houses.[9] Plaster of Paris has been more recently used in some commercial texture paints because it sets without shrinking and cracking.

In recent years there has been an important addition to the family of inorganic paint binders—potassium silicate. Although sodium and potassium silicates have been sporadically developed for a century or more, only in the last few decades have highly successful silicate paints been marketed. Based mainly on potassium silicate, these have been used as masonry coatings in Germany and are just now being imported to this country. Some are said to contain acrylic resin additives.

Potassium silicate solidifies by reaction with atmospheric carbon dioxide to form a continuous noncrystalline binder of essentially silicon dioxide. The great stability of silicon dioxide accounts for the extreme durability of silicate paints on masonry. Unlike whitewashes and cement paints, silicate paints may require added pigments to provide opacity.

PAINTS WITH ORGANIC BINDERS

Before discussing organically bound paints, other basic concepts must be explained, including the opacity of films and the molecular weight of organic binders.

All organic binders used in materials for contruction are transparent liquids during application and if used alone would dry to form transparent films, sometimes thin and penetrating. To produce bulk, opacity, color, and thus the protective and decorative effects required of paint, pigments—solid particles—have to be added. Pigments also have a hardening and reinforcing effect on organic films. Organic paint binders cannot serve as their own pigmentation, as can inorganic binders, which cure to form bulky opaque films.

OPACITY

Opacity, or hiding power, in paint materials is derived in two ways: absorption of light and scattering of light. These often occur together. Dark pigments absorb most or all of the light that strikes them, converting most of the light energy to heat, which is then dissipated. Pigments conventionally thought of as "colored," such as blues or yellows, absorb some frequencies of the light that strike them and reflect others: light of those frequencies that are not absorbed remains visible and results in the "color" of the pigment.

White pigments, on the other hand, derive their opacity by reflection and refraction of light, rather than absorption. White pigments are essentially transparent to all wavelengths of light. Light can pass through their particles with little or no loss by absorption. However, the light is broken up and deflected at the pigment surfaces. A reasonably thick film is impenetrable to light when there are large numbers of pigment particles contributing to the effect. This effect is known as scattering. Snow is an example of scattering: snowflakes, although actually composed of translucent ice, form in the aggregate an opaque white layer. All colored pigments except black "hide" partly by absorption and partly by scattering.

The reflection and refraction of light that add up to scattering occur only when the particles are surrounded by a material having a refractive index significantly different from that of the particles themselves. The refractive index of a material, designated as n, is inversely proportional to the ratio of the speed of light within the material to the speed of light in air: light passes more slowly through materials of higher refractive index. In the case of the highly porous, inorganic paints described here (whitewashes and cement paints), the particles are surrounded by air. Because air has a much lower refractive index ($n = 1$) than calcium carbonate or hydrated calcium silicate ($n = $ ca. 1.5), a whitewash or cement paint can be opaque for the same reason a layer of snow, which consists of myriad ice-air interfaces, is. If no absorbing (color) pigments are present and if the air spaces were filled instead with a material having a refractive index close to that of the lime or cement, the film would become much more transparent—just as snow becomes semitransparent when the spaces within it start to fill with water. When whitewashes or cement paints are wet with water or organic solvents, they usually turn darker and more transparent until the liquid evaporates.

With some notable exceptions, such as glue distemper paints, house paints based on organic binders are generally not highly porous. The organic binder fills or nearly fills the spaces between the pigment particles. Typical organic binders, such as linseed oil, have refractive indices close to that of calcium carbonate (around 1.5), so that in nonporous paints calcium carbonate cannot serve as an opaque white pigment, although it is used as a cheap transparent "extender." To provide opacity by means of the difference between the refractive index of pigment and binder, white pigments of higher refractive index are needed, such as white lead ($n = $ ca. 2.0) or titanium dioxide ($n = $ ca. 2.5).

Besides these fundamental optical principles affecting paint films, the concept of *molecular weight* is essential in considering organically bound paints. Organic compounds, as already explained, comprise atoms bonded to each other to form specific entities called molecules. The size of a molecule is most conveniently expressed as molecular weight, the sum of the atomic weights of the atoms in the molecule. Bonds between atoms within each molecule are strong (if the compound is a stable one), and breaking them is by definition a chemical reaction.

Weaker forces hold separate molecules together in liquid and solid masses of organic material that may contain many molecules. Several features of molecular structure, well summarized by Giorgio Torraca, influence the strength of these intermolecular attractions.[10] The separation of the molecules from each other does not constitute a reaction and often can be done easily. Besides structural features of the molecules, an important factor influencing the ease of separating them is their size: the smaller the molecules (and the lower the molecular weight), the lower the degree of entanglement and the strength of intermolecular forces and the more easily the molecules can be separated.

Organic substances made up of very small molecules, such as ethane (C_2H_6) **(fig. 2)** are usually gases.

The intermolecular attractive forces in gases are not strong enough to overpower the separative effect of molecular motion. As molecular weight increases, the forces of attraction increase and tend to draw molecules together into liquids, such as decane ($C_{10}H_{22}$) **(fig. 3)**.

Liquids of higher molecular weight tend to be more viscous (heavy-bodied and resistant to flow) than those made up of smaller molecules. As molecular weights further increase, increasing entanglement and attractive forces cause molecules to form solids. A type of very large molecule is made up of many repetitive smaller units; this type of molecule is called a polymer, meaning "many units." A resin is a polymer having certain properties.[11] The extreme example of high molecular weight is a polymer in which the molecules are linked to each other by chemical bonds: these are called cross-linked materials. An example in which all the molecules are linked together to form one giant molecule is Bakelite, the material used to form an automobile distributor cap.

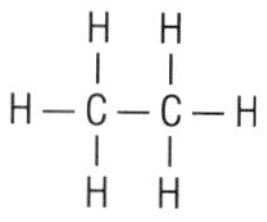

```
   H  H                          H   H   H   H   H   H   H   H   H   H
   |  |                          |   |   |   |   |   |   |   |   |   |
H—C—C—H                      H—C—C—C—C—C—C—C—C—C—C—H
   |  |                          |   |   |   |   |   |   |   |   |   |
   H  H                          H   H   H   H   H   H   H   H   H   H

   ethane                                      decane
```

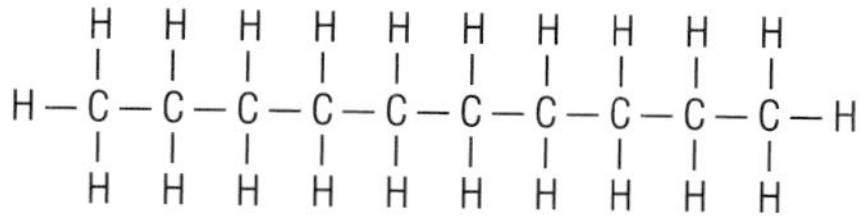

Figure 2. *The structure of a molecule of ethane.*

Figure 3. *The structure of a molecule of decane.*

With these concepts in mind, it is possible to visualize several ways in which organic paint binders and other similar organic products, including adhesives, varnishes, and consolidants, can be applied as liquids and then form solids. If the molecules of a solid are not all cross linked, the introduction of an appropriate liquid can cause them to separate from each other and float around as a liquid solution in a form that is convenient to mix with pigment and then apply as paint. This liquid is called a solvent. (Although most solvents are organic liquids, the solvent for any water-soluble polymer is water.)

After application, the solvent evaporates and the molecules become once again entangled and attracted, and a solid film or coating is formed. The molecules in such a situation have to be large enough that they will form a durable solid upon loss of the solvent. As a rule of thumb, the higher the molecular weight of a polymer, the greater will be its strength and toughness when dry and the more viscous (thicker) will be the solutions it forms when dissolved in a given amount of solvent. The strength of intermolecular attractions also affects these properties. An example of a paint that dries by loss of solvent from a polymer solution is glue distemper, which is based on animal glue. (Distempers are discussed in my chapter "A Victorian Trompe l'Oeil: The Restoration of Distemper Paints" in this volume.)

A second mechanism by which solid organic coatings can be formed from liquids is by chemical reactions causing the smaller molecules of the liquid to form primary chemical bonds with one another, thus creating the much larger molecules of a solid. Typically, these molecules consist of chainlike structures connected to one another by cross links. Examples of paint binders consisting of small molecules that cross link after application are linseed oil and typical epoxy resins. Once cross linked, the solidified binder cannot be dissolved and can be broken down only by a chemical reaction—the breaking of primary bonds between constituent atoms. Many paints dry initially by solvent loss and then achieve their final dry film properties by cross linking.

A third major mechanism of film formation of organic materials of construction is coalescence, which will be discussed in conjunction with the so-called "latex paints."

A few terms used to describe organic paint binders need clarification: *Binder* and *medium* refer to the material that holds pigment particles together. The term *vehicle* is currently used to describe the binder or medium of paints, particularly in their liquid state, as well as solvent that may be present. If solvent, which will evaporate on drying, is present, this is referred to as the *volatile* component of the vehicle. Material that is dissolved in the solvent and will remain in the dried film as solid binder is called the *nonvolatile* vehicle component.

PAINTS THAT FORM FILMS BY SOLVENT LOSS ONLY

By far the most common traditional American house paint that dries solely by evaporation of solvent is glue distemper, but other types, such as shellac paint, have been used.

GLUE DISTEMPER PAINTS

The term *distemper* has been used to refer to aqueous paints bound by many types of natural polymers. Glue distempers, specifically, are paints bound by animal glue. In architectural applications, glue distempers have frequently been called "calcimines." Glue distempers have had, by far, the most widespread use in American buildings of any type of paint that dries by solvent loss only. The solvent used in glue distempers is water.

Like many terms used in construction and art, the term *glue* can have both a general and a specific meaning: its general meaning is anything used as an adhesive; its specific meaning, as the term has been used traditionally in many fields, is animal glue.

COMPOSITION

Animal glue is largely protein and can be derived from various parts of land animals or fish. Glues vary widely in quality and properties. Glues derived from bones and hides have been especially common. The animal tissues contain not glue but collagen, from which are obtained ordinary glue and the particularly pure variety known as gelatin. Collagen is a fibrous protein, which imparts cohesion and strength to connective tissues, such as ligaments, in animals.[12]

Animal glue is a polymer consisting of a mixture of similar molecules of differing but generally high molecular weight. As already noted, a direct relationship exists between the molecular weights of polymers and the viscosities of the solutions they form at given concentrations—that is, given ratios of polymer to solvent. Because of its high average molecular weight and particularly because structural features of the gelatin molecule produce high levels of attraction between molecules, glue solutions quite low in polymer content (as little as 3 percent) form jellies at room temperature and often require warming in order to handle properly as paint binders.[13] By contrast, a solution of shellac (a lower molecular-weight polymer) in alcohol is highly fluid at 30 percent polymer content (or "solids"): this concentration is the widely used three-pound-per gallon "cut." For this reason glue distemper paints were commonly kept slightly warm during application. Heating lowers the viscosities of solutions by increasing molecular motion, the same means by which it causes many polymeric solids, like asphalt, to melt.

Even when warmed, typical glue (or gelatin) solutions do not handle well as paint binders above about 10 percent "solids": higher concentrations of glue make sticky paint. The optimum concentration of a glue solution to be used as a paint binder, in the author's limited experience, varies from about 2 to around 8 percent and, as repeatedly noted in old painters' manuals, depends heavily on the pigments used (different pigments have different handling properties and binding requirements) (see "A Victorian Trompe l'Oeil").

The vehicle of a glue distemper in the wet state consists mostly of water (90 percent or more) rather than glue (10 percent or less). When the water evaporates after application, the amount of glue present is insufficient to fill the spaces between the pigment particles. The dried film, therefore, is highly porous. This porosity—the fact that the spaces between the pigment particles are filled mostly with air—gives distempers the ability to "hide" (be opaque) very well by means of scattering without containing any expensive higher-refractive-index pigments such as white lead. For this reason whiting (calcium carbonate) has been by far the most common white pigment used in distempers. The refractive index difference between calcium carbonate (n = ca. 1.5) and air (n = 1) is sufficient to create effective scattering of light. Although only a small amount of glue is present, it is enough is to bind the pigment firmly because of another property of this polymer, its great strength.

Thus, calcium carbonate serves well as an opaque white in glue distempers, and because it is inexpensive it has been the most widely used white. Obtained by crushing limestone, the particular grade used is called "whiting." Whitewashes also consist ultimately of calcium carbonate, but in their case the calcium carbonate forms a matrix of interlocked crystals that act as the binder, while in glue distempers it exists as separate pigment particles.

Glue distempers were commonly used on historic wallpapers, which are nothing but painted papers (*papiers peints*, in French). Thus, it is impossible to be a "paint expert" in historic preservation and remain ignorant of other historic materials, such as wallpapers.

PROPERTIES

Glue distempers were widely used in American buildings from the earliest days until the mid-twentieth century because they were inexpensive, could be applied quickly, and could hide substrates well in one coat. Many color pigments that, when used in oil paint, do not handle well or do not produce bright tints will do both nicely in distempers. Well-applied distempers have a beautiful satiny appearance. Their binder—animal glue—is not subject to the pronounced yellowing observed in oil paints.

Because glue distempers remain soluble in hot water, they have the advantage of easy reversibility: plaster details that are becoming filled in with successive layers of distempers can be quickly restored to their original crispness by washing off the paint with warm water and sponges. (The water solubility of distempers is a property by which the investigator of old paint layers can quickly distinguish distempers from whitewashes, which are insoluble.) Now out of use, distempers may be missed by some older painters.

Unfortunately, glue distempers are weak and fragile. Also, because they are water soluble, they are susceptible to immediate damage or destruction by water and are difficult to clean. Weak even in the best of circumstances, they are further weakened by high or fluctuating levels of relative humidity. They make an unsound base for the application of stronger, moisture-resistant paints, such as oils, which when applied at later dates over distempers will often cause dramatic peeling. Glue distempers support mildew growth in any damp environment.

A problem facing the investigator of paints in an old building is that glue distempers were commonly washed off completely before repainting or papering. Washing off has always been considered the best practice in redecorating. For this reason finding and dating glue distemper paints in old buildings—or establishing whether they were once present and were later removed—usually involves much time, frustration, and uncertainty. Sometimes the only surviving samples of a glue distemper paint used on a plaster wall surface are on the abutting edges of woodwork, such as door casings; here small overlaps of glue distemper paint from the wall may have been sandwiched in between two layers of the oil paints that were used on the woodwork.

Although immune to yellowing, glue distempers are only as color stable as the pigments used in them, many of which were fugitive. In examining old paint layers, the investigator must be wary of another type of discoloration to which glue distempers are subject: drastic darkening when impregnated by the binder of an oil paint applied over them, as along the edges of woodwork painted in oil. This darkening is due to the partial filling of the pore spaces that through scattering had imparted lightness and opacity to the paint. The oil may also have yellowed. Another manner by which glue distempers have often become impregnated and thus darkened is through the application of a sizing of shellac or perhaps rosin, applied as a strengthener and sealer to make a glue distemper more suitable as a base for overpaint. Both these alterations make the glue distemper much more resistant to solution by water.

GOUACHES

Another type of paint worth brief mention in connection with buildings is gouache. Gouache is opaque paint bound primarily by vegetable gum, traditionally gum arabic or gum senegal. (Water-soluble natural polymers of vegetable origin are known as gums.) Dextrin is a common binder or supplementary binder in today's gouaches. Gouache is distinguished from watercolor, which uses the same binders, in that watercolor is transparent and derives whiteness not from white pigment but from the paper behind. One English use is known to me of gouache as a wall paint,[14] and gouache was sometimes used in printing wallpaper patterns.

I have used a particular brand of artists' gouache in one case where its superb handling, astonishing hiding power, and ready reversibility in water were vital to the task at hand: repainting the background (already repainted many times before) around original painted ceiling designs by Robert Adam.[15]

The polymers that bind gouaches are commonly found in higher proportions in relation to solvent than the glue in distemper paint. Handling properties are not adversely affected by this, and the higher proportion of polymer is needed to provide strength in the dried film. Thus, many gouaches are not porous, and high-refractive-index white pigments, such as white lead, are used to maximize scattering and opacity.

SOME OLDER TYPES OF LACQUERS

Like many terms in art and craft, *lacquer* has both more general and more specific meanings. In general, especially in modern commercial usage, the term implies any clear or pigmented coating that dries by solvent loss and is insoluble in water. The term is widely applied to opaque paints as well as clear or tinted transparent finishes. Lacquers are also called "solution coatings," a term clearly indicating that the binder is dissolved in solvent and dries by solvent loss.

The specific—and constantly changing—meanings of lacquer refer to particular binders. These have included the resinous exudation from a certain tree (the binder in Chinese lacquer), shellac, rosin, and cellulose nitrate. The last three have had some use as house paint binders and are worthy of brief mention. An important difference between these paint binders and the glue and gum binders discussed previously is that they are soluble not in water but in organic solvents, such as alcohol.

Shellac is a resin secreted by the lac insect and comes mainly from India. It is soluble in alcohol. An important use of unpigmented and pigmented shellacs has been as sealers to prepare knots or absorbent substrates for the application of oil paint or another type of paint. Since the 1970s, knot sealers based on synthetic resins have demonstrated superior moisture resistance in exterior applications.

Rosin, the residue left after turpentine has been distilled from pine balsam, is a cheap, brittle material that has served as a paint binder, at least in combination with other materials. It has been used in lacquers and in paints containing other binders that solidify by cross linking.

Cellulose nitrate is a resin made by treating cellulose with nitric and sulfuric acids. It was extensively used in the 1920s and 1930s as a binder for automotive and other paints.

Generally speaking, the resins used in these older types of lacquers are not nearly as resistant to photo-oxidative degradation as more modern synthetic resins such as poly(vinyl acetates) and acrylics.

ENCAUSTIC PAINT

A few late nineteenth-century decorators, most notably John La Farge, found reason to use encaustic paints—paints bound by mixtures of beeswax and other materials, mainly Venice turpentine (fig. 1). (Venice turpentine, unlike turpentine or spirits of turpentine, is not a solvent but rather the resinous exudate of the European larch tree.) Various complex encaustic brews have been used by decorative painting firms to this day. These paints were applied hot: their Greek name, *enkaustikos*, is taken from the verb *enkaiein*, meaning "to burn in." Thus, they dried largely by cooling and partly by loss of solvents such as turpentine and alcohol. The author's current involvement in the conservation of encaustic decorations by La Farge is proof that one should be prepared to encounter these relatively rare paints. The two examples of La Farge's encaustic paint of which the author has knowledge can be melted easily with a heat lamp and are soluble in virtually every organic solvent.

In an 1854 advertisement, P. A. Butler, a decorative painter of Lawrence, Massachusetts, particularly recommended "En Caustic" paint over oil and distemper: "Old walls, soiled and cracked, rough or smooth, can be made to look perfectly new, with a coating of this preparation. . . . it forms a surface, hard, like marble, that can be washed with soap and water without endangering or effacing its beauty."[16]

ACRYLIC LACQUERS

Coatings based on acrylic resins that are dissolved in organic solvents and that form solids by the evaporation of the solvents are lacquers or solution coatings. Acrylic solution coatings are quite different from acrylic "latex" coatings, which are discussed later. All acrylic resins are of synthetic origin: most are made from the reaction products of common alcohols and acrylic or methacrylic acids.

While other types of modern synthetic resins are used to make lacquers, only acrylic lacquers will be discussed because of the special importance in conservation work of the properties of highly stable acrylics. (Indeed, there are poor acrylics.) The best acrylic resins suitable for conservation purposes are highly stable chemically, colorless and resistant to yellowing, and hard enough not to absorb dirt but flexible enough not to crack in suitable applications. They meet the conservator's criterion of reversibility: they retain for very long periods the ability to be redissolved and removed in the same solvents in which they were applied. The great resistance of stable acrylics to loss of solubility over time is not shared by some other resins; it derives from the resistance of the molecules to the undesirable formation of cross links among one another.[17] However, when in-painting works of art, it is important to choose acrylics that dissolve in solvents that will not attack the underlying old paint.

Acrylic polymers used in typical solution coatings are of substantial molecular weight—around 200,000. This places them between higher-molecular-weight industrial polymers and many of the low-molecular-weight polymers mentioned earlier, such as dextrin and shellac. While sufficient to make the dried coating strong and durable, this level of molecular weight is also great enough to make acrylic solution coatings harder to handle by brush than shellac-based coatings, for example, unless they are greatly diluted with solvent. Conservators who use acrylic solution varnishes for coating (usually by spraying) pictures or who use pigmented acrylic solution paints for in-painting do not regularly complain of serious handling problems, but they would if they were trying to spread the materials by brush over large areas of wall. A task needed in architectural conservation is to formulate a wider choice of high-quality acrylic solution coatings that brush smoothly over large areas and can be used by decorative painters for striping and the other operations of their craft that require easy handling. Until then, in building restoration, acrylic lacquer paints are of value—or potential value—mainly in in-painting small losses in early paints and painted designs.

Unpigmented acrylic solutions are also widely used as penetrating consolidants for crumbling old materials and for other conservation purposes.

PAINTS THAT DRY BY CROSS LINKING

Oil paints and their cousins, alkyd resin paints, are the principal examples of house paints that dry by cross linking.

OIL PAINTS

Although oil paints have been the most important class of paints in American architecture, this discussion of them can be abbreviated somewhat because oils are treated in detail in "Historic and Modern Oil Paints" in this volume.

COMPOSITION AND DRYING MECHANISMS

By far the most common oil used in house painting has been linseed oil, which is extracted from flax seed. As detailed in Richard Newman's chapter "Historic and Modern Oil Paints" in this volume, the linseed oil molecule is based on a chain of three carbons (known as a glycerine backbone) from each of which branches a longer chain known as a fatty acid group. The chemical nature of the fatty acid groups within a given oil can vary. A typical linseed oil structure (fig. 4) would contain the glycerine backbone shown vertically at the left, one linoleic acid group shown horizontally at the top, and two linolenic acid groups. The molecular weight of this molecule is 874. The double hyphens in the three fatty acid chains represent double bonds between carbon atoms, in which not one pair but two pairs of electrons are shared by the adjacent carbons. The double bonds are points at which a complex series of chemical reactions involving atmospheric oxygen can occur, leading to the cross linking of oil molecules.

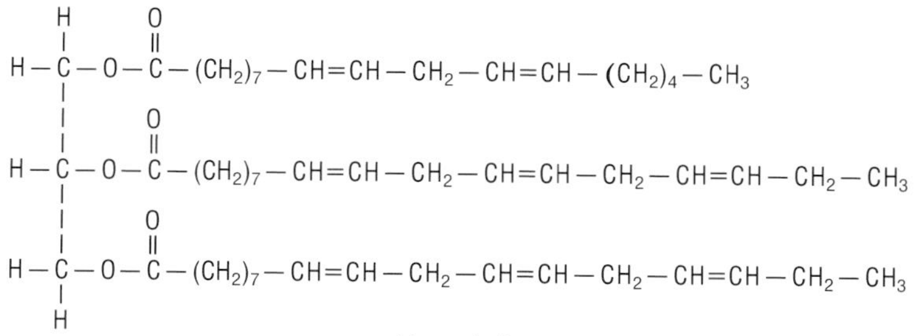

$$H-\overset{\displaystyle H}{\underset{\displaystyle H}{C}}-O-\overset{\displaystyle O}{C}-(CH_2)_7-CH=CH-CH_2-CH=CH-(CH_2)_4-CH_3$$

Linseed oil structure

Thus, linseed oil dries by oxidative cross linking. Any type of oil that does so, such as linseed oil or safflower oil, is called a drying oil. Linseed oil paints may contain a solvent to reduce viscosity of the fluid paint. When serving in this role—lowering the viscosity of a binder that would still be a liquid without solvent—a solvent is commonly called a diluent or thinner. Turpentine has been the most common thinner. Where oil paint is thus thinned, drying is a two-step process: initially by solvent loss and, much more slowly, by oxidation. Since the molecular weight of undried linseed oil is low, linseed oil paints handle well even with no added thinner, provided sufficient oil is present in relation to the amount of pigment.

The oxidative cross linking of drying oils is catalyzed (speeded up) by many metal ions. Compounds supplying these metals are known as driers. In the eighteenth and early nineteenth centuries the added driers were pigments. White lead (basic lead carbonate) not only served as the most common white pigment in oil paints but also had a drying effect. Red lead (lead oxide) was a far more potent drier. Umbers, which are among the iron-oxide earth pigments, enhanced drying through the presence of traces of manganese.

With the advent of commercially available chemical paint additives, liquid organometallic compounds were used as driers, mostly the colorless and transparent lead naphthenate or the purple cobalt naphthenate still found in art supply stores. Cobalt promotes a fast "top dry"; lead produces a "through dry." The two have commonly been used together.

Commercial linseed oil was often heated together with driers, in which case the oil was called "boiled oil" (as opposed to "raw"). This heating served to increase the molecular weight of the oil, which further enhanced the drying rate. The term *boiled oil* has also been used to describe oil to which driers have been added without heating.

Before the industrial era, the painter, using a stone slab and muller or ball and trough, ground white lead or any desired color pigments into the oil binder himself **(fig. 5)**. By the late nineteenth century the painter more commonly bought fully prepared and tinted oil paints or partially prepared paint called white lead paste. This last product, a thorough dispersion of white lead in a near-minimum amount of linseed oil, was available through house paint suppliers until the 1970s. A painter could easily work with the white lead paste, color pigments ground in oil, extra oil, turpentine, and driers to formulate and tint paints for every application, interior and exterior, matte and glossy.

Figure 4. *The structure of a molecule of linseed oil.*

Figure 5. *An oil-alkyd paint made by the author to replicate the original in a chamber of the Joseph Lloyd Manor House (1767), Huntington, N.Y. The paint is made using essentially the same pigments as the original and reproduces the very slight color variation that would have resulted from imperfect hand grinding of the Prussian blue pigment. Most of the color variation shown, however, is due to uneven lighting. (Morgan W. Phillips)*

Until the third quarter of this century the formulation of oil paints was a relatively simple matter. Gloss, for example, could be increased by using more oil and decreased by using the volatile turpentine instead of some of the oil. In the latter case the surface of the dried paint would not be so oil-rich, smooth, and shiny. The colorants—color pigments ground in oil—were perfectly serviceable paints in themselves and could be used in any amount in the paint. By contrast, the "universal colors" of today, made to custom-tint either oil- or water-based paints, do not dry and cannot be added to paint in more than a limited proportion.

PROPERTIES

Oil paints handle beautifully in the fluid state and dry to form rugged, adherent films. Unfortunately, oil paints embrittle with age through oxidative processes that continue beyond the point of optimum properties.

Oil paints are attacked (saponified) by alkali. For this reason fresh lime plaster, which is highly alkaline, was well aged and then usually neutralized with an acid salt before the application of oil paint. Today the recommended practice in painting fresh plaster or masonry is the application of an acrylic "latex" primer or some other type of alkali-resistant primer.

A great fault of oil paints—and a curse on those who study old oil paints—is that oils turn yellow, especially in the darkness created by later layers of paint. (A difference between oils and many natural resins is that the latter often yellow on exposure to light.) The reactions that produce yellowing are complex ones involving oxygen. Yellowing of oil is of no consequence when the original color of the paint is such as to mask the yellowing: blacks and dark reds and browns, for example, will not be affected. Paints of lighter colors and generally cooler colors change dramatically: white turns yellow; light blues turn green.

The problem of yellowing is greatest in the case of paints predating about 1820 because oil contents in these paints were typically high. Moreover, oil glazes (thin layers apparently containing oil and sometimes resins) were usually applied to early oil paints. When examining early oil paints, it is important to find thick protected drops of paint inside of which fugitive pigments have been protected from light and in which the yellowing problem is mitigated. Yellowing is reduced in the centers of such drops for two probable reasons: glazes high in oil content have not penetrated far into the drops, and the interiors of the drops have been somewhat protected from oxygen. On exposure to ordinary room light, yellowed oil paints, long protected from the light by overpaints, will slowly regain much of their clearer original tones.[18] Deliberate bleaching with light is a necessary part of the color study of oil paints. Systematic approaches to bleaching with light have not been developed; the process involves a degree of subjectivity. Thick samples that have discolored little can be bleached to much less yellow tones than badly discolored surface material.

The importance of finding and, if necessary, bleaching thick drops is insufficiently appreciated. Finding them is highly time-consuming, as only a few good samples may exist in a room—a drop that forms at the bottom of the barrel of a hinge or in a drilled ornamental hole in a cornice molding. A good sample is thick enough so that the interior is relatively consistent in color (surface discoloration tapers off for some distance inward). Drops that are thick enough to be good color samples are generally still too small to find and extract skillfully without the use in situ of a low-power stereomicroscope (ten to twenty power). It is desirable to find several thick samples that may be compared: close consistency among the internal colors of several samples is an indication that the samples have discolored relatively little. The fact that persistence, ingenuity, and a microscope used in situ are all required to find good samples of early oil paints greatly increases the cost of the work, as compared to random sampling and cross sectioning.

TRADITIONAL ENAMELS AND ALKYD RESIN PAINTS

Oil paints do not satisfy every user. Sometimes they are not hard enough and do not dry fast enough. Accordingly, two analogous modifications of oil paints—one old and the other dating from the 1920s—take important places in any outline of American architectural paints. These are the traditional enamels and the more recent alkyd resin paints.

Traditional enamels were paints bound by oil that had been cooked together with melted natural hard resins, such as copal. The product of this cooking is more than a mere solution of resin in oil; it is a reaction product of the two, to which a further quantity of oil could be added. Solvent is required to liquefy the oil-resin blend, which dries partly by solvent loss and partly by oxidative cross linking of the oil and fused resin-oil portion.

Unpigmented, these oil-resin blends were widely used as varnishes.[19] Pigmented, they were called enamels and found much use on kitchen woodwork and wherever extra ruggedness was required in a paint. As early as 1812 Hezekiah Reynolds recommended the addition of "Copal Varnish" to oil.[20]

COMPOSITION OF ALKYDS

Today, rather than cook up a compound of oil and a natural resin, resins of an analogous type—alkyds—are made by direct chemical combination of the fatty acids of drying oils with certain acids and alcohols. The acid and alcohol portions alone would form hard, largely insoluble resins somewhat akin to copal. The alcohol glycerine and the acid phthalic anhydride, for example, form just such a product, glyceryl phthalate, first synthesized about 1901.[21] The practicality of alkyds was greatly enhanced by the discovery, in the 1920s, that the incorporation of fatty acids (from oils) contributed solubility, flexibility, and the ability to dry by oxidative cross linking.

Because these resins were formed by the combination of alcohols and acids, they were at first called alcids and later, for phonetic reasons, alkyds. Without pigment they have been much used as varnishes; pigmented, this class of paints are the "oil" paints in use today.

The proportion of oil in the three-part molecule is called the oil-length. "Long-oil" or "long-long-oil" alkyds are the most common type in house paints, where flexibility is more important than hardness. Alkyd house paints often contain extra oil that does not constitute part of the three-part alkyd molecule.

PROPERTIES OF ALKYD RESIN PAINTS

Alkyd resin house paints are much faster drying than linseed oil paints. Like oils, they embrittle with age because of oxidative degradation, but they are more resistant to this than oils. They are stronger than oil paints, in inverse proportion to the oil length and proportion of added oil. They are lower in permeability to moisture and thus are useful as metal paints. The strength and low moisture permeability of alkyds are probably why they have frequently peeled when applied over old, weak, brittle, permeable oil paints on the exteriors of houses.

The variety of acids, alcohols, and oils used in alkyds has greatly increased since the 1930s, when alkyds began to be used widely. The choice of oil used in making an alkyd greatly influences the propensity to yellow: safflower alkyds are the best in this respect but are now rarely used; soya alkyds hold color almost as well as safflower alkyds and have better mechanical properties; linseed alkyds yellow much more than soya. Good brands of soya alkyds, widely popular today in house paints, yellow far less than linseed oil paint. An alkyd resin paint of very high quality is sold today as an artists' material.

MODERN SYNTHETIC RESIN PAINTS

A wide variety of resins have been developed in recent decades as binders for special high-performance coatings. Unlike the older alkyds, which are made in part from oils, the newer resins are entirely synthetic. Outstanding properties of high-performance coatings made using these resins might be great hardness, adhesion to glass or other substrates, or extreme weather resistance. Many of these coatings require critical surface preparation and are restricted largely to industrial use under carefully controlled factory conditions. Some require heat to cross link. Many of the binders are combinations of components of widely disparate natures; examples are siliconized polyesters and acrylic-melamine coatings.

Two types of synthetic resins are especially suitable for use in paints that are not difficult to apply in the field: epoxy resins and various urethane or acrylic-urethane resins. These have found their way into the market for architectural paints.

All that can be said about these resins in this chapter is that they vary widely. Some epoxies, the epoxy esters, are oil modified and dry by oxidative cross linking via the oil component when exposed to air. Others are two-part systems consisting of an epoxy component and amine; these cure by direct cross linking when the two components are mixed. These two-part epoxy paint binders are similar to two-part epoxies used for adhesives or for laying up fiberglass cloth or making solid castings.[22]

Urethanes include oil-modified types that dry by oxidation, moisture-curing ones that dry by reaction with atmospheric moisture, and two-pack systems that cure by reactions occurring when the two parts are mixed together.[23] Urethane resins that contain the benzene ring structure (six carbons joined in a ring by alternating or perhaps oscillating double bonds) are called aromatic and tend to turn yellow more drastically than resins of an aliphatic structure (not containing the benzene ring). Aliphatic moisture-curing urethanes form highly stable coatings, which are not reversible.

PAINTS THAT FORM FILMS BY COALESCENCE AND SOLVENT LOSS

"Latex" paints provide the principal example of film formation by coalescence and the subsequent evaporation of a minimum amount of solvent.

EMULSION PAINTS

Emulsion (latex) paints are paints bound by polymer emulsions, also called polymer dispersions. The term *latex* is somewhat inappropriately applied to polymer emulsion paint binders through association with rubber latex. The terms *emulsion* and *dispersion* are more precise and descriptive.

COMPOSITION AND SOLIDIFICATION MECHANISM

Robert L. Feller has written a succinct discussion of polymer emulsions: " . . . 'polymer emulsions' consist of minute particles of polymer dispersed in water. The typical volatile organic solvents are not present: the milky fluid is primarily water and tiny globules of polymer dispersed in it."[24] Polymer emulsions form dry films through evaporation of the water and merging, or coalescence, of the polymer particles, which are spherical. In this case the water is not a solvent for the polymer but merely the medium in which it is dispersed. If the polymer were water soluble, the spheres of polymer would dissolve into the water in the liquid paint, and also dried films of the paint would be soluble in rain water. Today a number of chemical classes of synthetic polymers are used in the emulsion form.

In polymer emulsion paints, the resin particles are suspended side by side with the pigment particles and entrap the pigment as the resin particles merge. Unpigmented polymer emulsions are used as adhesives, as adhesive additives for plaster and masonry materials, and for many other purposes. Elmer's Glue®, for example, is a polymer emulsion.

Besides the main constituents (polymer and water), many other ingredients are required in polymer emulsions. These include surface-active agents that prevent the polymer particles from touching and coagulating until the water evaporates. There are also "coalescing aids." These are slow-evaporating solvents, present in small amounts, that soften the particles to ensure that they merge during drying of the emulsion. These coalescing aids then gradually evaporate so that the film that is formed can develop full hardness. The complex formulas for emulsion paints include antifoam agents, mildewstats, and other additives.

The principal synthetic polymers that have been used in emulsion paints are of the acrylic, poly(vinyl acetate), and styrene-butadiene classes (and combinations of these). The molecular structure of good acrylic resins renders them more resistant to oxidative degradation than styrene-butadiene polymers and more resistant to water than poly(vinyl acetates). They are generally considered the best class of emulsion paints for general architectural use.

An older type of emulsion paint deserves mention because it did find widespread use in buildings from the early part of this century until the ascendancy of the synthetic resin types. These paints are based on drying oils, or alkyd resins, emulsified in water.[25] These oil-bound water paints formed films initially by coalescence as the water evaporated and then, like ordinary oil paints, by oxidative cross linking.

PROPERTIES

Polymer emulsions provide the convenience of application and cleanup with water, though waterproof when dry. A major factor leading to their increasing use in paints is their freedom from costly, toxic, and air-polluting solvents. In the emulsion form, non-water-soluble polymers can be mixed easily with water-based masonry and plaster materials.

A great advantage of emulsions is that high molecular weight can be used in the resin without raising the viscosity (thickness) of the emulsion or the paint made from it. This is because the viscosity is dependent mostly on the water between the particles rather than on the resin inside the particles. This situation contrasts with that of animal glue solutions, where the glue molecules, being entangled with each other throughout the solution, create jellies at a glue content of more than about 3 percent. Emulsions containing as much as 50 percent polymer by weight are typically so watery that in paints added thickeners are needed to make them handle well and form suitably thick films.

Resins used in emulsions generally have much higher molecular weights than resins used as solutions in organic solvents. Although high molecular weight enhances toughness and other properties of the dried film, it makes the resins much harder to dissolve in organic solvents when dried and thus less easily reversible. Because of the inherent chemical stability of good acrylic resins and because of the high molecular weight of emulsion resins, acrylic emulsion (acrylic latex) paints offer by far the highest degree of weather resistance of any type of paint in common use today on American buildings. Difficulties have occurred, however, when they are placed over unsuitable substrates, such as chalky old oil paints. Until very recently, emulsion paints have not exhibited good penetration and binding of old chalky paint surfaces: the polymer particles were too large to penetrate the pores in the old film, and the surface tension of the water in the emulsion detracted from the ability of the paint to wet and penetrate chalky substrates. However, there have reputedly been recent improvements in the performance of latex paints with respect to the penetration and binding of old paints. Further work is needed in designing latex and other durable modern paints specifically suited for overcoating old oil paints.

An advantage of acrylic emulsion paints is that the best ones are highly resistant to yellowing. Thus, if formulated with stable pigments, they are useful for in-painting missing portions of old decorative designs, where careful color matches must be expected to last many years. (Presumably the old paint, though perhaps an oil subject to yellowing, has reached an equilibrium level of yellowness depending on the level of illumination.) Emulsion paints become more transparent as they dry, and colored ones darken markedly. This effect is due to the fact that before drying the film contains polymer-water interfaces that scatter light, making the paint more reflective; these interfaces disappear as the paint dries. (This is the reason Elmer's Glue changes from milky white to clear as it dries.) Thus, emulsion paints must be test-dried to determine their color—an inconvenience when mixing many different colors for small areas being in-painted.

Besides color stability, a further advantage of the best emulsion paints is that they can be formulated so as never to coalesce completely: small remnants of the spaces occupied by water in the wet paint can remain permanently, and these allow moisture from inside a building to diffuse outward without becoming trapped behind exterior coatings. The application of successive coats over a period of years reduces this permeability to moisture.

MILK AND CASEIN PAINTS

The terms *milk paint* and *casein paint* are almost but not quite interchangeable. "Casein" is the more modern term and is used to describe any paint, ancient or modern, homemade or of commercial manufacture, that uses casein (the principal protein in milk) as the main binder. Sources before about 1900 use terms such as *milk painting* or *painting in milk* rather than *casein paint*. These earlier references describe the homemade paints that were the only milk products used for house painting before about the beginning of twentieth century, when commercially produced casein became widely available. Some of those homemade paints, like the commercial products, were made from casein that had been separated from the other ingredients of the milk. Others, however, were made directly from skim milk, which would have contained both casein and lactose (milk sugar), or apparently from whole milk, which would have contained casein, lactose, and fat, as roughly 3, 5, and 4 percent, respectively, of the milk.[26] Thus, some of the home-brewed milk paints would have been much less purely casein paints than others.

The variety of types of milk and casein paints that have been used is enormous, especially as many used other binders, such as linseed oil, in addition to casein. A good way to approach the subject is to start with more or less pure casein paints and then consider less pure versions and outright hybrids.

True casein paints have a history extending back to many civilizations of the ancient world; their use for house painting and decoration is recorded in ancient Hebrew texts.[27] Technological developments made possible the commercial preparation of large quantities of casein products starting in the late nineteenth century. The heyday of commercial casein paints was the second quarter of the twentieth century. In 1944, 5.7 million pounds of casein were used in paints in this country, 9.4 million pounds in adhesives (mainly for woodworking), and 26 million pounds in coatings for paper.[28] Most of the paint was used for interior plaster walls and ceilings; the term *calcimine* referred not only to glue distempers but also to casein paints.[29] Still in use in the 1980s in the paper industry, casein has been almost entirely supplanted by synthetic resins in paints and adhesives. Commercial casein paints are still used by artists and painters of theater scenery.

COMPOSITION AND SOLIDIFICATION MECHANISMS

Like animal glue (the binder in glue distemper paints), casein is a protein. Proteins are complex combinations of amino acids, which are nitrogen-containing acids. Casein contains about fifteen amino acids. Unlike animal glue, casein is only slightly soluble in water. In milk, casein is not dissolved but colloidally dispersed. (Casein is also insoluble in typical organic solvents, such as toluene; for this reason casein paints resist the action of solvent-based paint strippers.) Like all proteins, casein contains both acidic and basic chemical groups, permitting it to react either with bases or acids, respectively. Its acidic character is the more prevalent.

The effective use of casein as a binder in paints, adhesives, and other products is dependent on controlling the water solubility of casein by causing it to react with various materials. This is true of all commercial casein paints and most homemade milk paints to which I have found references. (As described later, there were also less sophisticated milk paints.)

In the preparation of commercial casein paints and other products, the degree of water solubility may be changed several times during the preparation of a product and in the course of its solidification after drying. Commercially prepared casein is precipitated from skim milk by treatment of the milk with an acid, usually hydrochloric, sulfuric, or lactic. (Casein can also be precipitated by allowing bacteria in the milk to produce lactic acid.) Reaction with acids lowers the water solubility of casein to its lowest level, which is reached at a pH of 4.6. The resulting precipitation is exactly what occurs when, as in making cheese, milk is curdled: the curds precipitated from the milk are essentially casein. Commercial casein is washed, dried, ground, and sold as a powder.

In this insoluble state, casein cannot be used as a liquid binder in a paint or other product. It must be made soluble in water. This is done by reaction with a base (alkali): as the pH is increased, the casein becomes water soluble and thus readily useful as a binder in a water-borne paint.

After application (in a paint or other product), the casein may or may not be converted back to a water-insoluble material, depending on the need for water resistance in the end product. There are several mechanisms by which insolubility of the dried casein product may be achieved. If, for example, the base used to solubilize the casein is highly volatile, it evaporates after application and the casein regains a substantial degree of insolubility. Ammonia (a solution of ammonium hydroxide in water) is the volatile base normally used with casein.

Nonvolatile bases used to solubilize casein remain bound to the casein molecule and can affect the water solubility of a dried casein paint film in various ways. If the base used is a substance that can form only a single chemical bond, such as sodium hydroxide, it causes the casein to remain water soluble. If, however, the base is polyvalent—that is, it can form two or more bonds—it may be able to form cross links between casein molecules, imparting a high degree of water insolubility in the dried film, far greater than that of the original casein. Thus, the base first solubilizes the casein and then renders it insoluble. The base most commonly used since ancient times to control the solubility of casein in this way is hydrated lime, $Ca(OH)_2$. Lime and casein react to form calcium caseinate, an insoluble substance having a cross-linked chemical structure.

The fact that hydrated lime serves to both solubilize and insolubilize the casein is not self-contradictory. The two phenomena occur at different times—solubilization first and then, after a "pot life" of some hours, insolubilization. Lime-casein solutions not used promptly will gel and become useless. Thus lime-casein paints sold as commercial products had to be packaged as dry powders, to which water was added just before use. Various other types of casein paint could be stored and marketed as wet pastes. True lime-casein paints are available today.

Compounds of polyvalent metals other than calcium—zinc and aluminum being the most important ones—have commonly been used to insolubilize casein. This explains the long-recognized usefulness of alum (aluminum salts) in hardening both casein and gelatin (animal glue). Reagents other than metal compounds, such as formaldehyde, have been widely used to insolubilize casein, sometimes by application to a casein film after it has dried.

Casein can be insolubilized by another mechanism besides cross linking: the "blocking" by a reagent of hydrophilic chemical groups on the casein molecule that would otherwise be attracted to water.[30] Formaldehyde and polyvalent metal compounds can insolubilize casein both by cross linking and by blocking hydrophilic groups.[31]

Many commercial casein paints incorporated drying oils, resins, waxes, and other supplementary binders. These materials were added to improve handling properties or durability. Presumably, they existed in the wet paint mainly as emulsions. In 1943 "oleocasein" paints represented "a considerable proportion of the commercial paints made with casein."[32] These supplementary binders made many casein paints into hybrids, with respect to composition, drying mechanisms, and final properties.

As this discussion suggests, the twentieth-century commercial producer of casein paints and other products could draw on a wide variety of ingredients that altered the character of the product in fundamental ways. Although the home-brewed casein paints used since ancient times were generally rather crude products not well understood by those who made them, some of the chemical mechanisms discussed here explain at least in part how archaic milk paints worked.

Of the types of casein paint discussed here, lime casein was the most widely described in American literature that predates the commercial manufacture of casein paints. Although well known in antiquity and the Middle Ages, caseins had declined in use after the invention of oil paints in the fifteenth century. Candee has shown that a late eighteenth-century French recipe, much published in America after 1800, was of central importance in popularizing milk paint, particularly lime casein paint, in this country.[33, 34] The key figure in the rediscovery and popularization of casein paints for architectural use was Antoine-Alexis Cadet-de-Vaux. During the French Revolution, Cadet-de-Vaux devised a formula for lime- casein paint for interior application in buildings and one for exterior use. These formulas were first published in English in 1801 in London. Another variation of lime casein paint was devised by M. Ludicke; this was first published in French in 1792 and seems to have been first published in English in 1805, again in London. Cadet-de-Vaux's recipe or adaptations thereof began to be published in America in the early nineteenth century. Around 1808 it was published in Connecticut as a "then new principle" and found lacking in durability.[35] The recipe was published again in the September 12, 1828, issue of *New England Farmer,* and in the next week's issue a correspondent reported that at the time of the recipe's publication in Connecticut he had tried the paint, with poor results. His remarks give an impression of the status of exterior milk painting at that time:

I think your correspondent in yours of September 12 has taken a too favorable view of milk paint. This is a revival of a subject on which some French chemists indulged opinions, which, to say the least, were hardly realized.... If so cheap a substitute for oil painting could be had, it would be a great benefit, extending a neatness of appearance through the country.[36]

In a painters' manual first published in Philadelphia in 1869, Henry Carey Baird repeated Cadet-de-Vaux's recipes for interior and exterior paints and implied that they—and apparently milk paints in general—had not yet become fully accepted for use in buildings:

In consequence of the injury which has often resulted to sick and weakly persons from the smell of common paint, the following method of painting with milk has been adopted by some workmen, which, for the interior of buildings, besides being as free as distemper from any offensive odour, is said to be nearly equal to oil-painting in body and durability.

Time only can prove how far this mode of painting is to be compared, for durability, with that in oil.... [37]

The Cadet-de-Vaux recipes differed in an important respect from the later formulas for commercial lime caseins and from Ludicke's 1792 recipe in that the casein was not precipitated out of the milk. Two quarts of skimmed milk were mixed directly with six ounces of hydrated lime putty, four ounces of a drying oil (caraway, linseed, or nut), five pounds of Spanish white (calcium carbonate pigment) and colored pigments, if desired. For exterior use, an additional two ounces each of lime and oil, plus two ounces of white burgundy pitch, were used.

Thus, Cadet-de-Vaux's recipes, containing not only lime and casein but also oil and sometimes pitch, were hybrids, like the later commercial oleocasein paints. The variety of hybrids that existed is suggested by the well-known use of milk as an additive to lime whitewashes: in this example, the principal solidification mechanism of the paint would be carbonation of the lime and crystal formation, as described at the beginning of this essay, but surely some calcium caseinate was also formed.

A complete history of commercial casein paints in America could readily be assembled from detailed industrial texts such as *Protective and Decorative Coatings* (see note 32), but the history of home-brewed milk paints requires more energetic detective work, both in analyzing paint films and in recording written and spoken references. In preparing this discussion of caseins, I happened on two personal recollections of the use of milk paints in rural America in the early 1930s, a time when economy was an especially important consideration. These tantalizing accounts indicate that painting with home-brewed milk paint did indeed become broadly popular.

Ruth Johnston-Feller, now of Oakland, Maryland, remembers her grandmother making milk paint in the kitchen and applying it to plaster walls of the kitchen and bedrooms of their farmhouse in Mount Morris, Illinois. She recalls no details about formulation.

Erle Ferson of North Perry, Maine, not only recalls in detail making milk paint in the early 1930s but stated that it was in common use for interiors and exteriors of all sorts of buildings in that area of Maine.[38] He said that his father and grandfather had made paint according to the same recipe he used and that his great uncle, a ships' carpenter in the mid-nineteenth century, had used milk paint on the interiors of the cabins of sailing ships.

Ferson's paint was made from buttermilk, which is the liquid left behind after the fat (butter) is extracted from cream. Although buttermilk has a strong flavor, it is similar to skim milk in composition.[39] A large quantity of buttermilk was put into an empty lime barrel in the cellar and left to stand for some months, into the fall of the year. During this time it would be acidified through the action of bacteria. The casein (curds) would precipitate out, leaving the whey, which was discarded. Whiting (calcium carbonate) was added for body and hiding power (whiteness). Increments of raw linseed oil would be added, with repeated stirring, over the course of a winter. The intended purpose of the linseed oil was to break up the mass of curds and impart workability. After the paint had achieved about the consistency of chocolate pudding, says Ferson, Dutch Boy brand white lead paste (white lead in linseed oil) was added to enhance body and hiding power. White was the principal color used for house exteriors. For painting barns, dry red ocher was ground in oil and added to the white base described here. Somehow, red rather than pink was achieved, in spite of the presence of white lead. Paints for interior use were often tinted with commercially prepared tube colors in oil. Ferson guesses that a batch of white paint would contain fifteen gallons of curd, ten pounds of whiting, three gallons of linseed oil, and twenty pounds (a modest amount by volume) of white lead in oil. As the last step, a cup of vinegar would be added to mask the unpleasant odor of the paint.

An important point regarding this paint is that it did not contain lime (calcium hydroxide), the highly reactive insolubilizing agent commonly used with casein. It may be that the whiting served the same purpose to some extent: in acidified milk, casein is sufficiently acidic to displace carbon dioxide from calcium carbonate and react with the calcium.[40] The oil in Ferson's paint undoubtedly contributed to the drying effect through oxidative cross linking.

Because it does not contain lime, Ferson's paint is an example of milk paints not corresponding to the much-published recipe of Cadet-de-Vaux. It appears that some other recipes did not contain any agents to control the solubility of casein during preparation, application, or drying of the film. These most primitive milk paints must have depended entirely for their film-forming effect on the simple drying and coagulation of milk. Richard Candee cites an account book of about 1801 that was published in 1943 and that noted: "For laying on of your Colering, for outdore work it must be mixed with linseed oil, but for indore work it may be mixed with Strong Beer or milk."[41]

There is a need for much more study of commercially prepared casein paints of this century and of homemade milk paints based on French recipes. The extent to which cruder milk paints were used, at what dates, and whether on furniture, objects, or buildings, should also be determined.

PROPERTIES

A great variety of casein paints have been made, as well as various hybrids containing casein as the major part of the binder. The properties of the dried films have likewise varied. We have already discussed the differing levels of water solubility of dried films of different kinds of casein paint. An important physical property is flexibility; pure casein paints tend to be brittle. Casein paper coatings and some casein paints have been made more flexible by additions of "plasticizers" (flexibilizing agents). Many of these, like glycerine, impart flexibility by retaining water in the film. Most plasticizers, like glycerine, can migrate out of the film in time, causing the film to embrittle.

Commercial casein paints have generally had a low content of casein—5 to 12 percent of the weight of the dried paint.[42] (Higher casein contents produced hard brushing.) Thus, unless additional binders are used, casein paints have a matte finish, and most dried caseins contain internal air spaces that provide hiding power in the absence of high-refractive-index pigments (see "A Victorian Trompe l'Oeil"). When tinted, caseins are said to exhibit cleaner and brighter colors than oil paints and do not suffer from the yellowing problem associated with oils.

Because they are brittle and porous, most casein paints have not generally been as resistant as oil paints to weathering and abrasion. Insofar as oils or resins were added to caseins, these aspects of durability were generally increased. Erle Ferson's paint, for example, contained a certain amount of oil. He states that in exterior application on wooden buildings, his paint would set "hard like cement" after a month, would last five to seven years, and had the desirable property of failing by wearing away rather than flaking.

Casein paints are subject to deterioration by fungal and bacterial growth. Preservatives are required for caseins marketed as wet pastes or for caseins that will be used in damp environments. There are many preservatives for casein.[43]

Altogether, the history of milk and casein paints, as applied not only to architecture but also to furniture and other objects, is a subject that deserves much more attention by historians and paint analysts.

Historic and Modern Oil Paints

COMPOSITION AND CONSERVATION

RICHARD NEWMAN

ocumentary sources suggest that various materials were used in oil paints from colonial times until the early part of the twentieth century. Particularly with the rise of the commercial paint industry beginning after the Civil War, the number of components that could have entered into paint binder formulations increased considerably. At first, most of these additional materials were also natural substances. The final stage in the development of oil paints was the invention of synthetic oils, or alkyd resins, around the time of World War I.

HISTORIC OIL PAINT COMPOSITION

Before about the third quarter of the nineteenth century, individual painters bought pigment, binder, and thinner and mixed their own paints (fig. 1). In urban areas pigments were available in dry form or ground in oil—that is, as thick pastes to be diluted with further medium or thinner. In rural areas only the dry pigments would have been readily available,[1] although paste colors could obviously have been ordered from urban merchants. As Matthew Mosca notes ("Paint Decoration at Mount Vernon: The Revival of Eighteenth-Century Techniques" in this volume), George Washington ordered several pigments "ground in oil" between 1757 and 1763 for Mount Vernon. Presumably these were paste paints that had to be further diluted on site by the painters. Orders for turpentine, which would have been used to thin the paint, are mentioned, although, curiously, additional oil is not. Ordinarily, paste paints would not have been ground with enough oil to form strong films when diluted with a thinner.

Ready-mixed oil paints did not become available until immediately after the Civil War,[2] and even by 1900 only about two-thirds of the paints in the United States were reportedly sold in this form.[3] Early ready-made paints are described by Roger Moss ("Nineteenth-Century Paints: A Documentary Approach" in this volume).

Linseed oil, from the seeds of the flax plant, was probably by far the major oil used from colonial times onward. Linseed oil was made in only a few places in early eighteenth-century America; most of the supply was imported.[4] After the American Revolution, when flax farming took place all along the eastern seaboard, linseed oil became more readily available.

Figure 1. Robert Gibbs, *Boston, 1670. The unknown painter of this early American portrait used many of the materials that would have been used in house paints of the same period, including drying oils (probably linseed) and pigments, although some pigments used by portrait painters were too expensive for common decorative use. (Museum of Fine Arts, Boston)*

Walnut and poppyseed oils, which were used in some artists' oil colors and higher-quality oil varnishes, were less readily available in quantity than linseed. Some twentieth-century paint manuals mention them as being too expensive for extensive use.[5] Nevertheless, a 1798 manual mentions walnut oil in an interior paint recipe,[6] and the 1812 pamphlet by Hezekiah Reynolds noted an unspecified oil (possibly linseed or nut) in interior and exterior oil paint recipes.[7] Reynolds's booklet is one of the few documentary sources predating the twentieth century to specifically describe the manufacture of paint, so it will be referred to a number of times in this chapter. Fish oil (probably sperm and other whale oils) is mentioned by Richard Candee as being common in eighteenth-century paints.[8]

During the second half of the nineteenth century and first quarter of the twentieth century, a number of other oils were introduced in paints.[9] In 1869–70 tung (Chinese wood) oil was first used in the United States but reportedly was not widely employed until after 1900. Oiticica oil was introduced as early as 1923, perilla oil somewhat earlier. All three oils were imported from the Orient.

Castor oil, which in its raw form does not dry, can be processed to form a drying oil; the earliest patent for such a process dates to 1888. Paint manufacturing manuals from the earlier part of this century also mention a number of other oils that could not have been used by themselves but were often mixed with more expensive drying oils such as linseed or perilla: these include the oils of hemp seed, nigerseed (from the seeds of a tropical African tree), sunflower, candlenut (from the seeds of a South American tree), corn, and rosin (from pine trees).[10]

Although documentary evidence is scant, it is probably safe to state that linseed oil would have been by far the principal oil in architectural paints. But clearly, other oils were occasionally used. Paints from the last quarter of the nineteenth century and later could have been based on mixtures of a number of different oils.

It is impossible to say how commonly "varnish" was incorporated in oil paints. Reynolds's book includes a recipe for an oil medium for interior painting directing the addition of four fluid ounces of "copal varnish" (or, alternatively, turpentine spirits) to a gallon of cooked oil.[11]

Oil-resin varnishes were quite popular throughout the period 1600–1850. The earlier varnishes may have been mostly restricted to copal and amber resins, both imported materials,[12] but more than a dozen other natural resins are also mentioned in European varnish formulas from about 1650 to about 1800.[13] The varieties of resins that appear to have been most common are briefly discussed in conjunction with the chemistry of resins.

Some varnishes were simple solutions of a resin in a solvent (most often turpentine) and did not contain any oil; these are traditionally referred to as "spirit varnishes." These form more brittle and less durable films than oil-based varnishes, but a small amount of such a varnish added to an oil paint probably would not have adversely affected the durability of the paint.

Although interior paints, most of which typically contained the pigment lead white, would have been quite opaque, there is evidence that transparent glazes were used in some cases to increase depth of color and add transparency to decorative painting schemes; they would also have resulted in a glossier surface. Morgan Phillips has described the extensive use of transparent green glazes based on the pigment verdigris in the 1796 Harrison Gray Otis House in Boston,[14] and similar green glazes at Mount Vernon are discussed by Mosca. Although the binder of these green glazes has not been analyzed, it could have included a substantial amount of natural resin. Candee has noted a preference for "shining colors" made with varnish glazes in early eighteenth-century decorative painting.[15]

Occasionally paints were based on resins alone, which would have formed rather brittle but shiny paint films. Abbott Lowell Cummings and Richard Candee discuss ceiling panels from about 1720 in a house near Dartmouth, Massachusetts, the medium of which was pine resin; they also note some other instances of a resin binder at Sturbridge, Massachusetts ("Colonial and Federal America: Accounts of Early Painting Practices" in this volume).

Oil paints intended for interior and exterior applications generally would have been similar in composition. However, Reynolds gave separate recipes for interior and exterior oil paints, the exterior recipe calling for a lower volume of oil in relation to the weight of pigment. Varnish would not likely have been used in exterior paints, as it decreases the durability of a dried paint film.

While ordinary architectural paint compositions may have been relatively simple, there is reason to think that some interior mural or decorative paintings were carried out in more complex combinations of media during the last half of the nineteenth century. The late nineteenth century was a period of renewed interest in classical painting among artists, and some experimented with the wax (encaustic) medium, which documentary sources suggest was important in classical antiquity. Delacroix, for example, is reported to have mixed wax with his oil paints for his canvas murals.[16] In America also some unusual mixtures of materials may have been experimented with by artists who carried out decorations in houses or buildings. American artist John La Farge executed some mural commissions in a mixed binder that according to the artist's notebooks contained oil, wax, and other ingredients.[17] A much more common type of mixed medium than that used by La Farge may have been milk-oil combinations; Phillips ("A Survey of Paint Technology: The Composition and Properties of Paints" in this volume) notes that such mixtures could be encountered in nineteenth-century paints.

For the moment, it is difficult to do more than speculate about what combinations of materials may have been used as media in different times and places. Documentary references are comparatively few and not often detailed. The picture will become clearer only as detailed analyses of the binders of older decorative paints are carried out.

COMPOSITION OF OIL PAINT COMPONENTS

The vehicle of oil paints consists mainly of drying oils. Additional components, one or more of which may be present in a given paint, include natural resins, thinners, and driers.

DRYING OILS

Oils, which belong to the broad class of organic compounds known as lipids, are extracted from a wide variety of seeds and nuts, as well as a few animal and fish sources. Oils are often broadly divided into three categories: drying oils (such as linseed, walnut, perilla, and poppyseed oils); semidrying oils (soybean, corn, and sunflower oils); and nondrying oils (olive and coconut oils). The drying oils will form firm, nonsticky films when exposed to air. Semidrying oils form solid films much more slowly, some even remaining tacky almost indefinitely. Nondrying oil films always remain liquid.[18]

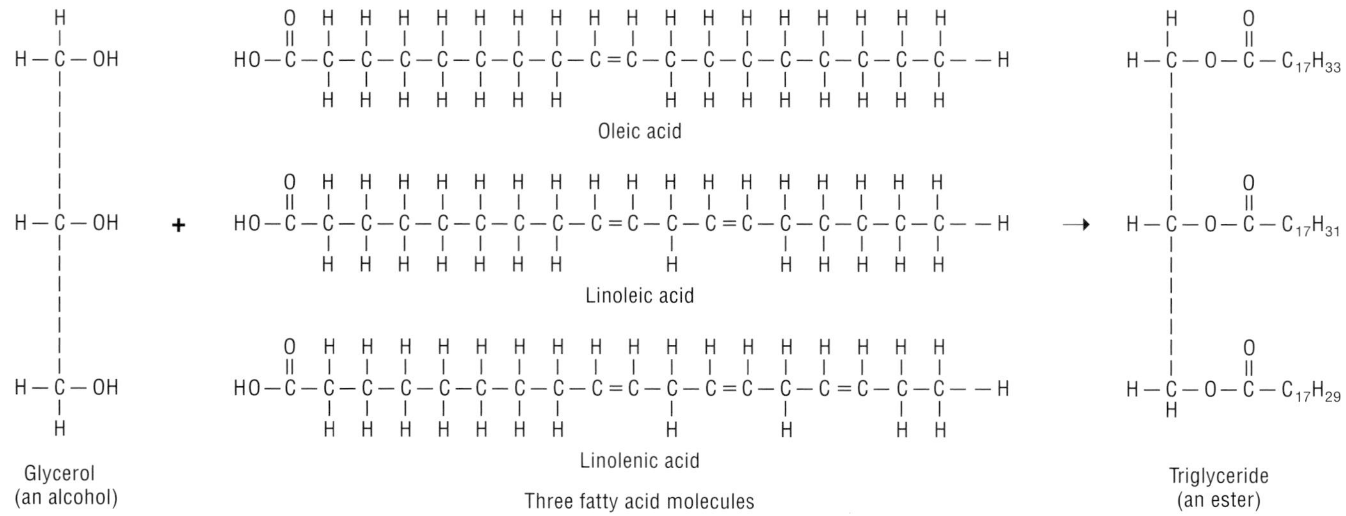

Glycerol
(an alcohol)

Oleic acid

Linoleic acid

Linolenic acid

Three fatty acid molecules

$H-C-O-C-C_{17}H_{33}$

$H-C-O-C-C_{17}H_{31}$

$H-C-O-C-C_{17}H_{29}$

Triglyceride
(an ester)

Figure 2. *Structure of a triglyceride molecule.*

The principal components of all these oils are triglycerides (fig. 2), esters formed by the reaction of glycerol (an alcohol) and fatty acids. While glycerol forms the backbone of all triglyceride molecules, the types of fatty acids in different oils vary considerably, as do their relative quantities. Nearly all naturally occurring fatty acids are long-chain molecules containing even numbers of carbon atoms. Some contain no carbon-carbon double bonds (saturated fatty acids), while others contain one, two, three, or occasionally more double bonds (unsaturated fatty acids).

The fatty acids most often encountered in oils are shown with their common and systematic names (table 1). The major fatty acids in the oils used as paint media are palmitic (sixteen carbons, no double bonds), stearic (eighteen carbons, no double bonds), oleic (eighteen carbons, one double bond), linoleic (eighteen carbons, two double bonds), and linolenic (eighteen carbons, three double bonds). The systematic names indicate the number of carbon atoms; numerical prefixes indicate the positions of the double bonds. Many organic compounds that contain carbon-carbon double bonds (including unsaturated fatty acids) can exist in two forms that are compositionally and structurally identical but differ in the geometry of the molecule: the prefixes *cis* and *trans* distinguish between the two forms (or diastereomers). The *cis* forms are the ones usually encountered in natural fatty acids.

The composition of fresh oils can be described from two points of view. In most oils four or five fatty acids are present (table 2). The number of triglycerides would actually be much greater than this, because there are three fatty acids in each triglyceride molecule. Physical properties (such as melting point) are primarily dependent on the triglyceride composition. It appears that fatty acids are not simply randomly distributed among the triglycerides in oils. Oils with quite similar overall types and amounts of fatty acids thus may vary in their physical properties if the distribution of these fatty acids differs substantially.

The second point of view from which fresh oil composition can be described is on the basis of their overall fatty acid contents (table 2). Fatty acids make up about 94 to 96 percent of

Table 1. *Names and Compositions of Some Fatty Acids*

Common name	Systematic name	Number of carbon atoms	Number of double bonds
Lauric	Dodecanoic	12	0
Myristic	Tetradecanoic	14	0
Palmitic	Hexadecanoic	16	0
Palmitoleic	9-Hexadecenoic	16	1
Stearic	Octadecanoic	18	0
Oleic	9-Octadecenoic	18	1
Linoleic	*cis,cis*-9,12-Octadecadienoic	18	2
Linolenic	*cis,cis,cis*-9,12,15-Octadecatrienoic	18	3
α-Eleostearic	*cis,cis,trans*-9,11,13-Octadecatrienoic	18	3
Arachidic	Eicosanoic	20	0
Behenic	Docosanoic	22	0

the overall weight of oils; they are the reactive portions of the triglycerides that determine the drying properties of different oils. Oils whose triglycerides on average contain a high proportion of unsaturated fatty acids dry when exposed to air, while those that contain a low proportion of unsaturated fatty acids cannot dry. The drying rates of different oils are a function of how rapidly the complex series of chemical reactions that constitute the "drying" process takes place. For reasons discussed later, rates are largely dependent on the overall number of double bonds in the fatty acids of an oil. Thus, perilla oil dries somewhat more quickly than linseed oil, which in turn dries more rapidly than walnut or poppyseed oil. Oils such as corn and sunflower contain much lower numbers of double bonds and dry very slowly, if at all. Departures from this simple classification of drying rate are due to structural differences in the fatty acids. In the most common fatty acids, double bonds are not conjugated (that is, they do not occur between alternating carbon atoms). But some of the rarer fatty acids contain conjugated carbon-carbon double bonds, and oils that contain such fatty acids will dry more rapidly than oils that contain unconjugated fatty acids, even though the overall number of double bonds may be virtually the same; examples are oiticica and tung oils.

The triglyceride composition and fatty acid composition just described apply only to characterization of fresh oil samples. Both the triglyceride and fatty acid compositions of a dried, aged oil film will be considerably different from that of the fresh oil.

Natural oils contain small amounts of materials other than triglycerides (in the case of refined oils, usually less than 2 percent). About half of this other material usually consists of sterols (in vegetable oils, there are three or four different ones). Traces of triterpene alcohols, fatty alcohols, and colorless hydrocarbons as well as colored compounds (mostly carotenoids) also occur. The most critical trace component is probably compounds of a type known as tocopherols, which have an influence on the drying behavior of oils.

Table 2. *Fatty Acid Composition of Oils*

Type of oil	Palmitic 16:0*	Stearic 18:0	Oleic 18:1	Linoleic 18:2	Linolenic 18:3	Others
Linseed	6–7	3–6	14–24	14–19	48–68	Arachidic, 0.3–1
Walnut	3–7	0.5–3	9–30	57–76	2–16	
Poppyseed	7–8	3–4	8–20	60–77		
Hempseed	6	2	7–14	46–69	16–28	
Soybean	7–11	2–6	15–33	43–56	5–11	Myristic and lower, trace-0.5
Sunflower	3–6	1–3	14–43	44–75		Arachidic, 0.6–4; behenic, trace-0.8
Candlenut	6	7	11	49	28	
Corn	8–19	0.5–4	19–50	34–62	2	Arachidic, 0.4–1; myristic, trace
Perilla	7	2	13	14	64	
Oiticica	7	5	6			Licanic, 78; hydroxy acids, 4
Tung	3	2	11	15		Conjugated 18:3, 69
Fish (menhaden)	17–29	3–4	11–23	1–3	1–2	Myristic, 7–16; 16:1, 7–18; 20:5, 0–14; 22:6, 3–14; others, 1–3
Safflower	3–6	1–4	13–21	73–79	trace	Myristic, trace; arachidic, trace-0.2
Rosin (tall)+			50	41		Palmitic and stearic, 2; conjugated 18:2, 7
Dehydrated castor			8			18:2, 65; conjugated 18:2, 22

Source: D. Swern (editor), *Bailey's Industrial Oil and Fat Products* (New York: Wiley, 1979–82), except walnut and linseed oils, which are from J. S. Mills and R. White, *The Organic Chemistry of Museum Objects* (London: Butter-worths, 1987).

* Number after name of fatty acid denotes number of carbon atoms and number of double bonds.

+ Fatty acids are present in free state rather than in triglycerides.

Until the end of the nineteenth century, seed and nut oils were extracted by crushing the nuts between stones, boiling them in water, and skimming the oil off the top. In addition to simmering or boiling the extracted oil, the only other type of refining carried out before the beginning of the nineteenth century was sun bleaching, which destroyed certain colored substances in the raw oils. Around the end of the eighteenth century, both sulfuric acid and caustic soda began to be used to eliminate impurities in raw oils.[19]

Extraction and treatment methods can affect the overall chemical composition of the oil in different ways and may influence the drying process. This is particularly the case with cooking or simmering methods.

NATURAL RESINS

A recent review by Robert Mussey of varnish recipes shows that European recipes from between 1650 and 1800 generally mention approximately the same fifteen resins in various combinations time and time again.[20] Virtually the same resins continued to be mentioned during the nineteenth century, with a few additions.

When a natural resin was introduced into an oil paint, the resin probably was in the form of a varnish, most probably an oil-resin varnish. Oil varnishes, among the most durable and popular of traditional furniture varnishes, consisted of natural resins usually put into solution by boiling in oil.

Most of the important resins came from conifers. Resins from such trees consist primarily of diterpenes, 20-carbon fused-ring compounds of which there are many specific types.[21] Two common resins in earlier oil-resin varnishes were amber and copal. Amber is a fossilized resin of great geological age (probably millions of years old) found principally on the shores of the Baltic Sea in Europe. Although the original botanical source of amber is not known, its chemical composition indicates that the source was most likely a conifer related to the present-day main coniferous genus of the southern hemisphere, the *Araucariaceae.*

Although the term *copal* is currently applied to a wide variety of resins originating in many different regions, the earliest copals were from Africa; these were semifossil resins from the family *Leguminosae.*

Amber and African copals consist for the most part of highly insoluble polymerized material. To be usable, these resins had to be "run," which involved heating to temperatures of 250 to 300 degrees Celsius, volatilizing a substantial amount of the original resin. The remaining residue could be put into solution by heating in oil.

Other conifer resins used in varnishes included kauri copal, Manila copal, Zanzibar copal, and rosin. Manila and kauri copals come from members of the *Araucariaceae* family. The former, collected primarily in the Phillipines, probably came onto the market before the nineteenth century; the latter, from New Zealand, came on the market early in the nineteenth century. Manila copal was collected from living trees, while kauri was often semifossil, probably hundreds to thousands of years old.

Rosin is the general term for resins that come from pines. The *Pinus* species is the major resin-producing conifer of the northern hemisphere. Some resins of other compositions are also mentioned—for example, the influential *Cabinetmakers Guide,* first published in Greenfield, Massachusetts, in 1825, mentions mastic and benzoin.[22] Mastic, a triterpenoid resin, comes from a member of the *Anacardiaceae* family and grows along many Mediterranean coasts, although the principal source has been the island of Chios. Benzoin, an example of a "balsamic resin," does not contain terpenes.

Some of these resins (notably pine and mastic) can also be prepared as spirit varnishes, because they are readily soluble in solvents such as turpentine. There is no reason that resin could not have been introduced into an oil paint in this form also.

THINNERS

Thinners were probably a common component of early oil paints, because they would have made the paints more easily brushable. Although they serve little or no function in the dried paint film, a substantial amount of thinner can have a flatting effect on the paint film. In the early nineteenth century, when flat finishes came into fashion, it became common to apply final paint layers that contained large amounts of turpentine and only small amounts of binders.[23]

Until about the last quarter of the nineteenth century, the only common thinner was turpentine, which was distilled from pine resins. Although consisting largely of a volatile compound (pinene), as a consequence of the ready oxidation of this material, a small amount of insoluble residue is always left as turpentine evaporates. Aside from allowing a thinner, more even layer of paint to be applied, turpentine would have had little effect on the properties of the dried paint film if used in small quantities. If an oil paint is diluted with a large amount of turpentine, the dried film will be weaker.

During the later nineteenth century, petroleum spirits were introduced, at first as a cheap substitute for turpentine.[24] Among other less common thinners were camphor oil, from a plant that grows mainly in Japan.

DRIERS

The drying time of oil paints can be considerably shortened by adding small amounts of certain types of inorganic compounds, and this was probably common practice. Reynolds's 1812 pamphlet, for example, directed that oil be boiled with some red lead (Pb_3O_4), a compound also used as a pigment, in a ratio of one-half pound of red lead to one gallon of oil for interior paints and one pound to four gallons for exterior paints.[25]

Many compounds have been used as driers, among which are other lead compounds (lead white pigment; "sugar of lead," or lead acetate; and other lead oxides such as litharge), "white copperas" (zinc sulfate), and salts of various multivalent metals (manganese, cobalt, chromium, and so forth).[26]

DRYING OF OIL PAINT FILMS

The process by which oil films dry can be regarded as a combination of two common general classes of organic chemical reactions: autoxidation and vinyl polymerization. Autoxidation, involving absorption of atmospheric oxygen, is the process by which oils and other foods spoil and by which many natural and synthetic resins and adhesives age and deteriorate. Vinyl polymerization is the process by which synthetic polymeric materials such as polyethylene, poly(vinyl chloride) and poly(methyl methacrylate) are manufactured. In the nomenclature of organic compounds, the "vinyl" position is a carbon atom that is doubly bonded to another carbon atom. Vinyl polymerization is so called because the reaction occurs at double bonds.

During the drying of an oil film, autoxidation occurs first. Autoxidation leads to the formation of various carbon-oxygen bonds within the triglyceride molecules. The oil film does not actually solidify during autoxidation, but reactions that occur during this stage are ultimately the cause of several problems of aged oil films, such as yellowing and embrittlement. As the autoxidation process slows down, vinyl polymerization begins to take place. Vinyl polymerization leads to complete solidification of the oil film as individual triglycerides combine to form larger polymeric units. A dried oil film falls somewhere between the two general varieties of polymers

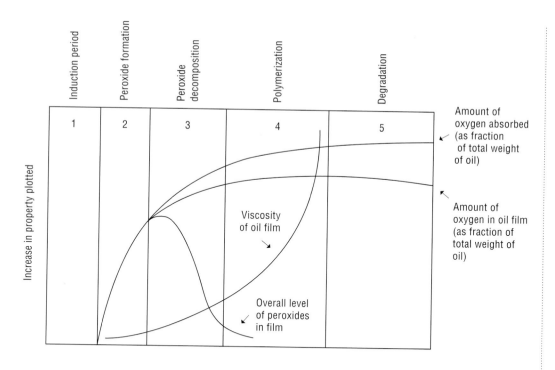

Figure 3. *Changes in oil films during various stages of the drying process. Adapted from* P. O. Powers, Industrial and Engineering Chemistry *41 (1949), pp. 304–9.*

discussed briefly by Phillips ("A Survey of Paint Technology: The Composition and Properties of Paint" in this volume): it is partly a network polymer and partly an agglomeration of many smaller polymeric (or even monomeric) molecules physically enmeshed.

The rate of drying and the actual chemical reactions that take place in the film can be heavily influenced by certain additives (including pigments), light, relative humidity, and temperature, as well as the method of preparation of the oil itself. Following is a brief review of current knowledge about the overall process, with a discussion of properties of the oil film during various stages of drying. More detailed reviews with references to the original chemical literature on drying oils are available elsewhere,[27] as are exhaustive bibliographies of early references and chemical research on linseed and other drying oils.[28]

The triglycerides of oils contain a variety of chemical bonds, only a few of which are particularly susceptible to reaction under normal circumstances. The fatty acids in triglycerides consist for the most part of stable carbon-carbon single bonds or carbon-hydrogen bonds. The double carbon-carbon bonds of unsaturated fatty acids are very reactive, and these sites are involved in the drying process.

A general sense of some of the changes a drying oil film undergoes can be gained from figure 3, adapted from an early study by P. O. Powers, who distinguished five stages in the drying process.[29] Initially for a short period ("induction," in Powers's terminology) the film appears to undergo little or no reaction, probably a consequence of small amounts of natural antioxidants (tocopherols) in the oil. This period can last a few minutes or a few hours, depending on the

Figure 4. *Chemical reactions*

involved in the drying of oils.

refining method used for the oil. Then follows a period ("peroxide formation") during which the oil film rapidly absorbs oxygen from the atmosphere and increases in weight, volume, and refractive index. During this time the film "sets to touch"—that is, it is no longer sticky when touched although it is still soft and liquid below the surface. Autoxidation is the principal chemical process occurring during this period. During the third stage, the peroxides formed during the second stage begin to decompose (in reality, peroxide decomposition would have begun as soon as peroxides began to form; in the second stage, the rate of formation was much greater than the rate of decomposition, whereas the rate of decomposition is greater in the third stage). The overall oxygen content of the film continues to rise but more slowly than during the second stage, indicating that peroxides are still being formed but that many of the previously formed peroxides are undergoing further reactions to form other types of carbon-oxygen bonds. The oil thickens slowly during the second and third stages, but the most dramatic changes in viscosity occur during the fourth stage. During this stage little additional oxygen is being absorbed, indicating that autoxidation is no longer the major reaction: vinyl polymerization is now the predominant process taking place in the oil film. After the fourth stage the oil is completely dried. The film continues to undergo additional chemical reactions during the fifth stage, but these take place at much slower rates than during the earlier four stages.

To give some indication of the duration of the first three stages, one study of a raw (unboiled) oil film found that the induction period lasted twenty to thirty hours and that maximum oxygen absorption had been reached after seven or eight days (this would correspond to a point during Powers's fourth stage).[30] The paint film feels dry to the touch after two to four days, virtually between the second and third stages, in the middle of the time during which the oil film is undergoing its most rapid changes in oxygen content and increase in weight and volume. Once again, the duration of these stages could vary considerably from oil to oil.

The final stage in the life of the oil film (Powers's fifth stage, "degradation") can also vary in duration. The oldest European oil paintings—a group of late thirteenth-century Norwegian altar frontals—are about seven hundred years old and are in reasonably good condition.[31] Oil films, however, degrade relatively rapidly if environmental conditions are adverse—for example, if they are exposed to the weather in an exterior setting or are subjected to extreme variations in temperature and humidity or to high levels of light.

Given this broad outline of changes that take place during the drying process, some of the chemical reactions can be considered in more detail. The initial addition of oxygen to the oil film probably occurs at double bonds in a limited number of triglyceride molecules, producing reactive free radicals **(fig. 4: 1a, 1b, 1c)**. By further reactions, hydroperoxides are eventually formed **(fig. 4: 2c)**; in this particular form the oxygen initially absorbed becomes part of the oil film. Through rearrangement, the reaction of oxygen with linoleic and linolenic acids (which are the major components of most drying oils) produces conjugated structures.

Autoxidation is an example of a chain reaction in which initially formed free radicals **(fig. 4: 2a)** react with other (previously unreacted) molecules to form additional free radicals **(fig. 4: 2b)** that propagate the reaction. Eventually the reaction is terminated by combinations of separate free radicals or by disproportionation, where a free radical breaks into two smaller fragments. Some combinations of free radicals produce polymers, which would be linked through

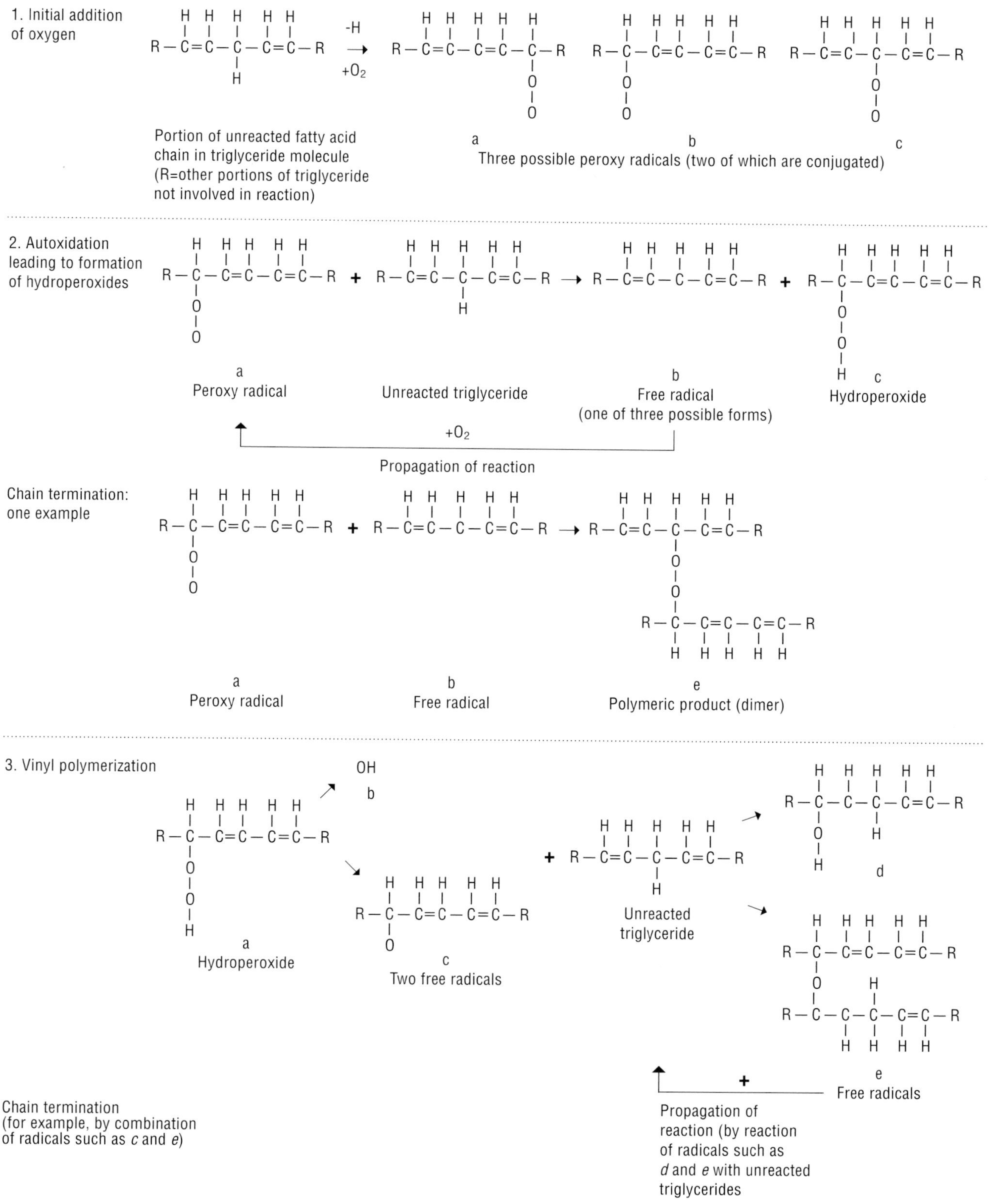

1. Initial addition of oxygen

Portion of unreacted fatty acid chain in triglyceride molecule (R=other portions of triglyceride not involved in reaction)

$-H$

$+O_2$

a
b
c

Three possible peroxy radicals (two of which are conjugated)

2. Autoxidation leading to formation of hydroperoxides

a
Peroxy radical

Unreacted triglyceride

b
Free radical (one of three possible forms)

c
Hydroperoxide

$+O_2$

Propagation of reaction

Chain termination: one example

a
Peroxy radical

b
Free radical

e
Polymeric product (dimer)

3. Vinyl polymerization

OH

b

a
Hydroperoxide

c
Two free radicals

$+$

Unreacted triglyceride

d

e

$+$

Free radicals

Propagation of reaction (by reaction of radicals such as d and e with unreacted triglycerides)

Chain termination (for example, by combination of radicals such as c and e)

a number of different functional groups, including peroxide groups (fig. 4: 2e). Hydroperoxides are not highly stable compounds, and eventually most of the initially formed hydroperoxides decompose or react further to form other functional groups. While the overall oxygen content and weight of the oil film is increasing, if examined in greater detail, the actual chemical reactions taking place would be many, some producing stable byproducts, others leading to breaking off of fragments of triglycerides.

During autoxidation, relatively few double bonds are probably consumed, and the viscosity of the oil does not increase substantially. Although some polymeric products are certainly formed, these apparently are comparatively few and small.

As the rate of oxygen absorption decreases, both a rapid increase in viscosity and a rapid decrease in the number of double bonds in the triglycerides (e.g., the overall degree of unsaturation) take place, the result of vinyl polymerization. This type of polymerization is initiated by small amounts of free radicals, probably formed by the breakdown of hydroperoxides (fig. 4: 3b, 3c). The free radicals add to double bonds, generating additional free radicals (fig. 4: 3d, 3e) that can further react with other unsaturated sites. The reaction is eventually terminated by combinations of free radicals. The final products of these reactions would be polymeric units mostly linked by carbon-carbon bonds.

As vinyl polymerization slows, most of the reactive sites in the triglycerides have been used up. Further reaction mainly involves the breaking down or further oxidation at relatively unstable functional groups formed during earlier stages. In a relatively short time the weight gain experienced by the drying oil mostly disappears, although the overall oxygen content remains greater than initially.

During the prolonged, final stage of the life of an oil film, overall oxygen content decreases very slowly, as does the weight and volume of the oil film, while the refractive index continues to increase slowly, indicating that chemical reactions continue to occur, although much more slowly than in the early stages of drying.

The dried oil film consists of a heterogeneous mixture of components. Some polymers with comparatively high molecular weights are present, having been formed by the cross-linking age of triglycerides principally during vinyl polymerization. Also present would be monomeric triglycerides and breakdown products. The overall structure of dried oil films is not well understood, but it seems that the size of the polymeric units formed is probably on the average not more than about three or four monomeric units (each monomer unit would consist of a single triglyceride molecule). Very small amounts of polymers with quite high molecular weights would be sufficient to link the entire film together. A leaching study of drying oil films showed that after about nine months, 20 percent of the film may be leached out in acetone.[32] The highly polymerized portion of the dried oil film would not be soluble, but the unreacted triglycerides and small breakdown products could easily be dissolved out of the film with various organic solvents. These smaller molecules, enmeshed in the framework of the polymeric film, appear to give aged oil films a certain degree of flexibility. Cleaning an oil paint film with a strong solvent and to a lesser extent with water could leach out some of the smaller molecular material and in some degree weaken the film as a result.

The increase in refractive index that occurs as the oil film ages can affect the transparency of paint layers, depending on the specific pigments that are present. Until the 1960s many architectural paints were based on lead white, a pigment of quite high refractive index; thus, changes in transparency would be negligible.

Another result of aging that can affect the appearance of the paint is yellowing; this results from the buildup of yellow-colored oxidation products. While the exact nature of these is not certain, there are probably several compounds that could cause the effect. Among those that have been suggested are ones that contain adjacent keto groups (for example, $C = O$ bonds on adjacent carbon atoms within larger molecules). Yellowing can be reversed by exposing a paint film to strong light but may recur when the paint film is returned to a fairly dark setting. Colors such as whites and blues are the most visibly affected by yellowing of an oil binder. Easel painters have apparently been aware from an early time that different oils yellow to various extents. In general, the tendency to yellow increases with the average degree of unsaturation of an oil: thus linseed oil yellows more as it ages than walnut or poppyseed. The lower yellowing tendency of the latter two oils was a major reason that they were preferred for clear varnishes and why painters preferred them for paint that is colored blue or white.

Driers and certain pigments that act as driers speed up the drying process, probably by catalyzing the breakdown of hydroperoxides. As noted earlier, these breakdown products of hydroperoxides initiate the vinyl polymerization process in the drying of oil paints.

During this century oils have often been heat-bodied—that is, heated in closed containers with oxygen excluded—before being used in paints. It is generally agreed that during heat-bodying, carbon-carbon double bonds are broken, and complex polymers are formed that are mainly bonded through carbon-carbon linkages. Heat-bodied oils, being partially polymerized, are more viscous than raw oils and dry more rapidly. The overall oxygen absorption of a heat-bodied oil will be considerably lower than that of a raw oil (less than about 3 percent for the heat-bodied oil versus 10 to 15 percent for the raw oil). Consequently, heat-bodied oil films are more stable and degrade less rapidly than raw oil films.

Recipes and paint manuals suggest that the oils used in decorative or architectural paints were usually prepared by boiling or simmering in open vessels, as Hezekiah Reynolds described. Depending on temperature and length of boiling time, oils thus prepared would be somewhat analogous to true heat-bodied oils, but because the treatment was carried out in the presence of oxygen, autoxidation would also take place during the boiling process. As a paint binder, such partially heat-bodied oils would have been somewhat more stable than raw oils; more rapid drying was enhanced by simmering the oil with a drier.

ANALYSIS OF BINDING MEDIA

When the binder of a paint sample is being analyzed it is always desirable to initially test for a variety of possible components (for example, oils, resins, proteins, carbohydrates, and waxes), following up with more specific tests for the class or classes of materials indicated by the preliminary analyses. Only tests for and analytical identification of oils and resins are discussed here, beginning with simple procedures that require no laboratory instrumentation and concluding with a brief discussion of three of the most common instrumental procedures for oil and resin identification, all of which require relatively expensive equipment. Although tests that should be carried out concurrently for other types of binders are not discussed, most of the general procedures described here can be extended to the other types of binders.

The simplest and least expensive identification procedures are microchemical or spot tests, which can be carried out on minute samples with or without the aid of a low-powered microscope. One useful test for drying oils is based on reaction with a mixture of equal parts of 30 percent hydrogen peroxide and concentrated ammonium hydroxide.[33] Foaming of the sample is indicative of drying oil. Some natural resins will also undergo this reaction but only to a limited extent; other common traditional binders will not react. Modern synthetic oil paints (alkyd resins) will react in the same way as natural drying oils. Another useful test for drying oils is designed to detect glycerol, the alcohol present in all triglycerides; the required chemicals and setup are fully described in a recent publication.[34]

There is no specific microchemical test for resins. If a natural resin is present in sufficient quantity in an oil paint sample, careful solubility tests might be able to suggest its presence.[35] In a 1977 article Elisabeth Martin suggested the use of a solution of Bromocresol purple on a fragment of paint to test for resin.[36] While this test can be useful for fairly pure resin samples, the results are difficult to interpret if aged oil is also present, because the oil will also give a positive result.

Examination of cross sections of a paint film with a reflected light microscope is often an important part of research on paint. Various biological stains have long been used to characterize the binders in cross sections. These stains are compounds that interact with certain types of organic molecules and not others, thus permitting general classification of binders. The traditional stains for lipids (oils), which include Sudan Black and Ponceau S,[37] have generally been abandoned by most researchers because of their poor reactivity with aged oil films and difficulties in interpreting staining results. More recently, fluorescent stains for lipids have been used; these react with oils to form complexes that fluoresce in ultraviolet light. The reaction of these stains on cross sections is observed under a reflected light microscope equipped with an ultraviolet fluorescence attachment. While they pose considerably less difficulty in interpretation than the stains used previously, their usefulness is somewhat limited by the fact that they sometimes do not react with older paint films (the limit in age seems to be quite variable but can be as little as fifty years). Two of the most commonly used fluorescent stains for lipids are Rhodamine B and 2,7-dichlorofluorescein; a discussion of their application can be found in an article by Richard Wolbers and Gregory Landrey.[38]

For detection of natural plant resins in cross sections, a solution of antimony pentachloride in chloroform can be applied and observed under a microscope with an ultraviolet fluorescence attachment.[39] If a substantial amount of oil and a relatively small amount of resin are present, it will be virtually impossible to draw any conclusions from this test.

At the moment no other technique can provide as much information on multilayered, small samples as staining of cross sections. Stains are attractive because they are relatively easy to use, although the type of microscope required to observe results of the fluorescent stains is comparatively expensive. Interpretation of results is not always straightforward, and preferably results should be confirmed by other analytical techniques if possible.

One such technique is infrared spectrometry, a highly versatile analytical technique for organic substances; oils, resins, and other binding materials (or mixtures of materials) in pure unpigmented or only slightly pigmented samples such as varnishes or tinted varnishes can frequently be readily distinguished. In the case of a typical paint sample, in which the medium makes up perhaps only 20 percent of the sample, interferences from pigments will at times make identification of the organic binder or binders difficult, although on modern Fourier transform infrared (FTIR) instruments pigment spectra can be subtracted out by computer, allowing binders to be more easily identified. Analysis can be carried out on quite minute samples (a speck of material), and with the use of an attached infrared microscope, analyses of individual layers of specially prepared thin cross sections can even be carried out. Several recently published papers demonstrate some applications of FTIR spectrometry in the identification of binders: a paper by Michelle Derrick is specifically concerned with oil–resin varnishes,[40] while a paper by Mary Orna and others is concerned with binders in medieval manuscripts.[41] Sample preparation is fairly simple, and much information can be gained from the examination of a single sample. Figure 5 shows infrared spectra of several natural resins, drying oil, and an oil–resin varnish.

At present, the most definitive identifications of aged oil binders are those carried out by gas chromatography.[42] The sample size can be on the order of a small paint cross section (a fraction of a millimeter across). Individual layers of multilayer samples would have to be separated to be analyzed, something virtually impossible to do when the layers are quite thin; this obviously limits the specific information that can be obtained by gas chromatography on some paint structures. The only portion of a dried oil film actually analyzed by this technique are the saturated fatty acids and smaller molecular fragments formed during the drying process. For identification purposes, the most useful information comes from the saturated fatty acids. As discussed earlier, these acids do not enter into any chemical reactions during the drying process. Palmitic and stearic acids are the only such acids in many oils, as can be seen in table 2. The ratios of these acids vary from oil to oil to a great enough extent that some oils can be distinguished from one another with considerable confidence by the ratio of the two acids (P/S), for example, this ratio in linseed oil ranges from about 1.1 to 2.1 and in walnut oil from 2.3 to 3.7.

There are many overlaps, however, and mixtures of more than one oil would be very difficult to identify. Although perilla oil (with P/S 3.5) could be distinguished from linseed oil, it has a similar ratio to that of walnut oil. Many semidrying oils that apparently were used as adulterants (such as sunflower or candlenut) have P/S ratios similar to or higher than that of

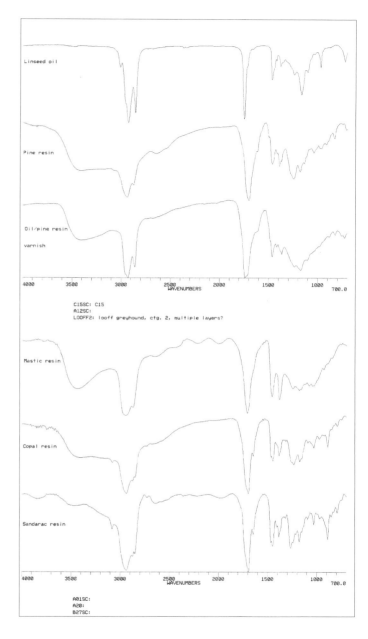

Figure 5. *Fourier transform infrared transmittance spectra of oil and several resins in the range 4000 to 700 wave numbers (cm-1).*

Figure 6. *Chromatograms from gas chromatography-mass spectrometry analyses of an aged oil paint sample and several natural plant resins. The major peaks in aged oils, as shown in the top chromatogram, are due to unsaturated fatty acids (palmitic and stearic) and a by-product of the drying process (azelaic acid); the ratio of palmitic to stearic acid (about 1.3 by peak area) is typical of linseed oil. Natural resins all contain numerous compounds, as shown by the representative chromatograms (each peak in a given chromatogram represents a different compound), some of which are found in more than one resin. Mastic resin is the only triterpenoid resin shown; it contains higher molecular weight compounds than the other resins shown, and thus its peaks appear later in the chromatogram.*

linseed oil. Mixtures of linseed oil and some of these oils would be difficult to identify with any certainty. Only traces of other saturated fatty acids occur in some oils, and these would not necessarily be detectable in small samples, although fish oil contains a level of myristic acid between that of palmitic and stearic acids.

While identification of the specific type of oil in a sample is not always possible, gas chromatographic analysis definitely could confirm the use of drying oil, and consideration of some of the other breakdown fragments (particularly, azelaic acid) can be used as evidence for whether nondrying oil is also present. Azelaic acid is not present in fresh oils; it forms as a result of oxidation of unsaturated fatty acids, and thus it is an important component of aged drying oil films. It is absent or present to a much lesser extent in more saturated (nondrying) oils. Figure 6 includes a typical chromatogram for an aged drying oil paint.

Resins can also be identified by gas chromatography, although they usually present more difficult problems.[43] The sample preparation techniques required to analyze oils by gas chromatography are those also used for resins, and thus mixtures of oil and resin could be simultaneously detected. Depending on the amount of sample available and the extent of aging, it is sometimes possible to identify the specific type of resin. In the case of aged samples, at best it may be possible only to note the presence of a diterpenoid (coniferous) resin or triterpenoid resin (such as mastic or dammar) in a sample. To date, the most certain identifications of residues of aged resins, whether in oil paints or by themselves, require the combined instrumental technique of gas chromatography-mass spectrometry. Some representative chromatograms for natural resins are shown in figure 6.

The detection and identification of natural resins in paint films remains a difficult problem to which there often are no certain answers. Presently, gas chromatography-mass spectrometry is probably the technique of choice for paint, while FTIR spectrometry can work quite well for unpigmented combinations of these materials.

Ultraviolet fluorescence microscopes are now relatively common in museum conservation or research laboratories and other large conservation facilities. FTIR spectrometers and FTIR microscopes are less readily available, as are gas chromatographs (GC) and gas chromatography-mass spectrometry (GC-MS) systems. While analyses by FTIR spectrometry or GC and GC-MS techniques can be costly (at least in relation to simple microchemical or spot tests), they provide invaluable detailed information on binder compositions. As already noted, the many gaps in our knowledge of the history of binders in American decorative paints can best be filled by detailed scientific analysis of paint samples. For this reason such analyses should be routinely included in historical research and conservation or preservation programs.

CONSERVATION AND PRESERVATION

The conservation problems posed by old oil paint films can be ascribed to a few simple sources, although treatment of these problems is usually far from simple. These problems will be described only in a somewhat abstract fashion; a review of actual treatment materials and procedures is beyond the scope of this chapter.

Old paint films rarely appear as they did when they were freshly applied. Visible changes in color are sometimes due to deterioration of the pigments used in the paint. In the case of oil paints, yellowing of the binder can substantially shift the hue of some tints (particularly whites and blues). Both pigment deterioration and binder yellowing are irreversible effects of aging. The tone and hue of paint films can also be altered by the buildup of soot or grime layers; these can usually be removed at least to some extent by cleaning.

An oil paint film, when freshly dried, can be stretched or compressed somewhat without breaking. Aged films, because of oxidation and other chemical reactions that continue to take place in the oil, are fairly fragile and brittle: they tend to respond by breaking rather than by deforming. There are two principal categories of cracks in paint films (using the nomenclature of painting conservators): (1) "premature cracks," which result from stresses produced in the oil film during the evaporation of thinners and loss of volatile byproducts produced during the drying process; and (2) "age" cracks, which are caused by movements of the substrate (in the case of architectural paints, the substrate would typically have been either wood or plaster).[44]

Another common problem that accompanies cracking is flaking. The bond between the paint film and substrate is often weak; if a wood substrate expands in humid weather, the paint film above it may respond not only by cracking but also by lifting and flaking away. Even if the paint has not become entirely detached, it may be very poorly adhered to the substrate and quite susceptible to mechanical damage—for example, by rubbing. Adhesion problems can also occur between successive paint layers, leading to losses in some of the upper layers while lower ones may remain more intact.

In the case of the fine arts (easel and wall paintings) there are many procedures to treat problems of cracking, flaking paint as well as surface grime and dirt layers. Not all these treatment procedures can be used on architectural paints. Some are very slow and labor intensive, making them unsuitable for large architectural settings for economic reasons, although they could be applied to smaller-scale projects. In addition, many fine arts treatments use toxic solvents or other chemicals that can be safely used in a laboratory with ventilation but that would pose health hazards in old houses or buildings.

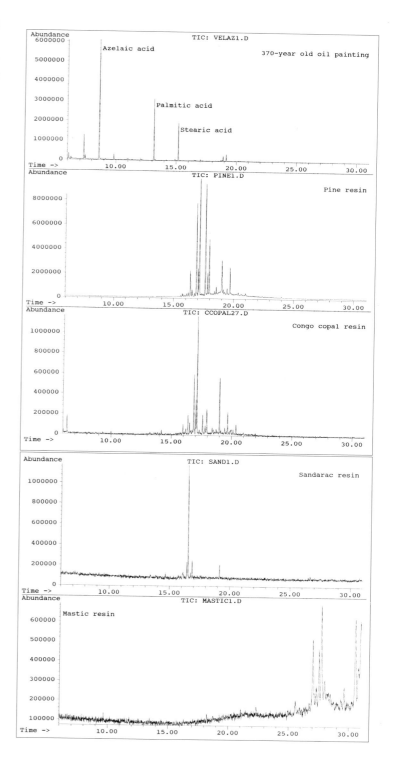

For these reasons fine arts conservation and architectural conservation diverge with respect to materials and procedures.

The extent to which adhesion problems exist in old oil paints varies considerably. Interior woodwork often has no adherence problems, unless environmental conditions have been quite severe (for example, the woodwork has been water damaged). Oil from the initial paint layer would have partially sunk into the wood, and oil from any original repainted layers would have sunk into the immediately underlying paint layers, creating fairly strong bonds between the substrate and the original paint layers. Drying oil films containing lead white as a major pigment are unusually strong compared with oil films based on most other pigments, another reason for the good condition of early oil paints in architectural settings. If flaking problems exist, they probably most often occur in overpainted layers.

Oil paint films on traditional lime plaster or mortar substrates often show cleavage and adhesion problems. This problem may be exacerbated or even be directly caused by the original application of sealing or isolating layers that were applied to the plaster before the oil paint to prevent binder from being absorbed into the plaster.

In the case of paint that shows adhesion problems, it is often desirable to consolidate the paint as well as readhere it in order to give the surviving paint greater strength. Given the porosity of oil paint films, certain resin or adhesive and solvent combinations can accomplish both consolidation and readhesion simultaneously. In the cases of cleavage where there is actually a visible space between paint chips and substrates, treatment can be carried out by flowing adhesive beneath the chips. As oil paints can be softened by gentle heating, some consolidation-readhesion treatments use adhesives in conjunction with heat (applied locally with a hot spatula) to gently reform flaking, cupped paint into plane.

A lime plaster substrate itself can be weakened and consolidation of it may be advisable. Vacuum impregnations have long been used in several areas of conservation involving porous materials. A vacuum removes air from the pores, allowing better penetration of solvent-resin solutions. For practical reasons, applications of such a treatment to architectural paint have been rare to date; one experimental application is described by Christy Cunningham-Adams ("An Early Colonial Mural: The Conservation of Wall Paintings" in this volume).

Another approach is to apply the adhesive solution under pressure, which aids penetration into the plaster substrate. Presently, this is a much more difficult procedure to carry out in architectural settings than vacuum impregnation.

Vacuum or pressure-aided consolidations have the advantage not only of permitting greater penetration of treatment solutions but allow consolidation of weak paint that may be partially adhered and cannot be treated readily by injecting adhesive material behind chips.

In addition to treating adhesion problems, cleaning old paint surfaces may also be desirable. Accumulations of grime or dirt are sometimes fairly superficial and readily removable with mild solvent or detergent solutions. Grime may be quite tenacious when it has penetrated somewhat into the surface of the paint, however. One successful cleaning treatment that has been used on architectural oil paints involves lime paste.[45] Although dried oil paints may appear to be inert, they can be leached by many types of solvents, as noted earlier; if extensive enough, leaching can seriously weaken the paint. In addition, oil paints can be chemically broken down by alkalis. Thus solvent and lime paste cleaning of oil paints inevitably will remove some portion (even if miniscule) of the original binder. More susceptible to solvents than oil paint layers would be the varnish glazes described earlier, which probably would have been bound by oil-resin mixtures.

Although not commonly encountered on architectural paints, some interior mural decorations could have been varnished either originally or at a later date, and removal of these varnishes may be required. Many cleaning systems could be used, ranging from simple solvents (or solvent mixtures) to specially designed soap gels and other formulations.

Varnishes are sometimes added as a final stage in the treatment and restoration of architectural paint. Varnishes serve two important functions: (1) adjusting the gloss of surfaces, which can become uneven during aging, and (2) protecting from further accumulations of dirt or soot. By isolating dirt and soot from the paint layer, varnishes make future cleaning much easier and safer to carry out.

Modern conservation practice encompasses three fundamental functions: examination, preservation, and restoration.[46] In any architectural painting treatment, careful preliminary examination of the original paint should be carried out to characterize its composition (pigments, binders, and layer structure) and understand its condition before a treatment is designed. To preserve the original paint, procedures and materials should be chosen that stabilize the original as necessary and leave it intact so that it will be available for future study.

The final function of conservation is restoration, which involves returning the damaged object undergoing treatment to its original form and appearance to the greatest extent without altering the structure or materials of the original. The restoration phase in architectural paint projects takes quite variable forms. In the Warner House murals described by Cunningham-Adams, the aim of the restoration phase of the treatment was mainly to fill and in-paint losses following stabilization and cleaning of the original paintings.[47] At the other extreme are treatments such as that carried out at Mount Vernon, in which the aim is primarily to replicate the original paint scheme by complete repainting, sometimes even using paints made by hand using traditional (period) pigments and binders.[48] In such cases the original paint, while still intact at least in places (although usually beneath layers of later paint), would not be visible after the treatment: fresh paint, constructed on the basis of preliminary examination of the remaining original paint, would be applied over the entire surface undergoing treatment. Between these two extremes would be instances in which some original paint would remain visible and other areas might be entirely overpainted.

Although extensive overpainting is generally not currently an acceptable practice in the treatment of fine arts artifacts, it is a part of architectural painting treatments at times for practical reasons. Even when this course is chosen, whatever remains of the original paint should be thoroughly examined and left intact for future research. The remains of original paint are likely to be the most important documents by which the history of earlier American architectural paints can be reconstructed.

House Paint Pigments

COMPOSITION AND USE, 1600 TO 1850

RICHARD NEWMAN AND EUGENE FARRELL

isted here are forty-four pigments most likely to have been used in house paints during the period 1600–1850, including three metallic materials. The pigments chosen for inclusion are based on unpublished research by Ian Bristow on English house paints (personal communication, January 21, 1990) and Frank Welsh's research on colonial American house paints ("The Early American Palette: Colonial Paint Colors Revealed" in this volume) and supplemented by research on some early American paintings by Pamela England and Lambertus Van Zelst in "A Technical Investigation of Some Seventeenth Century New England Portrait Paintings" (1982). The majority of these pigments would have been available during the entire period; many also had long histories of previous use, and some continued to be popular well after (fig. 1.). A large database of occurrences in historic houses would be required before useful statements regarding the popularity of various pigments could reasonably be made. The few comments of this nature here are based on statements by Bristow and Welsh.

NOMENCLATURE

Names are based on current standard terminology in international English-language literature on traditional artists' painting materials. Common synonyms and older names are in some instances included for convenience.

COMPOSITION

For inorganic compounds, composition is based on the most up-to-date information found in analytical studies of artists' materials. Most natural organic pigments contain several compounds, not all of which have necessarily been well characterized to date. For the organic pigments, the general class of organic compounds found in the material is usually given, along with the common name of the major specific compound.

HISTORY OF USE

Only brief comments are made on the historic use of most of the pigments (including beginning and terminal dates of use), based on notes derived from published research on traditional artists' materials. At the most, only brief notes on manufacturing techniques are

Figure 1. *Stencil pattern, first-floor corridor, northeast quadrant, New York State Capitol (1867–99), Albany. The color scheme reproduces the original decorative scheme of 1879, researched by Brian Powell of the Society for the Preservation of New England Antiquities. (Steven Fink; New York State Commission on the Restoration of the Capitol)*

included; details on specific pigments can be found in some chapters of this book and in many of the sources in the bibliography.

RED PIGMENTS

BRAZIL WOOD
COMPOSITION
Organic dyestuff, the principal coloring matter of which is brazilein, a hydroxyanthraquinone. Prepared as a lake for painting, usually mordanted on chalk.

HISTORY OF USE
The earliest brazil wood pigments used in Europe (ca. twelfth century) were prepared from a dye obtained from the wood of trees of the genus *Caesalpinia*, which grows in eastern Asia. Seventeenth-century sources of the raw material included South America (Brazil) and Jamaica.

COCHINEAL
COMPOSITION
Organic dyestuff, the principal coloring matter of which is carminic acid, a hydroxyanthraquinone. Usually precipitated onto a substrate such as aluminum hydroxide for use as a pigment (prepared as a lake).

HISTORY OF USE
Cochineal comes from the dried bodies of the female scale insect *Dactylopius coccus* L. costa, found on various cacti in Mexico and Central and South America. Cochineal insects were first imported into Europe by the Spanish in the mid-sixteenth century but had been widely used for the dying of textiles in pre-Columbian America for a considerable time before that. Indigenous to eastern Europe is Polish kermes, which contains carminic acid and a related compound, kermesic acid. Both Polish kermes and kermes itself (which contains only kermesic acid) were widely used in ancient Europe and the Middle East as dyestuffs well into the Middle Ages. The only other major traditional dyestuff from a scale insect is lac. Of all these materials, cochineal is the only one of importance in painting pigments from the period covered in this table. Because cochineal lakes are rather fugitive to light, they were probably not common in normal house paints.

IRON OXIDE REDS AND RED OCHERS
COMPOSITION
Usually colored by iron (III) oxide, most often Fe_2O_3 (the mineral hematite). Natural earth pigments (ochers) are a result of the extreme weathering of iron-containing rocks; consequently, in addition to the iron oxides that color them, most natural earth pigments also contain other (colorless) minerals, such as clays, micas, and quartz.

Natural red earth pigments were among the earliest materials used as pigments and have been identified in Paleolithic cave paintings in Europe. They were often marketed under names that referred to the source of the pigment (for example, Spanish red). Pure hematite has sometimes been used as a pigment. Red ochers can also be made, and probably often were, by heating yellow ochers or earth pigments. Artificial iron oxide reds may first have been produced in the second half of the seventeenth century from residues left during distillation of sulfuric acid from iron sulfate; in the later eighteenth century artificial iron oxide reds and yellows were widely produced. The initial product was yellow; red colors were produced by heating. These were usually marketed under the name of "Mars" colors, among others. These artificial pigments generally consist of relatively pure iron oxide, which is rarely the case with the natural earths.

RED LEAD, OR MINIUM

COMPOSITION

Principally lead tetroxide, Pb_3O_4, equivalent to the mineral minium.

HISTORY OF USE

Red lead, an artificial inorganic pigment made by heating yellow lead monoxide (litharge) or lead white (basic lead carbonate), was known as early as classical antiquity. This orange-yellow pigment was used in house paints and also in small quantities as a drier during the preparation of oils for oil-based paints.

VERMILION, OR CINNABAR

COMPOSITION

Mercury (II) sulfide, HgS, equivalent to the mineral cinnabar.

HISTORY OF USE

Cinnabar is the name for the naturally occurring mineral of this composition, the earliest known use of which as a pigment dates to the second century B.C. Vermilion refers to the synthetic pigment, which was probably first prepared in the eighth or ninth century. Vermilion was manufactured by combining liquid mercury and fused sulfur; the black compound thus formed was then sublimed to create the bright red pigment.

YELLOW PIGMENTS

CHROME YELLOW

COMPOSITION

Lead chromate, $PbCrO_4$, equivalent to the mineral crocoite.

The mineral crocoite was discovered in 1770, but its composition was not established until 1797. The artificial compound, which can vary in color from light yellow to orange-yellow, was first mentioned by Vauquelin in 1809. Commercial preparation of the pigment began about 1818, and probably by 1820 chrome yellow was already in common use in house paints.

GAMBOGE
COMPOSITION
A gum resin, containing one or more hydroxanthone-type compounds, the main one of which is gambogic acid.

HISTORY OF USE
This yellow gum resin is produced by various trees of the genus *Garcinia,* indigenous to south and southeast Asia. Possibly used as a pigment in Asian art as early as the eighth century, it was commercially available in Europe as early as the seventeenth century. While popular mainly as a watercolor pigment, it could have been used in house paints, but no instances have been noted to date.

IRON OXIDE YELLOWS AND YELLOW OCHERS
COMPOSITION
Colored by hydrated iron (II) oxide, usually the mineral goethite, FeOOH. As with red ochers, natural yellow ochers form by extensive weathering of rocks and consequently may also contain other minerals, such as quartz and clays.

HISTORY OF USE
Probably among the earliest pigments ever used, yellow ochers have been popular throughout history, as they continue to be. Among yellow ochers of specific origin is raw sienna; this somewhat orange variety of yellow ocher came from the Italian city of that name, but later the name was also applied to similar-appearing ochers from elsewhere; burnt sienna is a redder variety formed by heating the raw material. Artificial yellow ochers, usually known as "Mars" colors, were widely available by the later eighteenth century (see iron oxide reds and red ochers). Iron oxide yellows were used extensively in house paints.

LEAD-TIN YELLOW
COMPOSITION
The general name refers to two artificial pigments—one with the composition Pb_2SnO_4, the other with the approximate composition $PbSnO_3$ (this variety also usually contains some silicon).

The earliest occurrences of the pigment in Europe date to about 1300; the silicon-containing variety was the first to be used and was replaced by the other variety during the second quarter of the fifteenth century. The pigment was uncommon by the eighteenth century and went out of use by about 1750. It has been found in late eighteenth-century American portrait paintings and could have been used in house paints earlier, although no occurrences have been noted to date.

LITHARGE, OR MASSICOT
COMPOSITION

Litharge is the name for a yellowish orange mineral with the composition PbO, although the term is also used to refer to the material manufactured by direct oxidation of molten lead metal, which contains PbO as well as some red lead. Massicot is the name for a synthetic material of approximately the same composition made by gently roasting lead white pigment (see under white pigments).

HISTORY OF USE

Although known in Egyptian times, the history of the use of these compounds as pigments is largely unknown. Perhaps their most common use in house paints would have been as driers during the preparation of drying oils for use in oil paints.

NAPLES YELLOW
COMPOSITION

A synthetic pigment, lead antimonate, corresponding in composition and structure to the mineral bindheimate, $Pb_ySb_{2-z}O_7$ ($2<y<3$, $0<x<1$). Tin can substitute for antimony and has often been found in small quantities in Naples yellows.

HISTORY OF USE

Although used in antiquity as a glass colorant, the synthetic compound lead antimonate was first used as a pigment in the early eighteenth century. Probably used in house paints from about 1760 onward (although no American occurrences have been noted to date before 1800) but superseded by the cheaper pigment chrome yellow by about 1820.

ORPIMENT
COMPOSITION

Arsenic sulfide, As_2S_3.

HISTORY OF USE

Orpiment is a mineral that occurs in many places but never in large quantities. Used as a pigment during some periods in ancient Egypt, it has been found in medieval European paintings and continued to be used into the seventeenth century, although rarely. It was probably used in house painting, but the extent is uncertain. Only one occurrence of the related mineral pigment realgar has been noted in seventeenth-century American portrait paintings, and none of orpiment.

PATENT YELLOW

COMPOSITION
Hydrated lead chloride, $PbCl_2.5-7PbO$.

HISTORY OF USE
An artificial pigment first prepared by Carl Wilhelm Scheele about 1770. James Turner patented a process in England in 1781 for manufacturing the pigment from lead oxide and a sea salt solution. According to Bristow, it was extensively used in English house paints until about 1820 and thereafter was superseded by chrome yellow.

PERSIAN BERRIES LAKE

COMPOSITION
Organic dyestuff, the principal coloring matter of which is rhamnetin, a flavonoid. Prepared as a lake for use in painting or as a pseudolake on a substrate such as chalk.

HISTORY OF USE
This vegetable dyestuff, from the unripened berries of the buckthorn plant (genus *Rhamnus*), may first have become important as a pigment during medieval times in Europe. It was extensively used in English house painting, especially in a distemper (glue) medium. The pigment is relatively fugitive to light and can be quite difficult to identify in old paints that have been exposed to light, as it may have largely decomposed.

QUERCITRON LAKE

COMPOSITION
Organic dyestuff, consisting mainly of quercitrin, a glucoside that can be broken down into quercitin, a flavonoid. Prepared as a lake for use in painting.

HISTORY OF USE
The vegetable dyestuff comes from the inner bark of a species of oak indigenous to North America (black oak). First introduced in England in 1775, it was probably extensively used in house paints in the late eighteenth and early nineteenth century. Similar oak species grow in Europe, but North America seems to have been the source of the raw material. As with other yellow dyestuffs, confirmation of the presence of this compound by analysis of old paint samples would be difficult, because it is comparatively fugitive.

WELD LAKE

COMPOSITION

Organic dyestuff, the principal coloring matter of which is luteolin, a flavonoid. Prepared as a lake for use in painting.

HISTORY OF USE

The vegetable dyestuff comes from any number of brushlike plants. A popular textile dyestuff in medieval times in Europe and possibly used in easel paintings, the pigment was probably used in house paints in the early nineteenth century. A related pigment, probably much less commonly used, was Dyer's broom, from *Genista tinctoria L.*, which also contains the flavonoid luteolin. As with Persian berries, weld is fugitive to light.

BLUE PIGMENTS

AZURITE

COMPOSITION

Basic copper carbonate, $Cu_3(OH)_2(CO_3)_2$.

HISTORY OF USE

The mineral azurite, which is frequently associated in deposits with the green mineral malachite, has been a widely used pigment since classical antiquity. As an artist's pigment in Europe, azurite was used less during the latter half of the seventeenth century than it had been earlier and was comparatively uncommon during the eighteenth century. After about 1800 it virtually disappeared from artists' palettes. It may have been used in house paints in the seventeenth century and earlier but is not likely to be encountered in the eighteenth century, when the much cheaper Prussian blue had become available.

BLUE VERDITER

COMPOSITION

Usually basic copper carbonate, $Cu_3(OH)_2(CO_3)_2$.

HISTORY OF USE

An artificial pigment first produced during the Middle Ages in Europe, blue verditer is usually identical in composition and crystalline structure to azurite, although distinguishable microscopically. Because it was less expensive than azurite, it was probably more popular in house paints than its natural mineral counterpart, but like azurite it probably was rarely used during the eighteenth century.

INDIGO

COMPOSITION

Organic dyestuff, consisting mainly of indigo.

HISTORY OF USE

A vegetable dyestuff derived from the leaves of various plants of the genus *Indigofera*, indigo was first used as a pigment in classical antiquity. It probably was used fairly extensively in house paints during the seventeenth century but was superseded by Prussian blue during the eighteenth century. The colorant in indigo was first artificially synthesized in 1880 but probably did not become common until about 1900.

LAPIS LAZULI, OR NATURAL ULTRAMARINE

COMPOSITION

Primarily consists of lazurite, a sodium aluminum silicate with the following composition: $(Na,Ca)_3(AlSiO_4)_6(SO_4,S,Cl)_2$.

HISTORY OF USE

This natural pigment, colored by lazurite, is derived from the semiprecious stone lapis lazuli, which also contains calcite and iron pyrites. The material was apparently first used as a pigment in the sixth and seventh centuries in areas surrounding its earliest known source, mines in present-day northern Afghanistan. Among the most expensive of artists' pigments, lapis lazuli was used more sparingly than azurite or other blues in medieval and Renaissance European painting. Artificial ultramarine blue, essentially identical in composition to lazurite, was first synthesized in 1828 and was being manufactured shortly thereafter in factories in France and Germany. Because much cheaper alternatives were available, ultramarine blue is unlikely to be encountered in house paints.

PRUSSIAN BLUE

COMPOSITION

Variable in composition but usually ferric ferrocyanide, $Fe_4(Fe(CN)_6)_3$.

HISTORY OF USE

An artificial pigment, first made about 1704, it quickly displaced many of the blue pigments used earlier both in artists' paints as well as in house paints. Some varieties were extended with white pigments or other blue pigments and have been referred to by various names, such as Antwerp blue.

SMALT

COMPOSITION

Potassium glass, colored by cobalt oxide. Because it is a glass, smalt contains a variety of elements and can be highly variable in composition, depending on the raw materials used in its manufacture.

Although blue glasses colored by cobalt were used in ancient times, the artificial pigment smalt was not developed until the fifteenth century in Europe. It was used extensively in house paints up until about 1700, after which it was displaced by Prussian blue.

WOAD
COMPOSITION

Organic dyestuff, the principal coloring matter of which is indigo.

HISTORY OF USE

This vegetable dyestuff, from the flowers of the common woad plant *(Isatis tinctoria)*, which is indigenous to southern Europe, was used during the medieval period in Europe and probably in cheaper house paints during the seventeenth century.

GREEN PIGMENTS

COPPER RESINATE
COMPOSITION

A synthetic pigment that chemically consists of copper salts of natural resin acids. Copper resinate was typically manufactured by heating verdigris in a natural resin solution. Any number of resins could have been used, although recipes suggest that one of the more common may have been Venice turpentine, a natural balsam from a European larch.

HISTORY OF USE

Probably parallels that of verdigris itself. It was widely used in house paints, most commonly in transparent or glaze layers, and in easel paints.

EMERALD GREEN
COMPOSITION

A synthetic inorganic pigment, copper aceto-arsenite, $Cu(CH_3COO)_2 \cdot 3Cu(AsO_2)_2$.

HISTORY OF USE

Emerald green is an artificial pigment, first made in 1814 in Germany. It was probably used in house painting during the nineteenth century. The pigment viridian, a hydrated chromium oxide green that came into use in the second half of the nineteenth century, was commonly known as *vert emeraude* in French, which was occasionally translated into English as "emerald green"; this term, however, should be reserved for the copper aceto-arsenite.

GREEN VERDITER

COMPOSITION

A synthetic organic pigment, basic copper carbonate, $CuCO_3.Cu(OH)_2$.

HISTORY OF USE

Green verditer is an artificial pigment, chemically similar or identical to malachite. Probably used extensively in English house painting, it has not been identified in American house paints of this period to date.

MALACHITE

COMPOSITION

Basic copper carbonate, $CuCO_3.Cu(OH)_2$.

HISTORY OF USE

A natural mineral pigment used as early as classical antiquity, malachite was probably rarely used in seventeenth-century and later house paints as it has a rather dull color.

SCHEELE'S GREEN

COMPOSITION

A synthetic inorganic pigment, usually copper hydroarsenite, $CuHAsO_3$, but its composition may vary according to manufacturing procedures.

HISTORY OF USE

An artificial pigment, first prepared in 1773, Scheele's green was displaced by emerald green in the early nineteenth century. It may have been used in house paints.

VERDIGRIS

COMPOSITION

Basic or neutral copper acetate; four specific basic acetates may appear in a given variety of the pigment.

HISTORY OF USE

An artificial pigment, apparently first used in Roman times. It is the only green pigment identified to date in early American house paints, although in European easel paintings it lost favor during the later part of the seventeenth century and is rare in eighteenth-century paintings.

BLACK PIGMENTS

BONE BLACK

COMPOSITION

Primarily calcium phosphate, $Ca_3(PO_4)_2$, colored by a relatively small amount of carbon.

HISTORY OF USE

An artificial pigment made by charring bones in a closed chamber, bone blacks have a long history of use and were used extensively in house paints. Bone black was one of the principal black pigments in colonial American paints. Ivory black, quite similar in composition to bone black, is made by charring ivory, although the term may sometimes have been used to refer to bone blacks.

CHARCOAL BLACK

COMPOSITION

Nearly pure amorphous carbon.

HISTORY OF USE

A synthetic pigment made by charring woody material, charcoal blacks were widely used in English house paints, although they may not have been common in early American paints.

COAL BLACK

COMPOSITION

A natural "mineral" pigment, formed by long-term weathering and alteration of organic remains, coals vary in composition but typically contain hopane hydrocarbons, among other compounds.

HISTORY OF USE

Coal is mentioned as a black pigment in English sources from the beginning of the eighteenth century, although it was probably much less commonly used than the other black pigments.

LAMPBLACK, OR SOOT BLACK

COMPOSITION

Principally amorphous carbon.

HISTORY OF USE

A synthetic pigment made from the condensed smoke of burning oil or resin, it was used in classical antiquity, if not earlier, and extensively used in house paints. Along with bone black, this is a major black pigment in early American house paints.

MANGANESE BLACK

COMPOSITION

Manganese oxide, MnO_2 (the mineral pyrolucite), or various hydrous manganese oxides.

HISTORY OF USE

A natural mineral pigment, used at some prehistoric cave painting sites, manganese blacks may have occasionally been used in less expensive nineteenth-century house paints.

BROWN PIGMENTS

BURNT UMBER

COMPOSITION

Similar to raw umber, except much of the iron oxide is anhydrous.

HISTORY OF USE

Made by gently heating raw umber, burnt umber was used extensively in house paints.

RAW UMBER

COMPOSITION

A natural pigment formed by the extensive weathering of certain rocks. Contains hydrous iron oxide (goethite, $FeOOH$), manganese oxide, and other minerals such as quartz and clays. The presence of manganese oxides distinguishes the umbers from natural ochers, some of which can be brownish in color.

HISTORY OF USE

This natural pigment was probably used extensively in house paints.

WHITE PIGMENTS

ALUMINUM HYDROXIDE

COMPOSITION

A synthetic inorganic pigment, aluminum hydroxide, $Al(OH)_3$.

HISTORY OF USE

This artificial compound, while not used as a pigment, commonly served as a substrate or mordant for organic lake pigments.

BARIUM WHITE

COMPOSITION

A synthetic inorganic pigment, barium sulfate, BaSO4; the mineral equivalent is barite.

HISTORY OF USE

Introduced as an extender in paints in the nineteenth century, it was extensively used for that purpose in house paints of the nineteenth century. Most was probably synthetic, but the mineral itself could also have been used.

CALCIUM CARBONATE WHITES

COMPOSITION

Calcium carbonate, $CaCO_3$, usually equivalent to the mineral calcite.

HISTORY OF USE

Calcite occurs in many natural materials, a number of which have been used as a pigment. Chalk, a variety of limestone, consists mainly of microfossils (such as coccoliths). Other limestones or marble can also be ground for use as a pigment. "Shell white" refers to a pigment made by grinding mollusk shells. Artificially precipitated calcium carbonate (precipitated chalk) may also be used. Chalk has a long history of use and was used extensively as a white pigment in distemper paints (its transparency in oil precluded its use as a major white pigment in that medium).

LEAD WHITE

COMPOSITION

A synthetic inorganic compound, basic lead carbonate, $2PbCO_3.Pb(OH)_2$, or neutral lead carbonate, $PbCO_3$. These two lead carbonates are equivalent to the minerals hydrocerussite and cerussite, respectively.

HISTORY OF USE

Lead whites, referred to in older texts as white lead, are artificial pigments that have been used at least as early as classical antiquity. Extensively used in house paints, particularly oil-based ones, most consist entirely or predominantly of the basic carbonate.

ZINC WHITE

COMPOSITION

A synthetic inorganic pigment, zinc oxide, ZnO, equivalent to the mineral zincite.

HISTORY OF USE

This synthetic pigment was first prepared in the 1790s but did not become common until about 1830. It probably was not widely used in house paints until around 1840.

METALS USED AS PIGMENTS

GOLD

COMPOSITION

Metallic element, Au, but may be alloyed with other elements, such as silver and copper.

HISTORY OF USE

Widely used throughout history from the ancient Egyptian period. Gold may be used as leaf or as ground powder applied with a binder and was used extensively in decorative interior painting.

SILVER

COMPOSITION

Metallic element, Ag, but may contain some alloying elements, such as copper.

HISTORY OF USE

While not as popular as gold leaf, it too has a long history of use and can be found in decorative house painting.

DUTCH METAL

COMPOSITION

Common term for brass, an alloy principally of copper and zinc that is golden in color.

HISTORY OF USE

It could have been used as a cheap substitute for gold leaf or gold paint in some instances.

"Colonial and Federal America," Abbott Lowell Cummings and Richard M. Candee
The authors wish to thank the following persons for their assistance and contributions to this essay: Julia Bowers, Eugene Farrell, Charles Hammond, Bernard L. Herman, Fay Campbell Kaynor, James Kyprianos, Richard Newman, Morgan Phillips, Jane Porter, Brian Powell, Amy Snodgrass, and Myron Stachiw.

1. Sidney M. Gold, "A Study in Early Boston Portrait Painting Attribution: Augustine Clement, Painter-Stainer of Reading, Berkshire, and Massachusetts Bay," *Old-Time New England* 211 (Winter 1968): 61–78.

2. Virgil Barker, *American Painting: History and Interpretation* (New York: Macmillan, 1950), 16.

3. David S. Greenough Collection, Massachusetts Historical Society, folder 1716–25.

4. Massachusetts State Archives at Columbia Point, Office of the Secretary of State, Boston, Mass., 246:20 [hereafter Mass. Archives].

5. *Register of Pennsylvania*, vol. 3 (Philadelphia: Samuel Hazard, 1829), 310–12.

6. Manuscript, collection of Abbott Lowell Cummings.

7. The Gedney House and ceiling boards from an early house in Dartmouth, Mass., were analyzed for this symposium. Eugene Farrell and Amy Snodgrass, Analytical Report, March 7, 1989, Center for Conservation and Technical Studies, Fogg Museum, Harvard University, Cambridge, Mass., no. A88.64, includes four samples from the Gedney House and two from the Dartmouth ceiling now owned by the Harris family of Dover, Mass. Additional analysis of the pigments and binders from this ceiling was performed by Richard Newman, Museum of Fine Arts, Boston.

8. See Abbott Lowell Cummings, "Decorative Painters and House Painting at Massachusetts Bay, 1630–1725," *American Painting to 1776: A Reappraisal*, ed. Ian M. G. Quimby (Charlottesville: University Press of Virginia, 1971), 73–75.

9. Morgan Phillips to Peggy Armitage, Strawbery Banke, March 31, 1978, Correspondence Files, Society for the Preservation of New England Antiquities [hereafter SPNEA], Consulting Services.

10. Mass. Archives, 246:20.

11. *Arts Improvement: or Choice Experiments and Observations*, 2d ed. (London, 1725), 44; see also Richard M. Candee, "The Rediscovery of Milk-Based House Paints and the Myth of 'Brickdust and Buttermilk' Paints," *Old-Time New England* 211 (Winter 1968): 79–82.

12. Charles F. Montgomery, ed., *Joseph Moxen's Mechanick Exercises; Or, The Doctrine of Handy-Works* (New York: Praeger Publishers, 1970), 249.

13. Bernard L. Herman, Center for Historic Architecture and Engineering, University of Delaware, to Richard M. Candee, November 16, 1988.

14. Thomas T. Waterman, "The Province House Demolition," *Old-Time New England* 228 (Spring 1972): 113 and fig. 6.

15. Mass. Archives, 246:136.

16. Gibson Clough Papers, Essex Institute, Salem, Mass.

17. Henry D. Biddle, ed., *Extracts from the Journal of Elizabeth Drinker* (Philadelphia, 1889), 234.

18. Suffolk County Registry of Probate, Boston, Mass., 5:237 [hereafter Suf. Co. Prob. Records].

19. George Francis Dow, ed., *Records and Files of the Quarterly Courts of Essex County, Massachusetts* (Salem, Mass.: Essex Institute, 1911–75), 5:37.

20. *A Report of the Record Commissioners of the City of Boston Containing Miscellaneous Papers* (Boston, 1881), 71; Suf. Co. Prob. Records, 9:191.

21. Suffolk County Registry of Deeds, Boston, Mass., 13:86 [hereafter Suf. Co. Deeds].

22. Guildhall Library, London; Suf. Co. Prob. Records, 9:239.

23. Guildhall Library, London; Suffolk County Superior Court Files, Columbia Point, Office of the Secretary of State, Boston, Mass., no. 5670 [hereafter Suf. Co. Court Files].

24. Suf. Co. Court Files, no. 7024.

25. Suf. Co. Court Files, no. 10293.

26. Suf. Co. Deeds, 28:194.

27. Nina Fletcher Little, *American Decorative Wall Painting* (New York: Studio Publications, 1952), 33–35.

28. Historically the English guilds of "painter-stainers" monopolized the practice of oil painting by including within their ranks all painters from portrait artists to house decorators "except gentlemen painting for pleasure." See W.A.D. Englesfield, *The History of the Painter-Stainers Company of London* (London: Chapman and Dodd, 1923), 60–95. Toward the end of the seventeenth century the painter-stainers of York, England, voted that none of its members should work for "either Carpenter Joiner Bricklayers or any other undertakers of whatever business" and thereby aid crafts that had become competitive ("The Old and Ancient Ordinances, Articles, and Customes of the Mistery or Occupation of the Painters ... " MSS, Archives, Baker Library, Harvard Business School, 884/1810, 9).

29. Jonathan L. Fairbanks and Robert F. Trent, eds., *New England Begins: The Seventeenth Century* (Boston: Museum of Fine Arts, 1982) 3:477–78, and Cummings, "Decorative Painters," 92–117. See also Frederick W. Coburn, "Thomas Child, Limner," *The American Magazine of Art* 21, no. 6 (June 1930): 326–28.

30. For more detail about the Child-Stanbridge relationship, see Cummings, "Decorative Painters."

31. Suf. Co. Prob. Records, docket no. 6623.

32. *A Report of the Record Commissioners Containing Boston Births, Baptisms, Marriages, and Deaths, 1630–1699* (Boston, 1883), 175.

33. Suf. Co. Court Files, no. 7024.

34. "Journal, or Waste Book ... on Rebuilding the Meetinghouse," Archives, First Church, Boston, Mass., 21–22.

35. *A Volume of Records Relating to the Early History of Boston, Containing Miscellaneous Papers* (Boston, 1900), 223–24.

36. *A Report of the Record Commissioners of the City of Boston Containing the Records of Boston Selectmen, 1716 to 1736* (Boston, 1885), 147–48.

37. Suf. Co. Prob. Records, docket no.6958.

38. Chandler Robbins, *A History of the Second Church, or Old North, in Boston . . .* (Boston, 1852), 177.

39. David S. Greenough Collection, Massachusetts Historical Society, folder 1716–25.

40. *A Report of the Record Commissioners of the City of Boston, Containing the Boston Records from 1729 to 1742* (Boston, 1885), 60–64.

41. Frederick W. Coburn, "The Johnstons of Boston," *Art in America,* pt. 1 (December 1932): 27–36; pt. 2 (October 1933): 132–38. Also see Mabel M. Swan, "The Johnstons and Reas—Jappanners," *Antiques (*May 1943): 211–13. Both authors misread descriptions for common objects as more desirable goods; Coburn interpreted "ovals" painted for Paul Revere as portraits instead of tin ovals painted with street numbers to identify shops; Swan misread as "a piece of furniture" the charge for a "sett" of coffin hardware or "furniture."

42. Suf. Co. Prob. Records, 66:110–11.

43. Suf. Co. Prob. Records, 78:418–19.

44. *Letters and Papers of John Singleton Copley and Henry Pelham,* Massachusetts Historical Society Collections, 81:65–66.

45. Carl Bridenbaugh, *The Colonial Craftsman* (Chicago: University of Chicago Press, 1950), 102; also see George Francis Dow, *The Arts and Crafts in New England, 1704–1775, Gleanings from Boston Newspapers* (Topsfield, Mass.: Wayside Press, 1927), 1–36, 237–43, and *Everyday Life in the Massachusetts Bay Colony* (Boston: SPNEA, 1935), 22–25.

46. Pigments created after 1700 were Prussian blue (1704), patent or Turner's yellow (after 1785), and chrome yellow (after 1790). For information on the manufacture of all thirty-eight pigments available in this country before 1800, see Candee, *Housepaints in Colonial America: Their Materials, Manufacture, and Application,* reprinted from four parts in *Color Engineering* (September–October 1966, November–December 1966, January–February 1967, and March–April 1967) (Holland, Mich.: Holland-SUCO Color Company, 1967). See also Theodore Z. Penn, "Decorative and Protective Finishes, 1750–1850," *APT Bulletin* 16 (1984): 1, 3–46.

47. Candee, *Housepaints in Colonial America,* 9–10; Dow, *Arts and Crafts in New England,* 238.

48. "Letter Book of John Gore of Boston," 1773–76 (typescript), transcribed by Charles Hammond, former director, Gore Place, Waltham, Mass.

49. Suf. Co. Prob. Records, 84:656–61.

50. Richard Neve, *The City and Country Purchaser and Builder's Dictionary* (London, 1726; reprint ed. Newton Abbott, Devon: David and Charles, 1969), 212–13; William Salmon, *Vade Mecum, or the Complete and Universal Estimator,* 4th ed. (London: R. Crowder, 1760); *The Builder's Dictionary: or Architect's Companion* (London: A. Bettesworth and C. Hitch, 1734; reprint ed. 2 vols. Washington, D.C.: Association for Preservation Technology, 1981), vol. 2, "Painter's Work."

51. Suf. Co. Court Files, nos. 7024 and 7176.

52. Suf. Co. Court Files, no. 10293.

53. *150th Anniversary of the First Church in Pomfret, Connecticut* (Danielson, Conn., 1866), 43–44.

54. Ellen D. Larned, *History of Windham County, Connecticut* (Worcester, Mass., 1874–80), 2:81.

55. George Sheldon, *A History of Deerfield, Massachusetts (*Deerfield, Mass., 1895–96), 1:476.

56. Records of South Church, Portsmouth, N.H., vol. 4 (1749–1833), entry 25 April 1796.

57. Agreement between Jonathan Mansfield and Joseph McIntire and Samuel Luscomb, Jr., July 10, 1758, MSS collection, Essex Institute, Salem, Mass.

58. Building Contract, November 27, 1736, Hancock Papers, Baker Library, Harvard Business School, MSS 761/1728–1854/H234/v.6. The fireboard is owned by the Museum of Fine Arts, Boston.

59. Writings of Washington, Memorandum (Washington, D.C.: 1940) 40:263–64.

60. Adams and Roy Consultants, *Historic Structure Report, Porter-Phelps-Huntington House, Hadley, Mass.* (typescript), 1988.

61. Hancock Papers, Boston Public Library, 1720–49.

62. Account book (unnumbered pages), First Church, Ipswich, Mass.

63. MS bill, Joseph Simes to province of New Hampshire, New Hampshire Division of Records and Archives, Concord, N.H., Treasury Papers, Box 9. We wish to thank Jane Porter for sharing this document and its functional interpretation from her forthcoming study of New Hampshire lighthouses.

64. Foster Account: Pell vs. Foster, Suffolk County Inferior Court, Boston, Mass., Social Law Library; Henchman Account: Hancock Papers, Boston Public Library.

65. Mass. Archives, 246:159.

66. *Boston Gazette,* September 18, 1753.

67. Suf. Co. Court Files, no. 7176.

68. Hancock Papers, Boston Public Library, vol. 60 (1750–59).

69. Suf. Co. Prob. Records, 9:191.

70. Suf. Co. Court Files, no. 3350.

71. Accounts of Thomas Johnston and Daniel Rea, Jr., Boston, MSS 715/1764–1802/R 218, Baker Library, Harvard Business School [hereafter Rea Accounts], vol. 1 (unnumbered pages).

72. Little, *American Decorative Wall Painting,* 33–35.

73. Thomas T. Waterman, "The Smaller Virginia House" (typescript), chapter on "Interior Finish," 60. One of seven extant chapters (from an original nine) of this unpublished book, also titled "The Virginia House"; see Fay Campbell Kaynor, "Thomas Tileston Waterman: Student of American Colonial Architecture," *Winterthur Portfolio* 20, nos. 2–3 (Summer–Autumn 1985): 144–45.

74. Mary Kent Davey Babcock, *Christ Church, Salem Street, Boston, the Old North Church of Paul Revere Fame; Historical Sketches, Colonial Period, 1723–75* (Boston: Thomas Todd Company, 1947), 244.

75. For previous scholarship in this field, see Little, *American Decorative Wall Painting;* Edward B. Allen, *Early American Wall Painting 1710–1850* (New Haven, Conn.: Yale University Press, 1926); Janet Waring, *Early American Wall Stencils* (New York: William R. Scott, 1937); Jean Lipman, *Rufus Porter, Yankee Pioneer* (New York: Clarkson N. Potter, 1968), and *Rufus Porter Rediscovered: Artist, Inventor, Journalist, 1792–1884* (New York: Clarkson N. Potter, 1980); Robert L. McGrath, *Early Vermont Wall Paintings, 1790–1850* (Hanover, N.H.: University Press of New England, 1972); and Margaret Coffin, *Borders and Scrolls: Early American Brush-Stroke Wall Painting 1790–1820* (Albany, N.Y.: Albany Institute of History and Art, 1986).

76. Rea Accounts, 9 vols.

77. Only during the period 1781–85 did the number of entries charged to other craftsmen (49.3 percent) approach the level of Johnston's final years and more than equal the work done for the merchants and gentry of the town (40.6 percent). In addition to retaining his rank in this militia, Rea joined the St. Andrew's Masonic Lodge in 1779. Five years later Rea was one of twenty-three members who broke with the lodge's association with the Grand Lodge of Scotland and formed the nationalistic Rising States Lodge under Paul Revere and other patriot-members of the older lodge. Masonic members from both lodges accounted for forty of the shop's customers, although there is no statistical evidence that the schism affected his business.

78. Rea Accounts, 2:88.

79. Rea Accounts, Samuel Parkman, April 25, 1792; Jonathan Mosely, May 22, 1790.

80. George Davidson, MS Waste Book, Boston, 1793–99, call no. 1967, 27 BV,

Old Sturbridge Village Research Library, Sturbridge, Mass. Also see Nina Fletcher Little, *Floor Coverings in New England before 1850* (Sturbridge, Mass.: Old Sturbridge Village, 1967), 16–26.

81. Rea Accounts, ledger account with Stephen Gorham, November 1799, 4:20.

82. Suf. Co. Prob. Records, docket no. 6958.

83. Hezekiah Reynolds, *Directions for House and Ship Painting; Shewing in a plain and concise manner, The Best Method of Preparing, Mixing, and Laying the Various Colours Now in Use, Designed for the Use of Learners* (New Haven, Conn: Eli Hudson, 1812), 21–22.

84. See Abbott Lowell Cummings, ed., *Rural Household Inventories Establishing the Names, Uses, and Furnishings of Rooms in the Colonial New England Home, 1675–1775* (Boston: SPNEA, 1964).

85. Jack McLaughlin, *Jefferson and Monticello: The Biography of a Builder* (New York: Henry Holt and Company, 1988), 316.

86. McLaughlin, 321–22.

87. Rea Accounts, ledger account with Stephen Gorham, June 15, 1799, 4:20.

88. Rea Accounts, work for John Codman 1797–98; see also R. Curtis Chapin, "The Early History of the Codman House," *Old-Time New England* 258 (1981): 34–35.

89. Rea Accounts, vol. 3, William Wood, December 31, 1796.

90. Rea Accounts, vol. 2, April 30, 1798.

91. Edward G. Porter, "The Ship Columbia and the Discovery of Oregon," *New England Magazine* 12 (n.s. 6) (March–August 1892): 472–88. Also see Frederick C. Howay, ed., *Voyages of the "Columbia" to the Northwest Coast 1787–1790 and 1790–1793* (Boston: Massachusetts Historical Society, 1941), MHS Collections, vol. 79.

92. National Capital Sesquicentennial Commission, *American Processional 1492–1950* (Washington, D.C.: Corcoran Gallery of Art, 1950), 29, 238.

93. John Frazier Henry, *Early Marine Artists of the Pacific Northwest Coast, 1741–1841* (Seattle: University of Washington, 1984), 174.

94. Richard Candee wishes to thank Julia Bowers, a graduate student at Boston University, for making the initial connection between the manuscript and the artist, and also Myron Stachiw, then of the Old Sturbridge Village Research Department, for making available a copy of the manuscript.

95. Parsons (p. 480) notes that Yendell was the last survivor of the ship's crew, living to age ninety-two before his death in 1861; Henry (pp. 174, 231n) records a set then in the hands of a Popkins descendent and now at the Oregon Historical Society.

96. Caleb H. Snow, *A History of Boston* (Boston, 1825), 335–36.

97. MS additions to *The Rules of Work of the carpenters in the town of Boston* (Boston: By the Proprietors, 1800), Rare Book and Manuscript Division, Boston Public Library, call no. XH.99c.109. The MSS includes "Painters Rules, Boston 1800" and the longer 1815 version, as well as the signature "Perez Loring, April th 20, 1811" in the flyleaf. Master carpenters Braddock Loring and Jonathan Loring were appointed on August 21, 1800, to a larger committee to draw up the published rules.

98. MS Ledger of William Gray of Salem, Mass., and Portsmouth, N.H., 1774–1811, Essex Institute, Salem, Mass.

99. Edward Gray, "The William Grays in Salem in 1797," *Essex Institute Historical Collections*, 57:145–47.

100. *New Hampshire Gazette*, July 29, 1800, and March 21 and 31, 1801; *Portsmouth Oracle*, November 30, 1798, and February 12, 1799; William Gray also ran a boarding house advertised on June 14, 1802.

101. The Ebenezer Thompson house is noted in Candee, *Building Portsmouth: The Neighborhoods and Architecture of New Hampshire's Oldest City* (Portsmouth, N.H.: Portsmouth Advocates, 1992), 115.

102. This pamphlet, one of two known copies, at the American Antiquarian Society, Worcester, Mass., is available through the society in a 1978 facsimile reprint with an introduction by Richard M. Candee. Reynolds, 1.

103. Roger Welles, ed., *Early Annals of Newington [Conn.]: Comprising the First Records of the Newington Ecclesiastical Society, and of the Congregational Church Connected Therewith; with Documents and Papers Relating to the Early History of the Parish* (Hartford, Conn.: 1874), 143.

104. Thomas Green Fessenden, ed., *The New England Farmer and Horticultural Journal* 11, no. 48 (June 1833): 382.

105. Sylvanus Hayward, *Address Delivered at the Centennial of the Congregational Church at Gilsum, N.H.* (Dover, N.H., 1873), 19.

106. Middleboro-Taunton Society, Original Record Book, 1758–1800.

107. Contract, February 6, 1792, "Durham," Miscellaneous Town Records, New Hampshire Historical Society, Concord, N.H.

108. Richard Radis, "Thomas Rundle, Housewright" *Old-Time New England* 226 (Fall 1971): 53–56.

109. See cover, *Old-Time New England* 172 (Spring 1958); identification of James Kidder as the artist of the Medford estate is the result of documentary and visual research by James Kyprianos for the authors.

110. Henry Wansey, *An Excursion to the United States of North America, in the Summer of 1794* (Salisbury, England, 1798), 55.

111. Timothy Dwight, *Travels in New-England and New-York* (New Haven, Conn., 1821–22), 1:305.

112. Julian Ursyn Niemcewicz, *Under the Vine and Fig Tree: Travels through America in 1797–1799, 1805, with some further account of life in New Jersey*, trans. and ed. Metchie J. E. Budka (Elizabeth, N.J.: New Jersey Historical Society and Grassman Publishing, 1965), 5.

113. S. G. Goodrich [Peter Parley], *Personal Recollections of Poets, Philosophers and Statesmen* (New York, 1856), 34–35.

**"House Painting in Britain,"
Ian C. Bristow**

The arguments on which the general indications of house-painting practice given here are based are set out in full in the author's doctoral thesis, "Interior House Painting from the Restoration to the Regency," submitted to the University of York, England, in 1983. The technical material it contains is currently being revised for publication under the provisional title "House-Painting Colours and Technology 1615–1830" and will be complemented by a companion volume dealing with the architectural usage of color in interiors, provisionally titled "Architectural Colour in British Interiors 1615–1840."

1. MS. at Public Record Office (hereafter PRO), London, E.351/3251, M.xiiiv.

2. R. T. Gunther, ed., *The Architecture of Sir Roger Pratt* (Oxford, 1928), 67.

3. PRO, E.351/3261, M.xviiiv.

4. See, for example, account mentioning the supply of "spetches" in connection with repainting the Mansion House at Doncaster, Yorkshire, ca. 1800, cited by H.E.C. Stapleton, G. G. Pace, and J. E. Day, *A Skilful Master-Builder* (York, 1975), 58.

5. William Salmon (of Colchester), *Palladio Londinensis* (London, 1734), 59.

6. T. H. Vanherman, *Every Man His Own House-Painter and Colourman* (London, 1829), 51–53.

7. PRO, E.351/3259, M.xxviir.

8. PRO, WORK.5/22, f.114r.

9. PRO, E.351/3261, M.viv.

10. Jean Félix Watin, *L'Art du peintre, doreur, vernisseur*, 4th ed. (Paris, 1785), 71–78.

11. MS. at City of London Record Office, Mansion House accounts, box 5.

12. Cennino Cennini, *A Treatise on Painting*, translated by Mary Merrifield (London, 1844).

13. Gunther, p. 77; R. Neve [T. N. Philomath], *The City and Country Purchaser, and Builder's Dictionary* (London, 1703), 143 (s.v. Fresco).

14. Watin, 106–7.

15. Antoine Alexis Cadet-de-Vaux, "Memoir on a Method of Painting with Milk," *The Repertory of Arts and Manufactures* 15 (London, 1801), 411–21.

16. Cennini, cc.36 (with water) and 93 (with oil).

17. John Smith, *The Art of Painting in Oyl* (London, 1687), 1–4, 33–34.

18. British Museum, Print Room, Heal Collection, 89.54.

19. British Museum, Print Room, Heal Collection, 89.55.

20. British Museum, Print Room, Banks Collection, 89.9; reproduced by Rosamund Harley, *Artists' Pigments c.1600–1835* (London, 1970), pl.2; 2d ed. (London, 1982), fig. 8.

21. Andrew Ure, *A Dictionary of Arts, Manufactures, and Mines* (London, 1839), 916–17 (s.v. "Paints, Grinding of"); 5th ed., Robert Hunt, ed. (1860), vol. 3, 373–75 (s.v. "Paints, Grinding of").

22. P. F. Tingry, *The Painter's and Colourman's Complete Guide* (London, 1830), 273. .

23. Smith, 35.

24. PRO., E.351/3253, M.viiᵣ.

25. John Houghton, *A Collection for Improvement of Husbandry and Trade* (London, 1692–1703), no. 414 (1700).

26. Smith, 36.

27. Watin, 81–82; Tingry, *The Painter and Varnisher's Guide* (London, 1804), 442–43.

28. British Museum, Print Room, Heal Collection, 89.53.

29. Smith, 12.

30. Robert Dossie, *The Handmaid to the Arts* 1 (London, 1758), 164.

31. See, for example, Peter Nicholson, *The Mechanic's Companion* (Oxford, 1825), 407–9.

32. Gunther, 79.

33. Kensington: PRO., WORK.19/48/1, ff. 50 (iv), 64 (iii), 64 (iv); Montagu House: MS. book at Boughton House, Northamptonshire, of accounts of executors of First Duke of Montagu, vol. 1, 173.

34. Smith, 41.

35. Smith, 41.

36. André Félibien, *Des principes de l'architecture, de la sculpture, de la peinture* (Paris, 1676), 406.

37. *The Receipt Book of Elizabeth Raper . . . 1756–1770* (London, 1924), 81.

38. British Museum, Print Room, Heal Collection, 89.53.

39. See, for example, Dossie, vol. 1, 147–49.

40. Smith, 52.

41. Smith, 39; Dossie, vol. 1, 153–54.

42. Smith, 45.

43. Dossie, vol. 1, 52.

44. William Leyburn, *Architectonice: or, a Compendium of the Art of Building* (London, 1700), 71.

45. Nicholson, 407.

46. Smith, 54–55; Félibien, 405; Watin, 92.

47. British Museum, Print Room, Heal Collection 89.53.

48. PRO, WORK.5/3 (August 1662).

49. Dossie, vol. 1, 204.

50. British Museum, Print Room, Heal Collection 89.55; Tingry, *The Painter's and Colourman's Complete Guide*, 153–54.

51. See, for example, Tingry, *The Painter and Varnisher's Guide*, 464; Nicholson, 406.

52. Peter Nicholson, *An Architectural Dictionary* (1819), s.v. "Knotting," vol. 2, 202.

53. Smith, 5.

54. MS at Hertford Record Office, QSB/12, 387.

55. John Stalker and George Parker, *A Treatise of Japanning and Varnishing 1688 . . . with an introduction by H. D. Molesworth* (London, 1971), 9–10.

56. Watin, 239–42.

57. John Ray, *Historia Plantarum*, vol. 2 (1688), 1,846.

58. Stalker and Parker, 11.

59. See, for example, Tingry, *The Painter and Varnisher's Guide*, 120.

60. William Salmon (M.D.), *Polygraphice* (1672), 215.

61. Watin, 247.

62. Watin, 251.

63. Watin, 250.

64. Watin, 233, 291.

65. Watin, 287.

66. Stalker and Parker, 16–17.

67. Watin, 317–18.

68. Alfred Bartholomew, *Specifications for Practical Architecture*, 2d ed. (London: 1846), para. 1,500.

69. Stalker and Parker, xiv, 8, 19–26.

70. Watin, 93, 94, 241, 249, 295.

71. Tingry, *The Painter and Varnisher's Guide*, 389–408.

72. *Accounts of Chippendale Haig and Company for the Furnishing of David Garrick's House in the Adelphi* (London: Victoria and Albert Museum, 1920), 8.

73. See, for example, Morgan Phillips, "Discoloration of Old House Paints: Restoration of Paint Colors at the Harrison Gray Otis House, Boston," *Association for Preservation Technology Bulletin* 3 (1971): 40–47.

74. Smith, 74–75.

75. Ian C. Bristow, "Greenwich, the Queen's House: Report on an Investigation into the Seventeenth-Century Painted Finishes," unpublished typescript report prepared for the Property Services Agency, Department of the Environment (1986), 39–48.

76. British Museum, Print Room, Heal Collection, 89.53.

77. Bristow, "Ham House, Surrey: Report on a Further Investigation of Paint Samples," unpublished typescript report prepared for the Property Services Agency, Department of the Environment (1985), 1–2.

78. See quotations from manuscript accounts in Henry D. Roberts, *A History of the Royal Pavilion, Brighton* (London, 1939), 44, 46.

79. See Bristow, "Two Exterior Treatments to Imitate Stone," *ASCHB Transactions 1979* (Association for Studies in the Conservation of Historic Buildings, 1980), 3–9.

80. Peter Nicholson, *The New Practical Builder* (1823–25), 379, and "The Practical Builder's Perpetual Price-book" (supplement), 137.

81. See Bristow, "The Balcony Room at Dyrham," *National Trust Studies 1980* (1979), 140–46.

82. Smith, 47, 52.

83. Hezekiah Reynolds, *Directions for House and Ship Painting; Shewing in a plain and concise manner, The Best Methods of Preparing, Mixing, and Laying the Various Colours Now in Use, Designed for the Use of Learners* (New Haven, Conn.: Eli Hudson, 1812), 18–21.

84. Nathaniel Whittock, *The Decorative Painters' and Glaziers' Guide* (London, 1827), 32ff.; Vanherman, 58–64.

"Nineteenth-Century Paints," Roger W. Moss

1. For colonial colors, see Richard M. Candee, *Housepaints in Colonial America* (New York, 1967), and Theodore Zuk Penn, "Decorative and Protective Finishes, 1750–1850," *Association for Preservation Technology Bulletin* 16 (1984): 3–46. Howard Colvin calls Nicholson "one of the leading intellects behind nineteenth-century building technology" (*A Biographical Dictionary of British Architects, 1600–1840* [New York, 1978], 593–94). Several of Nicholson's books were reprinted in America, including the *Mechanic's Companion* (New York, 1831) and *An Architectural and Engineering Dictionary* (New York, 1835), which contained specific references to colors. Naturally, his books could have been seen by Americans in their original English editions dating from the previous two decades.

2. The Averill Chemical Paint Company was issued U.S. patent number 66,773 for ready-mixed paint on July 16, 1867. D. R. Averill's "patent" paint was not popular, however, because the pigments were improperly mixed and tended to sink in the can, causing the paint to streak when applied. This problem was not solved until 1876, when Henry A. Sherwin invented a new painting-grinding mill (Moss, *Century of Color* [Watkins Glen, N.Y., 1981], 11). Averill's paint was probably an inferior product because it used caustic soda and water. Early ready-mixed paint manufacturers were unregulated; some used sulfate of barium (Barytes) in place of lead, benzene rather than turpentine as thinner, and cheaper oils rather than linseed oil (George B. Heckel, *The Paint Industry* [St. Louis, 1931], 17–23). For the history of one early manufacturer, see William C. Bolger, *The John Lucas and Company Paint and Varnish Works* (Gibbsboro, N.J., 1982).

3. U.S. Bureau of the Census, *Statistical Abstract of the United States* (Washington, D.C., 1956), section 1.

4. An F. W. Devoe and Company dealer's scrapbook in the collection of the Athenaeum of Philadelphia contains correspondence and broadsides published in the 1860s and 1870s; these references are drawn from this ephemeral literature. William H. Ranlett specified "bronze or Paris green" shutters in the 1840s, and forty years later Charles L. Condit and Jacob Scheller could still write in *Painting and Painters' Materials* (New York, 1883), that "green is the most satisfactory color" for shutters (p. 403). According to Theodore Zuk Penn, Park Lawn Green was created by mixing yellow and blue pigments and was a substitute for Paris Green, an extremely poisonous color made from green arsenic pigments (Penn, 15–16).

5. The only recorded copy of the Averill color card of 1867, as reissued in 1869, is in the collection of the Athenaeum of Philadelphia.

6. Samuel Sloan, *The Model Architect* (Philadelphia, 1852), vol. 2, 85.

7. Arthur Channing Downs, "Downing's Newburgh Villa," *Association for Preservation Technology Bulletin* 4, nos. 3–4 (1972): 30–41, discusses the influences of Lugar and Goodwin on Downing. Downing lists the following "shades for outside painting"—fawn, drab, gray stone, brown stone, French gray, slate, sage, straw, and chocolate *(The Architecture of Country Houses* [New York, 1850], 198–206). See also Downing's *Cottage Residences* (New York, 1842), 22–23. Downing's influence on architecture and horticulture is discussed by several authors in George B. Tatum, ed., *Prophet with Honor: The Career of Andrew Jackson Downing, 1815–1852* (Washington, D.C., 1989).

8. For trade catalogues, see Lawrence B. Romaine, *A Guide to American Trade Catalogs, 1744–1900* (New York, 1960). A more detailed listing of paint company literature is contained in Samuel J. Dornsife, ed., *Exterior Decoration* (Philadelphia, 1976), 8–16.

9. *House Painting and Decorating* 1 (November 1885), 41–46. See also C. P. Sherwood, *A Few Words about Paint and Painting* (Wadsworth, Martinez and Longman, ca. 1884).

10. Hay's work is cited in the following sources: John C. Loudon, *Encyclopedia of Cottage, Farm, and Villa Architecture and Furniture* (London, 1833; New York, 1849; reprint ed., 1869), 1,274; Downing, *Architecture of Country Houses*, 400–02; "Art in Common Things," *Godey's Lady's Book* 79 (August 1869), 131–32; and John Masury, *House-painting: Plain and Decorative* (New York, 1868), 170–72.

11. For details, see Michel Eugène Chevreul, *The Principles of Harmony and Contrast of Colors and Their Applications to the Arts* (New York, 1967; based on the first English edition, 1854, and translated from the first French edition, 1839). See also *House Painting and Decorating* 1 (November 1885), 41–46.

12. For a discussion of Chevreul's influence on Victorian design, see Gail Caskey Winkler and Roger W. Moss, *Victorian Interior Decoration: American Interiors, 1830–1900* (New York: Henry Holt and Company, 1986), 128–44.

13. At the time of the 1976 reprint, only four copies of the original *Exterior Decoration* (1885) were known to have survived; subsequently two more have been discovered. The copy on which the reprint is based comes from the Samuel J. Dornsife Collection of the Victorian Society in America at the Athenaeum of Philadelphia. The project was funded by the Ella West Freeman Foundation, New Orleans, La., and the color chips were provided by the Matherson-Selig Company, Chicago, Ill.

14. Elizabeth Pomada and Michael Larson, *Painted Ladies: San Francisco's Resplendent Victorians (*New York, 1978); *Daughters of Painted Ladies: America's Resplendent Victorians* (New York, 1987); *The Painted Ladies Revisited: San Francisco's Resplendent Victorians Inside and Out* (New York, 1989); *How to Create Your Own Painted Lady: A Comprehensive Guide to Beautifying Your Victorian Home* (New York, 1989).

15. *Century of Color*, 7. *Century of Color* was published by the nonprofit American Life Foundation. The only relationship between Sherwin-Williams and the publisher was the paint card. In exchange for underwriting the paint card, Sherwin-Williams was provided with a documented line of authentic paint colors, which they named "Heritage Colors." That line was soon discontinued and replaced with one confusingly entitled "Heritage II," which had nothing to do with those used in *Century of Color*. Subsequently, Sherwin-Williams reissued some of the original colors, altered others to suit company perception rather than authenticity (although retaining the *Century of Color* names), and added colors with little historical basis. Scholarship and the profit motive rarely make congenial bedfellows.

16. Roger W. Moss and Gail Caskey Winkler, *Victorian Exterior Decoration: How to Paint Your Nineteenth-Century American House Historically* (New York: Henry Holt and Co., 1987); and Winkler and Moss, *Victorian Interior Decoration*). The difficulty of working with commercial color lines is that the manufacturers change them so often. Shortly after the first edition of *Victorian Exterior Decoration* appeared, the Benjamin Moore Company changed the numbering system of its entire color line. The paperback edition of *Victorian Exterior Decoration* (Henry Holt and Co., 1992) contains revised color charts coordinated to the colors and names available from the four manufacturers at that time.

17. Davis, *Rural Residences* (New York, 1837; reprint ed., 1980). Figure 5 is such an example.

18. Downing suggested that houses be painted in colors found in nature to harmonize with their surroundings. "Much of the beauty of landscapes depend on what painters call breadth of tone—which is caused by broad masses of colours that harmonize and blend agreeably together . . ," he explained in *The Architecture of Country Houses* (198–206).

19. John Riddell, *Architectural Designs for Model Country Residences* (Philadelphia, 1861, 1864, and 1867). Riddell is a figure who deserves more study; see Roger W. Moss and Sandra L. Tatman, *Biographical Dictionary of Philadelphia Architects, 1700–1930* (Boston, 1985), 659–62.

20. Ehrich Kensett Rossiter and Frank Ayers Wright, *Modern House Painting* (New York, 2d ed., 1883), 6–7. An excellent explanation of these processes is Bamber Gascoigne, *How to Identify Prints* (New York: Thames and Hudson, 1986).

21. *Exterior Decoration* (1976), 7.

22. The Munsell notations for the F. W. Devoe "Homestead Colors" card (ca. 1869) are found in *Century of Color*, 27. The Harrison Brothers and Company "Town and Country Ready Prepared Paints" (1871) are provided with National Bureau of Standards Color names and Munsell notations on p. 28.

23. Problems in attempting to follow historic paint formulas using modern pigments plagued one such effort discussed by Caroline Alderson, "Re-Creating a 19th Century Paint Palette,"*Association for Preservation Technology Bulletin* 16 (1984): 47–56.

24. The John Notman archive, including several of his mid-nineteenth-century specifications, is preserved at the Athenaeum of Philadelphia. The Glencairn drawings and specifications are reproduced in Constance M. Greiff, *John Notman, Architect* (Philadelphia, 1979), 152–57. For a more detailed discussion of the practices of sanding and striping, including photographs of the Athenaeum balcony roof and reproductions from *Villas on the Hudson* (New York, 1860), see Moss and Winkler, *Victorian Exterior Decoration*, 46–50, 57–64.

25. Moss and Winkler, *Victorian Exterior Decoration*, 60–63.

26. For a popular explanation of this phenomenon, see Bill Holm, "Old Photos Might Not Lie, But They Fib a Lot About Color," *American Indian Art Magazine* 10 (Autumn 1985): 44–49. A more technical discussion of orthochromatic photography is to be found in Paul N. Hasluck, ed., *The Book of Photography* (London, 1905), 439–53. I wish to thank Grant B. Romer, conservator, George Eastman House, Rochester, N.Y., and Daniel Fink, SUNY-Geneseo, N.Y., for their assistance with this problem.

**"The Early American Palette,"
Frank S. Welsh**

1. William Seale, *The President's House* (Washington, D.C.:The White House Historical Association, 1986), 76.
2. Seale, 77.
3. Ellen Wayles Randolph, April 14, 1808, Massachusetts Historical Society.
4. See Welsh, "Particle Characteristics of Prussian Blue in an Historical Oil Paint," *Journal of the American Institute for Conservation* 27 (1988): 55–63.
5. Marcus Whiffen, *The Eighteenth Century Houses of Williamsburg* (Williamsburg, Va.: Colonial Williamsburg Foundation, 1960), 201–202.

"Williamsburg Colors," Thomas H. Taylor, Jr., and Nicholas A. Pappas

1. W.A.R. Goodwin, "The Restoration of Colonial Williamsburg," *The National Geographic Magazine* 71, no. 4 (April 1937): 402.
2. Raymond B. Fosdick, *John D. Rockefeller, Jr.: A Portrait* (New York: Harper and Brothers, 1956), 272.
3. Alvin Moscow, *The Rockefeller Inheritance* (New York: Doubleday, 1977), 11.
4. Perry, Shaw and Hepburn, "Minutes of the Meeting Held at the Offices of the Williamsburg Holding Corporation, Williamsburg, Virginia," Wednesday, May 11, 1932, General Correspondence—Perry, Shaw and Hepburn—Williamsburg Meetings—Progress, Colonial Williamsburg Foundation Archive, Williamsburg, Va.

5. Thomas H. Taylor, Jr., "The Williamsburg Restoration and Its Reception by the American Public" (Ph.D. diss., George Washington University, 1989), 54–55 and 66–68.
6. The Department of Research and Record was established on March 29, 1930, under the direction of Perry, Shaw and Hepburn.
7. "The Williamsburg Colors Rooms," September 16, 1937, General Correspondence—Crafts—Distributor—McCutchen, Colonial Williamsburg Foundation Archive, n.p. See also "Memorandum of Information," August 23, 1935, General Correspondence—Paints—General, Colonial Williamsburg Foundation Archive.
8. After a structure was restored or reconstructed a use was quickly found for the building. In some cases a property was leased back to the family that sold it to the foundation for life tenancy rights. These people were often given greater voice in decisions concerning the interior and exterior finishes (Susan Higginson Nash, "Colonial Paint Colors in Williamsburg, Virginia," typed report dated May 19, 1936 [General Correspondence—Paints, Colonial Williamsburg Foundation Archive], 1). See also Nash to Branch Bocock, October 24, 1932, General Correspondence—Maintenance Paints), Colonial Williamsburg Foundation Archive, 16.
9. Susan Higginson Nash, "The Reminiscences of Susan Higginson Nash," typed transcript of a taped interview by James R. Short, June 18–20, 1956, Oral History Program, Colonial Williamsburg, 16.
10. Nash, 53–54.
11. Nash, 18–19.
12. Nash, 20.
13. A colorist is someone who is assigned the responsibility of mixing paint colors. The term was in common use in the 1920s and 1930s, when many painters were still mixing pigments in oil. A colorist not only had good color perception but knew which pigments were necessary to produce a desired color.
14. Edward K. Perry, paint contractor, was not related to William G. Perry, architect.

15. The 1929 correspondence between Edward K. Perry and Nash or one of the architects has not survived. The only reference to it was made by Nash in an interview in 1956 (Nash, 21–22).
16. Nash, 21–22.
17. Nash, 53.
18. Nash, 13.
19. Nash, 13.
20. Robert Trimble, Jr., to Perry, Shaw and Hepburn, May 2, 1931. Attached to this memo was "Survey of Exterior Paint on Buildings of the Williamsburg Restoration," prepared by Todd and Brown.
21. Nash to Orin M. Bullock, Jr., April 18, 1931, General Correspondence—Paints—General, Colonial Williamsburg Foundation Archive.
22. William G. Perry to Todd and Brown, February 25, 1932, General Correspondence—Paints General, Colonial Williamsburg Foundation Archive.
23. Perry, Shaw and Hepburn, "Minutes of the Meetings Held at the Offices of the Williamsburg Holding Corporation, Williamsburg, Virginia," meeting no. 4, January 27, 1931, and meeting no. 5, February 3, 1931, Perry, Shaw and Hepburn—Williamsburg Meetings—Progress, Colonial Williamsburg Foundation Archive.
24. The decision to hire a painter was made at a meeting of the foundation's administrative officers in Williamsburg on May 18, 1933 (Nash to Chorley, May 19, 1933, General Correspondence—Paints General, Colonial Williamsburg Foundation Archive). See also Edward K. Perry to Kenneth Chorley, October 4, 1933, General Correspondence—Manufacturer—Paints, Colonial Williamsburg Foundation Archive.
25. Nash to Chorley, June 5, 1933, General Correspondence—Paints—General, Colonial Williamsburg Foundation Archive.
26. Thrall was hired by Branch Bocock, director of the maintenance department, in 1935 (Susan Higginson Nash to Orin Bullock, May 2, 1932, General Correspondence—Paints—General, Colonial Williamsburg Foundation Archive.

27. Webb retired on November 30, 1962.
28. Albert Lucas, interview, February 21, 1989, Williamsburg, Va.
29. Since then the size of the paint work force has diminished. John V. O'Neal was paint shop superintendent from 1962 to 1972; Bruce Wildenberger was paint shop superintendent from 1972 to 1985; and Albert Lucas became the paint shop superintendent in 1985 (interview with Bruce Wildenberger, April 19, 1989, Williamsburg, Va.).
30. Nash to Orin M. Bullock, Jr., April 18, 1931, and May 7, 1931, General Correspondence—Paints—General, Colonial Williamsburg Foundation Archive.
31. M. N. Schuhman to Todd and Brown, September 29, 1933, General Correspondence—Paints—General, Colonial Williamsburg Foundation Archive.
32. Nash, 70.
33. Perry, Shaw and Hepburn, "Minutes of the Meetings held at the Offices of the Williamsburg Holding Corporation, Williamsburg, Virginia," meeting no. 80, May 24, 1933, Perry, Shaw and Hepburn—Williamsburg—Meetings—Progress, Colonial Williamsburg Foundation Archive.
34. Nash to Branch Bocock, November 3, 1933, and November 8, 1933, General Correspondence—Maintenance—Paints, Colonial Williamsburg Foundation Archive.
35. Nash to Bocock, October 13, 1933, General Correspondence—Maintenance—Paints, Colonial Williamsburg Foundation Archive, and William G. Perry to Anson B. Gardner, November 26, 1935, General Correspondence—Paints—General, Colonial Williamsburg Foundation Archive. This set of master paint samples was later sent to Masury and Son and Pittsburgh Paints.
36. Anson B. Gardner, "Memorandum for the Files," January 18, 1935, and May 1, 1935, General Correspondence—Paints—General, Colonial Williamsburg Foundation Archive.
37. Nash, 53–54.

38. In some cases the architects were able to persuade the owners of these houses to permit them to remove small samples of the woodwork. Several large wooden crates of wooden architectural fragments were collected. This architectural fragment collection has not been used in many years and is stored in one of the foundation's warehouses.

39. This assumption may have resulted in many misidentifications because recent paint investigations have shown that often the first coats of Spanish brown were actually finish coats and not merely primers.

40. Harold R. Shurtleff to Perry, Shaw and Hepburn, February 9, 1932, Block and Building Files, Block 28, Building 6—Peyton Randolph House—General, Colonial Williamsburg Foundation Archive. See also Joseph W. Geddes to Nash, March 25, 1932, Buildings—Peyton Randolph House—General, Colonial Williamsburg Foundation Archive.

41. This method is similar to the historic paint identification by layer exposure described by Andrea M. Gilmore, "Analyzing Paint Samples: Investigation and Interpretation" (in this volume).

42. Nash, "Paints, Furniture and Furnishings," *Architectural Record* 78, no. 6 (December 1935): 448.

43. For additional information on the solvent exposure method, see Gilmore "Analyzing Paint Samples."

44. Nash to Kenneth Chorley, September 19, 1933, General Correspondence—Maintenance—Paint, Colonial Williamsburg Foundation Archive.

45. W.A.R. Goodwin to Kenneth Chorley, September 13, 1933, General Correspondence—Maintenance—Paint, and Walter M. Macomber to Susan H. Nash, August 29, 1930, General Correspondence—Paints—General, Colonial Williamsburg Foundation Archive.

46. Although only two structures have undergone modern paint analysis, one of them, the Dr. Barraud House, was originally painted white. See Frank Welsh, "The Early American Palette: Colonial Paint Colors Revealed" (in this volume).

47. Walter M. Macomber to Susan Higginson Nash, August 29, 1930, General Correspondence—Paints—General, and Nash to Kenneth Chorley, September 19, 1933, General Correspondence—Maintenance—Paints), Colonial Williamsburg Foundation Archive.

48. Walter M. Macomber to A. H. Hepburn, June 4, 1932, General Correspondence—Paints—General, Colonial Williamsburg Foundation Archive.

49. Carroll and Herb Freeman did most of the paint investigation between February 26, 1951, and February 1973.

50. In 1933 Chorley wrote to the Williamsburg staff that some of the sample paint panels had faded and suggested that in the future samples should be stored in a dark place to prevent fading (Kenneth Chorley to Perry, Shaw and Hepburn, February 27, 1933, General Correspondence—Paints—General, Colonial Williamsburg Foundation Archive).

51. Bureau of Standards to Perry, Shaw and Hepburn, June 11, 1932, General Correspondence—Paints—General, Colonial Williamsburg Foundation Archive.

52. Singleton P. Moorehead to Deane B. Judd, April 26, 1948, General Correspondence—Building Materials—Paint, Colonial Williamsburg Foundation Archive. Moorehead reported receiving these documents at a divisional meeting held on April 19, 1948 (Meetings—Architecture, Construction, and Maintenance, Colonial Williamsburg Foundation Archive).

53. Moorehead also claimed that tenants had been allowed too much leeway in repainting, thus destroying the documentary work done in the 1930s.

54. One person Moorehead wrote concerning his search for a laboratory that would chemically analyze the paint on the wood fragments was Charles E. Peterson, architect, Independence National Historical Park in Philadelphia. See Moorehead to Peterson, June 13, 1952, General Correspondence—Building Materials—Paint, Colonial Williamsburg Foundation Archive.

55. Singleton P. Moorehead to Dr. Kenneth Conant, April 4, 1952, and Moorehead to Archibald G. Wenley, May 21, 1952, General Correspondence—Building Materials—Paint, Colonial Williamsburg Foundation Archive.

56. Richard D. Buck to Moorehead, May 5, 1952, and A. G. Wenley to Moorehead, June 4, 1952, General Correspondence—Building Materials—Paint, Colonial Williamsburg Foundation Archive.

57. Gettens visited Williamsburg on October 7, 1952 (Moorehead to Mario Campioli, October 7, 1952, General Correspondence—Building Materials—Paint, Colonial Williamsburg Foundation Archive).

58. Gettens's analysis was sent to Moorehead on January 18, 1953 (Moorehead to Gettens, March 4, 1953, General Correspondence—Building Materials—Paint, Colonial Williamsburg Foundation Archive).

59. E. B. Ankess [Stewart's secretary] to Charles E. Hackett, October 7, 1953, General Correspondence—Building Materials—Paint, Colonial Williamsburg Foundation Archive.

60. Orin M. Bullock, Jr., to E. K. Zimmermann, February 16, 1954, General Correspondence—Building Materials—Paint, Colonial Williamsburg Foundation Archive.

61. Bullock to Dunn, November 2, 1954, General Correspondence—Building Materials—Paint, Colonial Williamsburg Foundation Archives.

62. Kendrew to Sheldon Keck, July 7, 1959, General Correspondence—Building Materials—Paint, Colonial Williamsburg Foundation Archive.

63. W. E. Jacobs to Frank, Graham, Patrick, and Sparks, August 26, 1960, General Correspondence—Building Materials—Paint, Colonial Williamsburg Foundation Archive.

64. According to Vernon Hubbard, painter, and Albert Lucas, paint shop superintendent, the spectrophotometer was used during the paint investigations for Wetherburn's Tavern, although the instrument was seldom used after 1973 (interview, February 21, 1989, Williamsburg, Va.).

65. In 1983 the foundation acquired an XL-200 Colorimeter from Gardner Instruments and in 1987 a Minolta Chroma Meter CR-200. These instruments are used primarily to compare newly mixed paints with the refrigerated color cards.

66. Gen. Charles Cornwallis, the English commandant, had decreed that all structures between his fortifications and those of the colonists be demolished to preserve his lines of sight.

67. This was a particularly exciting discovery. Although it was known that the dark baseboard color was often continued across door surrounds in the eighteenth century, this was the first concrete evidence of this practice in Williamsburg.

68. A. Lawrence Kocher and Howard Dearstyne, "Architectural Report, Barraud House," Colonial Williamsburg Foundation Library, April 1949, 532.

69. Mary A. Stephenson, "Ludwell-Paradise House" (unpublished manuscript), Colonial Williamsburg Foundation Library, November 1948, 1.

70. Stephenson, 2.

71. Stephenson, 3.

72. Stephenson, 4.

73. The most expensive wood floor in eighteenth-century Virginia consisted of all edge-grain longleaf southern yellow pine boards of equal width that extended across the room in single lengths and were blind nailed and doweled. The floors in the Ludwell-Paradise House, which are original, meet none of these criteria.

74. Frank Welsh to Thomas Taylor, Jr., March 7, 1988, Foundation Architect's Office, Colonial Williamsburg Foundation.

75. In 1798 St. George Tucker wrote a long and detailed specification for the painting of his house. It specified that the body color of the exterior be a "pure white," the window frames and sash straw color, the doors and shutters "chocolate," the kitchen ocher, the brick foundations a "dark brick color," and the roof Spanish brown, mixed with fish oil and "enlivened with red lead."

76. The courthouse, which was completed in 1770, burned in 1911. The only surviving fabric is the exterior brick walls.

"Paint Decoration at Mount Vernon," Matthew J. Mosca

The Invoices and Letters of George Washington, a compilation of his writings, are mentioned thoughout these notes. A photocopy of this compilation is at the Library at Mount Vernon, where the author did much of his research; the original is at the Library of Congress.

1. Robert Dossie, *Handmaid to the Arts. Vol. 1: Teaching. A perfect knowledge of the materia pictoria: or the nature, use, preparation and composition of all the various substances employed in painting; as well as vehicles, dryers &c. as colours. . . .* (London: J. Nourse, 1758),4 and 5.

2. George Washington, Invoices and Letters. Mount Vernon Ladies' Association of the Union.

3. George Washington, Invoices and Letters, 175. Mount Vernon Ladies' Association of the Union.

4. *Webster's Revised Unabridged Dictionary of the English Language,* edited under the supervision of Noah Porter (Springfield, Mass.: G & C Merriam Company, 1890), 1261. A rundlet (also written runlet) is defined as "a small barrel of no certain dimensions. It may contain from 3 to 20 gallons, but it usually holds about 14 and one half gallons."

5. Washington, Invoices and Letters, 16. Mount Vernon Ladies' Association of the Union.

6. John C. Fitzpatrick, ed., *The Writings of George Washington from the Original Manuscripts Sources 1745–1799,* 39 vols., prepared under the direction of the U.S. George Washington Bicentennial Commission and published by the Authority of Congress (Washington, D.C.: U.S. Government Printing Office, 1931) 2:311.

7. Fitzpatrick, John C., ed., *The Diaries of George Washington from the Original Manuscripts Sources 1748–1799* (Boston and New York: Houghton Mifflin Company, 1925) 1:124.

8. Invoices and Letters, Vol. 10: Building Materials: Paints and Painting, 22, 23, 31, 37, 43, 99, 111, 126, 142. Mount Vernon Ladies' Association of the Union.

9. Invoice from Robert Cary and Company to George Washington, June 20, 1768, Invoices and Letters. Mount Vernon Ladies' Association of the Union.

10. William Salmon, Jr., *Palladio Londinensis or the London art of Building,* pt. 1 (London, 1734), 57. Hezekiah Reynolds, *Directions for House and Ship Painting,* facsimile reprint of the 1812 edition with an introduction by Richard M. Candee (Worchester, Mass.: American Antiquarian Society, 1978), 15.

11. Dossie, 149.

12. Rutherford J. Gettens and George L. Stout, *Painting Materials: A Short Encyclopedia* (New York: Dover Publications, 1942, 1966), 174–76.

13. Dossie, 121–24.

14. Dossie, 123–24.

15. Cenino d'Andrea Cenini, *Il Libro dell'Arte* (c. 1437), trans. Daniel V. Thompson, Jr. (1933; reprint, New York: Dover Publications, 1954, 1960), 53.

16. *The Artist's Repository. Vol. 2: A Compendium of Colors and other Materials used in the Arts of Drawing, Painting, Engraving, &c. in their Various Branches, with Remarks on their Natures and Uses* (London: C. Taylor, 1784), 81.

17. Dossie, 127.

18. Reynolds, 15.

19. Dossie, 104–6.

20. *Builder's Dictionary or Architect's Companion,* vol. 2 (1734; reprint, Washington, D.C.: Association for Preservation Technology, 1981), see "Timber work, painting of."

21. Dossie, 47, 48.

22. Dossie, 129.

23. Dossie, 151. Ralph Mayer, *The Artist's Handbook of Materials and Techniques,* 4th ed. (New York: Viking Press, 1981), 366–67.

24. *Builder's Dictionary or Architect's Companion,* see "Timber work, painting of."

25. Dossie, 52–53.

26. "Invoice of Sundry Goods Shipped by Richard Washington on board the Peggy and Elizabeth, bound to Virginia on the proper acet [sic] and risque of the honorable George Washington," November 1757 (unnumbered page), Invoices and Letters. Mount Vernon Ladies' Association of the Union.

27. Reynolds gives an elaborate recipe for mahogany color, which includes a red ocher ground with umber used for shading (Reynolds, 18). Extant mid-eighteenth-century examples of mahogany graining made in this manner survive on doors dating to 1745 at Graeme Park, Horsham, Pennsylvania, property of the Pennsylvania Historical and Museum Commission.

28. Alfred Coxe Prime, *The Arts and Crafts in Philadelphia, Maryland and South Carolina 1721–1785. Gleanings from Newspapers* (Topsfield, Mass.: The Walpole Society, 1929), 300.

29. Fitzpatrick, 3:155.

30. Transcription from the Lund Washington Account Book (W-693 bk.), 49. Archives Restoration files. Mount Vernon Ladies' Association of the Union.

31. George Washington to Mount Vernon manager, James Anderson, November 5, 1796: "Some years ago, I had brought from Point Comfort or some other place on the Bay of Chesapeake, a quantity of fine white Sand for the purpose of Sanding my house anew when the circumstances would enable me to give then a fresh coat of paint" (Fitzpatrick, 35:263–65).

32. Dossie, 93.

33. Dossie, 129.

34. Dossie, 147–50, and Reynolds, 7.

35. Archives Restoration files, Mount Vernon Ladies' Association of the Union.

36. Invoice of Goods, May 13, 1785, from the Washington Papers, Archives Restoration files. Mount Vernon Ladies' Association of the Union.

37. Dossie, 77–82.

38. *Encyclopedia Britannica or a Dictionary of Arts, Sciences and Miscellaneous Literature . . . Compiled from the writings of the best Authors, in several languages . . . The Third Edition in Eighteen Volumes, Greatly improved,* vol. 5 (Edinburgh: A. Bell and C. Macfarquhar, 1797), 158. Mount Vernon Ladies' Association of the Union.

39. Reynolds, 16.

40. Archives Restoration files, Mount Vernon Ladies' Association of the Union, and Historic Paint Research report, "The West Parlor: 1980," Matthew John Mosca. The few pigment particles that were observed under the microscope suggest that the yellow ocher component of the paint had virtually no effect on the finish color.

41. Cenini, 21.

42. Fitzpatrick, 29:246–47.

43. Cenini, 20 and 21.

44. Dossie, 149.

45. Reynolds, 13.

46. Fitzpatrick, 37:584.

47. *Builder's Dictionary or Architect's Companion,* vol. 2, see "Timber work, painting of."

48. June 16, 1786, Archives Restoration files. Mount Vernon Ladies' Association of the Union.

49. "Invoice of Sundry Goods shipped by Mr. Richard Washington, of London," April 15, 1757, Archives Restoration Files. Mount Vernon Ladies' Association of the Union.

50. Letters of Lund Washington to George Washington, September 29, October 15, and November 12, 1775, Archives Restoration Files. Mount Vernon Ladies' Association of the Union.

51. Letter of January 17, 1784, to Clement Biddle, Philadelphia. Fitzpatrick, 27:304–5.

52. Letter of February 5, 1785, to Samuel Vaughan. Fitzpatrick, 28:63–64.

53. Fitzpatrick 28:237–38.

54. *Maryland Gazette,* February 14, 1771, Archives Restoration Files. Mount Vernon Ladies' Association of the Union.

55. Letter to George Augustine Washington, July 1, 1787. Fitzpatrick, 29:239–42.

56. Letter to George Augustine Washington, July 15, 1787. Fitzpatrick, 29:246.

57. *Encyclopedia Britannica,* 158.

"The Color of Change," Myron O. Stachiw

1. See especially Jack Larkin, *The Reshaping of Everyday Life, 1790–1840* (New York: Harper and Row, 1988). The author wishes to acknowledge the assistance of his many colleagues at Old Sturbridge Village, especially John Worrell, David Simmons, Cariline Sloat, Jack Larkin, Nora Pat Small, John Curtis, and Tom Paske.

2. Blaine E. Taylor, ed., *Worcester County: America's First Frontier* (Worcester, Mass.: Isaiah Thomas Books and Prints, 1983), 160 (reprint of Peter Whitney, *The History of Worcester County, Massachusetts* [Worcester, Mass.: Isaiah Thomas, 1793]); John S. Yeomans, "Historical Sketches," in *The 150th Anniversary of the Organization of the Congregational Chyrch in Columbia, Connecticut, October 24th, 1866* (Hartford, 1867), 53.

3. Joseph S. Wood, "The New England Village as an American Vernacular Form," in *Perspectives in Vernacular Architecture II*, ed. Camille Wells (Columbia: University of Missouri Press, 1986), 54–63; Wood, "The Origin of the New England Village" (Ph.D. diss., Department of Geography, Pennsylvania State University, 1978), especially chapter 6; Patrick Shirreff, *A Tour through North America; together with a Comprehensive View of the Canadas and the United States* (Edinburgh, 1835), 40; Larkin, *The Reshaping of Everyday Life*, chapters 1, 3, 5. The term *factory village* refers to the rural hamlets created in the early nineteenth century at suitable water-power sites to accommodate such industries as textile manufacturing, metal working, and woodworking. They usually consisted of the factory and housing for employees and their families, as well as supporting craft shops, a sawmill, a gristmill, and a store.

4. Andrew H. Baker and Holly Izard Paterson, "Farmers' Adaptations to Markets in Early Nineteenth Century Massachusetts," in *The Farm, Annual Proceedings of the Dublin Seminar for New England Folklife*, vol. 11, ed. Peter Benes (Boston University, 1988), 88–108; Andrew H. Baker and Holly V. Izard, "New England Farmers and the Marketplace,

1780–1865: A Case Study," *Agricultural History* 65, no. 2 (Summer 1991: 29–52; Christopher Clark, "Household Economy, Market Exchange and the Rise of Capitalism in the Connecticut Valley, 1800–1860," *Journal of Social History* 13 (Winter 1979): 169–89; Robert A. Gross, "Culture and Cultivation: Agriculture and Society in Thoreau's Concord," *The Journal of American History* 69 (June 1982): 42–61; Richard M. Candee, "New Towns in the Early Nineteenth Century: The Textile Industry and Community Development in New England," Old Sturbridge Village Research Report, 1976 (unpublished), 1; Thomas Dublin, "Women's Work and the Family Economy: Textiles and Palm Leaf Hatmaking in New England, 1830–1850," *Tocqueville Review* (1983): 297–316; Mary H. Blewett, "Women Shoeworkers and Domestic Ideology: Rural Outwork in Early Nineteenth Century Essex County," *New England Quarterly* 60 (September 1987): 403–28; Caroline F. Sloat, "'A Great Help to Many Families': Strawbraiding in Massachusetts before 1825," in *Hearth and Home, Annual Proceedings of the Dublin Seminar in New England Folklife*, vol. 13 (Boston University, 1990); Myron O. Stachiw, "The Economy of the Countryside," Old Sturbridge Village Research Report, 1988 (unpublished); Stachiw, "Work at Home and for Hire," Old Sturbridge Village Research Report, 1988 (unpublished).

5. The archaeological, architectural, and documentary research for this project was carried out between 1984 and 1988 by the staff of Old Sturbridge Village as part of the Old Sturbridge Village research project "Tradition and Transformation: Rural Economic Life in Central New England, 1790–1850." In 1986 the house was partially dismantled and moved to the museum for restoration and interpretation as the home of an 1830s rural blacksmith and his family. The house opened as an exhibit in the living history component of the museum in April 1988. Research was funded in part by the National Endowment for the Humanities, RO-21015–85. Careful analysis of the composition and stratigraphy of

the paint layers and reconstruction of paint colors was conducted by Old Sturbridge Village staff and by the Conservation Center of the Society for the Preservation of New England Antiquities. Nora Pat Small, "Field Report: Recording the Bixby House," Old Sturbridge Village Research Report, 1986 (unpublished); Myron O. Stachiw, "Architectural Change in the Countryside: Evidence from the Bixby House," Old Sturbridge Village Research Report, 1986 (unpublished); John Worrell, Myron O. Stachiw, and David M. Simmons, "Archaeology from the Ground Up: The Bixby House and Site," in *Historical Archaeology and the Study of American Culture*, eds. Lu Ann de Cunzo and Bernard L. Herman (Winterthur, Del.: Henry F. Dupont Winterthur Museum, forthcoming); John Worrell, Myron O. Stachiw, and David M. Simmons, "The Total Site Matrix: Strata and Structure at the Bixby Site," in *Practices of Archaeological Stratigraphy*, eds. Edward C. Harris, Marley R. Brown III, and Gregory J. Brown (London and San Diego: Academic Press, 1993), 181–200; Myron O. Stachiw and Nora Pat Small, "Tradition and Transformation: Rural Society and Architectural Change in Nineteenth Century Central Massachusetts," in *Perspectives in Vernacular Architecture III*, eds. Thomas Carter and Bernard L. Herman (Columbia: University of Missouri Press, 1989); Myron O. Stachiw, "Tradition and Transformation: Emerson Bixby and the Social, Material and Economic World of Barre Four Corners," paper presented at the annual meeting of the Society for Historians of the Early Republic, Sturbridge, Mass., 1988.

6. Worcester County Land Records, vol. 184, p. 322 (hereafter WLR 184/322). The composition of the neighborhood and its craft industries is the result of extensive title reconstruction; compilation and cross-referencing of census, tax, probate, and school district records; and study of historic maps.

7. Andrew H. Ward, *History of the Town of Shrewsbury, Massachusetts, from Its Settlement in 1717 to 1829* (Boston, 1847), 308; Asa Hemenway, *A Genealogical Record of One Branch of the Hemenway

Family from 1634 to 1880* (Hartford, 1880), 25, 40–42.

8. Small, "Field Report"; Kathryn M. Carey and Sara B. Chase, "Historic Paint Analysis of the Sitting Room and Kitchen of the Bixby House," and "Addendum," Society for the Preservation of New England Antiquities, Conservation Center, 1987.

9. Small, "Field Report"; Stachiw, "Architectural Change in the Countryside."

10. Carey and Chase, "Historic Paint Analysis . . . Bixby House" and "Addendum;" Stachiw, "Architectural Change in the Countryside."

11. Stachiw, "Architectural Change in the Countryside." Because no microscopic inspection or infrared spectroscopy were carried out on the paints in this room, it is unknown if the brown iron oxide pigment was in an oil or resin medium. See Abbot Lowell Cummings, "Notes on Furnishing a Small New England Farmhouse," *Old-Time New England* 48, no. 3 (1958): 78, for a description of the polychrome furnishings in the best room of a small farmhouse.

12. Stachiw, "Architectural Change in the Countryside"; Carey and Chase, "Historic Paint Analysis . . . Bixby House."

13. WLR 246/492; WLR 252/272. Richard C. Nylander, Elizabeth Redmond, and Penny J. Sandler, *Wallpaper in New England* (Boston: Society for the Preservation of New England Antiquities, 1986), 132.

14. Richard M. Candee, *Housepaints in Colonial America: Their Materials, Manufacture, and Application* (reprint from *Color Engineering*, 1966–67): 15–18; Stachiw and Small, "Tradition and Transformation: Rural Society and Architectural Change;" Carey and Chase, "Historic Paint Analysis" and "Addendum"; Theodore Z. Penn, "Decorative and Protective Finishes, 1750–1850: Materials, Process, Craft" (M.A. thesis, University of Delaware, 1966), 51–55, 93–94; Robert Mussey," Transparent Furniture Finishes in New England, 1700–1820: A Documentary Study" (unpublished manuscript, 1980), 2–3, 7–8, 11–13. Sara Chase, in her report on the results of the infrared spectroscopy carried out by the Fogg Center for Conservation and Technical Studies, de-

scribed the use of pigmented varnishes as "unusual and unanticipated." A description of pigmented varnishes on interior architectural elements, found on a house in Rochester, New York, is in Marjorie Ward Selden, *Interior Paint of the Campbell-Whittlesey House, 1835–36* (Rochester: Society for the Preservation of Landmarks in Western New York, 1949), 7.

15. James Henry Maguire, "A Critical Edition of *Edward Parry's Journal, March 28, 1775 to August 23, 1777*" (Ph.D. diss., Indiana University, 1970), 72; I am indebted to Jack Larkin for this reference. John Trumbull, *Painters and Other Vagabonds* (Lebanon, Conn., n.d.), 271; Jane C. Nylander, "What about Floors?" (unpublished Old Sturbridge Village Report, 1982); Sarah Anna Emery, *Reminiscences of a Nonagenarian* (Newburyport, 1879), 10, 23; *Grandmother Tyler's Book; The Recollections of Mary Palmer Tyler (Mrs. Royall Tyler), 1775–1866,* eds. Frederick Tupper and Helen Tyler Brown (New York: G. P. Putnam's Sons, 1925); "A Country Wedding," M.R.G., *Lowell Offering* (March 1845); Harriet Beecher Stowe, *Old Town Folks* (Boston: Fields, Osgood & Co., 1869), 23, 61; Larkin, *The Reshaping of Everyday Life,* 137, 143; Rodris Roth, *Floor Coverings in Eighteenth Century America* (Washington, D.C.: Smithsonian Institution Press, 1967), 48; Nina Fletcher Little, *American Decorative Wall Painting, 1700–1850* (New York: E. P. Dutton & Co., 1972), 25, 76–79, 99, 116, 120; Nina Fletcher Little, *Floor Coverings in New England before 1850* (Old Sturbridge Village, 1967), 4–5, 18, 22, 24–26; Nina Fletcher Little, *Country Arts in Early American Homes* (New York: E. P. Dutton, 1975), 196–97, 203; Anthony N. Landreau, *America Underfoot: A History of Floor Coverings from Colonial Times to the Present* (Washington, D.C.: Smithsonian Institution Press, 1976), 3, 7, 15; Cummings, "Notes on Furnishing a Small

New England Farmhouse", 78; Richard M. Candee, "The Shop Records of the Reas and Johnstons, Painters of Boston: 1765–1795" (unpublished paper, 1968), 91–99; Brian Cullity, *Plain and Fancy: New England Painted Furniture* (Heritage Plantatin of New England, 1987); Edwin A. Churchill, *Simple Forms and Vivid Colors: An Exhibition of Maine Painted Furniture, 1800–1850* (Maine State Museum, 1983). William Rice placed an advertisement in the *Connecticut Courant* (April 16, 1816) for his services as a painter of signs, carriages, lettering, doors, graining, furniture, gilding, varnishing, and "floors painted in imitation of Italian Marble." See also the recent work of decorative arts historian Sumpter Priddy regarding the changing use and popularization of the term "fancy" in the early nineteenth century (personal communication, 1988).

16. Stachiw, "Architectural Change in the Countryside"; Small, "Field Report"; Carey and Chase, "Historic Paint Analysis" and "Addendum." For a discussion of the reorganization of yards and buildings closely tied to improvement and rural reform, see Thomas Hubka, *Big House, Little House, Back House, Barn* (Hanover, N.H.: University Press of New England, 1984), 70–80, and chapter 4. Another example of this sort of overall reorganization and improvement can be found in an 1840 letter from Mary Pease of East Boston to the modest Sturbridge, Massachusetts, farmer Pliny Freeman: " . . . I was glad to hear you have got your house painted and a door-yard . . . " (February 6, 1840, Freeman Family Papers, Old Sturbridge Village).

17. Stachiw, "Architectural Change in the Countryside"; Small, "Field Report." By 1840 painting floors was a common practice. Domestic advice books declared, "When they are not to be carpeted, it is an excellent plan to have the floors painted; as it preserves the wood, fills up the cracks, and saves much hard scrubbing" (Eliza Leslie, *The House Book* [Philadelphia, 1840], 335). In an 1843 edition of the book

Leslie wrote, "As a substitute for an oilcloth, the floor may be painted all over with several coats of common paint; yellow ochre being the cheapest, but slate-colour the best" *(The House Book* [Philadelphia, 1843], 228). See also Catherine Beecher, *A Treatise on Domestic Economy* (1841), 271, 367.

18. In 1837 Barre's five palm-leaf hat dealers recorded collecting 607,000 hats from farm families in the area (Secretary of the Commonwealth, *Statistical Tables: Exhibiting the Condition and Products of Certain Branches of Industry in Massachusetts* [Boston, 1837], 44–45.

19. Stachiw, "Tradition and Transformation: Emerson Bixby and the Social, Material and Economic World of Barre Four Corners."

20. The slackening of child-care responsibilities allowed Laura Bixby to devote more of her time to these pursuits as well. It is likely that the daughters and their mother were close partners in this transformation of the household economy. The diary of Jane Brigham, daughter of a neighboring carpenter and trading partner of Emerson Bixby, documents the changes in this young woman's social life from her early teenage years through the time of her marriage in 1860 and during the first few years of her married life. It reveals a significant increase and change in the frequency and nature of social activity as she entered her middle teenage years and courtship period. Not surprisingly, a number of changes were made to her house during these years; floors and ceilings were painted, traffic patterns in and out of the house were reordered, a flower garden was planted, and a pump and parlor stove were purchased. During this time she began braiding straw and working palm leaves, and her father purchased a horse for the first time (Karen Nelson, "Analysis of Jane Brigham's Diary," Old Sturbridge Village Research Report [unpublished], 1986; Jane Brigham diaries, 1837–63, Petersham, Massachusetts, at the Petersham Historical Society). On the new

values and material culture, see Richard D. Brown, "The Emergence of Urban Society in Rural Massachusetts, 1760–1820," *Journal of American History* 61 (June 1974): 29–51; Richard L. Bushman, "American High Style and Vernacular Cultures," in *Colonial British America: Essays in the New History of the Early Modern Era,* eds. Jack P. Greene and J. R. Pole (Baltimore, 1984), 345–83; Dell Upton, "Pattern Books and Professionalism: Aspects of the Transformation of Domestic Architecture in America, 1800–1860," *Winterthur Portfolio* 19 (Summer-Autumn 1984): 107–50; Sally McMurry, *Families and Farmhouses in Nineteenth Century America: Vernacular Design and Social Change* (New York: Oxford University Press, 1988); Bernard L. Herman, *Architecture and Rural Life in Central Delaware, 1700–1900* (Knoxville: University of Tennessee Press, 1987); Jack Larkin, "'Country Mediocrity' and 'Rural Improvement': Economic Transformation and the Domestic Environment in Central Massachusetts, 1775–1840," in *Everyday Life in the Early Republic,* ed. Catherine E. Hutchins (Winterthur, Del.: Henry F. Dupont Museum, forthcoming); Richard L. Bushman, *The Refinement of America: Persons, Houses, Cities* (New York: Knopf, 1992), especially chapter 8.

21. Worrell, Stachiw, and Simmons, "Archaeology from the Ground Up"; Worrell, Stachiw, and Simmons, "The Total Site Matrix"; David M. Simmons, "The Archaeology of Rural New England Craftsmen and Their Households," paper presented at the annual meetings of the Society for Historical Archaeology, 1989; Josiah Quincy, "An Adress Delivered before the Massachusetts Agricultural Society, at Brighton Cattle Show, October 12, 1819," *Massachusetts Agricultural Journal* 6 (January 1820), 1, as quoted in Larkin, "Country Mediocrity."

22. Andrew Jackson Downing, the self-proclaimed arbiter of taste in the mid-nineteenth century, expressed both the practical and symbolic meaning of having an entry lobby: "The principal entrance or front door should never open directly into an apartment of any kind, but always into a porch, a lobby, or entry of some kind. Such a passage not only protects the apartment against sudden draughts of air, but it also protects the privacy and dignity of the inmates" (*The Architecture of Country Houses* [New York, 1850], 44).

23. Larkin, *The Reshaping of Everday Life*, especially chapters 2, 4, 7; William J. Rorabaugh, *The Alcoholic Republic: An American Tradition* (New York: Oxford University Press, 1979); Ellen K. Rothman, *Hands and Hearts: A History of Courtship and Marriage in America* (New York: Basic Books, 1984); Paul E. Johnson, *A Shopkeeper's Millenium: Society and Revivals in Rochester, New York, 1815–1837* (New York: Hill and Wang, 1978).

"An Early Colonial Mural,"
Christy Cunningham-Adams

1. William Greenough Wendall, *The Warner House* (Portsmouth, N.H.: Author, 1966), 27.

2. M. T. Beck, "The Process of Restoration of Decorative Painting (of Two Indian Chiefs) on the North-East Wall in the Main Hall of the Warner House, Portsmouth, N.H." (November 1953) (Portsmouth, N.H.: Warner House Association).

"A Victorian Trompe l'Oeil,"
Morgan W. Phillips

1. Robert S. Radcliffe, "Casein Paints," *Protective and Decorative Coatings*, ed. Joseph Mattiello (New York: John Wiley and Sons, 1943), 3:466.

2. Radcliffe, 466.

3. F. N. Vanderwalker, *Interior Wall Decoration* (Chicago: Frederick J. Drake, 1924), 118.

4. Rutherford J. Gettens and George L. Stout, *Painting Materials: A Short Encyclopedia* (New York: Dover, reprint 1966 of 1942 original), 27.

5. Tsuneyuki Morita, "'Nikawa'— Traditional Production of Animal Glue in Japan," in *Adhesives and Consolidants, Preprints of the Contributions to the Paris Congress, 2–8 September, 1984*, eds. N. S. Bromelle et al. (London: International Institute for Conservation of Historic and Artistic Works, 1984), 121.

6. Gettens and Stout, 26.

7. Paulo Mora, Laura Mora, and Paul Philippot, *Conservation of Wall Paintings* (London: Butterworths, 1984), 124.

8. George Murray, M. R. Apted, and Ian Hodkinson, "Prestongrange and Its Painted Ceiling," part 3 of "The Paintings" (by Hodkinson), in *Transactions of the East Lothian Antiquarian and Field Naturalists' Society*, vol. 10 (Haddington, Scotland: East Lothian Antiquarian and Field Naturalists' Society, 1966), 35.

9. Ian Hodkinson, "Report and Estimate for Proposed Restoration of the Sixteenth-Century Painted Decorations in the Muses Room at Crathes Castle," unpublished report to National Trust for Scotland, 1967, 2, 3.

10. Act of Parliament (1, Jac I, c 20), as cited in Ian Bristow, *The Architect's Handmaid: Paint Colour in the Eighteenth-Century Interior*, catalogue of exhibition of Royal Institute of British Architects (London: RIBA, 1983), 8.

11. Richard M. Candee, "Materials Toward a History of Housepaints: The Materials and Craft of the Housepainter in Eighteenth Century America" (master's thesis, State University of New York, College at Oneonta, Cooperstown Graduate Programs, 1965), 119–21.

12. Catherine Lynn, "Colors and Other Materials of Historic Wallpaper," *Journal of the American Institute for Conservation of Historic and Artistic Works* 20, no. 2 (1981): 60–65.

13. Lynn, *Wallpaper in America from the Seventeenth Century to World War I* (New York: W. W. Norton, 1980), 41–51.

14. T. H. Vanherman, *Every Man His Own House-Painter and Colourman* (London, 1829), 59–61.

15. Anson Gilman, *Every Man His Own Painter* (Lewiston, Maine: Geo. A. Callahan, 1871), 14–16.

16. William E. Wall, *Graining, Ancient and Modern*, revised by F. N. Vanderwalker (New York: Drake Publishers, 1972; reprint), 141, 142.

17. Abbott Lowell Cummings, "Decorative Painters and House Painting at Massachusetts Bay, 1630–1725," in *American Painting to 1776: A Reappraisal* (Winterthur Conference Report, 1971) (Charlottesville, Va.: University Press of Virginia, 1971), 71–89.

18. Morgan W. Phillips, "Historic Finishes Analysis," in "Historic Structure Report, Morse-Libby Mansion, Portland, Maine," ed. Ann Beha Associates (unpublished report, 1989), 117–216.

19. The principal colorant in the bright green paint was identified by x-ray diffraction as copper chloride, or "Brunswick green," and that in the yellow paint as lead chromate, or chrome yellow. See Richard Newman, analytical report AL 85 24 (to SPNEA), Center for Conservation and Technical Studies, Fogg Art Museum, Harvard University, September 6, 1985.

20. Candee, "Materials," 32.

21. Ian Bristow, private communication, 1985.

22. Bristow, private communication, 1985.

23. Vanderwalker, 129.

24. Eugene Farrell and Amy Snodgrass, Analytical Report A 89.41, Center for Conservation and Technical Studies, Fogg Art Museum, June 19, 1989.

25. Morgan W. Phillips, "Experiences in the Use of Acrylic Plaster Adhesives," in *Case Studies in the Conservation of Stone and Wall Paintings, Preprints of the Contributions to the Bologna Congress, 21–26 September, 1986*, eds. N. S. Bromelle and Perry Smith (London: International Institute for the Conservation of Historic and Artistic Works, 1986), 34–37

26. M. F. Mecklenburg, "The Effects of Atmospheric Moisture on the Mechanical Properties of Collagen Under Equilibrium Conditions," in *Preprints of Papers Presented at the Sixteenth Annual Meeting, New Orleans, Louisiana, June 1–5, 1988* (Washington: American Institute for Conservation of Historic and Artistic Works, 1988), 231–44.

27. See Richard L. Kerschner, "A Practical Approach to Environmental Requirements for Collections in Historic Buildings," *Journal of the American Institute for Conservation of Historic and Artistic Works* 31, no. 1 (1992): 65–76.

28. Frank Preusser, private communication.

29. The formula used was 1 g. orthophenylphenol in a solution of 700 cc. isopropanol/300 cc. water. The importance of the water in this type of formulation is noted in Mary-Lou E. Florian, "Fungicide Treatment of Eskimo Skin and Fur Artifacts," *Journal of the International Institute for Conservation—Canadian Group* 2, no. 1 (1976): 13.

30. Vanderwalker, 118.

31. Franklin B. Gardner, *The Painters' Encyclopaedia* (New York: M. T. Richardson, 1887), 189.

32. Phillips, "Wallpaper on Walls: Problems of Climate and Substrate," *Journal of the American Institute for Conservation of Historic and Artistic Works* 20, no. 2 (1981): 85–86.

33. The use of swabs dampened with an aqueous cleaner is described in Charles H. Olin and Alexandra Riddleberger, "The Special Problems and Treatment of a Painting Executed in a Hot Glue Medium, 'The Public Garden' by Edouard Vuillard," in *Preprints of Papers Presented at the Eleventh Annual Meeting, Baltimore, Maryland, 25–29 May, 1983* (Washington, D.C.: American Institute for Conservation of Historic and Artistic Works, 1983), 102.

34. Robert L. Feller and Noel Kunz, "The Effect of Pigment Volume Concentration on the Lightness or Darkness of Porous Paints," in *Preprints of Papers Presented at the Ninth Annual Meeting, Philadelphia, Pennsylvania, May 27–31, 1981* (Washington, D.C.: American Institute for Conservation of Historic and Artistic Works, 1981), 66–74.

35. I am again indebted to the Smithsonian Institution, Carol Grissom in particular, for a computerized literature search. I also thank Faith Zieske of the Philadelphia Museum of Art for supplying the following reference, in which much more detail can be found about most of the consolidants and adhesives in this list, as well as other materials. "Consolidation/Fixing/Facing," Section 23 in *The Paper Conservation Catalog, AIC Book and Paper Group*, 5th ed. (Washington, D.C.: American Institute for Conservation of Historic and Artistic Works, 1988), 1–20. This article summarizes studies and practice by many conservators and reflects again the variety of materials used and advantages cited.

36. Robert L. Feller and M. Wilt, *Evaluation of Cellulose Ethers for Conservation*, Research in Conservation Series, no. 3. (Marina del Rey, Calif.: Getty Conservation Institute, 1990).

37. Olin and Riddleberger, 97, 101.

38. D. M. Burness and J. Pouradier, "The Hardening of Gelatin and Emulsions," in *The Theory of the Photographic Process*, ed. T. H. James, 4th ed. (New York: Macmillan, 1977), 77–87.

39. Pamela Hatchfield and Jane Carpenter, *Formaldehyde: How Great Is the Danger to Museum Collections?* (Cambridge, Mass.: Center for Conservation and Technical Studies, Harvard University Art Museums, 1987).

40. Sarah Wagner, "A Preliminary Study: Consolidation of Gelatin Glass Plate Negatives with Organosilanes," in *Topics in Photographic Preservation* 3 (Washington, D.C.: American Institute for Conservation/Photographic Materials Group, 1989), 69–85.

41. "Fluorad Fluorochemical Surfactant FC-120," technical data sheet, 3M Corporation, Commercial Chemicals Division, December 1983.

42. Elizabeth C. Welsh, "A Consolidation Treatment for Powdery Matte Paint," in *Preprints of Papers Presented at the Eighth Annual Meeting, San Francisco, California,* *May 22–25, 1980* (Washington, D.C.: American Institute for Conservation of Historic and Artistic Works, 1980), 141–50.

43. Elizabeth C. Welsh, private communication, 1989.

44. Eric F. Hansen, Michele R. Derrick, Michael Schilling, and Raphael Garcia, "The Effects of Solution Application on Some Mechanical and Physical Properties of Thermoplastic Amorphous Polymers Used in Conservation: Poly(vinyl Acetate)s," Journal of the American Institute for Conservation 30, no. 2. (1991): 203–13.

45. Tony Castro, private communication, 1989.

46. Vanderwalker, 118.

47. Candee, "Materials," 45–49.

48. Recent extensive research by the author into alkali-soluble acrylic resins has pointed to the possibility of their great utility in consolidating and replicating glue distemper paints. The research is directed mainly toward the development of consolidants for plaster and is being performed by the author under contract to the Getty Conservation Institute. A detailed publication on these resins and their possible applications in conservation is in progress.

"Analyzing Paint Samples,"
Andrea M. Gilmore

1. Joyce Plesters, "Cross-Sections and Chemical Analysis of Point Samples," *Studies in Conservation* 3 (April 1956), 137.

2. Morgan W. Phillips, "Discoloration of Old House Paints: Restoration of Paint Colors at the Harrison Gray Otis House, Boston," *Paint Color Research and Restoration of Historic Paint*, Association for Preservation Technology Publication Supplement (Ottawa: APT, 1977), 15.

3. Morgan W. Phillips, "Problems in the Restoration and Preservation of Old House Paints," in *Preservation and Conservation: Principles and Practices* (Washington, D.C.: Smithsonian Institution Press, for the National Trust for Historic Preservation,

1976), 275. As his source for this information Phillips cites Ruth M. Johnston and Robert Feller, "Optics of Paint Films: Glazes and Chalking," *Application of Science in Examination of Works of Art: Proceedings of a Seminar, September 7–16, 1965* (Boston: Museum of Fine Arts), 86–95.

4. Phillips, "Problems in the Restoration and Preservation of Old House Paints," 275.

"Pigments and Media,"
Eugene Farrell

The author wishes to thank Marlene Worhach for her research paper "'The Trout Brook' by Albert Bierstadt: A Technical Study," unpublished intern research report, Center for Conservation and Technical Studies, Harvard University Art Museums, 1990. All drawings are computer generated by the author.

1. Joyce Plesters, "Cross-Sections and Chemical Analysis of Paint Samples," *Studies in Conservation* 2, no. 3 (April 1956): 110–57.

2. E. E. Walstrom, *Optical Crystallography*, 2d ed. (New York: John Wiley and Sons, 1951).

3. W. C. McCrone and J. G. Delly, *The Particle Atlas* (Ann Arbor, Mich.: Ann Arbor Science Publishers, 1973), 3–114.

4. Robert L. Feller and M. Bayard, "Terminology and Procedures Used in the Systematic Examination of Pigment Particles with the Polarizing Microscope," in *Artists Pigments: A Handbook of Their History and Characteristics*, ed. Robert L. Feller (Washington, D.C.: National Gallery of Art, 1986).

5. McCrone and Delly, 72–74.

6. Walstrom, 69–92 and 143–73.

7. T. H. Behrens and P.D.C. Kley, *Organische Mikrochemische Analyse*, (Leipzig: Leopalk Voss, 1922). Translated by R. E. Stephens as *Microscopal Identification of Organic Compounds* (Chicago: Microscope Publications, 1969).

8. Emile M. Chamot and C. W. Mason, *Handbook of Chemical Microscopy*, vols. 1 and 2 (New York: John Wiley and Sons, 1958).

9. Alexander Eibner, "L'examen microchimique des agglutinauts," in *Moaseion* 20 (1932): 5–22.

10. Rutherford J. Gettens and George L. Stout, *Painting Materials: A Short Encyclopedia* (New York: Dover Publications, 1966).

11. Lyde S. Pratt, *The Chemistry and Physics of Organic Pigments*, 7th ed. (Amsterdam, London, and New York: Elsevier, 1966).

12. Fritz Feigl, *Spot Tests in Organic Analysis* (1937).

13. Plesters, 110–57.

14. Fred W. Billmeyer et al., "Pigment Analysis for Conservation" [conference preprint], Science and Technology in the Service of Conservation Conference, Washington, D.C., September 1982 (London: International Institute for Conservation of Historic and Artistic Works, 1982), 177–79.

15. Paul Whitemore, Appendix to *Mark Rothko's Harvard Murals*, ed. M. Cohn (Cambridge: Center for Conservation and Technical Studies, Harvard University Art Museums, 1988), 61–62.

16. H. Schweepe, "Nachweis von Farbstoffen auf alten Textilien," *Zeitschrift für Analytische Chemie*. 276 (1975): 291–96.

17. R. M. Barnes, *Emission Spectroscopy* (New York: Halsted Press, John Wiley and Sons, 1976).

18. L. Stodulski, "The Use of the Emission Spectrograph in the Conservation Laboratory," *Bulletin of the American Institute for Conservation* 15 (1975): 66–92.

19. J. Zussman, "X-Ray Diffraction," in *Physical Methods in Determinative Mineralogy*, ed. J. Zussman, 2d ed. (London, New York, and San Francisco: Academic Press, 1977), 391–473.

20. B. D. Cullity, *Elements of X-Ray Diffraction* (Reading, Mass.: Addison-Wesley, 1956).

21. H. P. Klug and L. E. Alexander, *X-Ray Diffraction Procedures* (New York: John Wiley and Sons, 1954).

22. L. V. Azaroff and M. J. Berger, *The Powder Method in X-Ray Crystallography* (New York: McGraw Hill, 1958).

23. C. S. Hurlbut and C. Klein, *Manual of Mineralogy,* 19th ed. (New York: John Wiley and Sons, 1977).

24. R. Ogolvie, "Applications of the Solid State X-Ray Detector to the Study of Art Objects," in *Application of Science in Examination of Works of Art* (Boston: Museum of Fine Arts, 1970), 84–87.

25. E. Atil, W. T. Chase, and P. Jett, "Notes Concerning the X-Ray Fluorescence Analysis" [appendix 1], in *Islamic Metalwork in the Freer Gallery of Art* (Washington, D.C.: Smithsonian Institution, 1985), 257–64.

26. V. F. Hanson, "Quantitative Elemental Analysis of Art Objects by Energy-Dispersive X-ray Fluorescence Spectroscopy," *Applied Spectroscopy* 27, no. 5 (1973): 309–34.

27. J. J. Hren et al, *Introduction to Analytical Electron Microscopy* (New York: Plenum Press, 1979).

28. J. I. Goldstein et al., *Scanning Electron Microscopy* (New York and London: Plenum Press, 1981).

29. D. Stulik and E. Doehne, "Applications of Environmental Scanning Electron Microscopy in Art Conservation and Archaeology," in *Materials Issues in Art and Archaeology,* Symposium Proceedings, vol. 185 (Pittsburgh: Materials Research Society, 1991), 23–29.

30. M. T. Baker and D. W. von Endt, "Use of FTIR-Microspectrometry in Examinations of Artistic and Historic Works," in *Materials Issues in Art and Archaeology,* ed. E. Sayre et al. (Pittsburgh: Materials Research Society, 1988), 71–76.

31. K. Krishnan and S. L. Hill, "FT-IR Microsampling Techniques," in *Practical Fourier Transform Infrared Spectroscopy,* ed. J. R. Ferraro and K. Krishnan (San Diego and New York: Academic Press, 1990), 103–65.

32. M. Baker, D. von Endt, W. Hopwood, and D. Erhardt, "FT-IR Microspectrometry: A Powerful Conservation Analysis Tool,"

in *AIC Preprints of the Sixteenth Meeting, New Orleans, June 1988* (Washington, D.C.: American Institute for Conservation of Historic and Artistic Works, 1988), 1–13.

33. R. J. Meilunas, J. G. Bentsen, and A. Steinberg, "Analysis of Aged Paint Binders by FTIR Spectroscopy," *Studies in Conservation* 35 (1990): 33–51.

34. M.J.D. Low and N. S. Baer, "Application of Infrared Fourier Transform Spectroscopy to Problems in Conservation," *Studies in Conservation* 22 (1977): 116–28.

35. Richard Newman, "Some Applications of Infrared Spectroscopy in the Examination of Painting Materials," *Journal of the American Institute of Conservation* 19 (1980): 42–62.

36. M. R. Derrick, J. M. Landry, and D. C. Stulik, Methods in Scientific Examination of Works of Art: Infrared Microspectroscopy (Los Angeles: Getty Conservation Institute, 1991).

37. Liliane Masschelein-Kleiner, J. Heylen, and F. Tricot-Marckx, "Contribution Á L'Analyse Des Liants, Adhésifs et Vernis Anciens," *Studies in Conservation* 13 (1968): 105–21.

38. Liliane Masschelein-Kleiner, "Analysis of Paint Media Varnishes and Adhesives," in *Scientific Examination of Easel Paintings,* ed. R. van Schaute and H. Verougstraete-Marco, Pact 13 (Strasbourg: 1986), 185–206.

39. John S. Mills and Raymond White, *Organic Chemistry of Museum Objects* (London: Butterworths, 1987).

40. Mills and White, 141–58.

41. Wilhelm, Ostwald (trans. H. Zeishold), "Iconoscopic Studies, 1. Microscopic Identification of Homogeneous Binding Mediums," *Technical Studies* 4 (1935): 135–44.

42. Arthur P. Laurie, *Pigments and Mediums of the Old Masters* (New York: Macmillan, 1914), 153.

43. Rutherford J. Gettens, "Identification of Pigments and Media" (unpublished notebooks of Rutherford John Gettens) (Cambridge, Mass.: Center for Conservation and Technical Studies, Harvard University Art Museums).

44. R. H. de Silva, "The Problem of Binding Medium Particularly in Wall Painting," *Archaeometry* 6 (1963): 5–62.

45. De Silva, 56–64.

46. Richard Wolbers and Gregory Landry, "The Use of Direct Reactive Fluorescent Dyes for the Characterization of Binding Media in Cross Sectional Examinations" (Washington, D.C.: American Institute for Conservation Preprints, 1987), 168–202.

47. Meryl Johnson and Elisabeth Packard, "Methods Used for the Identification of Binding Media in Italian Paintings of the Fifteenth–Sixteenth Centuries," *Studies in Conservation* 16 (1971): 145–64.

48. Elizabeth Martin, "Some Improvements in Techniques of Analysis of Paint Media," *Studies in Conservation* 22 (1977): 63–67.

49. R. Talbot, "The Fluorescent Antibody Technique in the Identification of Proteinaceous Materials," in *Papers Presented by Conservation Students at the Third Annual Conference of Art Conservation Training Programmes* (Ontario: Queens University, 1982), 140.

"A Survey of Paint Technology," Morgan W. Phillips

1. Therald Moeller et al., *Chemistry, with Inorganic Qualitative Analysis* (New York: Academic Press, 1980), 7, 8.

2. *Webster's New Collegiate Dictionary* (Springfield, Mass.: G. C. Merriam Company, 1976), 667.

3. Robert S. Boynton, *Chemistry and Technology of Lime and Limestone,* 2d ed. (New York: John Wiley and Sons, 1980), 2, 192–94.

4. Boynton, 10–11.

5. Boynton, 169.

6. Michael Fortin, private communication, 1989.

7. George Troxell, Harmer Davis, and Joe Kelly, *Composition and Properties of Concrete* (New York: McGraw Hill, 1968), 27.

8. Geoffrey Frohnsdorff, "Portland Cements, Blended Cements and Mortars," in *Encyclopaedia of Materials Science and Engineering,* ed. M. Bever (New York: Pergamon, 1986), 3849.

9. Henry Carey Baird, *The Painter, Gilder, and Varnisher's Companion* (Philadelphia: Henry Carey Baird, 1873), 21, 22.

10. Giorgio Torraca, *Solubility and Solvents for Conservation Problems* (Rome: International Centre for the Study of the Preservation and the Restoration of Cultural Property, 1975), 6–8.

11. Feller explains some of the confusing ways in which the related terms *resin* and *polymer* are used. In my chapter *resin* is used to mean any of a wide variety of materials, natural or synthetic, water-soluble or water-insoluble, that are or can form a polymeric solid with certain physical properties. See Robert L. Feller, Nathan Stolow, and Elizabeth Jones, *On Picture Varnishes and Their Solvents,* rev. enlarged ed. (Washington, D.C.: National Gallery of Art, 1985), 119.

12. Richard E. Dickerson and Irving Geis, *The Structure and Action of Proteins* (Menlo Park, Calif.: W. A. Benjamin, 1969), 40.

13. O. F. Hutchinson and C. L. Pearson, "Animal Glues and Gelatins," in *Protein Binders in Paper and Paperboard Coating,* ed. R. Strauss, TAPPI Monograph no. 36 (Atlanta: Technical Association of the Pulp and Paper Industry, 1975), 101.

14. Richard Wolbers, private communication concerning analysis of wall paint from the drawing room of Lansdowne House.

15. Morgan W. Phillips, "The Repainting: Materials and Colors," in "Drawing Room from Lansdowne House," *Bulletin of the Philadelphia Museum of Art* (Summer 1986): 47–51.

16. *The Practical Dentist* (Portsmouth, N.H.), November 15, 1854.

17. Feller, Stolow, and Jones, 155–59. This work includes authoritative studies of various acrylic resins for conservation.

18. Phillips, "Problems in the Restoration and Preservation of Old House Paints," *Preservation and Conservation: Principles and Practices* (Washington, D.C.: Smithsonian Institution Press, for the National Trust for Historic Preservation, 1976), 273–85.

19. Robert D. Mussey, "Early Varnishes," *Fine Woodworking* 35 (July-August 1982): 54–57. This article describes the ingredients and characteristics of eighteenth-century varnishes.

20. Hezekiah Reynolds, *Directions for House and Ship Painting,* facsimile reprint of the 1812 edition with an introduction by Richard M. Candee (Worcester, Mass.: American Antiquarian Society, 1978), 13.

21. James R. Blegen, *Alkyd Resins,* Federation Series on Coatings Technology, unit 5 (Philadelphia: Federation of Societies for Coatings Technology, 1967), 7.

22. Henry Lee and Kris Neville, *Handbook of Epoxy Resins* (New York: McGraw-Hill, 1967).

23. Gunther Oertel, *Polyurethane Handbook,* (New York: Danser, 1985).

24. Feller, 218.

25. Wayne R. Fuller, *Formation and Structure of Paint Films,* Federation Series on Coatings Technology, unit 2 (Philadelphia: Federation of Societies for Paint Technology, 1965), 16–17.

26. Frank B. Morrison, *Feeds and Feeding,* 9th ed., abridged (Clinton, Iowa: Morrison Publishing Company, 1961), 377.

27. Rutherford J. Gettens, *Painting Materials: A Short Encyclopaedia* (New York: Dover, 1966; reprint of 1942 work), 8.

28. F. P. Nabenhauer, "Manufacture of Casein," in *Protein and Synthetic Adhesives for Paper Coating,* TAPPI Monograph Series no. 9 (New York: Technical Association of the Pulp and Paper Industry, 1952), 14.

29. F. N. Vanderwalker, *Interior Wall Decoration* (Chicago: Frederick J. Drake, 1924), 118.

30. Harold K. Salzberg and William L. Marino, "Casein in Coating Paper and Paperboard," in *Protein Binders in Paper and Paperboard Coating,* ed. R. Strauss, TAPPI Monograph Series no. 36 (Atlanta: Technical Association of the Pulp and Paper Industry, 1975), 35.

31. Salzberg and Marino, 40.

32. Robert S. Radcliffe, "Casein Paints," in *Protective and Decorative Coatings,* vol. 3, ed. Joseph Matiello (New York: John Wiley and Sons, 1943), 465.

33. Richard M. Candee, "Materials Toward a History of Housepaints: The Materials and Craft of the Housepainter in Eighteenth-Century America" (master's thesis, State University of New York, College at Oneonta, 1965), 123–28.

34. Richardd M. Candee, "The Rediscovery of Milk-based House Paints and the Myth of 'Brickdust and Buttermilk' Paints," *Old-Time New England* 58, no. 3 (Winter 1968): 79–81.

35. *New England Farmer,* September 19, 1828.

36. *New England Farmer,* September 19, 1828.

37. Henry Carey Baird, 97, 98.

38. I am indebted to Roger Reed for the opportunity to interview Mr. Ferson.

39. Morrison, *Feeds,* table 1.

40. Radcliffe, 464.

41. Candee, "Materials," 126.

42. Radcliffe, 468.

43. Salzberg and Marino, 33.

**"Historic and Modern Oil Paints,"
Richard Newman**

1. Richard M. Candee, Introduction to *Directions for House and Ship Painting; Shewing in a plain and concise manner, The Best Method of Preparing, Mixing, and Laying the Various Colours Now in Use, Designed for the Use of Learners,* by Hezekiah Reynolds (1812. Reprint. Worcester, Mass.: American Antiquarian Society, 1978).

2. J. J. Mattiello, ed., *Protective and Decorative Coatings* (New York: Wiley, 1941–43), 3:271.

3. Mattiello, 1:34.

4. Robert Mussey, "Transparent Furniture Varnishes in New England, 1700–1820: A Documentary Study," in *Canadian Conservation Institute Proceedings of the Furniture and Wooden Objects Symposium, July 2–3, 1980* (Ottawa: Canadian Conservation Institute, 1980), 77–101.

5. See, for example, J. G. Bearn, *The Chemistry of Paints, Pigments, and Varnishes* (London: Ernest Benn, 1923). See also Candee, "Materials Toward a History of House Paints: The Materials and Craft of the Housepainter in Eighteenth Century America" (M.A. thesis, State University of New York, College at Oneonta, 1965), 117–18; and Theodore Z. Penn, "Decorative and Protective Finishes 1750–1850: Materials, Process, and Craft" (M.A. Thesis, University of Delaware, 1966), 59ff. Portions of Candee's thesis were published in abbreviated form as "Housepaints in Colonial America," *Color Engineering* 4, no. 5 (1966): 26–29, 32–34; 4, no. 6 (1966): 24–26, 30; 5, no.1 (1967): 24–26; 5, no. 2 (1967): 32–42.

6. Candee, "Materials and Craft," 35

7. Reynolds, *Directions,* 7–8, 13–14.

8. Candee, "Materials and Craft," 117–18.

9. Mattiello, 1:16–21.

10. Bearn, 184ff.

11. Reynolds, *Directions,* 13.

12. Mattiello, 1:1–8.

13. Mussey, "Early Varnishes: The Eighteenth Century's Search for the Perfect Film Finish," *Fine Woodworking* 35 (July-August 1982): 54–57.

14. Morgan W. Phillips, "Discoloration of Old House Paints: Restoration of Paint Colors at the Harrison Gray Otis House, Boston," *Association for Preservation Technology Bulletin* 3 (1971): 40–47.

15. Candee, "Materials and Craft," 40–41.

16. Paolo Mora, Laura Mora, and Paul Philippot, *Conservation of Wall Paintings* (London: Butterworths, 1984), 158–59.

17. For a brief note on his technique, see Holly Hotchner, Robert Sawchuck, and Paula Volent, "The Conservation of an Oil/Encaustic-on-Canvas Mural: The Ascension by John La Farge, 1886/88," papers presented at the seventeenth annual meeting of the American Institute for Conservation [Abstracts], Cincinnati, Ohio, May 31–June 4, 1989 (Washington, D.C.: 1989), 9–11.

18. The chemistry of oils is described in detail in several chapters of D. Swern, ed., *Bailey's Industrial Oil and Fat Products,* 4th ed., 2 vols. (New York: John Wiley and Sons, 1979–82).

19. Mattiello, 1:65–66.

20. Mussey, "Early Varnishes," 56–57.

21. For reviews of the history of use and chemistry of resins, see John S. Mills and Raymond White, *The Organic Chemistry of Museum Objects* (London: Butterworths, 1987), 83–110; and John S. Mills and Raymond White, "Natural Resins of Art and Archaeology: Their Sources, Chemistry, and Identification," *Studies in Conservation* 22 (1977): 12–31.

22. Mussey, "Transparent Furniture Varnishes," 90.

23. Penn, 78ff.

24. N. Heaton, *Volatile Solvents and Thinners* (London: Ernest Benn, 1925), 17.

25. Reynolds, *Directions,* 7, 13.

26. Bearn, 238; Candee, "Materials and Craft," 115–16.

27. See Swern.

28. The bibliography has appeared in several parts: Norbert S. Baer and Norman Indictor, "Linseed Oil and Related Materials: An Annotated Bibliography," *Art and Archaeology Technical Abstracts* 9, no. 1 (1972): 153–240, and no. 2 (1972): 159–241; and *Art and Archaeology Technical Abstracts* 10, no. 1 (1973): 155–256. Additional parts have appeared as "Lipids and Works of Art," *Proceedings of the 13th International Society for Fat Research Congress* (Marseille, 1976), 17–31; and *Proceedings of the 14th International Society for Fat Research Congress* (Brighton, 1978), 31–49.

29. P. O. Powers, "Mechanism of the Oxidation of Drying Oils," *Industrial and Engineering Chemistry* 41 (1949): 304–9.

30. E. R. Mueller and Clara D. Smith, "Effects of Driers on Linseed Oil and Varnish Films," *Industrial and Engineering Chemistry* 49 (1957): 210–19.

31. Leif E. Plahter, E. Skaug, and Unn Plahter, *Medieval Art in Norway.* Vol. I, *Gothic Painted Altar Frontals from the Church of Tingelstad: Materials, Technique, Restoration* (Oslo: Universitetsforlaget, 1974). An abbreviated version of this research is available: Leif E. Plahter and Unn Plahter, "The Technique of a Group of Norwegian Gothic Oil Paintings," in *Conservation and Restoration of Pictorial Art,* eds. Norman Brommelle and Perry Smith (London: Butterworths, 1976), 36–42. Analytical evidence suggests that the binder is actually a mixture of drying oil and protein (perhaps egg), rather than a drying oil alone.

32. Robert L. Feller, Nathan Stolow, and Elizabeth H. Jones, *On Picture Varnishes and Their Solvents* (1971. Reprint. Washington, D.C.: National Gallery of Art, 1985), 47–116.

33. For one application of this test, see Hermann Kühn, "A Study of the Pigments and the Grounds Used by Jan Vermeer," *Report and Studies in the History of Art* (Washington, D.C.: National Gallery of Art, 1968), 155–202.

34. Dusan Stulik and Henry Florsheim, "Binding Media Identification in Painted Ethnographic Objects," *Journal of the American Institute for Conservation* 31 (1992): 275–88, particularly 276–77.

35. Lack of complete reaction with a basic solution was used to suggest the possible presence of resin by Paul Coremans, Rutherford J. Gettens, and Jean Thissen, "La technique des 'Primitifs flamands,'" *Studies in Conservation* 1 (1952): 1–29. If resin is present, it can often be extracted from a chip of paint with strong solvents, such as acetone or chloroform, leaving a ring of transparent material behind that fluoresces in ultraviolet light; this test was used by Joyce Plesters, "Cross-sections and Chemical Analysis of Paint Samples," *Studies in Conservation* 2 (1955–56): 130.

36. Elisabeth Martin, "Some Improvements in Techniques of Analysis of Paint Media," *Studies in Conservation* 22 (1977): 63–67.

37. There are numerous articles in the conservation literature on the use of such stains. For one discussion of the preparation and application of these, see Meryl Johnson and Elizabeth Packard, "Methods Used for the Identification of Binding Media in Italian Paintings of the Fifteenth and Sixteenth Centuries," *Studies in Conservation* 16 (1971): 145–64.

38. Richard Wolbers and Gregory Landrey, "The Use of Direct Reactive Fluorescent Dyes for the Characterization of Binding Media in Cross-Sectional Examination," preprints of papers presented at the fifteenth annual meeting, American Institute for Conservation, Vancouver, British Columbia, May 20–24, 1987, 168–202.

39. Wolbers and Landrey, 178.

40. Michelle Derrick, "Fourier Transform Infrared Spectral Analysis of Natural Resins Used in Furniture Varnishes," *Journal of the American Institute for Conservation* 28 (1989): 43–56.

41. Mary V. Orna, Patricia L. Lang, J. E. Katon, Thomas F. Matthews, and Robert S. Nelson, "Application of Infrared Microspectroscopy to Art Historical Questions about Medieval Manuscripts," in *Archaeological Chemistry IV,* ed. Ralph O. Allen (Washington, D.C.: American Chemical Society, 1989), 265–88.

42. For gas chromatographic analysis of paint samples, see Mills and White, *Organic Chemistry,* 141–46.

43. Mills and White, *Organic Chemistry,* 144–46, 149–52.

44. An excellent general review of the mechanical properties of paint films is Sheldon Keck, "Mechanical Alteration of the Paint Film," *Studies in Conservation* 14 (1969): 9–30.

45. Morgan W. Phillips and Brian Powell, "Several Experiences Using Lime Paste as a Cleaning Agent for Oil Paint," *Association for Preservation Technology Bulletin* 14, no. 2 (1982): 31–33.

46. This general definition of the functions of conservation is a common one although there are variations in specific definitions of the functions. For a discussion of these terms, although in a context unrelated to architectural treatments, see Arthur Beale, "The Varying Role of the Conservator in the Care of Outdoor Monuments," *Sculptural Monuments in an Outdoor Environment,* Virginia N. Naudé, ed. (Philadelphia: Pennsylvania Academy of Fine Arts, 1985), 39–50.

47. One complex example, involving transfer of the original paintings, is Ian Hodkinson, "Conservation and Transfer of an Early 19th Century Painted Room," *Association for Preservation Technology Bulletin* 14 (1982): 17–35.

48. For other discussions of the uses of such "replication" paints, see Morgan W. Phillips, "Acrylic Paints for Restoration: Three Test Applications," *Association for Preservation Technology Bulletin* 15, no. 2 (1983): 3–11, and "Problems in the Restoration and Preservation of Old House Paints," *Preservation and Conservation: Principles and Practices* (Washington, D.C.: Smithsonian Institution for the National Trust for Historic Preservation, 1976), 273–85.

BIBLIOGRAPHY

Albee, Peggy A. "A Study of Historic Paint Colors and the Effects of the Environmental Exposures on Their Colors and Their Pigments." *Association for Preservation Technology Bulletin* 16, nos. 3 and 4 (1984): 3–25.

———. "Technology Trends: Hue & Pry ... to Determine an Historic Property's True Colors." *Technology and Conservation* 7, no. 4 (1982): 5–8.

Allen, Edward B. *Early American Wall Painting 1710–1850*. New Haven, Conn.: Yale University Press, 1926.

Allen, Eugene. "Paint Color Research and House Painting Practices." *Association for Preservation Technology Newsletter* 1, no. 2 (1969): 5–19.

Barker, Virgil. *American Painting: History and Interpretation*. New York: Macmillan, 1950.

Barr, James K. "Commentary." In *Preservation and Conservation: Principles and Practices*, 304–6. Proceedings of the North American International Region Conference, Williamsburg, Va., and Philadelphia, September 10–16, 1976. Washington, D.C.: Smithsonian Institution Press for the National Trust for Historic Preservation.

Batcheler, Penelope Hartshorne. "Commentary." In *Preservation and Conservation: Principles and Practices*, 300–303. Proceedings of the North American International Regional Conference, Williamsburg, Va., and Philadelphia, September 10–16, 1972. Washington, D.C.: Smithsonian Institution Press for the National Trust for Historic Preservation, 1976.

———. "Paint Color Research and Restoration." Technical Leaflet, no. 15. *History News* 23, no. 10 (1968).

Bearn, J. G. *The Chemistry of Paints, Pigments, and Varnishes*. London: Ernest Benn, 1923.

Benes, Peter. *New England Meeting House and Church: 1630–1850*. Vol. 4, The Dublin Seminar for New England Folklife: Annual Proceedings, June 26 and 27, 1979. Boston: Boston University, 1980.

Bolger, William C. *The John Lucas and Company Paint and Varnish Works*. Gibbsboro, N.J., 1982.

Bristow, Ian. *The Architect's Handmaid: Paint Colour in the Eighteenth-Century Interior* [exhibition catalogue]. London: Royal Institute of British Architects, 1983.

———. "Repainting Eighteenth-Century Interiors." *Transactions of the Association for Studies in the Conservation of Historic Buildings* 6 (1981): 25–33.

Brommelle, Norman S. "Colour and Conservation." *Studies in Conservation* 2, no. 2 (1955): 76–85.

Brommelle, Norman S., and Perry Smith, eds. *Case Studies in the Conservation of Stone and Wall Painting*. Preprints of the Contributions to the Bologna Congress, September 21–26, 1986. London: International Institute for the Conservation of Historic and Artistic Works, 1986.

Bullock, Helen Duprey. "Paint Color and Whitewash in Williamsburg and Virginia." Research Report Series, no. 132. Colonial Williamsburg Foundation Library, Williamsburg, Va., 1932. Bound photocopy.

Butler, Marigene. "Polarized Light Microscopy in the Conservation of Painting." Reprinted from the Centennial Volume, State Microscopical Society of Illinois, 1970.

Candee, Richard M. *Housepaints in Colonial America: Their Materials, Manufacture, and Application*. Compilation of a four-part article appearing in *Color Engineering*: vol. 4, no. 5 (1966): 26–29, 32–34; vol. 4, no. 6 (1966): 24–26, 30; vol. 5, no. 1 (1967): 24–26; vol. 5, no. 2 (1967): 32–42. New York: Chromatic Publishing Company, 1967.

———. "The Rediscovery of Milk-Based House Paints and the Myth of 'Brickdust and Buttermilk' Paints." *Old-Time New England* 58, no. 3 (1968): 79–81.

Canning, John. "Covering-Encapsulating Decorative Wall Treatments to Ensure Long-term Preservation Options." In *The Interiors Handbook for Historic Buildings*, vol. 2, edited by Michael Auer, Charles E. Fisher, Thomas Jester, and Marilyn Kaplan, 6-23–6-27. Washington, D.C.: Historic Preservation Education Foundation, 1993.

Chamot, Emile Monnin, and Clyde Walter Mason. *Handbook of Chemical Microscopy*. 2 vols. Vol. 1, New York: John Wiley and Sons, 1983. Vol. 2, Chicago: McCrone Research Institute, 1989.

Chappell, Edward A. "Architects of Colonial Williamsburg." In *Encyclopedia of Southern Culture*, edited by Charles Reagan Wilson and William Ferris, 59–61. Oxford, Miss.: Center for the Study of Southern Culture, University of Mississippi Press, 1989.

Chevreul, Michel Eugène. *The Principles of Harmony and Contrast of Colors and Their Applications to the Arts*. Based on the first English edition, 1854 and translated from the first French edition, 1839. New York: Van Nostrand Reinhold, 1967.

Condit, Charles L., and Jacob Schelle. *Painting and Painters' Materials*. New York, 1883.

Cummings, Abbott Lowell. "Decorative Painters and House Painting at Massachusetts Bay, 1630–1725." In *American Painting to 1776: A Reappraisal*, edited by Ian M. G. Quimby, Winterthur Conference Report 1971. Charlottesville: University Press of Virginia, 1971.

Davis, Alexander Jackson. *Rural Residences*. New York, 1837.

de la Rie, E. Rene. "Fluorescence of Paint and Varnish Layers." Parts 1–3. *Studies in Conservation* 27, no. 1 (1982): 1–7; no. 2 (1982): 65–69; no. 3 (1982): 102–8.

Doerner, Max. *The Materials of the Artist and Their Use in Painting, with Notes on the Techniques of the Old Masters.* Translated by Eugen Neuhaus. 1934. New York: Harcourt Brace Jovanovich, 1962.

Doonan, Nancy Locke. "Historic Exterior Paints: Guidelines for Establishing Whether a Sample Contains a Layer Original to the Building's Construction." *Association for Preservation Technology Bulletin* 14, no. 2 (1982): 26–29.

Dornsife, Samuel J., ed. *Exterior Decoration, Victorian Paint for Victorian Houses.* Reprint of 1885 F. W. Devoe and Company counter top display book. Philadelphia: The Athenaeum of Philadelphia, 1976.

Dossie, Robert. *The Handmaid to the Arts.* London: J. Nourse, 1758.

Downing, Andrew Jackson. *The Architecture of Country Houses.* New York, 1850.

————. *Cottage Residences.* New York, 1842.

Downs, Arthur Channing, Jr. "The Introduction of American Zinc Paints, ca. 1850." *Association for Preservation Technology Bulletin* 6, no. 2 (1974): 36–37.

————. "Zinc for Paint and Architectural Use in the Nineteenth Century." *Association for Preservation Technology Bulletin* 8, no. 4 (1976): 80–99.

Eiseman, Alberta. "A Painter's Passion: Connecticut's Ornate Capitol Inspired Painter John Canning's Reverent Three-Year Restoration." *Historic Preservation* 41, no. 2 (1989): 22–27.

England, Pamela A., and Lambertus van Zelst. "A Technical Investigation of Some Seventeenth Century New England Portrait Paintings." In *Preprints of Papers Presented at the Tenth Annual Meeting, American Institute for Conservation, Milwaukee, Wisconsin, 26–30 May, 1982,* 85–95. Washington, D.C.: American Institute for Conservation, 1982.

Faloon, Dalton B. *Zinc Oxide: History, Manufacture, and Properties as a Pigment.* New York: D. Van Nostrand Company, 1925.

Feller, Robert L. "Analysis of Pigments." In *American Painting to 1776: A Reappraisal,* edited by Ian M. G. Quimby. Winterthur Conference Report 1971. Charlottesville: University Press of Virginia, 1971.

————. "The Deterioration of Organic Substances and the Analysis of Paints and Varnishes." In *Preservation and Conservation: Principles and Practices,* 287-99. Proceedings of the North American International Regional Conference, Williamsburg, Va., and Philadelphia, September 10–16, 1972. Washington, D.C: Smithsonian Institution Press for the National Trust for Historic Preservation, 1976.

————. "Scientific Examination of Artistic and Decorative Colorants." *Journal of Paint Technology* 44, no. 566 (1971): 51–58.

Feller, Robert L., ed. *Artists' Pigments: A Handbook of Their History and Characteristics..* Washington, D.C.: National Gallery of Art, 1986.

Feller, Robert L., Nathan Stolow, and Elizabeth H. Jones. *On Picture Varnishes and Their Solvents.* 1959. Cleveland, Ohio: Case Western Reserve University Press, 1971.

Fischer, William von, ed. *Paint and Varnish Technology.* 2d ed. New York: Reinhold Publishing Company, 1950.

Flynt, William A., and Joseph Peter Sprang. "Exterior Architectural Embellishments." *The Magazine Antiques* 127, no. 3 (1985): 632–39.

Fram, Mark. *Well-Preserved: The Ontario Heritage Foundation's Manual of Principles and Practice for Architectural Conservation.* Ontario: Boston Mills Press, 1988.

Gagne, Cole. "Glossary of Historic Paints." *Old-House Journal* 14, no. 4 (1986): 178–79.

Gardner, F.B. *Everybody's Paint Book.* New York, 1886.

Gardner, Henry Alfred, and George G. Sward. *Physical and Chemical Examinations of Paints, Varnishes, Lacquers, and Colors.* Washington, D.C.: Institute of Paint and Varnish Research, 1946.

Gettens, Rutherford J. "Malachite and Green Verditer." *Studies in Conservation* 19 (1974): 2–23.

Gettens, Rutherford J., Robert L. Feller, and W. Thomas Chase. "Vermilion and Cinnabar." *Studies in Conservation* 17 (1972): 45–69.

Gettens, Rutherford J., and Elisabeth W. FitzHugh. "Azurite and Blue Verditer." *Studies in Conservation* 11 (1966): 54–61.

Gettens, Rutherford J., Elisabeth W. FitzHugh, and Robert L. Feller. "Calcium Carbonate Whites." *Studies in Conservation* 19 (1974): 157–84.

Gettens, Rutherford J., Hermann Kühn, and W. Thomas Chase. "Lead White." *Studies in Conservation* 12 (1967): 125–39.

Gettens, Rutherford J., and George L. Stout. *Painting Materials: A Short Encyclopedia.* 1942. New York: Dover Publications, 1966.

"A Glossary of Painted Finishes." *Old-House Journal* 16, no. 1 (1988): 34–37.

Goodwin, W.A.R. "The Restoration of Colonial Williamsburg." *The National Geographic Magazine* 71, no. 4 (1937).

Green, Teresa Osterman. "The Birth of the Paint Industry." Master's thesis, University of Delaware, 1975.

Greiff, Constance M. *John Notman, Architect, 1810-1865.* Philadelphia: The Athenaeum of Philadelphia, 1979.

Harley, Rosamund D. *Artists' Pigments c. 1600–1835: A Study in English Documentary Sources.* 2d ed. London: Butterworths, 1982.

Hasluck, Paul N., ed. *The Book of Photography.* London, 1905.

Hawkes, Pamela W. "Economical Painting: The Tools and Techniques Used in Exterior Painting in the Nineteenth Century." In *The Technology of Historic American Buildings: Studies of the Materials, Craft Processes, and the Mechanization of Building Construction,* edited by Ward Jandl. Washington, D.C.: Foundation for Preservation Technology, 1983.

———. "Paints for Architectural Cast Iron." *Association for Preservation Technology Bulletin* 11, no. 1 (1979): 17–36.

Heckel, George B. *The Paint Industry.* St. Louis, Mo., 1931.

Hodkinson, Ian. "Conservation and Transfer of an Early Nineteenth-Century Painted Room." *Association for Preservation Bulletin* 14, no. 1 (1982): 17–35.

Holley, Clifford Dyer. *Analysis of Paint Vehicles, Japans, and Varnishes.* New York: John Wiley and Sons, 1920.

Holm, Bill. "Old Photos Might Not Lie, but They Fib a Lot about Color," *American Indian Art Magazine* 10 (Autumn 1985): 44-49.

Hosmer, Charles B., Jr. "Williamsburg and the American Preservation Movement, 1926–1949." Talk given at Principia College, Elsah, Ill., November 12, 1976. Colonial Williamsburg Foundation Library, Williamsburg, Va. Photocopy of edited manuscript.

Keck, Sheldon. "Mechanical Alteration of the Paint Film." *Studies in Conservation* 14 (1969): 9–30.

Kocher, A. Lawrence. "Color in Early American Architecture, with Special Reference to the Origin and Development of House Painting." *Architectural Record* 64 (October 1928): 278–90.

Kocher, A. Lawrence, and Howard Dearstyne. "Approved Methods of Restoration at Colonial Williamsburg." Research Report Series, no. 12. Colonial Williamsburg Foundation Library, Williamsburg, Va., 1949. Bound photocopy.

———. "Architectural Report, Barraud House." Colonial Williamsburg Foundation Library, Williamsburg, Va., April 1949. Bound typescript.

Kühn, Hermann. "Lead-tin Yellow." *Studies in Conservation* 13 (1968): 7–33.

———. "Verdigris and Copper Resinate." *Studies in Conservation* 15 (1970): 12–36.

Laurie, Arthur P. *The Materials of the Painter's Craft in Europe from the Earliest Times to the Seventeenth Century with Some Accounts of Their Preparation and Use.* Edinburgh: T. N. Foulis, 1910.

———. *The Painter's Methods and Materials.* 1926. New York: Dover Publications, 1967.

———. *The Pigments and Mediums of the Old Masters.* London: Macmillan, 1914

Little, Nina Fletcher. *American Decorative Wall Painting, 1700–1850.* New York: Studio Publications, 1952. New York: E. P. Dutton, 1972.

Loudon, John Claudius. *Encyclopedia of Cottage, Farm, and Villa Architecture and Furniture.* London, 1833; New York, 1849.

Lounsbury, Carl R. "A Brief Architectural History of the Dr. Barraud House." Colonial Williamsburg Foundation Library, Williamsburg, Va., July 1988. Bound typescript.

———. *A Glossary of Early Southern Architecture and Landscape.* Oxford: Oxford University Press, 1993.

Loth, Calder. "A Mid-Nineteenth Century Color Scheme." *Association for Preservation Technology Bulletin* 9, no. 2 (1977): 83–88.

MacDougall, Elisabeth B., and George B. Tatum, eds. *Prophet with Honor: The Career of Andrew Jackson Downing, 1815-1852.* Washington, D.C.: The Athenaeum of Philadelphia and Dumbarton Oaks Research Library and Collection, 1989.

Macomber, Walter M. "The Interpretation of Evidence." In *Old Cities of the New World: Proceedings of the Pan American Symposium of Historic Monuments, St. Augustine, Florida, June 20–25, 1965.* San Augustin, Antigua: Pan American Symposium on the Preservation and Restoration of Historic Monuments, 1967.

Massey, Robert. *Formulas for Painters.* New York: Watson-Guptill Publications, 1967.

Masury, John W. *House-painting: Plain and Decorative.* New York, 1868.

———. *How Shall We Paint Our Houses?* New York, 1868.

Matero, Frank G. "Methodologies for Establishing Appropriate Decorative Finish Treatments." In *The Interiors Handbook for Historic Buildings,* vol. 1, edited by Charles E. Fisher, Michael Auer, and Anne Grimmer, 3-45–3-48. Washington, D.C.: Historic Preservation Education Foundation, 1988.

Matero, Frank G., and Constance Silver. *Examination and Analysis of the Interior Architectural Finishes of Room H144, House of Representatives, U.S. Capitol Building.* Washington, D.C.: Office of the Architect of the Capitol, 1988.

Matero, Frank G., and Joel C. Snodgrass. "Understanding Regional Painting Traditions: The New Orleans Exterior Finishes Study." *Association for Preservation Technology Bulletin* 24, nos. 1 and 2 (1992): 36–52.

Mattiello, Joseph J. *Protective and Decorative Coatings.* 5 vols. New York: John Wiley and Sons, 1941–46.

Mayer, Ralph. *The Artist's Handbook of Materials and Techniques.* 4th ed., rev. New York: Viking Press, 1981.

———. *The Painter's Craft: An Introduction to Artists' Methods and Materials.* New York: D. Van Nostrand and Company, 1966.

McCrone, Walter C. "The Microscopical Identification of Artists' Pigments." *Journal IIC-CG,* 7, nos. 1 and 2:11–34.

McCrone, Walter C., Lucy B. McCrone, and John Gustav Delly. *Polarized Light Microscopy.* Ann Arbor, Mich.: Ann Arbor Science Publishers, 1979.

McCrone, Walter C., John Gustav Delly, et al. *The Particle Atlas.* Vols. 1–5. 2d ed. Ann Arbor, Mich.: Ann Arbor Science Publishers, 1973.

McKinstry, E. Richard. *Trade Catalogues at Winterthur: A Guide to the Literature of Merchandising, 1750–1980.* New York and London: Garland Publishing, 1984.

Meilunas, R. J., J. G. Bentsen, and A. Steinberg. "Analysis of Aged Paint Binders by FTIR Spectroscopy. *Studies in Conservation* 35 (1990): 33–51.

Miller, Kevin H., ed. *Paint Color Research and Restoration of Historic Paint.* Ottowa: Association for Preservation Technology, 1977.

Milley, John. "Experimental Paint Color Research with Solvents at Independence National Historical Park, Philadelphia." *Association for Preservation Technology Newsletter* 1, no. 2 (1969): 19–20.

Mills, John S., and Raymond White. *The Organic Chemistry of Museum Objects.* London: Butterworths, 1987.

Minhinnick, Jeanne. "Some Personal Observations on the Use of Paint in Early Ontario." *Association for Preservation Technology Bulletin* 7, no. 2 (1975): 13–31.

Moorehead, Singleton P. "Ludwell-Paradise House Architectural Report." Colonial Williamsburg Foundation Library, Williamsburg, Va., March 1933. Bound typescript.

———. "Problems in Architectural Restoration . . . Colonial Williamsburg." *Arts in America* 43 (April 1955): 23–29.

Mora, Paolo, Laura Moro, and Paul Philippot. *Conservation of Wall Paintings.* London: Butterworths, 1984.

Morton, W. Brown, III, et al. *The Secretary of the Interior's Standards for Rehabilitation and Illustrated Guidelines for Rehabilitating Historic Buildings.* Washington, D.C.: National Park Service, 1992.

Mosca, Matthew J. "Historic Paint Research: Determining the Original Colors." *Old-House Journal* 9, no. 4 (1981): 81–83.

———. "The House and Its Restoration." *The Magazine Antiques* 135 (February 1989): 462–73.

Moss, Roger W. *Century of Color: Exterior Decoration for American Buildings, 1820-1920.* Watkins Glen, N.Y.: American Life Foundation, 1981.

———. "Color Consulting for Historic Buildings." In *Color Consulting: A Survey of International Color Design,* Harold Linton, ed. 1-15. New York: Van Nostrand Reinhold, 1991.

Moss, Roger W., et al. *Detroit Historic Districts Style and Color Guild.* Detroit: Detroit Historic District Commission, 1984.

Moss, Roger W., and Gail Caskey Winkler. *Victorian Exterior Decoration: How to Paint Your Nineteenth-Century American House Historically.* New York: Henry Holt and Company, 1987; revised paperback edition, 1992.

Mühlethaler, B., and Jean Thissen. "Smalt." *Studies in Conservation* 14 (1969): 47–61.

Munsell, A. H. *The Munsell Book of Color.* 2 vols. Baltimore: Macbeth, 1976.

Nash, Susan Higginson. "Paints, Furniture, and Furnishings." *Architectural Record* 78, no. 6 (1935): 447–58.

Nelson, Lee H., ed. "Paint Color Research and House Painting Practices. " *Association for Preservation Technology Newsletter* 1, no. 2 (1969): 5–19.

Newman, Richard. "Some Applications of Infrared Spectroscopy in the Examination of Painting Materials." *Journal of the American Institute of Conservation* 19 (1980): 42–62.

Painting and Decorating Contractors of America. *Painting and Decorating Craftsman's Manual and Textbook.* 5th ed. Falls Church, Va.: 1975.

Palenik, Skip. "The Polarizing Microscope: A Valuable Analytical Instrument in Conservation." *Technology and Conservation* (June 1977): 28–33.

Pandich, Susanne Brendel. "Restoration of the Abbey Murals at the Pennsylvania State Capitol." *Association for Preservation Technology Bulletin* 24, nos. 1 and 2 (1992): 14–20

Pappas, Nicholas A. "Paint Research Leads to More Authentic Look for Historic Area." *Colonial Williamsburg News* 41, no. 8 (1988): 3.

Patton, Temple C., ed. *Pigment Handbook.* Vol. 1. New York: John Wiley and Sons, 1973.

Peck, Amelia, ed. *Alexander Jackson Davis: American Architect, 1803-1892.* New York: Rizzoli, 1992.

Penn, Theodore Z. "Decorative and Protective Finishes, 1750–1850: Materials, Process, and Craft." *Association for Preservation Technology Bulletin* 16, no. 1 (1984): 3–45.

Perrault, Carole L. "Techniques Employed at the North Atlantic Historic Preservation Center for the Sampling and Analysis of Historic Architectural Paints and Finishes." *Association for Preservation Technology Bulletin* 10, no. 2 (1978): 6–46.

Perry, William Graves. "Notes on the Architecture [of Colonial Williamsburg]." *Architectural Record* 78 (December 1935): 363–81.

Peterson, Charles E. "Early Sanded Paint Finish." *Journal of the Society of Architectural Historians* 9, no. 3 (1950): 23–24.

Phillips, Morgan W. "Acrylic Paints for Restoration: Three Test Applications." *Association for Preservation Technology Bulletin* 15, no. 1 (1983), 3–11.

———. "Brief Notes on the Subjects of Analyzing Paints and Mortars and the Recording of Moulding Profiles." *Association for Preservation Technology Bulletin* 10, no.2 (1978): 77–89.

———. "Discoloration of Old House Paints: Restoration of Paint Colors at the Harrison Gray Otis House, Boston." *Association for Preservation Technology Bulletin* 3, no. 4 (1971): 40.

———. "Problems in the Restoration and Preservation of Old House Paints." In *Preservation and Conservation: Principles and Practices*, 273–85. Proceedings of the North American International Regional Conference, Williamsburg, Va., and Philadelphia, September 10–16, 1972. Washington, D.C.: Smithsonian Institution Press for the National Trust for Historic Preservation, 1976.

Phillips, Morgan, and Brian Powell. "Several Experiences Using Lime Paste as a Cleaning Agent for Oil Paint." *Association for Preservation Technology Bulletin* 14, no. 2 (1982): 31–33.

Phillips, Morgan W., and Norman R. Weiss. "Some Notes on Paint Research and Reproduction." *Association for Preservation Technology Bulletin* 7, no. 4 (1975): 14–16.

Phillips, Morgan, and Christopher Whitney. "Restoration of Original Paints at the Otis House." *Old-Time New England* 62, no. 1 (1971): 25–28.

Plesters, Joyce. "Cross-Sections and Chemical Analysis of Paint Samples." *Studies in Conservation* 2, no. 3 (1956): 110–57.

———. "Ultramarine Blue, Natural and Artificial." *Studies in Conservation* 11 (1966): 62–91.

Pomada, Elizabeth, and Michael Larsen. *Painted Ladies: San Francisco's Resplendent Victorians*. New York: E.P. Dutton, 1978.

———. *Daughters of Painted Ladies: America's Resplendent Victorians*. New York: E.P. Dutton, 1987.

———. *The Painted Ladies Revisited: San Francisco's Resplendent Victorians Inside and Out*. New York: E.P. Dutton, 1989.

———. *How to Create Your Own Painted Lady: A Comprehensive Guide to Beautifying Your Victorian Home*. New York: E.P. Dutton, 1989.

Pratt, L. S. *The Chemistry and Physics of Organic Pigments*. London and New York: John Wiley and Sons, 1947.

Reynolds, Hezekiah. *Directions for House and Ship Painting; Shewing in a plain and concise manner, The Best Method of Preparing, Mixing, and Laying the Various Colours Now in Use, Designed for the Use of Learners*. 1812. Facsimile reprint, with an introduction by Richard Candee. Worcester, Mass.: American Antiquarian Society, 1978.

Riddell, John. *Architectural Designs for Model Country Residences*. Philadelphia, 1861.

Rossiter, Ehrick K., and Frank A. Wright. *Modern House Painting*. New York, 1882.

Rowe, Linda H. "Exterior Painting." Research Report Series, no. 76. Colonial Williamsburg Foundation Library, Williamsburg, Va., 1983. Bound photocopy.

Sabin, Alvah Horton. *Industrial and Artistic Technology of Paint and Varnish*. 2d ed. New York: Wiley, 1917.

"The Saga of the Painted Ladies," *Qualified Remodeler* 2 (August 1985): 34-49.

Schlichting, Carl. "In-Situ Treatment of Paints: A Ukrainian Catholic Church." *Association for Preservation Technology Bulletin* 10, no. 4 (1988): 14–18.

Schur, Susan E. "Conservation Training Profile: The National Trust Restoration Workshop." *Technology and Conservation* 5, no. 2 (1980): 36–39.

———. "Laboratory Profile: The National Park Service's North Atlantic Region Preservation Laboratory." *Technology and Conservation* 1, no. 2 (1976): 18-19, 23, and 28.

Seale, William. *The President's House: A History*. 2 vols. Washington, D.C.: White House Historical Association, 1986.

Seldon, Marjorie Ward. *The Interior Paint of the Campbell-Whittlesey House, 1835–1836*. Rochester, N.Y.: Landmark Society of Western New York, 1970.

Smith, John. *The Art of Painting in Oyl*. 1687. 4th ed. London, 1705.

Standard Operating Procedures for the Analysis of Historic Building Materials at the Building Conservation Branch. Cultural Resources Center, North Atlantic Region, National Park Service, 1991.

Stephenson, Mary A. "Barraud House History." March 1947. Revised and expanded by Emma L. Powers, July 1988. Colonial Williamsburg Foundation Library, Williamsburg, Va. Bound typescript.

———. "Ludwell-Paradise House." Colonial Williamsburg Foundation Library, Williamsburg, Va., November 1948. Bound typescript.

———. "Supplementary Report to Paint Color and Whitewash in Williamsburg and Virginia." Research Report Series, no. 166. Colonial Williamsburg Foundation Library, Williamsburg, Va., 1952. Bound photocopy.

Taylor, Thomas H., Jr. "The Williamsburg Restoration and Its Reception by the American Public: 1926–1942." Ph.D. diss., The George Washington University, 1989.

Tingry, P. F. *The Painter's and Colourman's Complete Guide*. London, 1830.

———. *The Painter and Varnisher's Guide*. London: G. Kearsley, 1804.

Ure, Andrew. *A Dictionary of Arts, Manufactures, and Mines*. London, 1839.

Vanderwalker, F. N. *Interior Wall Decoration*. Chicago: Frederick S. Drake, 1924.

Vaux, Calvert. *Villas and Cottages*. New York, 1857.

Villas on the Hudson. New York, c. 1860.

Voltz, John. "Paint Bibliography." Supplement, *Association for Preservation Technology Newsletter* 4, no. 1 (1975).

Wainwright, Nicholas, *Colonial Grandeur in Philadelphia*. Philadelphia: The Historical Society of Pennsylvania, 1964.

Wehlte, Kurt. *The Materials and Techniques of Painting.* Translated by Ursus Dix. New York: Van Nostrand Reinhold, 1967.

Welsh, Frank S. "Architectural Metallic Finishes in the Late Nineteenth and Early Twentieth Centuries. The Great Imitators: Aluminum and Bronze." *The Interiors Handbook for Historic Buildings,* vol. 1, edited by Charles E. Fisher, Michael Auer, and Anne Grimmer, 3-37–3-44. Washington, D.C.: Historic Preservation Education Foundation, 1988.

———. "The Art of Painted Graining." *Historic Preservation* 29, no. 3 (1977): 32–37.

———. "Courthouse Project Paint Analysis." Foundation Architect's Office, Colonial Williamsburg Foundation, Williamsburg, Va., May 30, 1989. Unbound photocopy.

———. "Dr. Barraud House Paint Analysis." Foundation Architect's Office, Colonial Williamsburg Foundation, Williamsburg, Va., May 1987. Bound photocopy.

———. "Documentation of the 1902 Paint Colors of the Florida State Capitol." *Association for Preservation Technology Bulletin* 12, no. 2 (1980): 117–21.

———. Eighteenth-Century Black Window Glazing in Philadelphia." *Association for Preservation Technology Bulletin* 12, no. 2 (1980): 122–23.

———. "Microchemical Analysis of Old Housepaints with a Case Study of Monticello." *The Microscope* 38, no. 3 (1990): 247–57.

———. "Paint Analysis." *Association for Preservation Technology Bulletin* 14, no. 4 (1982): 29–30.

———. "Paint and Color Restoration." *Old House Journal* 3, no. 8 (1975): 1, 8–11.

———. "Particle Characteristics of Prussian Blue in an Historical Oil Paint." *Journal of the American Institute for Conservation* 27, no. 2 (1988): 55–63.

———. "The Peter Wentz House: Eighteenth-Century Sponge Painting in Pennsylvania." *Association for Preservation Technology Bulletin* 7, no. 2 (1975): 124–30.

———. "Report on an Early Wall Stencil in Philadelphia." *Association for Preservation Technology Bulletin* 5, no. 2 (1973): 54–62.

———. "Who Is an Historic Paint Analyst? A Call for Standards." *Association for Preservation Technology Bulletin* 18, no. 4 (1986): 4–5.

Welsh, Frank S., and Charles L. Grandquist. "Restoration of the Exterior Sanded Paint at Monticello." *Association for Preservation Technology Bulletin* 15, no. 2 (1983): 2–10.

Wheatcroft, Andrew, ed. *Adhesives and Coatings.* New York: Routledge, 1992.

Whiffen, Marcus. *The Eighteenth Century Houses of Williamsburg.* Williamsburg, Va.: Colonial Williamsburg Foundation, 1960.

"Williamsburg: What It Means to Architecture, to Gardening, to Decoration." *House and Gardening* 72 (November 1937): 37–67.

Winkler, Gail Caskey, and Roger W. Moss. *Victorian Interior Decoration: American Interiors, 1830–1900.* New York: Henry Holt and Company, 1986; paperback edition, 1992.

Wolbers, Richard, and Gregory Landrey. "The Use of Direct Reactive Fluorescent Dyes for the Characterization of Binding Media in Cross-Sectional Examination." In *Preprints of Papers Presented at the Fifteenth Annual Meeting, American Institute for Conservation, Vancouver, British Columbia, May 20–24, 1987.* Vancouver: American Institute for Conservation, 1987.

Zucker, Joyce, and Deborah Gordon. "Decorative Finishes: Aspects of Conservation and Cleaning." In *The Interiors Handbook for Historic Buildings,* vol.1, edited by Charles E. Fisher, Michael Auer, and Anne Grimmer, 3-23–3-30. Washington, D.C.: Historic Preservation Education Foundation, 1988.